The Loyal Subject

The German Library: Volume 64

Volkmar Sander, General Editor

Heinrich Mann

THE
LOYAL SUBJECT

Edited by Helmut Peitsch

CONTINUUM · NEW YORK

1998
The Continuum Publishing Company
370 Lexington Avenue, New York, NY 10017

The German Library
is published in cooperation with Deutsches Haus,
New York University.
This volume has been supported by Inter Nationes.

Der Untertan by Heinrich Mann. Copyright 1919
Kurt Wolff Verlag, Leipzig. All rights reserved
S. Fischer Verlag GmbH, Frankfurt am Main.

New English translation Copyright © 1998 by
The Continuum Publishing Company, by arrangement
with S. Fischer Verlag GmbH, Frankfurt am Main
Introduction © 1998 by Helmut Peitsch

Printed in the United States of America

Library of Congress Cataloging-in-Publication Data

Mann, Heinrich, 1871–1950.
[Untertan. English]
The loyal subject / Heinrich Mann ; edited by Helmut Peitsch.
p.   cm. — (The German library ; v. 64)
ISBN 0-8264-0954-7. — ISBN 0-8264-0955-5 (pbk.)
I. Peitsch, Helmut ; Translated by Ernest Boyd — adapted, with new portions
translated by Daniel Theisen. II. Title. III. Series.
PT2625.A43U513   1998

833'.912—dc21   97-22094
                                                                 CIP

Contents

Translated by Ernest Boyd
Adapted, with New Portions Translated
by Daniel Theisen

Introduction

"As soon as the Germans have lost a war they print my *Untertan*," Ludwig Marcuse's obituary in *Books Abroad* (1950) quoted the author from a Californian afternoon conversation.[1] The changing titles of the English translation indicate, too, what kind of interest the American or British public has been supposed to have in reading Heinrich Mann's novel. From *The Patrioteer* (1921) to *Little Superman* (1945) and *Man of Straw* (1947, 1972, 1984), the suggested interpretation has shifted from German nationalism to fascism and, finally, to the authoritarian personality. It was not until 1977 that an article in *The Nation* made the case for the literal translation: "The Loyal Subject."[2]

Even if some critics would argue that this very political cycle might mirror the political rather than literary quality of the text, it could also be regarded as proof that only after things in Germany went wrong the importance of the work was recognized. As long as outside observers see Germany doing business as usual they are not much interested in the way a satirist denounces the way *Germanness* was constructed in Imperial Germany.

In the history of the American reception of *The Loyal Subject*, historians and social scientists have played a more prominent role than Germanists. The dominant academic view has been a rather negative one, always measuring Mann's novel against what was regarded—actually for the time being, but formulated with great security about the timelessness of these values—literature in the true sense. The 1937 volume of Columbia's *Germanic Review*, for instance, contrasted a strong critique of the exiled Heinrich Mann as an intellectual isolated from German society with approving portrayals of two authors who lived and published successfully in Nazi Germany, Agnes Miegel and Erwin Guido Kolbenheyer who were seen as real poets because of being rooted in either German soil and blood or German metaphysics.[3] An influential *History of*

German Literature, which in 1949 only mentioned *Der Untertan* as one of the author's novels "which hardly justify a place for them in literary history"[4] extended this evaluation in a new, 1959 edition by adding that the novel "goes beyond the bounds of art in its polemics."[5] About the same time, another American literary historian linked the "limpid prose style" of *The Loyal Subject* unfavorably with the "aggressive liberal" author's French narrative models and his later belief in "Russian communism."[6] Whereas this literary historian, Ernst Rose of New York University, held up as late as 1960 the yardstick of the "translucent style"[7] of a Hermann Stehr, in general the main aesthetic argument against *Der Untertan* turned from the "true literature" heralded by the Nazis to high modernism. Even in Roy Pascals's insightful social and political history of German literature *From Naturalism to Expressionism* where—as far as mentioning is concerned Heinrich Mann comes fifth—(equal with Rilke),—right after his brother, Gerhart Hauptmann, Hofmannsthal, and George, and well before Hesse and the Expressionist poets and playwrights—a remark of the following kind seemed indispensable to the author in 1973: "*Der Untertan* might have profited from greater formal subtlety."[8] This supposed lack of "innovation" was the point of departure for those critics who tried to introduce Heinrich Mann into the canon of "20th Century Classics"—where the *The Loyal Subject* arrived only in 1984 when Penguin published it in the series of this name. "The artist in Heinrich Mann will long survive the politician," Ulrich Weisstein had pleaded in *Books Abroad* in 1959.[9] Since then, critical attention shifted from *Der Untertan* to the oeuvre of the author. This is documented by the first monograph on Heinrich Mann in English, Rolf N. Linn's 1967 contribution to Twayne's World Authors Series, which is—alongside W. E. Yuill's 1963 article in *German Men of Letters*[10]—still the best introduction available in English although it took a then-timely stance on *The Loyal Subject:* Linn "acknowledged its artistic merits without, however, ranking it as part of the canon of twentieth century German literature. To this day, most of those who have occasion to refer to it are cautious not to appear too enthusiastic over a work written with so much acerbity as this one is."[11]

As early as 1950, an obituary had lamented by quoting the writer himself that he was seen as "a man of one book."[12] This "one book's" satirical structure fitted into neither the realist tradition nor its modernist challenge. In order to rescue the whole work of Heinrich Mann much critical scrutiny went into the aestheticism of his pre-1910 work and the *Greisenavantgardismus* (old age's avant-gardism) for which his brother praised the post-1945 novels.

In Heinrich Mann's biography, commonly, five phases are distinguished. The eldest son of a Lübeck merchant started his literary career—after leaving school early and breaking off an apprenticeship in the book trade—not only with novellas and novels, but with journalism. When the articles he wrote in 1895–96 for the journal *The Twentieth Century* were rediscovered, they disturbed admirers of the later Heinrich Mann not only because of their reactionary politics of "cultural despair," but particularly because of their anti-Semitism. The linking of a cultural-political program close to *Heimatkunst*—one of the forerunners of Nazi "blood-and-soil" literature—and a way of writing on contemporary society inspired by Friedrich Nietzsche's and Paul Bourget's criticism of "decadence" was given up when Heinrich Mann separated on the one hand the celebration of "heightened life" (aesthetically idealizing, for instance, the Renaissance in *The Goddesses* [1903]) and on the other hand the satirical portrayal of big-city and small-town life in *In the Land of Cockaigne* (1900) and *Small Town Tyrant* (1905). In these two novels some, but not yet all, of the social and political ideals Heinrich Mann had championed in his early journalism came under satirical attack. In one of the essays marking his democratic-liberal politicization, Heinrich Mann stated it a requirement for the satirist to have once been involved in what he is later criticizing.

Whereas the essays of *Spirit and Action* (1910) refer to the French Revolution as a model for what is lacking in German society and literature, the novel *The Small Town* (1909) idealizes Italian middle-class democracy. It was less Mann the novelist than the literary essayist who exercised a remarkable influence upon those Expressionist writers who named themselves *activists,* taking up Mann's terminology for turning spirit into action. This influence was particularly strong during World War I, when Mann was among the very few writers who refused to take part in the nationalistic outrage against Western "civilization" (economic liberalism, political democracy, rationalistic thinking) in the name of German "culture" (of allegedly superior inwardness). Heinrich Mann's opposition to the so-called ideas of 1914 heralding a specific German, neither liberal nor democratic, neither capitalistic nor socialist way into modernity, became publicly most visible in his hostile exchange with his brother. Heinrich Mann's *Zola* (1915) and Thomas Mann's *Reflections of a Nonpolitical Man* (1918; 1983) reveal their mutual perception as the politically committed Western intellectual and the specifically German unpolitical poet.

Heinrich Mann's Empire Trilogy—"the history of the German public soul under William II"—on which he started work in 1906 with the inception of *The Loyal Subject,* concluded in 1914, but published after the November revolution in 1918, made the author a representative of the new republic (only gradually joined in this role by his brother). Even the very mixed critical reception of this first volume, which in terms of copies sold was highly successful, shed some light on the state of Weimar. The utmost hostile reaction of the conservative literary establishment brought out the critics' antirepublican sentiments in aesthetic disguise. The two following volumes—*The Poor* and *The Chief* (1925)—as well as the social novels Heinrich Mann published later in the 1920s, were less successful. Nevertheless, he had established himself as a prophet of things to come to whom attention must be paid. After the appearance of *The Patrioteer* some of Heinrich Mann's pre-World War I novels were translated into English, not by chance those that suited the image of the German republican best, the satirical *In the Land of Cockaigne* (1929) and *Small Town Tyrant,* as well as the idyllic *The Little Town* (1931): by the end of the 1920s, however, most of Heinrich Mann's new novels were quickly translated, upon publication.

When the Nazis came to power, Heinrich Mann in pleading for common action of social democrats and communists anticipated some of his politics after being forced into exile. In early 1933, his former aestheticist admirer Gottfried Benn was behind the scenes of the Literary Section of the Prussian Academy of the Arts when Heinrich Mann was made to resign from its presidency because of allegedly violating the autonomy of art in his anti-Nazi call for action. In his French exile, the number of political essays Mann published increased because of the urgency he felt to fight against fascism and imminent war. The titles of the volumes of collected essays—*The Hatred* (1933), *The Day Will Come* (1936), and *Courage* (1939)—speak for themselves. Heinrich Mann also actively participated in the attempt to build up a popular front, at least among the exiled intellectuals. His not shying away from collaboration with communists, even during the Stalinist "purges" and show-trials, contributed to the official fame he and his work were to enjoy after World War II in East Germany.

The anti-Hitler coalition, however, also allowed his reputation in the United States—where he lived since fleeing from France in 1940—to reach a peak in the final years of the war against Nazi Germany, and in the immediate postwar period before the outbreak of the cold war. In December 1945, Lewis Mumford in an open letter to a German writer, which was commissioned by the Office of War Information, singled out the author of *The Loyal Subject*— together with Heinrich Heine—as the exception among the German writers; Mumford asked his addressee:

> Is it not strange that your philosophy and your literature, so rich in other respects, should be so impoverished in the literature of self-criticism? What have you to put alongside Milton's "The Tenure of Kings and Magistrates," alongside Thomas Paine's *Common Sense,* alongside Thoreau's "Essay on Civil Disobedience," alongside Carlyle's "Past and Present"? Who among your men of letters has indicted your social system, your historic tradition, as soberly and as unflinchingly as Walt Whitman, the prophet of democracy, indicted his own country in "Democratic Vistas?" During the last century two writers stand out, among a bare handful one might name: Heinrich Heine and Heinrich Mann. These men dared to challenge Germany. When they attacked they did not graze a few hairs: they aimed at the fatty tissue around the heart. I wonder if you recall that it was Heinrich Mann that you yourself used as a symbol of the impure artist, whose work was unpleasantly discolored by his democratic political opinions? (. . .) In its plot, the book was prophetic. Anyone who read *Der Untertan* in 1918, when it came out, would have been fully prepared for all that happened in 1933 (. . .). He would have been prepared, provided he accepted Heinrich Mann's satire as the expression of an essential truth—admittedly not the whole truth or the best truth—about German society. You were not prepared, dear Alfons: you attributed to Heinrich Mann's political philosophy the discoloration that actually existed on the face of Germany.[13]

For a short while, Heinrich Mann could be regarded as an example of what intellectuals should do not only in the West, but also in the East where the leading Marxist critic Georg Lukács hailed the historical novels *Young Henry of Navarre* (1935, English 1937) and *Henry Quartre, King of France* (1938, English 1939) as representing the highlights of "critical realism" and "democratic humanism."[14] When Heinrich Mann died in 1950 after having finished an autobiography—in which Roosevelt and Stalin figure with equal prominence as intellectual leaders—and two rather experimental novels dealing with the downfall of France in 1940 and with life in Hollywood, the cold war shaped the response. The obituaries in American journals came from fellow exiles and were on the defensive because Heinrich Mann had accepted the offer of the presidency of the (East) German Academy of the Arts and decided to settle in the former German Democratic Republic. *Books Abroad* printed the rather short article by Ludwig Marcuse on the same page with an illustrated and much longer one on Ernst Wiechert, who was defended eloquently against the charges of being "escapist" and having "much in common with the professed ideologies of National Socialism"; Wiechert, not Heinrich Mann, was presented to the American reader as "pointing a way into the future without breaking with what is best in the past—a way distinctly German, distinctly Christian." The reason for this view was given in the evermore popular equation of fascism and socialism: Wiechert was "undaunted by encroachments from rightist as well as leftist authoritarianism."[15]

During the cold war, the conviction that a political satire did not belong in the realm of art could unite conservatives, who rejected the criticism of their values in *The Loyal Subject,* with liberals, who meant to defend the autonomy of art itself against its politicization. When the former argued the datedness of *Der Untertan,* since Germans as depicted in Heinrich Mann's novel had never existed or had only existed in cartoons, the latter saw the form of the realist social novel as hopelessly belated with regard to the complexity of the self-conscious, auto-referential narration achieved by Döblin, Kafka, Musil, Broch, and perhaps, Thomas Mann during Heinrich Mann's lifetime. The academic and journalistic construction of the canon of classical modernism, however, excluded not only "realism" in terms of thematic concern with social reality, but also diminished the importance of satire within the canonized texts in order to put all the stress on the representation of consciousness—thereby staying firmly within the boundaries of German inwardness, which was to a degree westernized by being elevated to "the modern condition." Real objects worthy of attack did not fit into the calm skepticism of cold war criticism.

Whereas Heinrich Mann's protagonist denounces the genre of the "Roman" (novel) as "no art, at least no German art, as its name already proves," the author's claim to the "social novel of topicality" (*sozialer Zeitroman*) nevertheless related to various traditions of the nineteenth-century German novel. It could be argued that *The Loyal Subject* is a kind of summary of the nineteenth-century German novel: a satirical attempt to bring its *Sonderweg* to a democratic end. By taking up traditional types of the genre, Heinrich Mann breaks with them. The topical novel since the 1830s concerned itself mostly with the discussion of contemporary ideas, which is why it has been described often negatively as a Salon or Feuilleton novel. In the social novel, as it emerged in the 1840s, the description of pauperism often took refuge in the pattern of the adventure novel. But Heinrich Mann did not go beyond the limitations of these traditions by following the lines of the French social novel only, although his departure from the German novel of good society is no less obvious. There are, however, not only echoes of Fontane's *Delusions, Confusions* (see The German Library, Volume 47)—most visible in Diederich's and Agnes's excursion—but Heinrich Mann also keeps the same time distance from his own present as that preferred by Fontane. The main plot is set in the years 1892–97, although the author actually wrote the text between 1911 and 1914. Perhaps more significant is an allusion to Gustav Freytag's *Debit and Credit,* the programmatical social novel of German so-called poetic realism. In Freytag's novel, the "poetry" of trade is presented in exactly the way Heinrich Mann's hero ascribes poetry to the drinking of beer in his students' corps. This is not merely an intertextual polemic against a liberal, but also a nationalistic German writer; the "drunken ecstasy" the beer is bringing Diederich into is intrinsically intertwined with specific forms of sexuality, business, and politics. What is venerated as poetic in the dominant German tradition, in *Der Untertan* becomes the object of satirical attack.

The narrator's comment on the end of Diederich's "apprenticeship" recalls Goethe's *Wilhelm Meister* and so brings out that *The Loyal Subject* begins as an inverted version of the Bildungsroman. Seemingly, Diederich arrives at the harmony between individual and society that Meister is searching for, but only at the expense of any individual development in the traditionally humanist sense. Nevertheless, the Bildungsroman's love episode with Agnes is the one in which the positive ideal to which the satire everywhere else implicitly refers is stated most clearly; the other being the final speech of old Buck. It becomes obvious: on the private level, mutual love functions as a metonomy for the self-respect that implies the recognition of the human dignity of everyone in public life. Diederich's *pseudo-Bildung* represses this "true nature" in favor of "manly idealism," which brings together sadomasochistic sexuality, capitalist business, and the ideology of German imperialism.

The fact that the *Wilhelm Meister* allusion comes rather early—after just a quarter of the text—should serve as a warning against the now-dominating way of reading the novel: if the psychological interest in the "authoritarian personality" were the only one, the book could well end here. But its remaining larger part can make clear that the mechanism allowing Diederich to succeed in the conquest of Netzig is at least equally important.

The Loyal Subject can be seen as the best of the Berlin novels that began to be written in the 1880s, although only one and one half chapters are set in Berlin. The basic satirical motif of identifying the Emperor and his loyal subject undermines the ideological opposition of city and country, metropolis and province, which were at the heart of the so-called *Heimatkunst*. *Der Untertan* successfully subverts the notion of a healthy, rural, preindustrial, pure German "land" as opposed to a big city intoxicated by industrialization, finance, capitalism, liberal democracy, and socialism—for all of which "the Jew" was presented as responsible. Heinrich Mann's former editor-in-chief at *The Twentieth Century* was one of the many who depicted this *Judaized* Berlin in novels and essays at the beginning of the century. The small-town hero's status is reduced to the one who introduces the imperialist ideology and politics that govern Berlin into the liberal Netzig still lying behind the capital. His dependence on social and political forces beyond his control prevents him from being mythologized. If he is laughable, he is also frightening. But the readers attention is always directed to those power-relations of which he has to make use.

How these economic, social, political, and ideological forces make it possible for Diederich and his allies to deconstruct a liberal consensus by applying a strictly polarizing strategy of German identity vs. its enemy, is still worth study. Jews, women, and workers are the obvious victims, but nevertheless for some of them the option of compliance is shown as available so long as they accept the self-destructive consequences of the definition of Germanness as "violent maleness." The main means of satirical attack are the identification of Hessling and William II, which proves the individual as symptom of a system. This is achieved, first, by the wealth of documentary details that refer to recorded events in Imperial Germany: the riots of February 1892, the Lück case, the anti-Semitic agitation of the court's chaplain Stoecker, the scandal around the court's master of ceremonies who was blamed in 1894 for circulating pornographic letters, the Emperor's travel to Rome in 1895, his publication of a poem "Song to Aegir" that was followed by a series of trials for *lèse majesté*, and the erection of numerous monuments to William I between 1897 and 1900. Second, the language of the narrator as well as of Hessling (and his friendly antagonist Wolfgang Buck) is full of quotations from the speeches and telegrams of William II; the ironic stand, however, taken by the narrator in mixing free indirect speech, direct speech, commenting, describing, and reporting, makes it often difficult to determine who is actually speaking. Third, the identity of the Emperor and his loyal subject is brought out by the plot. Five of the six chapters end on an identification of the pair; two times, invented encounters of the Emperor and Hessling are told—and both times William II is laughing at Diederich; two chapter endings stress the physiognomic identity of William II and Hessling in terms of the stony as well as flashing face of power, which is compared to that of a male cat; the other two chapters close with Diederich inventing something the Emperor—so Hessling claims—has uttered, which in the end is confirmed by the official press as indeed the Emperor's own saying. This exchange of the high and the low level of imperial society, the center and the periphery, goes along with a drastically comic way of bringing down the supposedly highest and holiest "goods": the smell of sublime power is constantly close to defecation. It is Hessling's toilet paper which, appropriately enough, propagates "world power." The satire aims at mobilizing revulsion: *Ekel*.

For destroying the respect of "power" by reducing its high and low representatives to self-interest and hypocrisy, the novel has been applauded by liberal and leftist writers from Tucholsky and Brecht to Böll: "Fifty years after the book appeared I recognize still the forceful model of a subservient society."[16] Not by coincidence, all three of them were also satirists who appreciated the ridicule of the seemingly sublime by familiarizing it. Böll's 1969 statement, however, brings into the open one problem foreign readers could have from the first publication in 1921 onward: namely, the richness of denotation appealed to an everyday knowledge of life in Imperial Germany, perhaps even not available to later readers in the two former postwar Germanies. The translator of the English edition of 1921, for instance, had missed most of the quotes from William II's speeches and therefore destroyed, by using varying English words for, e.g., *zerschmettern* (to crush, to dash, to destroy), the leitmotifs of Heinrich Mann's text; but the original translator did not stop there. By cutting most of the sex scenes and several of the episodes containing the political business between Hessling, Wulckow, and Fischer he showed some of the good taste to which the former West Germany's leading literary critic referred when he rejected the book and the author vehemently in 1958: "What he lacks is a category of highest ranking, although we deal with it condescendingly: taste."[17] Between 1933 and 1958, however, this so-called tasteless novel was not available for readers in those regions that became the Federal Republic of Germany in 1949. And although even after the extension of this state of 1990 the 1964 paperback edition has been available, the novel and its author have come under renewed attack, both because of his "un-German Westernness" and his admiring of Stalin in the early 1940s. Once again these political objections are supposed to prove *The Loyal Subject* dated.[18] Already in 1979, when the rise of a neonationalism could be seen in the former Federal Republic of Germany, the leading West German critic Karl Heinz Bohrer, in reviewing Gordon C. Graig's *Germany 1866–1945*, took the role Heinrich Mann's *Der Untertan* played in Craig's history as evidence of its belatedness. Whereas Craig's book was dismissed as mere repetition of Heinrich Mann's (and Brecht's) well-known caricatures, Bohrer praised another American historian instead for in his book "encouraging the Germans once again to proclaim their loyalty to their specific tradition, their grand style."[19]

Following unification, Heinrich Mann's *The Loyal Subject* can do a good job in making such loyal subjugation a little bit more difficult.

H. P.

Notes

1. Ludwig Marcuse, "Farewell to Heinrich Mann," *Books Abroad*, 24, 1950, 248.
2. Michael Kowal, "Heinrich Mann and *Der Untertan*," *The Nation*, October 8, 1977, 347.

3. Hans W. Rosenhaupt, "Heinrich Mann und die Gesellschaft," *Germanic Review*, 12, 1937, 278.

4. J. G. Robertson, *A History of German Literature,* sixth impression, new and rev., Edinburgh and London, 1949, 636.

5. ———— and Edna Purdie, *A History of German Literature,* third edition, Edinburgh and London, 1959, 547–48.

6. Ernst Rose, *A History of German Literature,* New York, 1960, 298.

7. Ibid., 299.

8. Roy Pascal, *From Naturalism to Expressionism: German Literature and Society from 1870 to 1918,* London, 1973, 147.

9. Ulrich Weisstein, "Heinrich Mann in America: A Critical Survey," *Books Abroad,* 33, 1959, 284.

10. W. E. Yuill, "Heinrich Mann," Alex Natan, ed., *German Men of Letters,* vol. 2, London, 1963, 197–224.

11. Rolf N. Linn, *Heinrich Mann,* New York, 1967, 68.

12. F. S. Grosshut, "Heinrich Mann," *Books Abroad,* 24, 1950, 359.

13. Lewis Mumford, "Letter to a German Writer," *Saturday Review of Literature,* December 8, 1945. Reprinted in Mumford, *Values for Survival: Essays, Addresses, and Letters on Politics and Education.* New York, 1946, 275–76, 277–78.

14. Georg Lukács, *The Historical Novel,* Boston, 1963, 231–350.

15. Gunther M. Bonnin, "Wiechert and Christian Humanism," *Books Abroad,* 24, 1950, 250.

16. *Bis zu mir reichende Wirkungen.* In *Akzente* 10, 1969, 403

17. *Frankfurter Allgemeine Zeitung,* December 13, 1958.

18. Cf. Joachim Fest, "Ein Unpolitischer wird besichtigt," *FAZ,* October 16, 1982; Marcel Reich-Ranicki, "Ein Abschied nicht ohne Wehmut," *FAZ,* August 15, 1987.

19. Karl Heinz Bohrer, "Ein Schuldspruch und ein Freispruch," *FAZ,* January 27, 1979.

Chapter 1

Diederich Hessling was a dreamy, delicate child, frightened of everything, and troubled frequently by earaches. In winter he hated to leave the warm room, and in summer the narrow garden, which smelled of rags from the paper factory, and where laburnum and elder-trees were overshadowed by the half-timbered gables of the old houses. Diederich was often terribly frightened when he raised his eyes from his story book, his beloved fairy tales. A toad half as big as himself had been sitting on the seat beside him, just as plain as day! Or over there against the wall a gnome, sunk to his waist in the ground, was staring at him!

His father was even more terrible than the gnome and the toad, and moreover he was compelled to love him. Diederich loved him. Whenever he had pilfered, or told a lie, he would come cringing shyly like a dog to his father's desk, until Herr Hessling noticed that something was wrong and took his stick from the wall. Diederich's submissiveness and confidence were shaken by doubts when his misdeeds remained undiscovered. Once when his father, who had a stiff leg, fell downstairs, the boy clapped his hands madly—and then ran away.

The workmen used to laugh when he passed the workshops after having been punished, crying loudly, his face swollen with tears. Then Diederich would stamp his feet and put out his tongue at them. He would say to himself: "I have got a beating, but from my papa. You would be glad to be beaten by him, but you are not good enough for that."

He moved among the men like a capricious potentate. Sometimes he would threaten to tell his father that they were bringing in beer, and at others he would coquettishly allow them to wheedle out of him the hour when Herr Hessling was expected to return. They were on their guard against the boss; he understood them, for he has been a workman himself. He had been a vat-man in the old mills where every sheet of paper was made by hand. During that time he had served in all the wars, and after the last one, when everybody had made money, he was able to buy a paper machine, which together with a beater and a cutter constituted the equipment of his plant. He himself counted the sheets. He kept his eye on the buttons which were taken from rags. His little son would often accept a few from the women, on condition that he did not betray those who took some away with them. One day he had collected so many buttons that he thought of exchanging them with the grocer for sweets. He succeeded—but in the evening Diederich knelt in his bed, and as he swallowed the last piece of barley-sugar, he quaked with fear and prayed to Almighty God to leave the crime undetected. He nevertheless allowed it to leak out. His father had always used the stick methodically, his weather-beaten face reflecting an old soldier's sense of honor and duty. This time, however, his hand trembled and a tear rolled down, trickling over the wrinkles on to one side of his silvery mustache. "My son is a thief," he said breathlessly, in a hushed voice, and he stared at the child as if he were a suspicious intruder. "You lie and you steal. All you have to do now is to commit a murder."

Frau Hessling tried to compel Diederich to fall on his knees before his father and beg his pardon, because his father had wept on his account. Diederich's instinct, however, warned him that this would only have made his father more angry. Hessling had no sympathy whatever with his wife's sentimental attitude. She was spoiling the child for life. Besides, he had caught her lying just like little Diederich. No wonder, for she read novels! By Saturday night her week's work was often not completed. She gossiped with the servant girl instead of exerting herself. . . . And even then Hessling did not know that his wife also pilfered food, just like a child. At table she dared not eat her fill, but then crept surreptitiously to the cupboard afterward. Had she dared to go into the workshop she would also have stolen buttons.

She prayed with the child "from the heart," and not according to the prescribed forms, and that always brought a flush to her face. She, too, used to beat him, but with wanton fury, her face contorted in a grimace of vengeance. On such occasions she was frequently in the wrong, and then Diederich threatened to complain to his father. He would pretend to go into the office and, hiding somewhere behind a wall, would rejoice at her terror. He exploited his mother's tender moods, but felt no respect for her. Her resemblance to himself made that impossible, for he had no self-respect.

The consequence was that he went through life with a conscience too uneasy to withstand the scrutiny of God.

Nevertheless mother and son spent twilight hours overflowing with sentiment. From festive occasions they jointly extracted the last drop of emotion by singing, piano-playing and storytelling. When Diederich began to have doubts about the Christ Child he let his mother persuade him to go on believing a little while longer, and thereby he felt relieved, faithful and good. He also believed obstinately in a ghost up in the Castle, and his father, who would not hear of such a thing, seemed too proud, and almost deserving of punishment. His mother nourished him with fairy tales. She shared with him her fear of the new, busy streets, and of the tramway which crossed them and she took him past the town wall toward the Castle, where they enjoyed thrills of dread.

At the corner of Meisestrasse you had to pass a policeman, who could take you off to prison if he liked. Diederich's heart beat nervously. How gladly he would have made a detour! But then the policeman would have noticed his uneasy conscience and seized him. It was much better to prove that one felt pure and innocent—so with trembling voice Diederich asked the policeman the time.

After so many fearful powers, to which he was subjected: after the fairy-tale toad, after his father, God, the ghost of the Castle and the police; after the chimney-sweep, who could drag him right up through the flue until he, too, was quite black, and the doctor, who could paint his throat and shake him when he cried—after all these powers, Diederich now fell under the sway of one even more terrible, one which swallowed people up completely—the school. Diederich went there in tears, and because he had to cry he could not even answer the questions which he knew. Gradually he learned how to exploit this tendency to cry whenever he had not learned his lessons, for his fears did not make him more industrious or less dreamy. And thus, until the teachers saw through the trick, he was able to avoid many of the unpleasant consequences of his idleness. The first teacher who saw through it earned at once his whole-hearted respect. He suddenly stopped crying and gazed at him over the arm which he was holding bent in front of his face, full of timid devotion. He was always obedient and docile with the strict teachers. On the good-natured ones he played little tricks, which could be proved against him only with difficulty and about which he would boast. With much greater satisfaction he bragged about his bad marks and severe punishments. At table he would say: "Today Herr Behnke flogged three people again." And to the question: Whom?

"I was one of them."

Diederich was so constituted that he was delighted to belong to an impersonal entity, to this immovable, inhumanly indifferent, mechanical organization which was the school, the *Gymnasium*. He was proud of this power, this grim power, in which he participated, if only as its passive object. On the headmaster's birthday the desk and the blackboard were festooned with garlands. Diederich even decorated the cane.

In the course of years two catastrophes that befell the all-powerful filled him with a holy and wonderful horror. An assistant master was reprimanded in front of the class by the Principal and dismissed. A senior master became insane. On these occasions still higher powers, the Principal and the lunatic asylum, wrought fearful havoc with those who had hitherto wielded so much power. From beneath, insignificant but unharmed, one could raise one's eyes to these victims, and draw from their fate a lesson which rendered one's own lot more easy.

In relation to his younger sisters Diederich represented the power which held him in its mechanism. He made them take dictation, and deliberately make more mistakes than they naturally would, so that he could make furious corrections with red ink, and administer punishment. His punishments were cruel. The little ones cried— and then Diederich had to humble himself so that they would not betray him.

He had no need of human beings in order to imitate the powers ruling him. Animals, and even inanimate objects, were sufficient. He would stand at the rail of the papermaking machine and watch the drum shredding the rags. "So that one is gone! Look out, now, you blackguards!" Diederich would mutter, and his pale eyes glared. Suddenly he flinched, almost falling into the tub of chlorine. A workman's footsteps had interrupted his vicious enjoyment.

Only when he himself received a beating did he feel free from unease and sure of his position. He hardly ever resisted the temptation. At most he would beg a comrade: "Not on the back, that's unhealthy."

It was not that he was lacking in a sense of his rights and a love of his own advantage. But Diederich believed that the blows which he received brought no practical profit to the striker and no real loss to himself. These purely ideal values seemed to him far less serious than the cream puff which the head waiter at the Netziger Hof had long since promised him, but had never produced. Many times Diederich walked seriously up Meisestrasse to the market place, and called upon his swallow-tailed friend to deliver the goods. One day, however, when the waiter denied all knowledge of his promise, Diederich declared, as he stamped his foot in genuine indignation: "This is really too much of a good thing. If you don't give me it immediately, I'll report you to the boss!" Thereupon George laughed and brought him the cream puff.

That was a tangible success. Unfortunately Diederich could enjoy it only in haste and fear, for he was afraid that Wolfgang Buck, who was waiting outside, would come in and demand the share which had been promised to him. Meanwhile Diederich found time to wipe his mouth clean, and at the door he broke into violent abuse of George, whom he called a swindler who had no cream puff. Diederich's sense of justice, which had just manifested itself so effectively to his own advantage, did not respond to the claims of his friend, who could not, at the same time, be altogether ignored. Wolfgang's father was much too important a personage for that. Old Herr Buck did not wear a stiff collar, but a white silk neck-cloth, and above that a great white mustache. How slowly and majestically he struck the pavement with his gold-topped walking-stick! He wore a silk top hat, too, and the tails of his dress coat often showed under his overcoat, even in the middle of the day! For he went to public meetings, and looked after the affairs of the whole town. Looking at the bathhouse, the prison, and all the public institutions, Diederich would think: "That belongs to Herr Buck." He must be tremendously wealthy and powerful. All the men, including Herr Hessling, took off their hats most respectfully to him. To deprive his son of something by force was a deed the dangerous consequences of which could not be foretold. In order not to be utterly crushed by the mighty powers, whom he so profoundly respected, Diederich had to go quietly and craftily to work.

Only once, when he was in the Lower Third—Diederich forgot all prudence, acted blindly and became himself an oppressor, drunk with victory. As was the usual approved custom he had bullied the only Jew in his class, but then he proceeded to an unfamiliar manifestation. Out of the blocks which were used for drawing he built a cross on the desk and forced the Jew on to his knees before it. He held him tight, in spite of his resistance; he was strong! What made Diederich strong was the applause of the bystanders, the crowd whose arms helped him, the overwhelming majority within the building and in the world outside. He was acting on behalf of the whole Christian community of Netzig. How splendid it was to share responsibility, and to have a collective sense of duty. When the first flush of intoxication had waned, it is true, a certain fear took its place, but all his courage returned to Diederich when he saw the face of the first master he met. It was full of embarrassed good will. Others showed their approval openly. Diederich smiled up at them with an air of shy understanding. Things were easier for him after that. The class could not refuse to honor one who enjoyed the favor of the headmaster. Under him Diederich rose to the head of the class and secretly acted as monitor. At least, he claimed, later on, to have done so. He was a good friend to all, laughed when they planned their escapades, an unreserved and hearty laugh, as befitted an earnest youth who could yet understand frivolity—and then, during the lunch hour, when he brought his notebook to the professor, he reported everything. He also reported the nicknames of the teachers and the rebellious speeches which had been made against them. In repeating these things his voice trembled with something of the voluptuous terror which he had experienced as he listened to them with half-closed eyes. Whenever there was any disparaging comment on the ruling powers he had a guilty feeling of relief, as if something deep down in himself, like a kind of hatred, had hastily and furtively satisfied its hunger. By sneaking on his comrades he atoned for his own guilty impulses.

For the most part, however, he harbored no personal antagonism against the pupils whose advancement was checked by his activities. He acted as the conscientious instrument of dire necessity. Afterwards he could go to the culprit and quite honestly sympathize with him. Once he was instrumental in catching someone who had been suspected of copying. With the knowledge of the teacher, Diederich gave this fellow pupil a mathematical problem, the working out of which was deliberately wrong, while the final result was correct. That evening, after the cheat had been exposed, some of the older boys were sitting in the garden of a restaurant outside the gates singing, as they were allowed to do after their gymnastics lesson. Diederich had taken a seat beside his victim. Once, when they had emptied their glasses, he slipped his right hand into that of his companion, gazed trustfully into his eyes, and began to sing in a bass voice that quivered with emotion:

I once had a comrade,
A truer one you'll never find. . . .

For the rest, with increasing school experience he could make a good show in most subjects, without going beyond what was required of him in any one, or learning anything in the world which was not prescribed in the curriculum. German composition was his most difficult subject, and anyone who excelled at it inspired him with an inexplicable mistrust.

Since he had been promoted to the highest form his matriculation at a university was certain, and his father and teachers felt that he ought to continue his studies. Old Hessling, having marched through the Brandenburger Tor in 1866 and in 1871, decided to send Diederich to Berlin.

As he did not care to venture far from the neighborhood of Friedrichstrasse he rented a room in Tieckstrasse, so that he had only to walk straight down and could not miss the University. As he had nothing else to do, he went there twice a day, and in the intervals he often wept from homesickness. He wrote a letter to his father and mother thanking them for his happy childhood. He seldom went out unless he had to. He scarcely dared to eat; he was afraid to spend his money before the end of the month, and he would constantly feel his pocket to see if it was still there.

Lonely as he was, he still did not go to Blücherstrasse with his father's letter to Herr Göppel, the cellulose manufacturer, who came from Netzig and did business with Hessling. He overcame his shyness on the fourth Sunday, and hardly had the stout red-faced man, whom he had so often seen in his father's office, waddled up to meet him than Diederich wondered why he had not come sooner. Herr Göppel immediately asked after everybody in Netzig, especially about old Buck. Although his beard was now grey he still respected old Buck as he had done when he was a boy like Diederich, only it was for different reasons. He took off his hat to such a man, one of those whom the German people should esteem more highly than certain persons whose favorite remedy was blood and iron, for which the nation had to pay so dearly. Old Buck was a Forty-Eighter! and had actually been condemned to death. "It is to such people as old Buck," said Herr Göppel, "that we owe the privilege of sitting here as free men." And, as he opened another bottle of beer: "Nowadays we are expected to let ourselves be trampled on with jackboots. . . ."

Herr Göppel admitted that he was a Liberal opponent of Bismarck. Diederich agreed with everything that Göppel said: he had no opinion to offer about the Chancellor, the young Emperor and freedom. Then he became uncomfortable, for a young girl had come into the room, and at the first glance her elegance and beauty frightened him.

"My daughter Agnes," said Herr Göppel.

A lanky youth, wearing a flowing frock coat, Diederich stood there, blushing furiously. The girl gave him her hand. No doubt she wanted to be polite, but what could one say to her? Diederich said yes, when she asked him if he liked Berlin; and when she asked if he had been to the theatre, he said no. He was perspiring with nervousness, and was firmly convinced that his departure was the only thing which would really interest the young lady. But how could he get out of the place? Fortunately a third person appeared, a burly creature named Mahlmann, who spoke with a loud Mecklenburg accent, and seemed to be a student of engineering and a lodger at Göppel's. He reminded Fräulein Agnes of a walk they had arranged to take. Diederich was invited to accompany them. In dismay he pleaded the excuse of an acquaintance who was waiting for him outside and went off at once. "Thank God," he thought, "she already has an admirer," but the thought hurt him.

Herr Göppel opened the door for him in the dark hall and asked if his friend was also new to Berlin. Diederich lied, saying his friend was from Berlin. "For if neither of you know the city you will take the wrong bus. No doubt you have often lost your way in Berlin." When Diederich admitted it, Herr Göppel seemed satisfied. "Here it is not like in Netzig; you can walk about for half a day. Just fancy when you come from Tieckstrasse here to the Halle Gate you have walked as far as three times through the whole of Netzig. . . . Well, now, next Sunday you must come to lunch."

Diederich promised to come. When the time came he would have preferred not to go; he went only because he was afraid of his father. This time he had a *tête-à-tête* with the young lady. Diederich behaved as if absorbed in his own affairs and under no obligation to entertain her. She began again to speak about the theatre, but he interrupted her gruffly, saying he had no time for such things. Oh, yes, her father had told her that Herr Hessling was studying chemistry.

"Yes. As a matter of fact that is the only science which can justify its existence," Diederich asserted, without exactly knowing what put that idea into his head.

Fräulein Göppel let her bag drop, but he stooped so reluctantly that she had picked it up before he could get to it. In spite of that, she thanked him softly and almost shyly. Diederich was annoyed. "These coquettish women are horrible," he reflected. She was looking for something in her bag.

"Now I have lost it—I mean my sticking plaster. It is bleeding again."

She unwound her handkerchief from her finger. It looked so much like snow that Diederich thought that the blood on it would sink in.

"I have some plaster," he said with a bow.

He seized her finger, and before she could wipe off the blood, he licked it.

"What on earth are you doing?"

He himself was startled, and wrinkling his brow solemnly he said: "Oh, as a chemist I have to do worse things than that."

She smiled. "Oh, yes, of course, you are a sort of doctor . . . How well you do it," she remarked as she watched him sticking on the plaster.

"There," he said, pushing her hand away and moving back. The air seemed to have become close and he thought: "If it were only possible to avoid touching her skin. It is so disgustingly soft." Agnes stared over his head. After a time she tried again: "Haven't we mutual relations in Netzig?" She compelled him to discuss a few families and they discovered they were cousins.

"Your mother is still living, isn't she? You should be glad of that. Mine is long since dead. I don't suppose I shall live long either. One has premonitions"—and she smiled sadly and apologetically.

Silently Diederich decided that this sentimentality was ridiculous. Another long interval, and as they both hastened to speak, the gentleman from Mecklenburg arrived. He squeezed Diederich's hand so hard that the latter winced, and at the same time he looked into his face with a smile of triumph. He drew a chair unconcernedly close to Agnes's knee, and with an air of proprietorship began talking animatedly about all sorts of things which concerned only the two of them. Diederich was left to himself and he discovered that Agnes was not so terrible, when he could contemplate her undisturbed. She wasn't really pretty; her flattened nose was too small, and freckles were plainly visible on its narrow bridge. Her light brown eyes were too close together, and they blinked when she looked at anyone. Her lips were too thin, as indeed was her whole face. "If she had not that mass of reddish brown hair over her forehead and that white complexion. . . ." He noted, too, with satisfaction that the nail of the finger which he had licked was not quite clean.

Herr Göppel came in with his three sisters, one of whom was accompanied by her husband and children. Her father and her aunts threw their arms round Agnes and kissed her fervently, but with solemn composure. The girl was taller and slimmer than any of them, and as they hung about her narrow shoulders she looked down on them with an air of distraction. The only kiss which she returned, slowly and seriously, was her father's. As Diederich watched this he could see in the bright sunlight the pale blue veins in her temples overshadowed by auburn hair.

Diederich was asked to take one of the aunts into the dining room. The man from Mecklenburg had taken Agnes's arm. The silk Sunday dresses rustled round the family table, and the gentlemen took precautions not to crush the tails of their frock coats. While the gentlemen rubbed their hands in anticipation and cleared their throats, the soup was brought in.

Diederich sat at some distance from Agnes, and he could not see her unless he bent forward—which he carefully refrained from doing. As his neighbor left him in peace, he ate vast quantities of roast veal and cauliflower. The food was the subject of detailed conversation and he was called upon to testify to its excellence. Agnes was warned not to eat the salad, she was advised to take a little red wine, and she was requested to state whether she had worn her galoshes that morning. Turning to Diederich, Herr Göppel related how he and his sisters somehow or other had got separated in Friedrichstrasse, and had not found one another until they were in the bus. "That's the sort of thing that would never happen in Netzig," he cried triumphantly to the whole table. Mahlmann and Agnes spoke of a concert to which they said they must go, and they were sure papa would let them. Herr Göppel mildly objected and the aunts supported him in chorus. Agnes should go to bed early and soon go for a change of air; she had over-exerted herself in the winter. She denied it. "You never let me go outside the door. You are terrible."

Diederich secretly took her side. He was overcome by a sense of chivalry: he would have liked to make it possible for her to do everything she wished, to be happy and to owe her happiness to him. . . . Then Herr Göppel asked him if he would like to go to the concert. "I don't know," he said indifferently, looking at Agnes who leaned forward. "What sort of a concert is it? I go only to concerts where I can get beer."

"Quite right," said Herr Göppel's brother-in-law.

Agnes had shrunk back, and Diederick regretted his remark.

They were all looking forward to the custard but it did not come. Herr Göppel advised his daughter to have a look. Before she could push away her plate Diederich had jumped up, hurling his chair against the wall, and rushed to the door. "Marie! the custard!" he bawled. Blushing, and without daring to look anyone in the face, he returned to his seat, but he saw only too clearly how they smiled at one another. Mahlmann actually snorted contemptuously. With forced heartiness the brother-in-law said: "Always polite; as a gentleman should be." Herr Göppel smiled affectionately at Agnes, who did not raise her eyes from her plate. Diederich pressed his knees against the leaf of the table until it shook. He thought: "My God, my God, if only I hadn't done that!"

When they wished each other *"gesegnete Mahlzeit"* he shook hands with everybody except Agnes, to whom he bowed awkwardly. In the drawing-room for coffee he carefully chose a seat where he was screened by Mahlmann's broad back. One of the aunts tried to look after him.

"What are you studying, may I ask, young man?" she said.

"Chemistry."

"Oh, I see, physics?"

"No, chemistry."

"Oh, I see."

Auspiciously as she had begun, she could not get any further. To himself Diederich described her as a silly goose. The whole family was impossible. In moody hostility he looked on until the last relative had departed. Agnes and her father had seen them out, and Herr Göppel returned to the room and found the young man, to his astonishment, still sitting there alone. He maintained a puzzled silence and once dived his hand into his pocket. When Diederich said goodbye of his own accord, without trying to borrow money, Göppel displayed the utmost amiability. I'll say good-bye to my daughter for you," he said, and when they got to the door he added, after a certain hesitation: "Come again next Sunday, won't you?"

Diederich was determined never to set foot in the house again. Nevertheless, he neglected everything for days afterwards to search the town for a place where he could buy Agnes a ticket for the concert. He had to find out beforehand from the posters the name of the virtuoso whom Agnes had mentioned. Was that he? Hadn't the name sounded something like that? Diederich decided, but he opened his eyes in horror when he discovered that it cost four marks fifty. All that good money to hear a man make music! Once he had paid and got out into the street, he became indignant at the swindle. Then he recollected that it was all for Agnes and his indignation subsided. He went on his way through the crowd feeling more and more mellow and happy. It was the first time he had ever spent money on another human being.

He put the ticket in an envelope, without any covering message, and, in order not to give himself away, he inscribed the address in his best calligraphy. While he was standing at the mailbox, Mahlmann came up and laughed derisively. Diederich felt that he had been found out and looked earnestly at the hand which he had just withdrawn from the box. But Mahlmann merely announced his intention of having a look at Diederich's rooms. He found that the place looked as if it belonged to an elderly lady. Diederich had actually brought a coffee pot from home! Diederich was hot with shame. When Mahlmann contemptuously opened and shut his chemistry books Diederich was ashamed of the subject he was studying. The man from Mecklenburg plumped down on the sofa and asked: "What do you think of the little Göppel girl? Nice kid, isn't she? Oh, look at him blushing again! Why don't you go after her? I am willing to retire, if it is any satisfaction to you; I have fifteen other strings to my bow."

Diederich made a gesture of indifference.

"I tell you she is worth while, if I am any judge of women. That red hair!—and did you ever notice how she looks at you when she thinks you can't see her?"

"Not at me," said Diederich even more indifferently. "I don't care a damn about it anyhow."

"So much the worse for you!" Mahlmann laughed boisterously. Then he proposed that they should take a stroll, which degenerated into a round of bars. By the time the street lamps were lit they were both drunk. Later on, in Leipzigerstrasse, without any provocation, Mahlmann gave Diederich a tremendous box on the ear. "Oh," he said, "you have an infernal—" He was afraid to say "cheek." "All right, old chap, among friends, no harm meant," cried the Mecklenburger, clapping him on the shoulder. And finally he touched Diederich for his last ten marks ... Four days later he found him weak from hunger, and magnanimously shared with him three marks he had meanwhile borrowed elsewhere. On Sunday at Göppel's—where Diederich would perhaps not have gone if his stomach had not been so empty—Mahlmann explained that Hessling had squandered all his money and would have to eat heartily that day. Herr Göppel and his brother-in-law laughed knowingly, but Diederich would rather never have been born than meet the sad, inquiring eyes of Agnes. She despised him. In desperation he consoled himself with the thought: "She always did. What does it matter?" Then she asked if it was he who had sent the concert ticket. Everyone turned to look at him. "Nonsense! Why on earth should I have done that?" he returned, so gruffly that they all believed him. Agnes hesitated a little before turning away. Mahlmann offered the ladies sugar-almonds and placed what was left in front of Agnes. Diederich took no notice of her, and ate even more than on the previous occasion. Why not, since they all thought he had come there for no other reason? When someone proposed that they should go out to Grunewald for their coffee, Diederich invented another engagement. He even added: "With someone whom I cannot possibly keep waiting." Herr Göppel placed his stout hand on his shoulder, smiled at him, with his head a little on one side, and said in an undertone: "Of course you know it's my treat." But Diederich indignantly assured him that had nothing to do with it. "Well, in any case you will come again whenever you feel inclined," Göppel concluded, and Agnes nodded. She appeared to wish to say something, but Diederich would not wait. He wandered about for the rest of the day in a state of self-satisfied grief, like one who has achieved a great sacrifice. In the evening he sat in an overcrowded beer-hall, with his head in his hands, and nodded his head at his solitary glass from time to time, as if he now understood the ways of destiny.

What was he to do about the masterly manner in which Mahlmann accepted his loans? On Sunday the Mecklenburger had brought a bouquet for Agnes, though Diederich, who came with empty hands, might have said: "That is really from me." Instead of that he was silent, and was more resentful toward Agnes than toward Mahlmann. The latter commanded his admiration when he ran at night after some passer-by and knocked in his hat— although Diederich was by no means blind to the warning which this procedure implied for himself.

At the end of the month he received for his birthday an unexpected sum of money which his mother had saved up for him, and he arrived at Göppel's with a bouquet, not so large as to give himself away, or to challenge Mahlmann. As she took it the girl was embarrassed, and Diederich's smile was both shy and condescending. That Sunday seemed to him unusually gay and the proposal that they should go to the Zoological Gardens did not surprise him.

The company set out, after Mahlmann had counted them: eleven persons. Like Göppel's sisters, all the women they met were not dressed as they were on weekdays, as though they belonged today to a higher class, or had come into a legacy. The men wore frock coats, only a few wore dark trousers like Diederich, but many had straw hats. The side streets were broad, uniform and empty, not a soul was to be seen, no horse-droppings littered the pavement. In one street, however, a group of little girls in white dresses and black stockings bedecked with ribbons, were singing shrilly and dancing in a ring. Immediately afterward, in the main thoroughfare, they came upon perspiring matrons storming a bus, and the faces of the shop assistants, who struggled ruthlessly with them for seats, looked so pale beside their strong red cheeks that one would have thought they were going to faint. Everyone pushed forward, everyone rushed to the one goal where pleasure would begin. On every face was plainly written: "Come on, we have worked enough!"

Diederich became the complete city man for the benefit of the ladies. He captured several seats for them in the tram. One gentleman was on the point of taking a seat when Diederich prevented him by stamping heavily on his foot. "Clumsy fool!" he cried and Diederich answered in appropriate terms. Then it turned out that Herr Göppel knew him, and scarcely had they been introduced when both exhibited the most courtly manners. Neither would sit down lest the other should have to stand. .

When they sat down at a table in the Zoological Gardens, Diederich succeeded in getting beside Agnes—why was everything going so well today?—and when she proposed to go and look at the animals immediately after they had had their coffee, he enthusiastically seconded the proposal. He felt wonderfully enterprising. The ladies turned back at the narrow passage between the cages of the wild animals. Diederich offered to accompany Agnes. "Then you'd better take me with you," said Mahlmann. "If a bar really did break—"

"Then it would not be you who would put it back into its place," retorted Agnes, as she entered, while Mahlmann burst out laughing. Diederich went after her. He was afraid of the animals who bounded toward him on both sides with nary a sound but the noise of their breathing. And he was afraid of the young girl whose perfume attracted him. When they had gone some distance she turned round and said,

"I hate people who boast."

"Really?" Diederich asked, joyfully moved.

"You are being nice for a change today," said Agnes; and he: "I always want to be nice."

"Really?"—and now it was her voice that trembled slightly. They looked at one another, each with an expression suggesting that they had not deserved all this. The girl said complainingly:

"I can't stand the horrible smell of these animals."

Then they went back.

Malhmann greeted them. "I was curious to see if you were going to give us the slip." Then he took Diederich aside. "Well, how did you find her? Did you get on all right? Didn't I tell you that no great arts are required?"

Diederich made no reply.

"I suppose you made a good beginning? Now let me tell you this: I shall be only one more term in Berlin, then you can take her on after I am gone, but meanwhile, hands off—my little friend!" As he said this, his small head looked malicious on his immense body.

Diederich was dismissed. He had received a terrible fright and did not again venture near Agnes. She did not pay much attention to Mahlmann, but shouted over her shoulder: "Father! it is beautiful today and I really feel well."

Herr Göppel took her arm between his hands, as if he were going to squeeze it tight, but he scarcely touched it. His bright eyes laughed and filled with tears. When the rest of the family had gone, he called his daughter and the two young men, and declared that this was a day that must be celebrated; they would go to Unter den Linden and afterward get something to eat.

"Father is becoming frivolous!" cried Agnes, looking at Diederich. But he kept his eyes fixed on the ground. In the tram he was so clumsy that he got separated far from the others, and in the crowd in Friedrichstrasse he walked behind alone with Herr Göppel. Suddenly Göuppel stopped, fumbled nervously at his waistcoat and asked:

"Where is my watch?"

It had disappeared along with the chain. Mahlmann said:

"How long have you been in Berlin, Herr Göppel?"

"Ah, yes"—Göppel turned to Diederich.

"I have been living here for thirty years, but such a thing has never happened to me before." Then, with a certain pride: "Such a thing couldn't happen in Netzig."

Now, instead of going to a restaurant, they had to go to the police station and lodge a complaint. Agnes began to cough, and Göppel gave a start. "It would make us too tired after this," he murmured. With forced good humor he said good-bye to Diederich, who ignored Agnes's hand, and lifted his hat awkwardly. Suddenly, with surprising agility, he sprang on to a passing bus, before Mahlmann could grasp what was happening. He had escaped. Now the holidays were beginning and he was free of everything. When he got to his house he threw his heaviest chemistry books to the floor with a crash, and he was preparing to send the coffee pot after them. But, hearing the noise of a door, he began at once to gather up everything again. Then he sat down quietly in a corner of the sofa, and wept with his head in his hands. If it had only not been so pleasant before! She had led him into a trap. That's what girls were like; they led you on solely for the purpose of making fun of you with another fellow. Diederich was deeply conscious that he could not challenge comparison with such a man. He contrasted himself with Mahlmann and would not have understood if anyone had preferred him to the other. "How conceited I have been," he thought. "The girl who falls in love with me must be really stupid." He had a great fear lest the man from Mecklenburg come and threaten him more seriously. "I don't want her at all. If I only could get away!" Next day he sat in deadly suspense with his door bolted. No sooner had his money arrived than he set off on his journey.

His mother, jealous and estranged, asked him what was wrong. He had grown up in such a short time. "Ah, yes, the streets of Berlin!"

Diederich grasped at the chance, when she insisted that he go to a small university and not return to Berlin. His father held that there were two sides to the question. Diederich had to give him a full account of the Göppels. Had he seen the factory? Had he been to his other business friends? Herr Hessling wanted Diederich to spend his holidays learning the papermaking process in his Father's workshops. "I am not as young as I used to be, and my old wound hasn't given me this much trouble in quite some time."

Diederich disappeared as soon as he could, in order to wander in the Gäbbelchen wood, or along the stream in the direction of Gohse, and to feel himself one with Nature. This pleasure was now open to him. For the first time it occurred to him that the hills in the background looked sad and seemed full of longing. The sun was Diederich's warm love and his tears the rain that fell from heaven. He wept a great deal, and even tried to write poetry.

Once when he was in the chemist's shop his school friend, Gottlieb Hornung, was standing behind the counter. "Yes, I am playing the pharmacist a bit here during the summer months," he explained. He had even succeeded in poisoning himself by mistake, and had twisted backwards like an eel. It had been the talk of the town. But he would be going to Berlin in the autumn to set about the thing scientifically. Was there anything doing in Berlin? Delighted with his advantage, Diederich began to brag about his Berlin experiences. "The two of us will paint the town red," the chemist vowed.

Diederich was weak enough to agree. The idea of a small university was abandoned. At the end of the summer Diederich returned to Berlin. Hornung had still a few days to serve in the shop. Diederich avoided his old room in Tieckstrasse. From Mahlmann and the Göppels he fled out as far as Gesundbrunnen. There he waited for Hornung. But the latter, who had announced his departure from home, did not arrive. When he finally came he was wearing a green, yellow and red cap. He had been immediately captured by a fellow student for a students' corps. Diederich would have to join them also; they were known as the Neo-Teutons, a most select body, said Hornung; there were no fewer than six pharmacy students in it. Diederich concealed his fright under a mask of contempt, but to no effect. Hornung had spoken about him to the members of the corps, and he could not let him down; he would have to pay at least one visit.

"Well, only one," he said firmly.

That one visit lasted until Diederich lay under the table and they carried him out. When he had slept it off they took him for the *Frühschoppen,* for although not a member of the corps, he had been admitted to the privilege of drinking with them.

This suited him well. He found himself in the company of a large circle of men, not one of whom interfered with him, or expected anything of him, except that he should drink. Full of thankfulness and good will he raised his glass to everyone who invited him. Whether he drank or not, whether he sat or stood, spoke or sang, rarely depended on his own will. Everything was ordered in a loud voice, and if you followed orders you could live at peace with yourself and all the world. When Diederich remembered for the first time not to close the lid of his beer-mug at a certain stage in the ritual, he smiled at them all, nearly abashed at his own perfection!

That, however, was nothing compared with his confident singing! At school Diederich had been one of the best singers, and in his first song book he knew by heart the numbers of the pages on which every song could be found. Now he had only to put his finger between the pages of the *Kommersbuch*, which lay in its nail-studded cover in the pool of beer, and he could find before anyone else the song which they were to sing. He would often hang respectfully on the words of the president for a whole evening, in the hope that they would announce his favorite song. Then he would intone bravely: *The devil they know what freedom means.*

Beside him he heard Fatty Delitzsch bellowing, and felt cozily ensconced in the shadow of the low-ceilinged room, decorated in Old German style, with the students' caps on the wall. Around him was the ring of open mouths, all singing the same songs and drinking the same drinks, and the smell of beer and human bodies, from which the heat drew the beer again in the form of perspiration. When the hour turned late, he felt as though he were sweating, together with the others, from the same body. He had sunk his personality entirely in the students' corps, whose will and brain were his. And he was a real man, who could respect himself and who had honor, because he belonged to it. Nobody could separate him from it, or attack him individually. Let Mahlmann dare to come there and try. Twenty men, instead of one Diederich, would stand up to him! Diederich only wished Mahlmann were there now, he felt so courageous. He should preferably come with Göppel, then they would see how grand Diederich had become. What a splendid revenge that would be!

Diederich found a friend in the most harmless member of the whole crowd, Fatty Delitzsch. There was something deeply soothing about this smooth, white, humorous lump of fat, which inspired confidence. His corpulent body bulged far out over the edge of the chair and rose in a series of rolls, until it reached the edge of the table and rested there, as if it had done its uttermost, incapable of making any further movement other than raising and lowering the beer glass. There Delitzsch was in his element more than any of the others. To see him sitting there was to forget that he had ever stood on his feet. He was constructed for the sole purpose of sitting at the beer table. In any other position his trousers hung loosely and despondently, but now they swelled majestically and assumed their proper shape. It was only when Delitzsch's posterior face came thus to life that his anterior one did likewise, bright with the joy of life, and he became witty.

It was a tragedy when a young freshman played a joke on him by taking his glass away. Delitzsch did not move, but his glance, which followed the glass wherever it went, suddenly reflected all the stormy drama of life. In his high-pitched Saxon voice he cried: "For goodness' sake, man, don't spill it! Why on earth do you want to take from me the staff of life! That is a low, malicious threat to my very existence, and I could have you jailed for it!"

If the joke lasted too long Delitzch's fat cheeks sank in, and he humbled himself beseechingly. But as soon as he got his beer back, how all-embracing was his smile of forgiveness, how he brightened up! Then he would say: "You are a decent devil after all: Your health! Good luck!" He emptied his mug and rattled the lid for more beer.

A few hours later Delitzsch would turn his chair round and go and bend his head over the basin under the water tap. The water would flow. Delitzsch would gurgle chokingly, and a couple of others would rush into the lavatory drawn by the sound. Still a little pale, but with renewed good humor, Delitzsch would draw his chair back to the table.

"Well, that's better," he would say; and: "What have you been talking about while I was busy elsewhere? Can you not talk of a damn thing except women? What do I care about women?" and louder: "They are not even worth the price of a stale glass of beer. I say! Bring another!"

Diederich felt he was quite right. He knew women himself and was finished with them. Beer stood for incomparably higher ideals.

Beer! Alcohol! You sat there and could always get more. Beer was homely and true and not like coquettish women. With beer there was nothing to do, to wish and to strive for, as there was with women. Everything came by itself. You swallowed, and already something was accomplished; you were raised to a higher sense of life, and you were a free man, inwardly free. Even if the whole place were surrounded by police, the beer that was swallowed would turn into inner freedom, and you felt that examinations were as good as passed. You were through and had got your degree. In civil life you held an important position and were rich, the head of a great postcard or toilet paper factory. The products of your life's work were in the hands of thousands. From the beer table one spread out over the whole world, realized important connections, and became one with the spirit of the time. Yes, beer raised one so high above oneself that one had a glimpse of deity!

Diederich would have liked to go on like that for years. But the Neo-Teutons would not allow this. Almost from the very first day they had pointed out to him the moral and material advantages of full membership in the corps. But gradually they set out to catch him in a less indirect fashion. Diederich referred in vain to the fact that the had been admitted to the recognized position of a drinking guest, to which he was accustomed and which he found quite satisfactory. They replied that the aim of the association of students, namely, training in manliness and idealism, could not be fully achieved by mere drinking, important as that was. Diederich shivered, for he knew only too well what was coming. He would have to fight duels! It had always affected him unpleasantly when they had shown him the swordstrokes with their sticks, the strokes which they had taught one another; or when one of them wore a black skull cap on his head and smelt of iodine. Panic-stricken he now thought: "Why did I stay as their guest and drink with them? Now I can't retreat."

That was true. But his first experience soothed his fears. His body was so carefully padded, his head and eyes so thoroughly protected, that it was impossible for much to happen to him. As he had no reason for not following the rules as willingly and as carefully as when drinking, he learned to fence quicker than the others. The first time he was pinked he felt weak, as the blood trickled down his cheek. Then when the cut was stitched he could have jumped for joy. He reproached himself for having attributed wicked intentions to his kind adversary. It was that very man, whom he had most feared, who took him under his protection and became a most well-meaning instructor.

Wiebel was a law student, and that fact alone ensured Diederich's submissive respect. It was not without a sense of his own inferiority that he saw Wiebel's English tweeds and his colored shirts, of which he always wore several in succession, until they all had to go to the laundry. What abashed him most was Wiebel's manners. When the latter drank Diederich's health with a graceful bow, Diederich would go to pieces—the strain giving his face a tortured expression—spill one half of his drink and choke himself with the other. Wiebel spoke with the soft, insolent voice of a feudal lord.

"You may say what you will," he was fond of remarking, "good form is not a vain illusion."

When he pronounced the letter *f* in the word *form*, he contracted his mouth to a small, dark mousehole, and emitted the sound in a slow crescendo. Every time Diederich was thrilled by so much refinement. Everything about Wiebel seemed so cultivated to him: his reddish moustache which grew high up on his lip, and his long, curved nails, which curved downward, not upward as Diederich's did; the strong masculine odor given off by Wiebel, his prominent ears, which heightened the effect of the carefully drawn part in his hair, and the catlike eyes deeply set in his face. Diederich had always observed these things with a wholehearted feeling of his own unworthiness. But, since Wiebel had spoken to him, and become his protector, Diederich felt as if his right to exist had now been confirmed. If he had had a tail, he would have wagged it gratefully. His heart swelled with happy admiration. If his wishes had dared to soar to such heights, he would also have liked to have such a red neck and to perspire constantly. What a dream to have Wiebel's purring lisp!

It was now Diederich's privilege to serve him; he was his fag. He was always in attendance when Wiebel got up, and got his things for him. As Wiebel was not in the good graces of the landlady, because he was irregular with his rent, Diederich made his coffee and cleaned his boots. In return, he was taken everywhere. When Wiebel visited the lavatory Diederich stood on guard outside the door, and he only wished he had his sword with him so that he might shoulder it.

Wiebel would have deserved such attention. The honor of the corps, in which Diederich's honor and his whole consciousness were rooted, had its finest representative in Wiebel. On behalf of the Neo-Teutons he would fight a duel with anyone. He had raised

the dignity of the corps, for he was reputed once to have reprimanded a member of the most exclusive corps in Germany. He
had also a relative in the Emperor Franz Josef second regiment of
Grenadier Guards, and every time Wiebel mentioned his cousin,
von Klappke, the assembled Neo-Teutons felt flattered, and bowed.
Diederich tried to imagine a Wiebel in the uniform of an officer of
the Guards, but his imagination reeled before such distinction.
Then one day, when he and Gottlieb Hornung were returning
highly perfumed from their daily visit to the barber's, Wiebel was
standing at the street corner with a paymaster. There could be no
doubt that it was a paymaster, and when Wiebel saw them coming
he turned his back. They also turned and walked away stiffly and
silently, without looking at one another or exchanging any remarks. Each supposed that the other had noticed the resemblance
between Wiebel and the paymaster. Perhaps the others were long
since aware of the true state of affairs, but they were all sufficiently
conscious of the honor of the Neo-Teutons to hold their tongues,
indeed, to forget what they had seen. The next time Wiebel mentioned "my cousin, von Klappke," Diederich and Hornung bowed
with the others, as flattered as ever.

By this time, Diederich had learned self control, a sense of good
form, *esprit de corps*, and zeal for things of a higher nature. He
thought with reluctance and pity of the miserable existence of the
common herd to which he had once belonged. Order and duty had
now been brought into his life. At regularly fixed hours he put in
an appearance at Wiebel's lodgings, in the fencing hall, at the barber's, and at *Frühschoppen*. The afternoon walk was a preliminary
to the evening's drinking, and every step was taken in common,
under supervision and with the scrupulous observance of prescribed forms and mutual deference, which did not exclude a little
playful roughness. A fellow student, with whom Diederich had
hitherto had only official relations, once bumped into him at the
door of the lavatory, and although both of them could barely stand,
neither would take precedence over the other. For a long time they
stood bowing and scraping—until suddenly, overcome by the same
need at the same moment, they burst through the door, charging
like two wild boars, and knocked their shoulders together. That
was the beginning of a friendship. Having come together in such
human circumstances, they drew nearer at the official beer table as
well, drank one another's health, and called each other *pig-dog*
and *hippopotamus*.

The life of the students' corps also had its tragic side. It demanded sacrifices and taught them to suffer pain and grief with a manly bearing. Delitzsch himself, the source of so much merriment, brought bereavement to the Neo-Teutons. One morning when Wiebel and Diederich came to fetch him, he was standing at his washstand and he said: "Well, are you as thirsty today as ever?" Suddenly, before they could reach him he fell, bringing down the crockery with him. Wiebel felt him all over, but Delitzsch did not move again.

"Heart failure," said Wiebel shortly. He walked firmly to the bell. Diederich picked up the broken pieces of crockery and dried the floor. Then they carried Delitzsch to his bed. They maintained a strictly disciplined attitude in the face of the landlady's vulgar tears. As they proceeded to attend to the next of their duties—they were marching in step—Wiebel said with stoical contempt of death: "That might have happened to any of us. Drinking is no joke. We should always remember that."

Together with the others, Diederich felt inspired by Delitzsch's faithful devotion to duty, by his death on the field of honor. They proudly followed the coffin, and every face seemed to say: "The Neo-Teutons for ever!" In the churchyard, with their black-draped swords lowered, they all wore the introspective expression of the warrior whose turn may come in the next battle, as his comrade's had come in the one before. And when the leader praised the deceased, who had won the highest prize in the school of manliness and idealism, each of them was moved as if the words applied to himself.

This incident marked the end of Diederich's apprenticeship. Wiebel left, he was preparing to be called to the bar, and from now on Diederich had to stand alone for the principles Wiebel had laid down, and inculcate them in the younger generation. He did this very strictly and with a sense of great responsibility. Woe to the freshman who incurred the penalty of drinking so many pints in succession. After no more than five minutes of this, the miscreant would have to grope his way out along the wall. The worst offense was for one of them to walk out of the door in front of Diederich. His punishment was eight days without beer. Diederich was not guided by pride or vanity, but solely by his lofty idea of the honor of his corps. He himself was a mere individual, and therefore nothing; whatever rights, whatever dignity and importance he enjoyed, were conferred upon him by the corps. He was indebted to it even for his physical advantages: his broad white face, his paunch which inspired the freshmen with respect, and the privilege of appearing on festive occasions in top boots and wearing a cap and sash, the joy of a uniform! It is true he had still to give precedence to a lieutenant, for the corps to which a lieutenant belonged was obviously a higher one. But, at all events, he could fearlessly approach a tram conductor without running the risk of being barked at. His manly courage was threateningly inscribed on his countenance in the slashes which grooved his chin, streaked his cheeks and cut their way into his close-cropped skull. What a satisfaction it was to exhibit these constantly to everyone! Once unexpectedly a brilliant occasion arose. He and two others, Gottlieb Hornung and the landlady's servant, were at a dance in Halensee. The two friends had for some months been sharing a flat which included a rather pretty servant. Both of them gave her small presents, and on Sundays they went out with her together. Whether Hornung had gone as far with her as he had was a matter about which Diederich had his private opinion. Officially and as a member of the corps he knew nothing.

Rosa was rather nicely dressed and she found admirers at the ball. In order to dance another polka with her, Diederich had to remind her that it was he who had bought her gloves. He had made a polite bow as a preliminary to the dance when suddenly a third person thrust himself between them and danced off with Rosa. Considerably taken aback, Diederich looked after them with the somber conviction that this was a case where he must assert himself. But, before he could move, a girl had rushed through the dancing couples, slapped Rosa, and dragged her roughly from her partner. It was the work of a moment for Diederich, when he had seen this, to dash up to Rosa's captor.

"Sir," he said, looking him straight in the eye, "your conduct is unworthy of a gentleman."

"Well, what about it?"

Astonished by this unusual turn to an official conversation Diederich stammered: "Dog."

"Hog," replied the other promptly with a laugh. Completely bewildered by this absence of the good form prescribed by the corps, Diederich prepared to bow and retire. But the other gave him a punch in the stomach and immediately they rolled on the floor. Amidst screams and encouraging shouts they fought until they were separated. Gottlieb Hornung, who was helping to find

Diederich's eyeglasses, cried, "There he goes"—and rushed after him, with Diederich following. They were just in time to see him and a companion getting into a cab, and they took the next one. Hornung declared that the corps could not allow such an insult to pass unpunished. "The swine runs away and does not even trouble to look after his lady."

Diederich said: "As far as Rosa is concerned, I consider the matter closed."

"So do I."

The chase was exciting. "Shall we overtake them? Our old nag is lame. Suppose this lout is not of high enough rank to fight a duel with us Neo-Teutons?" In that case they decided that the affair would be officially considered never to have happened.

The first carriage stopped before a nice-looking house in the West End. Diederich and Hornung got to the door just as it was shut. They posted themselves with determination in front of it. It grew cold and they marched up and down in front of the house, twenty paces to the right and twenty paces to the left, always keeping the door in view and repeating the same profound and serious remark. This was a case for pistols! This time the Neo-Teutons would buy their honor dearly! Provided he was not a prole!

At last the concierge appeared, and they interrogated him. They tried to describe the two gentleman, but found that neither of them had any special marks. Hornung maintained, even more passionately than Diederich, that they must wait, and for two more hours they marched up and down. Then two officers came out of the house. Diederich and Hornung stared, uncertain whether there might not be some mistake. The officers started, and one of them seemed to turn slightly pale. That settled the matter for Diederich. He walked up to the one who had turned pale.

"I beg your pardon, sir—"

His voice faltered. The embarrassed Lieutenant replied, "You must be mistaken."

Diederich managed to say:

"Not at all. I demand satisfaction. You have—"

"I don't know you at all," stammered the Lieutenant. But his comrade whispered something in his ear: "That won't do," and taking his friend's card, together with his own, he handed them to Diederich, who gave the man one of his. Then he read: "Albrecht Count Tauern-Bärenheim." He did not bother to read the other card, but began to make zealous little bows. Meanwhile the second officer turned to Gottlieb Hornung.

"Of course, my friend meant no harm by the little joke. Needless to say, he is perfectly ready to give you satisfaction and fight a duel, but I wish to state that no insult was intended."

The other, at whom he glanced, shrugged his shoulders. Diederich stuttered: "Thank you very much."

"That settles the matter, I suppose," said the friend; and the two gentlemen went off.

Diederich remained standing there, his brow moist and his senses reeling. Suddenly he gave a deep sigh and smiled slowly.

This incident was the sole subject of conversation afterward at their drinking parties. Diederich praised the true knightly conduct of the count to his comrades.

"A real nobleman always reveals himself."

He contracted his mouth until it was the size of a mousehole and brought out in a slow crescendo:

"Good f-form is not a vain illusion."

He repeatedly appealed to Gottlieb Hornung as the witness of his great moment.

"He wasn't a bit stuck up, was he? Even a rather daring joke is nothing to a gentleman like that. He preserved his dignity all through. Simply *impeccable,* I tell you! His Excellency's explanation was so thoroughly satisfactory that it was impossible for me to—after all, we aren't ruffians, are we?"

Everyone understood and assured Diederich that the Neo-Teutons had come off quite well in this affair. The cards of the two noblemen were handed round by the juniors and were stuck between the crossed swords over the Emperor's portrait. There was not a Neo-Teuton that night who went home sober.

That was the end of the term, but Diederich and Hornung had no money to travel home. For some time past they had had no money for most things. In view of his duties as a corps member, Diederich's allowance had been raised to two hundred and fifty marks, but still he was up to his eyes in debt. All sources from which a loan could be expected were exhausted, and only the most harried prospect stretched out forbiddingly before them. Finally they were obliged to consider the question of recovering what they themselves had lent in the course of time to their comrades, little as this accorded with knightly practice. Many old friends must meanwhile have come into money, but Hornung could find none. Diederich remembered Mahlmann.

"He will be easy," he declared. "He is not a member of any corps, a common roughneck. I'll beard him in his den."

As soon as Mahlmann saw him, he at once burst into that tremendous laugh which Diederich had almost forgotten, and which brought about an immediate and irresistible drop in his spirits. Mahlmann had no tact. He should have felt that all the Neo-Teutons were morally present in his office with Diederich, and on their account he should have shown Diederich more respect. The latter had the sensation of having been roughly torn from that powerful unit, and of standing here as one isolated individual before another. This was an unforeseen and uncomfortable position. He felt all the less compunction in mentioning his business. He did not want any money back, such conduct would be unworthy of a comrade. He simply asked if Mahlmann would be so kind as to back a loan for him. Mahlmann leaned back in his desk-chair and said plain and straight: "No."

Diederich was astonished: "Why not?"

"It is against my principles to back a loan," Mahlmann explained.

Diederich flushed with indignation. "But I have gone security for you, and then the bill came to me and I had to hand over a hundred marks. You took care not to show up."

"So you see! And if I were to go security for you now, you wouldn't pay up either."

Diederich could only gape in astonishment.

"No, my young friend," Mahlmann concluded, "if I ever want to commit suicide I can do so without your help."

Diederich pulled himself together and said in a challenging fashion:

"I see you have no conception of a gentleman's honor."

"No," Mahlmann repeated with a monstrous laugh.

With the utmost emphasis Diederich declared:

"You appear to be a regular swindler. I understand that there is a good deal of swindling in the patent business."

Mahlmann stopped laughing. The eyes in his little head had taken on a threatening expression and he stood up. "Now, get out of here," he said quietly. "Between ourselves, I suppose, it doesn't matter; but my employees are in the next room, and they must not hear such talk."

He seized Diederich by the shoulders, turned him around, and shoved him along. Every time he tried to break loose Diederich received a powerful cuff.

"I demand satisfaction," he shrieked. "I challenge you to a duel!"

"I am at your service. Have you not noticed it? Then I'll get somebody else for you." He opened the door. "Friederich!" Then Diederich was handed over to one of the packers, who sent him sprawling down the stairs. Mahlmann called after him:

"No hard feelings, my young friend. Whenever you have anything else on your mind, be sure to call again!"

Diederich put his clothes in order and left the building in proper style. So much the worse for Mahlmann if he made such a boor of himself. Diederich had nothing to reproach himself with, and would have been brilliantly vindicated by a court of honor. The fact remained that it was most objectionable for an individual to allow himself such liberties. Every corps member had been insulted in the person of Diederich. Yet it could not be denied that Mahlmann had reawakened considerably Diederich's old respect for him. "A low dog," Diederich reflected. "But that's the way one has to be. . . ."

At home he found a registered letter.

"Now we can be off," said Hornung.

"What do you mean, we? I need my money for myself."

"You must be joking. I can't stay here alone."

"Then go and find someone else to keep you company!"

Diederich burst into such a laugh that Hornung thought he was crazy. Thereupon Diederich left for home.

On the way he noticed for the first time that his mother had addressed the letter. That was unusual. . . . Since her last card, she said, his father had been much worse: Why had Diederich not come?

"We must be prepared for the worst. If you want to see your dearly beloved father again, do not delay any longer, my son."

These expressions made Diederich feel uncomfortable. He decided simply not to believe his mother. "I never believe women anyhow, and mother is not quite right in her mind."

Nevertheless, Herr Hessling was breathing his last when Diederich arrived.

Overcome by the sight, Diederich immediately burst into a most undignified wailing as he crossed the threshold. He stumbled to the bedside, and his face at that moment was as wet as if he had been washing it. He flapped his arms a number of times, like a bird beating its wings, and let them fall helplessly to his side. Suddenly he noticed his father's right hand on the coverlet, and knelt down and kissed it. Frau Hessling, silent and shrinking, even at the last breath of her master, did the same to his left hand. Diederich remembered how this black, misshapen fingernail had hit his cheek, when his father boxed his ears, and he wept aloud. And the thrashings when he had stolen the buttons from the rags! This hand had been terrible, but Diederich's heart ached now that he was about to lose it. He felt that the same thought was in his mother's mind and she guessed what was passing in his. They fell into one another's arms across the bed.

When the visits of condolence began, Diederich was himself again. He stood firm before the whole of Netzig as the representative of the Neo-Teutons, secure in his knowledge of gentlemanly behavior. He almost forgot he was in mourning, so great was the attention he aroused. He went all the way out to the hall door to receive old Herr Buck. The bulky person of Netzig's leading citizen was majestic in his fine frock coat. With great dignity he carried his upturned silk hat in front of him in one hand, while the other, from which he had taken his black glove to shake hands with Diederich, felt extraordinarily soft. His blue eyes gazed warmly at Diederich and he said:

"Your father was a good citizen. Strive to become one, too, young man. Always respect the rights of your fellow citizens. Your own human dignity demands that of you. I trust that we shall work here together in our town for the common welfare. You will be graduating soon, no doubt?"

Diederich could scarcely answer yes, he was so stricken by a sense of reverence. Old Buck asked in a lighter tone:

"Did my youngest son look you up in Berlin? No? Oh, he must do that. He is also studying there now. I expect he'll soon have to do his year's military service. Have you got that behind you?"

"No"—and Diederich turned very red. He stammered his excuses. It had been quite impossible for him hitherto to interrupt his studies. But old Buck shrugged his shoulders as if the subject were hardly worth discussing.

By his father's will Diederich was appointed, together with the old bookkeeper, Sötbier, as the guardian of his two sisters. Sötbier informed him that there was a capital of seventy thousand marks which was to serve as a dowry for the two girls. Even the interest could not be touched. In late years the average net profit of the factory had been nine thousand marks. "That's all?" asked Diederich. Sötbier looked at him, horrified at first and then reproachful. If the young gentleman only knew how his late lamented father and Sötbier had worked up the business! Of course there was still room for improvement. . . .

"Oh, all right," said Diederich. He saw that many changes would have to be made here. Was he expected to live on one quarter of nine thousand marks? This assumption on the part of the deceased made him indignant. His mother stated that the dear departed had expressed the hope on his deathbed that he would live on in his son Diederich, that Diederich would never marry, and always care for the family, but Diederich burst out: "Father was not a sickly sentimentalist like you," he shouted, "and he wasn't a liar either." Frau Hessling thought she could hear the voice of her husband again and bowed to the inevitable. Diederich seized the opportunity to raise his monthly allowance by fifty marks.

"First of all," he said roughly, "I must do my year's military service. That's an expensive business. Afterwards you can come to me with your petty money questions."

He insisted on reporting for military service in Berlin. The death of his father had filled him with wild notions of freedom. But at night he had dreams in which the old man came out of his office. His face was as grey as when he lay in his coffin—and Diederich awoke in a sweat of terror.

He departed with his mother's blessing. He had no further use for Gottlieb Hornung and their common property, Rosa, so he moved. He notified the Neo-Teutons in due form of his altered circumstances. The happy days of student life were over. The farewell party! They drank toasts of mourning which were intended for the old gentleman, but which also applied to Diederich and the first flowering of his freedom. Out of sheer devotion he finished up under the table, as on the night when he had first drunk with them as a guest. He had now joined the ranks of the old boys.

The next day, he was standing before the military doctor with a severe hangover and a crowd of other young men, all stark naked like himself. The medical officer looked disgustedly at all this manly flesh exposed to view, but when he saw Diederich's paunch his expression was one of contempt. At once they all grinned, and Diederich could not help looking down at his reddened stomach

... The medical officer had become quite serious again. One of the volunteers, who did not hear as well as the regulations prescribed, had a bad time, as they knew the tricks of the shirkers. Another, who had the misfortune to be called Levysohn, was told: "If you ever come to bother me here again, you might at least take a bath first!"

To Diederich the doctor said: "We'll soon massage the fat off you. After four weeks' training I guarantee you'll look like an upright Christian."

With that he was accepted. Those who had been rejected hastened into their clothes as if the barracks were on fire. The men who were considered fit for service looked at one another suspiciously out of the corners of their eyes and went off hesitantly, as if they expected to feel a heavy hand come down on their shoulders. One of them, an actor, who looked as if everything was a matter of indifference, went back to the doctor and said in a loud voice, carefully enunciating each word: "I beg to add that I am also homosexual."

The medical officer recoiled and went very red. Voicelessly he said:

"We certainly don't want such swine here."

To his future comrades Diederich expressed his indignation at this shameless conduct. Then he spoke again to the sergeant who had previously measured his height against the wall, and assured him that he was delighted. Nevertheless, he wrote home to Netzig to the general practitioner, Dr. Heuteufel, who used to paint his throat as a boy, asking if he could not certify that he was suffering from scrofula and rickets. Diederich could not be expected to destroy himself with military drudgery. But the reply was that he should not try to weasel out, that the training would do him no end of good. So Diederich gave up his room again and drove off to the barracks with his suitcase. Since he had to put in fourteen days there, he might as well save that much rent.

They at once began with horizontal-bar exercises, jumping, and other breathless exertions. They were herded in companies into corridors, which were called "departments," where they were "broken in." Lieutenant von Kullerow displayed a supercilious indifference, screwing up his eyes whenever he looked at the volunteers. Suddenly he shouted, "Instructor!", gave his orders to the sergeant and turned on his heels contemptuously. The sole object of the exercises on the barrack square, forming ranks, opening out, and changing places, was to keep these "dogs" on the jump. Diederich fully realized that everything here, their treatment, the language used, the whole military system, had only one end in view, to degrade one's personal dignity to a minimum. And that impressed him. Miserable as he was, indeed precisely on that account, it inspired him with deep respect and a sort of suicidal enthusiasm. The principle and the ideal were obviously the same as those of the Neo-Teutons, only the system was carried out more cruelly. There were no more comfortable intervals when one could remember one's humanity. Rapidly and inevitably one degenerated to the status of an insect, of a part in the machine, of so much raw material to be moulded by an omnipotent will. It would have been ruin and folly to rebel, even in one's secret heart. The most that one could do, against one's own convictions, was to shirk occasionally. When they were running Diederich fell and hurt his foot. It was not quite bad enough to make him limp, but he did limp, and when the company went out route marching, he was allowed to remain behind. In order to do this he had first gone to the Captain in person. "Please Captain—" What a catastrophe! In his innocence he had boldly addressed a power from which one was expected to receive orders silently and metaphorically on one's knees! A power whom one could approach only through the intermediary of a third person. The Captain thundered so loudly that the non-commissioned ranks came running, with expressions of horror at having witnessed such blasphemy. The result was that Diederich limped still more and had to be relieved of duty for another day.

Sergeant Vanselow, who was responsible for the misdemeanors of his recruits, only said to Diederich: "And you call yourself an educated man!" He was accustomed to seeing all his misfortunes come from the volunteers. Vanselow slept in their dormitory behind a screen. When lights were out they would tell dirty stories until the outraged sergeant yelled at them: "And you fellows call yourselves men of education!" In spite of his long experience he always expected more intelligence and better conduct from the one-year volunteers than from other recruits, and every time he was disappointed. Diederich he regarded as by no means the worst. Vanselow's opinion was not influenced solely by the number of drinks they brought him. He set even more store by the military spirit of ready submission, and that Diederich had. When they received instruction he could be held up as a model for the others. Diederich showed himself to be inspired by the military ideals of bravery and honor. When it came to differences of rank and stripes, he seemed to have an innate sense of these things. Vanselow would say: "Now I am the general commanding," and immediately Diederich would act as if he believed it. When he said: "Now I am a member of the Royal Family," then Diederich's attitude was such as to coax from the sergeant a smile of megalomania.

In private conversation in the canteen Diederich confided to his superior that military life filled him with enthusiasm. "The glory of being swallowed up in a great unit!" he would say. He could ask for nothing better in the world than to stay in the army. He was sincere, but that did not prevent him, when they were exercising on the parade ground that afternoon, from having no other wish than to lie down in his grave and die. The uniform, which was already cut to fit too closely, for reasons of smartness, was like an instrument of torture after eating. It was no consolation that the Captain appeared unspeakably warlike and daring as he gave his commands from his horse, when one could feel the undigested soup slopping about in one's stomach as one ran around breathlessly. The enthusiasm which Diederich was fully prepared to feel was tempered by his personal hardships. His foot was aching again, and Diederich waited for the pain in anxious hope, mixed with self-contempt, that it would get worse, so bad that he could not go route marching again. Perhaps he might not even have to exercise any more on the barrack square, and they would have to give him his discharge!

Things came to the point where he called one Sunday on the father of one of his college friends, who was an advisory member of the Medical Council. Red with shame Diederich confessed that he had come to ask for his support. He loved the army, the whole system, and would gladly follow that career. He would be part of a great mechanism, an element in its strength, so to speak, and would always know what he had to do, which was a splendid feeling. But now his foot was paining him. "I can't let it become too bad. After all, I have to support my mother and sisters." The doctor examined him. "The Neo-Teutons forever," he said. "It so happens your Surgeon-Major is a friend of mine." That fact was known to Diederich; his friend had told him. He took his leave full of anxious hope.

The effect of this hope was that he was barely fit to fall in the next morning. He reported sick. "Who are you? And why are you bothering me?" And the medical officer looked him up and down. "You look as fit as a fiddle, your waistline has even diminished."

But Diederich stood to attention and remained sick. The officer in charge had to come and make an examination. When the foot was uncovered the latter declared that if he did not light a cigar he would be ill. Still, he could find nothing wrong with the foot. The doctor pushed him impatiently from the chair. "Fit for duty, that's all, dismissed—"And Diederich was released. In the middle of drill he gave a sudden cry and collapsed. He was taken into the sick ward for slight cases where there was nothing to eat and a powerful smell of humanity. In this place it was difficult for the volunteers to procure their own food, and he got none of the other men's rations. Driven by hunger he reported himself cured. Cut off from all human protection, and from all the social privileges of civil life, he endured his dismal fate. But one morning, after he had lost all hope, he was called away from drill to the room of the Surgeon-Major-General. This important official wished to examine him. He spoke in an embarrassed, human kind of way, and then broke again into military gruffness which sounded no less affected. He too seemed to find nothing definite, but the result of his examination sounded somewhat different. Diederich was only to carry on "temporarily" until further notice. "With a foot like that . . ."

A few days later a hospital orderly came to Diederich and took an impression of this fateful foot on black paper. Diederich was ordered to wait in the consulting room. The Surgeon-Major happened to be passing and took the opportunity to express his complete contempt. "The foot is not even flat! All it wants is to be washed!" Just then the door was pushed open and the Surgeon-Major-General came in with his cap on his head. His step was firmer and surer than usual, he looked neither to the right nor to the left, stood silently in front of his subordinate, and glared gloomily and severely at his cap. The latter was embarrassed. He obviously found himself in a position which did not permit the usual comradeship of colleagues. But he realized the situation, took off his cap and stood at attention. His superior then showed him the paper with the tracing of Diederich's foot, spoke to him in a low tone but with emphasis and commanded him to see something that was not there. The Surgeon-Major blinked alternately at his commanding officer, at Diederich and at the paper. Then he clicked his heels; he had seen what he was ordered to see.

When the Major-General had gone, the Major approached Diederich. With a slight smile of understanding he said politely:

"Of course, the case was clear from the beginning. Because of the men we had to . . . you understand, discipline. . . ."

Diederich stood at attention as a sign that he understood.

"But," continued the Major, "I need hardly say I knew how your case stood."

Diederich thought: "If you didn't know it before you know it now." Aloud he said: "I trust you will pardon me for asking, sir, but I shall be allowed to continue my service, shall I not?"

"I cannot guarantee that," said the doctor, turning away.

From that time on Diederich was relieved of heavy duty. He was excused from route marches. His conduct in barracks was all the more friendly and willing. At roll-call in the evening the Captain came from the mess, a cigar in his mouth, and slightly tipsy, to confine to cells those who had wiped their boots instead of polishing them. He never found fault with Diederich. On the other hand, he vented his righteous wrath all the more severely on a volunteer who, now in his third month, had to sleep in the men's dormitory as a punishment because he had not slept there, but at home, during his first fortnight's service. At the time he had a high fever and would probably have died if he had done his duty. Well, let him die! The Captain's face assumed an expression of proud satisfaction every time he looked at this volunteer. Standing in the background, small and unnoticed, Diederich thought: "You see, my boy, the Neo-Teutons and an Advisory Member of the Medical Council are more useful than a fever of one hundred four degrees . . ." As for Diederich, the official formalities were one day happily fulfilled, and Sergeant Vanselow informed him that he had received his release. Diederich's eyes at once filled with tears and he shook his hand warmly.

"Just my luck for this to happen to me, and I had"—he sobbed—"such a happy time."

Then he found himself outside in the street.

He remained at home four whole weeks and studied hard. When he went out to meals he looked round anxiously lest an acquaintance should see him. Finally he felt he would have to visit the Neo-Teutons. He assumed a challenging attitude. "Until you have been in the army you have no idea what it's like. There, I can tell you, you see the world from a very different standpoint. I would have stayed altogether, my qualifications were so excellent that my superior officers advised me to do so. But then—"

Here he assumed a pained expression.

". . .came the accident with the horse. That was the result of being too good a soldier. The Captain used to get someone to drive in his dogcart to exercise the horse, and that is how the accident happened. Of course, I did not nurse my foot properly and resumed duty too soon. The thing got very much worse, and the doctor advised me to prepare my relatives for the worst."

Diederich spoke these last words tersely and with manly restraint.

"You should have seen the Captain; he came to see me every day, after the long marches, just as he was, his uniform still covered with dust. That's something that only happens in the army. During those days of suffering we became real comrades. Here, I still have one of his cigars. When he had to confess that the doctor had decided to send me away, I assure you it was one of those moments in a man's life which he can never forget. Both the Captain and I had tears in our eyes."

The whole company was deeply moved. Diederich looked bravely around at them.

"Well, now I suppose I must try to find my way back into civilian life. Your health."

He continued to cram, and on Saturdays he drank with the Neo-Teutons. Wiebel also turned up. He had become an assistant judge, on the way to becoming a state's attorney, and could only talk of "subversive tendencies," "enemies of the fatherland," and "Christian socialist ideas." He explained to the freshmen that the time had come to take politics seriously. He knew it was considered vulgar, but their opponents made it necessary. Real feudal aristocrats, like his friend, von Barnim, were in the movement. Herr von Barnim would shortly honor the Neo-Teutons with his company.

When he came he won all hearts, for he treated the students as equals. He had dark, slicked-back hair, the manner of a conscientious bureaucrat, and spoke in matter-of-fact tones, but at the end of his address his eyes had taken on a fanatical gaze, and he said good-bye quickly, pressing their hands fervently. After his visit the Neo-Teutons all agreed that Jewish Liberalism was the harbinger of social democracy and German Christians should rally to the Imperial Chaplain Stoecker. Like the others, Diederich did not connect the expression "harbinger" with any definite idea, and he understood "social democracy" to mean a general division of wealth. And that was enough for him. But Herr von Barnim had invited those who desired further information to come to him, and

Diederich would never have pardoned himself if he had missed so flattering an opportunity.

In his cold, old-fashioned, bachelor apartment Herr von Barnim held a private and confidential conclave. His political objective was a permanent system of popular representation as in the happy Middle Ages: knights, clergy, craftsmen and artisans. As the Emperor had rightly insisted, the crafts would have to be restored to the dignity which they had enjoyed before the Thirty Years' War. The guilds were to cultivate morals and the fear of God. Diederich expressed the warmest approval. The idea fully corresponded with his desire, as a member of a profession and a gentleman, to take his stand in life collectively rather than individually. He already pictured himself as the representative of the paper industry. Herr von Barnim frankly excluded their Jewish fellow citizens from his social order. Were they not the root of all disorder and revolution, of confusion and disrespect, the principle of evil itself? His pious face was convulsed with hatred and Diederich felt with him.

"When all is said and done," he remarked, "we wield the power and can throw them out. The German army—"

"That's just it," cried Herr von Barnim, who was walking up and down the room. "Did we wage the glorious war in order that I might sell my family estate to some Herr Frankfurter?"

While Diederich maintained a disturbed silence, there was a ring and Herr von Barnim said:

"This is my barber; I must work on him as well."

He noticed Diederich's look of disappointment and added: "Of course with such a man I talk differently. But each one of us must do his bit against the Social Democrats, and bring the common people into the camp of our Christian Emperor. You must do yours!"

Thereupon Diederich took his leave. He heard the barber say:

"Another old customer, sir, has gone over to Liebling just because Liebling now has marble fittings."

When Diederich reported to Wiebel the latter said:

"That is all very well, and I have a particular regard for the idealistic viewpoint of my friend, von Barnim, but in the long run it will not get us anywhere. Stöcker, you know, also made his damned experiments with democracy at the Ice Palace. Whether it was Christian or un-Christian democracy, I don't know. Things have got too far for that. Today only one course is still open: to hit out hard so long as we have the power."

Greatly relieved, Diederich agreed with him. To go around converting Christians had at once struck him as a rather embarrassing task.

"'I will attend to the Social Democrats,' the Emperor has said." Wiebel's eyes gleamed with a catlike ferocity. "Now what more do you want? The soldiers have been given their orders, and it may happen that they will have to fire on their beloved relatives. What do you think of that? I tell you, my dear fellow, we are on the eve of great events."

Diederich showed signs of excited curiosity.

"My cousin, von Klappke—"

Wiebel paused and Diederich clicked his heels:

"—has told me things which are not yet ripe for publication. Suffice it to say that His Majesty's statement yesterday, that the grumblers should kindly shake the dust of Germany from the soles of their feet, was a damned serious warning."

"Is that a fact? Do you really think so?" said Diederich. "Then it is the devil's own luck that I have to leave His Majesty's service just at this moment. I would have done my duty against the enemy inside Germany. One thing I do know, the Emperor can rely upon the army."

During those cold, damp days of February 1892, he went about the streets expecting great events. Along Unter den Linden something was happening, but what it was could not yet be seen. Mounted police stood guard at the ends of the streets and waited. Pedestrians pointed to this display of force. "The unemployed!" People stood still to watch them approaching. They came from a northerly direction, marching slowly in small sections. When they reached Unter den Linden they hesitated, as if lost, took counsel by an exchange of glances, and turned off toward the Emperor's palace. There they stood in silence, their hands in their pockets, while the wheels of the carriages splashed them with mud, and they hunched up their shoulders beneath the rain which fell on their faded overcoats. Many of them turned to look at passing officers, at the ladies in their carriages, at the long fur coats of the gentlemen hurrying from Burgstrasse. Their faces were expressionless, neither threatening nor even curious: not as if they wanted to see, but as if they wanted to be seen. Others never moved an eye from the windows of the palace. The rain trickled down from their upturned faces. The horse of a shouting policeman drove them on farther across the street to the next corner—but they stood still again, and the world seemed to sink down between those broad hollow faces, lit by the livid gleam of evening, and the stern walls beyond them which were already enveloped in darkness.

"I do not understand," said Diederich, "why the police do not take more energetic measures. That is certainly a rebellious crowd."

"Don't you worry," Wiebel replied, "they have received exact instructions. Believe me, the authorities have their own well-developed plans. It is not always desirable to suppress at the outset such excrescences on the body politic. When they have been allowed to ripen, then a radical operation can be performed."

The ripening process to which Wiebel referred increased daily, and on the twenty-sixth it was completed. The demonstrations showed that the unemployed were now more conscious of their objective. When they were driven back into one of the northern streets they overflowed into the next, and before they could be cut off, they surged forward again in increasing numbers. The processions all met at Unter den Linden, and when they were separated they ran together again. They reached the palace, were driven back, and reached it again, silent and irresistible, like a river overflowing its banks. The traffic was blocked, the stream of pedestrians was banked up until it flowed over slowly into the flood which submerged the square; into this turbid, discoloured sea of poverty, rolling up in clammy waves, emitting subdued noises and thrusting up, like the masts of sunken ships, poles bearing banners: "Bread! Work!" Here and there a more distinct rumbling broke out of the depths: "Bread! Work!" Swelling above the crowd it rolled off like a thunder cloud: "Bread! Work!" The mounted police attacked, the sea foamed up and subsided, while women's voices rose shrilly like signals above the uproar: "Bread! Work!"

They were swept along, carrying with them the curious spectators standing on the Friedrich monument. Their mouths were wide open; dust rose from the minor officials whose way to the office had been blocked, as if their clothes had been beaten. A distorted face, unknown to Diederich, shouted at him: "Here's something different! Now we are going for the Jews!"—and the face disappeared before he realized that it was Herr von Barnim. He tried to follow him, but in a big rush was thrown far across the road in front of a café, where he heard the crash of broken windows and a workman shouting: "They pushed me out of here lately with my thirty pfennig, because I didn't have a silk hat on." With him

Diederich was forced in through the window, between the over-turned tables, where they tripped over broken glass, crushing against one another and howling, "No more room in here! We must have air!" But still others poured in. The police pressed forward. In the middle of the street, a free passage was miraculously made, as if for a triumphant procession. Then someone cried: "There goes Emperor Wilhelm!"

Diederich found himself once more on the street. No one knew how it happened that they could suddenly move along in a solid mass the whole width of the street, and on both sides, right up to the flanks of the horse on which the Emperor sat—the Emperor himself. The people looked at him and followed. Shouting masses were dissolved and swept along. Everyone looked at him. A dark pushing mob without form, with plan, without limit, and gleaming above it a young man wearing a helmet: the Emperor. They saw. They had brought him down from his palace. They had shouted: "Bread! Work!" until he had come. Nothing had been changed, except that he was there, and yet they were marching as if to a review of the troops at Tempelhof.

On the outskirts, where the crowds were thinner, respectably dressed people were saying to each other: "Well, thank God, he knows what he wants!"

"What does he want then?"

"To show that mob who is in power! He tried treating them kindly. He even went too far in remitting sentences two years ago; they have become impertinent."

"He is certainly not afraid, you have to admit that. My word, this is an historical moment!"

Diederich listened and was thrilled. The old gentleman who had spoken turned to him. He had white side-whiskers and wore the Iron Cross.

"Young man," he said, "what our magnificent young Emperor is now doing will be taught the children one day in their school-books. Wait and see."

Many people had thrust-out chests and solemn faces. The gentle-men who rode behind the Emperor kept their eyes fixed decisively in front of them, but they guided their horses through the crowd as if all these folk were extras ordered to appear in some royal spectacle. At times they glanced sideways at the public to see how the people were impressed. The Emperor was aware only of himself and his own performance. Profound seriousness turned his features to stone and his eyes glared over the thousands whom he had fascinated. He measured himself against them, he, the master by the grace of God, and they his rebellious slaves. Alone and unprotected he had dared to come among them, strong only in the sense of his mission. They might lay violent hands upon him if that were the will of the Almighty. He offered himself as sacrifice to his own sacred cause. He would show them whether God was on his side. Then they would carry away the impression of his action and the eternal memory of their own impotence!

A young man wearing a wide-brimmed hat passed near Diederich and said: "Old stuff. Napoleon in Moscow fraternizing alone with the people."

"But this is splendid!" asserted Diederich, and his voice faltered with emotion. The other shrugged his shoulders.

"Theatrics, and not even good ones at that."

Diederich looked at him and tried to glare like the Emperor.

"I suppose you are one of them yourself."

He could not have explained what he meant by "them". He simply felt that here, for the first time in his life, he had to defend law and order against hostile criticism. In spite of his agitation, he had another look at the man's shoulders; they were not imposing. The bystanders, too, were expressing disapproval. Then Diederich asserted himself. With his huge stomach he pressed the enemy against the wall and battered in his hat. Others joined in pummelling him, his hat fell to the ground, and soon the man himself lay there. As he moved on, Diederich remarked to his fellow combatants:

"That fellow has certainly not done his military service. He hasn't even got scars on his face; he has never fought a duel."

The old gentleman with the side-whiskers and the Iron Cross turned up again and shook Diederich's hand.

"Bravo, young man, bravo!"

"Isn't it enough to make you angry," said Diederich, still panting, "when a fellow tries to spoil our historical moment?"

"You have been in the army?" queried the old gentleman.

"I would have liked nothing better than to stay there," Diederich replied.

"Ah, yes, the Battle of Sedan doesn't happen every day." The old gentleman touched his Iron Cross. "That's what we did!"

Diederich drew himself up and pointed to the Emperor and the subdued crowd.

"That is as good as Sedan!"

"Hm, hm," said the old gentleman.

"Allow me, sir," cried someone, waving a notebook. "We must publish this story. A touch of atmosphere, y'understand? I suppose it was a damned radical you bashed?"

"Oh, a mere trifle"—Diederich was still panting. "As far as I am concerned this would be the time to go straight for the enemy at home. We have our Emperor with us."

"Fine," said the reporter as he wrote: "In the wildly agitated throng people of all classes were heard expressing their devoted loyalty and unshakable confidence in His Majesty."

"Hurrah!" shouted Diederich, for everyone was shouting and, caught in a great surge of shouting people, he was carried along to the Brandenburg Gate. A few steps in front of him the Emperor was riding through. Diederich could see his face, its stony seriousness and glaring eyes, but he was shouting so loudly that his sight was blurred. An intoxication, more intense and nobler than that stimulated by beer, raised his feet off the ground and carried him into the air. He waved his hat high above all heads in enthusiastic madness, in a heaven where our finest feelings move. There on the horse rode Power, through the gateway of triumphal entries, with dazzling features, but graven as in stone. The Power which transcends us and whose hooves we kiss, the Power which is beyond the reach of hunger, spite and mockery! Against which we are impotent, for we all love it! Which we have in our blood, for in our blood is submission. We are an atom of that Power, a minuscule molecule of something it has spit out. Each one of us is as nothing, but massed in ranks as Neo-Teutons, soldiers, bureaucrats, priests and scientists, as economic organizations and conglomerations of power, we taper up like a pyramid to the point at the top where Power itself stands, with features of stone and glaring eyes! In it we live and have our being, merciless towards those who are remote beneath us, and triumphing even when we ourselves are crushed, for thus does power justify our love for it!

...One of the policemen lined up to keep a clear passage through the gateway gave Diederich a blow in the chest that took his breath away, but his eyes were full of the tumult of victory, as if he himself were riding away over all these wretches who had been cowed into swallowing their hunger. Let us follow him! Follow the Emperor! They all felt as Diederich did. A chain of policemen was too weak to restrain so much feeling. The people broke through.

Beyond the gate was another chain, so they had to make a detour, find a gap, and reach the Tiergarten by a roundabout way. Only a few succeeded, and Diederich was alone when he stumbled on to the riding path in the direction of the Emperor, who was also alone. Diederich looked like a man in a very dangerous state of fanaticism, dirty and torn, with wild eyes—from his horse the Emperor flashed his eyes in a glance which went straight through him. Diederich snatched his hat off, his mouth was wide open, but not a sound came from it. As he came to a sudden stop he slipped and sat down violently in a puddle, with his legs in the air, splashed with muddy water. Then the Emperor laughed. The fellow was a monarchist, a loyal subject! The Emperor turned to his escorts, slapped his thigh, and laughed. From the depths of his puddle, Diederich stared after him, his mouth still open.

Chapter 2

He brushed his clothes as best he could and turned back. A lady was sitting on a bench, and Diederich did not want to pass in front of her. To make matters worse, she kept looking toward him. "Silly fool," he thought angrily, but then he noticed an expression of great shock on her face and he recognized Agnes Göppel.

"I have just met the Emperor," he began at once.

"The Emperor?" she asked abstractedly. With large, unaccustomed gestures he began to pour out the emotions which were choking him. Our magnificent young Emperor, all alone in the midst of a mob of revolutionaries! They had smashed up a café, and Diederich himself had been in it! He had fought bloody fights in Unter den Linden for his Emperor! They ought to have turned cannons on them!

"I suppose the people are hungry," said Agnes shyly. "They, too, are human beings."

"Do you call them human?" Diederich rolled his eyes. "They are the enemy from within, that's what they are!"

But he grew a little calmer when he saw Agnes start again with fear.

"No doubt it amuses you to find all the streets barred on account of that mob."

No, that was most inconvenient for Agnes. She had had some errands in the city, but when she had wanted to go back to Blücherstrasse no buses were running, and she could not get through anywhere. She had been pushed back to the Tiergarten. It was cold and wet; her father would be anxious; what was she to do? Diederich assured her that he would make it all right. They continued their way together. All of a sudden he felt tongue-tied and kept looking about him as if he had lost his way. They were alone among the bare trees and the piles of wet, withered leaves. Where was all the manly rapture which had previously filled him? Diederich was embarrassed, as he had been during that last walk with Agnes, when Mahlmann had warned him, and he had jumped on to a bus, torn himself away, and disappeared. Agnes was just saying: "It is a very, very long time since you came to see us. Didn't papa write to you?"

Diederich explained awkwardly that his own father had died. Agnes hastened to express her sympathy. Then she went on to ask why he had suddenly disappeared three years ago.

"Isn't that so? It is nearly three years now."

Diederich recovered his self-possession, and explained that life in the students' corps had taken up all his time, that it was a very strenuous business. "And then I had to do my military service."

"Oh!"—Agnes stared at him. "What a great man you have become! And now I suppose you have taken your doctor's degree?"

"That will come very soon."

He gazed discontentedly in front of him. The scars on his face, his stately girth, all the signs of his well-earned manliness—were these nothing to her? Did she not even notice them?

"But what about you?" he said suddenly. A faint blush suffused her thin, pale face and even the bridge of her small, flattened nose, with its freckles.

"Yes, sometimes I don't feel very well, but I'll be all right again."

Diederich expressed his regrets.

"Of course I meant to say that you have become prettier,"—and he looked at her red hair which welled forth from under her hat, and seemed thicker than formerly because her face had become so thin. He was reminded of his former humiliations and of how different things were now. Defiantly he asked:

"How is Herr Mahlmann?"

Agnes assumed an air of contempt.

"Do you still remember him? If I were to see him again, I should not be particularly pleased."

"Really? But he has a patent office and could very easily marry."

"Well, what of it?"

"But you used to be interested in him."

"What makes you think that?"

"He was always giving you presents."

"I would have preferred not to take them, but then—" she looked down at the ground, at the wet fallen leaves—"then I could not have accepted your presents."

She was frightened and said nothing more. Diederich felt that something serious had happened and was silent also.

"They were not even worth talking about," he said finally, "a few flowers." And, with returning indignation: "Mahlmann even gave you a bracelet."

"I never wear it," said Agnes. His heart began to beat violently as he managed to say: "And if I had given it to you?"

Silence. He held his breath. Softly he heard her whisper: "In that case, yes."

With that they began to walk more quickly and without speaking a word. They came to the Brandenburg Gate, saw that Unter den Linden was threateningly full of police and hurried past it, turning into Dorotheenstrasse. Here there were few people about. Diederich walked more slowly and began to laugh.

"It is really very funny. Every present Mahlmann gave you was paid for with my money. I was still a greenhorn and he took everything from me."

They stood still. "Oh!"—and she gazed at him, her golden-brown eyes tremulous. "That's dreadful. Can you forgive me?"

He smiled in a superior way, and said that was ancient history, youthful follies.

"No, no," she said, quite disturbed.

Now, he said, the principal thing was: how was she to get home? They could not go any farther this way either, and there were no more buses to be seen. "I am very sorry, but you will have to put up with my society a little longer. In any case, I live near here. You could come up to my flat, at least you would be dry there. But, of course, a young lady can't do such a thing."

She still had that beseeching look.

"You are too kind," said she, breathlessly. "You are so noble." And as they entered the house, she added: "I know I can trust you, can't I?"

"I know what I owe to the honor of my corps," Diederich declared.

They had to pass the kitchen, but there was no one in it. "Won't you take off your coat until you go out again?" said Diederich graciously. He stood there without looking at Agnes, and while she was taking off her hat he stood first on one foot and then on the other.

"I must go and find the landlady and ask her to make some tea." He had turned towards the door, but started back, for Agnes had seized his hand and kissed it. "Agnes," he murmured, terribly frightened, and he put his arm around her shoulder as if to console her. Then she nestled against him. He pressed his lips to her hair, and pressed them fairly hard, because he felt that was the right thing to do. Under that pressure her whole being quivered and shook, as if she had been struck. Through her thin blouse her body felt warm and moist. Diederich felt hot. He kissed Agnes's neck, but suddenly her face was turned up to his, with her lips parted, her eyes half closed and with an expression which he had never seen before and which made his senses reel. "Agnes! Agnes! I love you," he cried, as if compelled by some deep anguish.

She did not answer. Light, warm, panting breaths came from her open mouth, and he felt that she was falling; as he carried her, she seemed to melt away.

She sat on the sofa and cried. "Don't be angry with me, Agnes," Diederich begged. Her eyes were wet and she looked at him.

"I am crying with joy," she said. "I have waited so long for you."

"Why," she asked, when he began to button her blouse. "Why do you cover me so soon? Do you no longer find me beautiful?"

He protested: "I am fully conscious of the responsibility I have undertaken."

"Responsibility?" Agnes queried. "Whose is it? I have loved you for three years, but you did not know it. It must have been our fate."

With his hands in his pockets Diederich was thinking that such is the fate of light-minded women. At the same time he felt the need of hearing her repeat her protestations. "So I am really the only man you ever loved?"

"I saw that you did not believe me. It was terrible when I knew that you had stopped coming, and that everything was over. It was dreadful. I wanted to write to you, to go and see you. I lost courage each time, because you might not want me any more. I was so run down that papa had to take me away."

"Where to?" asked Diederich, but Agnes did not answer. She drew him to her again. "Be good to me, I have no one but you!"

"Then you haven't got much," thought Diederich, embarrassed. Agnes appeared greatly diminished in his eyes, and lowered in his estimation, since he had proof that she loved him. He also said to himself that one could not believe everything a girl said who behaved like that.

"And Mahlmann?" he queried mockingly. "There must have been something between you and him—Oh, well, we'll say no more about it," he concluded, as she drew herself up dumbfounded with horror. He tried to put things right again, saying that he too was still completely overpowered by his joy.

She dressed very slowly. "Your father will not know what has happened to you," said Diederich. She merely shrugged her shoulders. When she was ready and he had opened the door, she stood for a moment and looked back into the room with a long glance, full of fear.

"Perhaps," she said, as if talking to herself, "I shall never come back again. I feel as if I were going to die tonight."

"Why do you say that?" asked Diederich aggrievedly. Instead of replying she clung to him again, her lips pressed to his, their two bodies from their hips to their feet so closely held together that they seemed but one. Diederich waited patiently. She broke away from him, opened her eyes and said:

"You must not think that I expect anything from you. I loved you and that is enough."

He offered to call a cab for her, but she preferred to walk. On the way he inquired after her family and other acquaintances. But by the time they had reached the Belle Alliance Platz he began to feel uneasy, and in rather muffled tones he said:

"Of course you must not think that I want to evade my responsibility to you. But, you understand, at present I am not earning anything, and I must make plans and get into harness at the factory . . ."

Agnes answered quietly and gratefully, as if she had been paid a compliment:

"How nice it would be if I could one day become your wife."

When they turned into Blücherstrasse he stopped. Hesitatingly he suggested it would probably be better if he turned back.

"Because someone might see us? That wouldn't matter at all, for I must explain at home that I met you and that we waited together in a café till the streets were clear."

"She is certainly a clever liar," thought Diederich. She added: "You are invited to dinner on Sunday, you must be sure to come."

This was too much for him, he started. "I must—? I am invited to—?"

She smiled softly and slyly. "It cannot be avoided. If anyone ever saw us—. Do you not want me to come to you again?"

Oh, yes, he did. Nevertheless, she had to coax him before he would promise to come on Sunday. In front of her house, he said good-bye with a formal bow, and turned quickly away. "Women of that type," he thought, "are horribly shrewd. I certainly won't be putting up with her for long." Meanwhile he noticed with reluctance that it was time to meet his friends for a drink. For some reason he was longing to be at home. When he had shut the door of his room behind him he stood and stared into the darkness. Suddenly he raised his arms, turned his face upward and breathed a long sigh:

"Agnes!"

He felt entirely changed, as light as if he trod on air. "I am terribly happy," was his thought, and, "Never in my life again shall I experience anything so wonderful!" He was convinced that until then, until that moment, he had looked at things from a wrong angle, and had estimated them wrongly. Now his friends were drinking and giving themselves an air of importance. What did it matter about the Jews and the unemployed? Why should he hate them? Diederich even felt prepared to love them! Was it really he who had spent the day in a struggling mob of people whom he had regarded as enemies? They were human beings; Agnes was right. Was it really he who, for the sake of a few words, had beaten somebody, had bragged, lied and foolishly over-exerted himself, and who had finally thrown himself, torn and stunned, in the mud before a gentleman on horseback, the Emperor, who had laughed at him? He recognized that, until Agnes came, his life had been poor and meaningless. Efforts which seemed to have been made by someone else, feelings which shamed him, and nobody whom he could love—until Agnes came! "Agnes! my sweet Agnes, you do not know how much I love you!" But she would have to know. He felt that he would never again be able to tell her as well as in this hour, and he wrote a letter. He wrote that he, too, had waited for her these three years, and that he had had no hope because she was too fine, too good, too beautiful for him; that he had said what he did about Mahlmann out of cowardice and spite, that she was a saint, and, now that she had condescended to him, he lay at her feet. "Lift me up, Agnes, I can be strong. I know I can, and I will dedicate my whole life to you!" He began to cry, pressing his face into the sofa cushion where her perfume still lingered, and sobbing like a child he fell asleep.

In the morning, it is true, he was astonished and irritated at not finding himself in bed. His great adventure came back to his mind and sent a delicious thrill through his blood to his heart. At the same time the suspicion seized him that he had been guilty of unpleasant exaggerations. He re-read his letter. It was all well and good and a man could really lose his head when he suddenly had an affair with such a fine girl. If she had only been there now he would have treated her tenderly. Still, it was better not to send that letter. It was imprudent in every way. In the end Papa Göppel would intercept it . . . Diederich shut the letter up in his desk. "I forgot all about eating yesterday!" he ordered a substantial breakfast. "I did not smoke either in order to preserve her perfume. But that's absurd; such things aren't done." He lit a cigar and went off to the laboratory. He resolved to release what was weighing on his heart in music rather than in words, for such lofty words were unmanly and uncomfortable. He hired a piano and tried to play Schubert and Beethoven with more success than at his music lessons.

On Sunday when he rang at the Göppels', Agnes herself opened the door. "The maid seemed in no hurry to leave the kitchen range," she said: but her glance told him the real reason. Not knowing what to say, Diederich allowed his eyes to wander to the silver bracelet which she rattled as if to draw attention.

"Do you not recognize it?" Agnes whispered. He blushed.

"The present from Mahlmann?"

"The present from you. This is the first time I have worn it."

Suddenly he felt the warm pressure of her hand, then the door of the drawing room opened. Herr Göppel turned to meet him: "Here is the man who deserted us!" But scarcely had he seen Diederich than his manner altered and he regretted his familiarity.

"Really, Herr Hessling, I should hardly have recognized you!"
Diederich looked at Agnes as much as to say: "You see, he notices that I am no longer a callow youth."

"Everything is unchanged here," Diederich observed, and he greeted the sisters and brother-in-law of Herr Göppel. In reality he found them all appreciably older, especially Herr Göppel, who was not so lively, and whose cheeks were unhealthily fat. The children had grown and someone seemed to be missing from the room.

"Yes, indeed," concluded Herr Göppel, "time passes, but old friends always meet again."

"If you only knew in what circumstances," Diederich thought with embarrassment and disdain as they went in to dinner. When the roast veal was brought on, it finally dawned upon him who used to sit opposite him. It was the aunt who had so haughtily asked him what he was studying, and who did not know that chemistry and physics were two entirely different things. Agnes, who sat on his right, explained to him that his aunt had been dead for two years. Diederich murmured words of sympathy, but his private reflection was: "Well, that's one less chatterbox." It seemed to him as if everyone present had been punished and buffeted by fate, he alone had been raised up by it in accordance with his merits. He swept Agnes from head to foot with a glance of possession.

As on the former occasion, they had to wait again for dessert. Agnes kept looking uneasily at the door and Diederich saw a shadow in her lovely pale eyes, as if something serious had happened. He suddenly felt the deepest sympathy for her and an immense tenderness. He rose and shouted through the door:

"Marie! the custard!"

When he returned Herr Göppel drank to him. "You did the same thing before. You are like one of the family. Isn't that so, Agnes?" Agnes thanked Diederich with a glance which stirred his heart to the depths. He had to control himself to prevent tears from coming into his eyes. How kindly her relatives smiled at him. The brother-in-law clinked glasses with him. What good-hearted people! and Agnes, darling Agnes, loved him! He was unworthy of so much kindness! His conscience pricked him and he vaguely resolved to speak to Herr Göppel afterward.

Unfortunately, after dinner Herr Göppel began to talk about the riots. When we had at last shaken off the pressure of the Bismarckian jackboot there was no necessity to irritate the workers with flamboyant speeches. The young man (that was how Herr Göppel referred to the Emperor!) will talk until he has brought about a revolution . . . Diederich felt himself called upon to repudiate such fault-finding most sharply, on behalf of the young men who were steadfast, and true, to their magnificent young Emperor. His Majesty himself had said: "I welcome heartily those who want to help me. I will smash those who oppose me." As he said this Diederich tried to glare. Herr Göppel declared that he would await events.

"In these tough times," Diederich continued, "everyone must stand his ground." He struck an attitude in front of the admiring Agnes.

"What do you mean by tough times?" Herr Göppel said. "The times are tough only when we make life difficult for one another. I have always got on perfectly well with my workmen."

Diederich expressed his determination to introduce entirely different methods at home in his factory. There would be no room for Social Democrats, and on Sunday the people would have to go to church! "Is that what things are coming to?" said Herr Göppel. He could not expect such a thing from his people, when he himself went only on Good Friday. "Am I supposed to lie to them? Christianity is all well and good, but nobody believes the parsons any longer." Then Diederich's countenance assumed the most superior expression.

"My dear Herr Göppel, all I can say is this: what the powers that be, and especially my esteemed friend, Assessor von Barnim, consider it right to believe, I also believe—unconditionally. That's all I have to say."

The brother-in-law, who was a civil servant, suddenly took Diederich's side. Herr Göppel was already considerably excited when Agnes interrupted with coffee. "Well, how do you like my cigars?" Herr Göppel tapped Diederich's knee. "Don't you see, we are at one where human interests are concerned."

Diederich thought: "Especially as I am, so to speak, one of the family." He gradually relaxed his uncompromising attitude, it was all so very cozy and comfortable. Herr Göppel wanted to know when Diederich would be "finished" and a doctor. He could not understand that a chemistry thesis took two years and more. Diederich launched into phrases which nobody understood about the difficulties of reaching a solution. He had the impression that Herr Göppel, for definite reasons of his own, was most anxious that he should finish his degree. Agnes seemed to notice this, too, for she intervened and changed the subject. When Diederich had said good-bye she accompanied him to the door and whispered: "To-morrow, at three o'clock at your rooms."

From sheer joy he seized her and kissed her, between the two doors, while in the very next room the servant was clattering the dishes. She asked sadly: "Don't you realize what would happen to me if someone were to come now?" He was taken aback, and as a proof that she had forgiven him, he asked for another kiss. She gave it to him.

At three o'clock Diederich would normally return to the laboratory from the café. Instead he was back in his room at two, and she came before three o'clock. "Neither of us could wait! We love one another so much!" It was nicer, much nicer than the first time. No more tears nor fears, and the room was flooded with sunshine. Diederich spread out Agnes's hair in the sun and buried his face in it.

She stayed until it was almost too late to make the purchases which had served as an excuse at home. She had to run. Diederich, who ran with her, was greatly concerned lest any harm should come to her. But she laughed, looked rosy, and called him her bear. And so ended every day on which she came. They were always happy. Herr Göppel noticed that Agnes was looking better than ever and this made him feel younger. For that reason the Sundays were also jollier. They stayed on till evening, then punch was made. Diederich played Schubert or he and the brother-in-law sang students' songs while Agnes accompanied them. Sometimes these two glanced at each other and it seemed to them both that it was their happiness which was being celebrated.

It came about that in the laboratory the porter would come and inform him that a lady was waiting outside. He got up at once, blushing proudly under the knowing looks of his colleagues. Then they wandered off, went to the cafés and to the waxworks. As Agnes was fond of pictures Diederich discovered that there were such things as art exhibitions. Agnes loved to stand in front of a picture that pleased her, a placid, festive landscape from a more beautiful country, and with half-closed eyes to share her dreams with Diederich.

"Just look, you'll see that it is not a frame, it is a gate with golden stairs and we are going down them and across the road; we are bending back the hawthorn bushes and stepping into the

boat. Don't you feel it rock? That's because we're trailing our
hands in the water, it is so warm. Up there, on the hill, the white
speck, you know, is our house, that's where we're going. Look, do
you see?"

"Oh, yes," said Diederich with enthusiasm. He screwed up his
eyes and saw everything that Agnes wished. He was so enthusiastic
that he seized her hand to dry it. Then they sat in a corner and
talked of the journeys they would take, of untroubled happiness in
distant sunny lands, and of love without end. Diederich believed
everything he said. Deep down, he knew very well that he was
destined to work and to lead a practical existence without much
leisure for such enthusiasms. But what he said here was true in a
higher sense than everything that he knew. The real Diederich, the
man he should have been, spoke the truth. But when they stood
up to go, Agnes was pale and seemed tired. Her lovely golden eyes
had a brightness that made Diederich feel uncomfortable, and in
a trembling whisper she asked: "Supposing our boat overturned?"

"Then I would rescue you!" replied Diederich with resolution.
"But it is far from the shore and the water is frightfully deep."
And when he seemed powerless to make any suggestion:
"We'd have to drown. Tell me, would you like to die with me?"
Diederich looked at her and shut his eyes.
"Yes," he said with a sigh.

But afterward he regretted having talked like that. He had noticed why Agnes suddenly got into a cab and drove home. She was
flushed and pale by turns and tried to hide how much she was
coughing. Then Diederich regretted the whole afternoon. Such
things were unhealthy, led nowhere except to unpleasantness. His
Professor had begun to hear about the lady's visits. It wouldn't do
for her to take him from his work whenever the whim seized her.
He explained the whole matter to her patiently. "I suppose you are
right," she said. "Normal people must have regular hours. But
what if I must come to you now at half-past five when I feel inclined
to love you most at four?"

He sensed mockery in this, perhaps even contempt, and was
rude. He had no use for a sweetheart who wished to hinder him
in his career. He had not counted on that. Then Agnes begged his
pardon. She would be quite humble and would wait for him in his
room. If he still had anything to do, he need have no consideration
for her. Diederich was shamed by this, he softened and abandoned
himself with Agnes in complaints against the world which was not

made entirely for love. "Is there no alternative?" Agnes asked. "You have a little money and so have I. Why worry about making a position for yourself? We could be so happy together." Diederich agreed, but afterward he resented her attitude. Now he kept her waiting, sometimes even deliberately. He even declared that going to political meetings was a duty which took precedence over his meetings with Agnes. One evening in May, as he returned home late, he met a young man at the door in a volunteer's uniform, who looked at him in a hesitating manner. "Herr Diederich Hessling?" "Oh, yes," Diederich stammered. "You are Herr Wolfgang Buck, aren't you?"

The youngest son of the great man of Netzig had at last decided to obey his father's orders and call on Diederich. He took him upstairs, as he could not think at once of an excuse to get rid of him, and Agnes was upstairs! On the landing he raised his voice so that she could hear him and hide. In fear and trembling he opened the door. There was nobody in the room, even her hat was not on the bed, but Diederich knew very well that she had been there a moment previously. He knew it by the chair which was not in its exact place. And he felt it in the air which seemed still to reverberate gently from the swish of her skirts. She must have gone into the little windowless room where his washstand was. He pushed a chair in front of it and with peevish embarrassment grumbled about his landlady who hadn't cleaned his room. Wolfgang Buck hinted that perhaps his visit was untimely. "Oh, no!" Diederich assured him, and he asked his visitor to be seated and got some cognac. Buck apologized for calling at such an unusual hour, but his military service left him no choice. "Oh, I quite understand that," said Diederich, and, in order to anticipate awkward questions, he began at once to explain that he had a year's service behind him, that he was delighted with the army, for it was the best life. How lucky were those who could stay in it! He, unfortunately, had family responsibilities. Buck smiled, a gentle, sceptical smile which irritated Diederich. "Well, of course, there were the officers; they, at least, were people with good manners."

"Do you see much of them?" Diederich asked with ironical intention. Buck explained simply that he was invited from time to time to the officers' mess. He shrugged his shoulders. "I go because I think it is useful to see everything. On the other hand, I mix a good deal with Socialists." He smiled again. "Sometimes I think I'd like to be a general, and sometimes a Labor leader. I am curious to know on which side of the fence I shall come down," he concluded, emptying his second glass of cognac. "What a disgusting person," thought Diederich. "And Agnes is in the dark room!" Then he said: "With your means you could be elected to the Reichstag or do anything else you like. I am destined for practical work. Anyhow, I regard the Social Democrats as my enemies, for they are the enemies of the Emperor."

"Are you quite sure about that?" queried Buck. "I rather suspect the Emperor of having a secret affection for the Social Democrats. He himself would like to have become the chief Labor leader. But they wouldn't have him."

Diederich fumed, saying it was an insult to His Majesty. But Buck was not in the least put out. "Don't you remember how he threatened Bismarck that he would withdraw military protection from the rich? In the beginning, at least, he had the same grudge against the rich as the workers, though, of course, for very different reasons, namely, because he cannot stand anyone else having power."

Buck anticipated the protest which he read in Diederich's face. "Please don't imagine," he said with animation, "that I speak with any antipathy. It is tenderness, rather, a sort of hostile tenderness, if you wish."

"I don't follow you," said Diederich.

"Well, you know, the sort of thing one feels for a person in whom one recognizes one's own defects or, if you like, virtues. At all events, we young men are all like our Emperor nowadays, we want to develop our own personality, but we know very well that the future belongs to the masses. There will be no more Bismarcks and no more Lassalles. Perhaps it is the more gifted among us who would like to deny this today. The Emperor would certainly deny it. And for anyone with so much power falling into his lap, it would be really suicidal not to exaggerate his personal value. But in the depths of his soul he must certainly have his doubts about the part which he has decided to act."

"The part?" Diederich asked, but Buck did not hear him.

"It is a role which can lead him very far, for it must appear quite a paradox in the world as it is today. The world expects nothing more from one individual than from another. What matters is status, not distinction; least of all great men."

"I beg your pardon!" cried Diederich, striking his chest. "And what about the German Empire? Should we have had that without great men? The Hohenzollerns are always great men." Buck screwed up his mouth in a melancholy and sceptical smile. "Then they had better look out for themselves and so had we. In his own sphere the Emperor is facing the same question as I. Shall I become a general and live my whole life preparing for a war which, so far as we can see, may well never happen? Or shall I become a more or less gifted Labor leader, at a time when the people can do without men of genius? Both would be romantic, and romanticism, as everyone knows, ends in bankruptcy." Buck drank two more glasses of cognac in succession. "What, then, am I to become?"

"A drunkard," thought Diederich. He debated with himself whether it was not his duty to begin a quarrel with Buck. But Buck was in uniform! Besides, the noise might have frightened Agnes out of her hiding place. Then, goodness knows what could happen! In any case he decided to make an exact note of Buck's remarks. Did the man actually hope to make a career for himself with opinions like that? Diederich remembered that in school Buck's German compositions had aroused in him a deep, if inexplicable, mistrust; they were too clever. "That's it," he thought, "he has remained the same, an intellectual, and so is the whole family." Old Buck's wife was a Jewess and had been an actress. Diederich felt humiliated in retrospect by the benevolent condescension of old Buck at his father's funeral. The son also humiliated him constantly and in all things: by his superior phrases, by his manners, by his friendships with officers. Was he a von Barnim? He was only from Netzig like Diederich himself. "I hate the whole lot of them!" From beneath his half-closed eyelids Diederich observed his fleshy face with its gently curved nose and moist, dreamy eyes. Buck rose: "Well, we'll meet again at home. I shall pass my examination next term, or the term after, and then what is there to do but play the lawyer in Netzig? And you?" he asked. Diederich solemnly explained that he did not intend to waste his time and would finish his doctor's thesis by the summer. Then he saw Buck to the door. "You are only a silly fool after all," he said to himself, "you didn't notice that I had a girl with me." He returned, pleased at his superiority to Buck, and to Agnes who had waited in the darkness and had not uttered a sound.

When he opened the door, however, she was leaning over a chair, her breast was heaving and with her handkerchief she was stifling her gasps. She looked at him with reddened eyes, and he saw that she had almost suffocated in there, and had cried—while he was sitting out here drinking and talking a lot of nonsense. His first impulse was one of immense remorse. She loved him! There she sat, loving him so much, that she endured everything! He was on the point of raising his arms and throwing himself before her, weeping and begging her pardon. He restrained himself just in time; he was afraid of the scene and the ensuing sentimental mood which would cost him several days of work and would give her the upper hand. He would not give her that satisfaction. For, of course, she was exaggerating on purpose. So he kissed her hastily on the forehead and said: "Here already? I did not know you had come." She gave a start, as if she were going to reply, but she remained silent. Whereupon he explained that someone had just gone out. "What a Jewboy, trying to make himself so important! Simply disgusting." Diederich rushed about the room. In order not to look at Agnes, he went quicker and quicker and talked with increasing vehemence. "Those people are our deadliest enemies! With their so-called refined education they paw everything which is sacred to us Germans! A damn Jewboy like that may consider himself fortunate when we put up with him. Let him pore over his law books and keep his mouth shut. I don't care a rap for his highbrow cleverness!" he screamed still louder, with the intention of hurting Agnes. As she did not answer, he tried a new line of attack. "It all comes because everyone now finds me at home. On your account I am constantly obliged to hang around the place!"

Agnes replied timidly: "We have not seen one another for six days. On Sunday again, you didn't come. I am afraid you don't love me any more." He stopped in front of her. Very condescendingly: "My dear child, it is hardly necessary for me to assure you anymore that I love you. But it is quite another question whether that means that I wish to watch your aunts crochet every Sunday, and to talk politics with your father who doesn't understand the slightest thing about it." Agnes bowed her head. "It used to be so nice. You got on so well with Papa." Diederich turned his back on her and looked out of the window. That was just it: he was afraid of being on too good terms with Herr Göppel. He knew from his bookkeeper, old Sötbier, that Göppel's business was going downhill. His cellulose was no good, and Sötbier no longer gave him any orders. Clearly a son-in-law like Diederich would have fit most conveniently into his plans. Diederich felt as if he were being ensnared by these people. By Agnes, too. He suspected her of working in conjunction with the old man. Indignantly he turned to her again. "Another thing, my dear child, let us be honest: what we two do is our affair, isn't it? So let's not bring your father into it. The relations which exist between us must not be mixed up with a family friendship. My moral sense demands that the two be kept entirely separate."

A moment passed, then Agnes rose as if she at last understood. Her cheeks were crimson. She walked toward the door and Diederich caught up to her. "But I didn't mean it like that, Agnes. It was only because I have too much respect for you—and I shall really be able to come on Sunday." She let him talk, unmoved. "Now, do be pleasant again," he begged. "You haven't even taken off your hat." She did so. He asked her to sit down on the sofa and she obeyed. She kissed him, too, as he desired. But though her lips smiled and kissed, her eyes were staring and unresponsive. Suddenly she seized him in her arms; he was frightened, for he did not know if it was hate that moved her. But then he felt that she loved him more passionately than ever.

"Today was really beautiful, wasn't it, my dear, sweet little Agnes?" Diederich asked, happy and contented.

"Good-bye," said she, hastily seizing her bag and umbrella while he was still dressing himself.

"You're in a great hurry."—"I suppose there is nothing more I can do for you?" She was already at the door, when suddenly she fell with her shoulder against the door post and did not move. "What's wrong?" When Diederich approached he saw that she was sobbing. He touched her. "Hey, what's the matter?" Then she began to cry loudly and convulsively. She did not stop. "Agnes, dear," said Diederich from time to time. "What has happened all of a sudden? We were so happy." He did not know what to do. "What have I done to you?" Between spasms of crying which half choked her, she managed to say: "I can't. I'm sorry." He carried her to the sofa. When the crisis was over Agnes was ashamed. "Forgive me. I can't help it." "Is it my fault?" "No, no. It is my nerves. I am sorry!"

Full of patience and sympathy he saw her to a cab. Looking back on it, however, the affair seemed to him half play-acting, and one of the tricks devised to ensnare him in the end. He could not get rid of the feeling that plans were being laid against his freedom and his future. He defended himself with gruff behavior, insistence upon his manly independence, and by his coldness whenever her mood was sentimental. On Sunday at Göppel's he was on his guard as though in an enemy's country; he was correct and unapproachable. When would his research work be finished? they would ask. He might find a solution the next day or in two years, he himself didn't know. He stressed the fact that he would remain financially dependent upon his mother. For a long time yet he would have no time for anything but business. When Herr Göppel reminded him of the ideal values in life, Diederich repelled him sharply. "Only yesterday I sold my edition of Schiller. I'm not crazy and I'm nobody's fool, either." Whenever, after such speeches, he felt the silent reproach of Agnes's glance upon him, he would feel for a moment as if someone else had spoken and he was walking in a fog, speaking falsely and acting against his own will. But that feeling passed off.

Whenever he sent for her, Agnes came, and she left whenever it was time for him to go off to work or to drink. She no longer enticed him to daydreams in front of pictures after he had once stopped in front of a sausage shop, and had declared that this spectacle was for him the highest form of artistic enjoyment. At last it occurred even to him that they saw one another very seldom. He reproached her because she no longer insisted on coming more often. "You used to be quite different." "I must wait," she said. "Wait for what?" "Until you are again as you used to be. Oh, I am quite certain that you will be." He remained silent for fear of an argument. Nevertheless, things came about as she had predicted. His thesis was finally finished and accepted. He had still to pass only an unimportant oral examination, and he was in the exalted frame of mind of one who has passed a turning point. When Agnes came with her congratulations and some roses he burst into tears and vowed that he would love her always and for ever. She announced that Herr Göppel was just starting on a business trip for several days. "And the weather is so perfectly lovely just now. . . ." Diederich at once accepted the hint. "We have never had such an opportunity. We must make use of it." They decided to go out into the country. Agnes knew of a place called Mittenwalde; it must be lonely there and as romantic as the name.

"We shall be together all day long!" "And the whole night, too," added Diederich.

Even the station from which they started was out of the way and the train was small and old-fashioned. They had the carriage to themselves. The day slowly darkened, the conductor lit a dim lamp for them, and, held close in one another's arms, they gazed silently with wide-open eyes at the flat, monotonous fields. Oh, to go out there on foot, far away, and lose oneself in the kindly darkness! They almost got out at a little village with a handful of houses. The jovial conductor held them back, asking if they wanted to sleep under a hayrick all night. Then they reached their destination. The inn had a great yard, a spacious dining room lit with oil lamps hanging from the rafters, and a general innkeeper, who called Agnes *"gnädige Frau,"* with a sly, Slavic smile, full of secret sympathy and understanding. After eating they would have liked to go upstairs at once, but they did not dare to do so and obediently turned the pages of the magazines which their host laid before them. As soon as he had turned his back, they exchanged a glance and in the twinkling of an eye they were on the stairs. The lamp had not yet been lit in the room and the door was still open, but they already lay in one another's arms.

Very early in the morning the sun streamed into the room. Down in the yard the chickens were pecking and fluttering on the table in front of the summer house. "Let us have breakfast there!" They went downstairs. How delightfully warm it was. A delicious smell of hay came from the barn. Coffee and bread tasted fresher than ever. Their hearts were so free and life stood open before them. They wanted to walk for hours and the innkeeper told them the names of the streets and villages. They joyfully praised his house and his beds. He assumed they were on their honeymoon. "Quite right," they said, laughing heartily.

The cobblestones of the main street stretched their peaks upwards and were gaily dappled by the summer sun. The houses were uneven, crooked, and so small that the street between them gave the impression of a field dotted with stones. The bell in the general store tinkled for a long time after the strangers had left. A few people, dressed in semifashionable style, glided among the shadows and turned to look after Agnes and Diederich, who felt proud, for they were the most elegantly dressed couple in the place. Agnes discovered the milliner's shop with hats for fine ladies. "It is incredible! Those were the fashion in Berlin three years ago!" Then they went through a rickety gate in the town wall and out into the country. The mowers were at work in the fields. The sky was heavy and blue and the swallows swam in the heavens as if in slow-moving water. The peasants' cottages in the distance were bathed in a hot, shimmering haze, and a wood stood out darkly with blue pathways. Agnes and Diederich took one another's hands and without premeditation they began to sing a song for wandering children, which they remembered from their schooldays. Diederich assumed a deep voice to excite Agnes's admiration. When they could not remember any more of the text their faces met and they kissed as they walked.

"Now I can see properly how pretty you are," said Diederich, looking tenderly into her rosy face, her bright eyes glittering like stars beneath their fair lashes. "Summer weather always agrees with me," replied Agnes with a deep breath which swelled her blouse. She looked slim as she walked along, with slender hips, her blue scarf floating behind her. It was too warm for Diederich, who first took off his coat, then his waistcoat, and finally admitted that he would have to seek out the shade. This they found along the edge of a field in which the corn was still standing, and under an acacia which was in bloom. Agnes sat down and laid Diederich's head in her lap. They played for a while with each other and joked: suddenly she noticed that he had fallen asleep.

He woke up, looked about him, and when he saw Agnes's face he beamed with delight. "Dearest," said she, "what a good-natured, silly old face you are making." "Come now, I can't have slept more than five minutes. What, really have I been asleep for an hour? Were you bored?" But she was more astonished than he that the time had passed so quickly. He withdrew his head from beneath the hand which she had laid upon his hair when he fell asleep.

They went back among the fields. In one place a dark mass was lying. When they peered through the stalks, they saw it was an old man in a fur cap, rusty coat and reddish corduroy trousers. He was crouching on his haunches and had twisted his beard round his knees. They bent down lower to get a better look at him. Then they noticed that he had been gazing at them for some time with dark, glowing eyes like live coals. In spite of themselves they hastened on, and the glances which they exchanged revealed the fear of frightened children. They looked about them: they were in a vast strange land, away in the distance behind them the little town loomed ominous and sleepy in the sun, and judging by the sky it seemed as if they had been traveling day and night.

How romantic was their lunch in the summer house of the inn, with the sun, the chickens, and the open kitchen window through which the plates were passed out to Agnes! Where was the bourgeois orderliness of Blücherstrasse, where Diederich's familiar pub-table? "I will never leave here," declared Diederich, "and I won't let you leave." "Why should we?" she answered. "I will write to father and have the letter sent to him by my married friend in Küstrin. Then he will think I am there."

Later they went out for a walk again in the other direction, where the sails of three windmills stood out on the horizon. A boat lay on the canal, and they hired it and drifted along. A swan came toward them. Their boat and the swan glided past one another noiselessly, the former coming to a stop of its own accord beneath the overhanging bushes. Suddenly Agnes asked about Diederich's mother and sisters. He said that they had always been good to him and that he loved them. He was going to have his sisters' photographs sent. They had grown up into pretty girls, or perhaps not pretty, but so decent and gentle. One of them, Emmi, read poetry like Agnes. Diederich was going to look after them both and get them married. But he would keep his mother with him, for he owed her all that was best in his life until Agnes came. He told her about the twilight hours, the fairy tales beneath the Christmas trees of his childhood, and even about their prayers "from the heart". Agnes listened, sunk in thought. At last she sighed: "I would like to meet your mother. I never knew my own." Full of pity he kissed her respectfully and with an obscure sense of uneasy conscience. He felt that he should now say one word which would console her forever. But he could not speak, and he put it off. Agnes gave him a profound look. "I know," she said slowly, "you are good at heart, but sometimes you need to go about things differently." Her words made him start. Then she concluded by way of apology: "I am not afraid of you at all today."

"Are you afraid at other times?" he questioned remorsefully. "I am always afraid when other people are jolly and in the highest spirits. With my friends I often used to feel as if I could not keep pace with them, and that they would notice it and despise me. But they did not notice anything. When I was a child I had a doll with big blue glass eyes, and when my mother died I had to sit in the next room with my doll. It kept staring at me with its hard, wide-open eyes that seemed to say to me: 'Your mother is dead. Now everyone will look at you as I do.' I would like to have laid it on its back so that the eyes would close. But I didn't dare. Could I have laid the people too on their backs? They all have eyes like that and sometimes—" She hid her face on his breast. "Even you have."

He felt a lump in his throat. His hand sought her neck and his voice trembled. "Agnes! my sweetest, you cannot know how much I love you . . . I was afraid of you, indeed I was! For three whole years I longed for you, but you were too beautiful for me, too fine, too good . . ." His heart melted and he told her everything that he had written to her after her first visit, in the letter which still lay in his desk. She had raised herself and was listening to him enchanted, with her lips parted. Softly she rejoiced: "I knew it, you are like that, you are like me!"

"We belong together," said Diederich, pressing her to him, but he was frightened by his own words.

"Now," he thought, "she will expect me to speak!" He wanted to do so, but felt powerless. The pressure of his arms around her back grew weaker . . . She made a movement and he knew that she no longer expected him to speak. They drew away from one another with averted faces. Suddenly Diederich buried his face in his hands and sobbed. She did not ask why, but soothingly stroked his hair for many minutes.

Speaking over his head into space, Agnes said: "Did I ever really believe this would last? It had to end badly because it has been so beautiful."

He broke out in desperation: "But it is not over!" "Do you believe in happiness?" she asked.

"Never again, if I lose you!"

She murmured: "You will go away out into the world and forget me."

"I would rather die!" and he drew her closer. She whispered against his cheek:

"Look how wide the stream is here, like a lake. Our boat has got loose and we have drifted far out. Do you still remember that picture? And that lake on which we once sailed in a dream? Where to, I wonder?" And more softly: "To where are we drifting?"

He did not answer. Wrapped in one another's arms, and lips pressed against lips, they sank backward deeper and deeper over the water. Was she pushing him? Was he dragging her? Never had they been so united. Now, Diederich felt, it was right. He had not been noble enough, not trustful enough, not brave enough, to live with Agnes. Now he had risen to her standards, and all was well.

Suddenly came a bump and they started up. Diederich's movement was so violent that Agnes fell from his arms to the bottom of the boat. He drew his hand across his forehead. "What on earth was that?" Shivering with fright he looked away from her, as if he had been insulted. "One should not be so careless in a boat." He allowed her to get up by herself, seized the oars at once and rowed back. Agnes kept her face turned towards the shore. Once she ventured to glance at him, but he looked at her with such harsh, mistrustful eyes that she shuddered.

In the darkening twilight they walked faster and faster back along the high road. Towards the end they were almost running. Not until it was dark enough to hide their faces did they speak. Perhaps Herr Göppel was coming home early the next morning. Agnes had to get back ... As they arrived at the inn, the whistle of the train could be heard in the distance. "We can't even eat together again," cried Diederich, with forced regret. In a terrible fluster they got their things, the bill was paid and they were off. They had scarcely taken their seats when the train started. It was fortunate that it took them some time to get their breath and to talk over the pressing matters of the last quarter of an hour. They had nothing more to say, and there they sat alone under the dim light as if stunned by a great misfortune. Was it that same somber country out there which had once enticed them and promised happiness? Was that only yesterday? It was now irrevocably past. Would the lights of the city never come to release them?

By the time they had arrived they had agreed that it was not worth while getting into the same cab. Diederich took the tram. With the merest glance and touch of the hands they separated.

"Phew!" exclaimed Diederich, when he was alone. "That takes care of that!" He said to himself: "It might just as well have gone wrong." Then, indignantly: "Such an hysterical person!" She would probably have clung to the boat. He would have taken the bath alone. She had only come up with the trick in the first place because she wanted to be married at all costs! "Women are so cunning and they have no inhibitions. We men cannot keep up with them. This time, by God, she played me for even more of a fool than she did Mahlmann. Well, let it be a lesson to me for life. Never again!" With an assured gait he went to the Neo-Teutons. Henceforth he spent every evening there, and in the daytime he studied for his oral examination, not at home, as a precaution, but in the laboratory. When he did come home he found it laborious to mount the stairs, and he had to admit that his heart was beating abnormally. Tremblingly he opened the door of his room—nothing. In the beginning, after it had become a little easier, he ended regularly by asking the landlady if anyone had called. Nobody had called.

A fortnight later a letter came. He opened it without thinking, then he felt inclined to throw it into the drawer of his desk without reading it. He did so, but then took it out again and held it in front of his face at arm's length. His hasty and suspicious glance caught a line here and there. "I am so unhappy . . ." "We've heard all that before," Diederich thought in reply. "I am afraid to come to you . . ." "So much the better for you!" "It is dreadful to think we have become strangers to one another. . . ." "Well, you've grasped that much, anyhow." "Forgive me for what has happened, if anything has happened . . ." "Quite enough!" "I cannot go on living . . ." "Are you beginning that all over again?" Finally he hurled the sheet of paper into the drawer with the other letter which he had filled with exaggerations during a night of madness, but which he had fortunately not posted.

A week later, as he was coming home late, he heard steps behind him which sounded familiar. He turned around with a start and the figure stood still with raised hands stretched out empty before it. While he opened the street door and stepped in he could still see her standing in the shadow. He was afraid to turn on the light in the room. While she stood out there in the dark, looking up, he was ashamed to light up the room which had belonged to her. It was raining. How many hours had she been waiting? She was probably still there, waiting with her last hope. This was more than he could stand. He was tempted to open a window, but he refrained. Then he suddenly found himself on the stairs with the key of the street door in his hand. He had just enough will power to turn back. He shut his door and undressed. "Pull yourself together, old chap!" This time it would not be so easy to extricate oneself from the affair. No doubt the girl was to be pitied, but after all it was her doing. "Above all, I must remember my duty to myself." The next morning, having slept badly, he even held it as a grievance against her that she had once more tried to make him deviate from his proper course. Now, of all times, when he was about to take his examination! It was just like her to behave in this irresponsible fashion. That scene in the night, when she had appeared as a beggar in the rain, had transformed her into a suspicious and uncanny apparition. He regarded her as definitely fallen. "Never again, not on your life!" he assured himself, and he decided to change his lodgings for the short time which he still had to stay, "even at a pecuniary sacrifice." Fortunately, one of his colleagues was just looking for a room. Diederich lost nothing and moved at once far out on to the North Side. Shortly afterward he passed his examination. The Neo-Teutons celebrated the occasion with a *Frühschoppen* which lasted until the evening. When he reached home, he was told that a gentleman was waiting in his room. "It must be Wiebel," thought Diederich, "coming to congratulate me." Then with swelling hope, "Perhaps it is Assessor von Barnim?" He opened the door and jumped back, for there stood Herr Göppel.

The latter was at a loss for words at first. "Well, well, why in evening dress?" he said, then with hesitation: "Were you by any chance at our house?"

"No," replied Diederich, starting again in fear. "I have just taken my doctoral examination."

"My congratulations," said Göppel. Then Diederich managed to say: "How did you find out my address?" And the other replied, "Certainly not from your former landlady, but there are other sources of information." Then they looked at one another. Göppel's voice had not been raised, but Diederich felt terrible threats in it. He had always refused to think about this catastrophe, and now it had happened. He had to sit down.

"As a matter of fact," began Göppel, "I have come because Agnes is not at all well."

"Oh, really," said Diederich with an effort of frantic hypocrisy. "What's wrong with her?" Mr Göppel wagged his head sorrowfully. "Her heart is bad, but, of course, it is only her nerves . . . of course," he repeated, after he had waited in vain for Diederich to say something. "Now apathy has driven her to melancholia and I would like to cheer her up. She is not allowed to go out. But won't you come and see us, tomorrow will be Sunday?"

"Saved!" thought Diederich. "He knows nothing." He was so pleased that he became quite diplomatic and scratched his head. "I had fully determined to do so, but now I am urgently required at home, our old manager is ill. I cannot even pay farewell calls on my professors, for I am leaving early in the morning."

Göppel laid his hand on his knee. "You should think it over, Herr Hessling. Often one has duties to one's friends as well."

He spoke slowly and his glance was so searching that Diederich's eyes could not meet it. "I only wish I could come,"he stammered. Göppel replied:

"You can. In fact, you can do everything that the present situation requires."

"What do you mean?" Diederich shivered inwardly. "You know very well what I mean," said the father, and, pushing back his chair a little: "I hope you do not think that Agnes has sent me here. On the contrary, I had to promise her I would do nothing and leave you in peace. But then I began to think that it would be really too silly for us two to go on playing hide-and-seek with one another, seeing that we are friends, and that I knew your late lamented father, and that we have business connections and so forth."

Diederich thought: "These business connections are a thing of the past, my dear man." He steeled himself.

"I am not playing hide-and-seek with you, Herr Göppel."

"Oh, well, then everything is all right. I can easily understand, no young man, especially nowadays, wants to take the plunge into matrimony without going through a period of hesitation. But then the matter is not always so simple as in this case, is it? Our lines of business fit into one another, and if you wanted to extend your father's business Agnes's dowry would be very useful." In the next breath, he added, while his glance faltered: "At this moment, it is true I can only put my hands on twelve thousand marks in cash, but you can have as much cellulose as you want."

"So, you see," thought Diederich, "and even the twelve thousand would have to be borrowed—that is, if you could raise a loan." . . . "You misunderstand me, Herr Göppel," he explained. "I am not thinking of marriage, that would require too much money."

Herr Göppel laughed, but his eyes were full of anxiety as he said: "I can do more than that . . ."

"You needn't trouble yourself," said Diederich in a tone of dignified refusal.

Göppel became more and more bewildered.

"Well, then, what do you really want?"

"I? Nothing. I thought you wanted something, since you have called on me."

Göppel pulled himself together. "That won't do, my dear Hessling, after what has happened, especially as it has gone on for so long."

Diederich looked the father up and down, and the corner of his mouth curled. "So, you knew about it, did you?"

"I was not certain," murmured Göppel. With great condescension Diederich retorted: "That would have been rather remarkable."

"I had every confidence in my daughter."

"That's where you were mistaken," said Diederich, determined to use every weapon in self-defense. Göppel's forehead flushed. "I also had confidence in you."

"In other words, you thought I was naive." Diederich stuck his hands in his trousers pockets and leaned back.

"No!" Göppel jumped up. "But I did not take you for the dirty cad that you are!"

Diederich stood up with an air of formal restraint. "Are you trying to get me to challenge you to a duel?" he asked. Göppel shouted:

"No doubt that is what you'd like! To seduce the daughter and shoot the father. Then your honor would be satisfied."

"You understand nothing about honor." Diederich in his turn became excited. "I did not seduce your daughter. I did what she wanted, and then I could not get rid of her. In this she takes after you." With great indignation: "How do I know that you were not in league with her from the beginning? This is a trap!"

Göppel's face looked as if he were going to shout still louder. He gave a sudden start, and in his ordinary tone, but with a voice that shook, he said: "We are becoming too heated, the subject is too important for that. I promised Agnes that I would remain quiet."

Diederich laughed derisively. "You see what a swindler you are, you said before that Agnes did not know you were here."

The father smiled apologetically. "In the end people can always agree in a good cause, isn't that so, my dear Hessling?"

But Diederich felt that it was dangerous to become amiable again. "What the hell do you mean by your 'dear Hessling?'" he yelled. "To you I am *Doctor Hessling!*"

"Of course," retorted Göppel, still with rage. "I suppose this is the first time that you have been able to be called Doctor. You may be proud of so auspicious an occasion."

"Do you wish to make any insinuations against the honor of my profession as well?" Göppel made a gesture of dissent.

"I make no insinuations. I am simply wondering what we have done to you, my daughter and I. Must you really have so much money when you marry?"

Diederich felt that he was blushing, and he proceeded with all the more assurance.

"Since you insist upon my telling you: my moral sense forbids me to marry a girl who is no longer pure when she marries."

Göppel was clearly on the point of another outburst, but his strength failed him, he could only stifle a sob.

"If you had seen her misery this afternoon. She confessed to me because she could not stand it any longer. I believe she does not even love me any more, only you. I suppose it is natural, you are the first."

"How do I know that? Before me a gentleman named Mahlmann frequented your house." Göppel shrank back as if he had received a blow on the chest.

"Yes, how can you tell? A person who tells lies cannot be believed."

He continued: "Nobody can expect me to make such a woman the mother of my children. My sense of duty to society is too strong." With this, he turned round and, stooping over the trunk that stood open, he began to fill it with his things.

Behind him he could hear the father who was now really sobbing—and Diederich could not help feeling moved himself by the manly noble sentiments which he had expressed, by the unhappiness of Agnes and her father which his duty forbade him to alleviate, by the painful memory of his love and this tragic fate . . . He listened with an anxious heart to Herr Göppel opening and closing the door, creeping along the passage, and heard finally the noise of the street door closing behind him. Now it was all over—then Diederich fell on his knees and wept passionately into his half-packed trunk. That evening he played Schubert.

That was a sufficient concession to sentiment. He must be strong. Diederich speculated, not without self-reproach, as to whether Wiebel had ever become so sentimental. Even a common bounder like Mahlmann had given Diederich a lesson in ruthless energy. It seemed to him highly unlikely that any of the others still had some soft spots left in them. He alone was so afflicted, by the influence of his mother. A girl like Agnes, who was just as crazy as his mother, would have rendered him completely unfit for these tough times. These tough times, the phrase always reminded Diederich of Unter den Linden with its mob of unemployed, women and children, of want and fear and disorder—and all that quelled, tamed into cheering, by the power, the all-embracing inhuman power, massive and glaring, which seemed to place its hooves upon those heads.

"It can't be helped," he said to himself in enthusiastic submission. "That's the way one has to be." So much the worse for those who were not, they fell under the hooves. Had the Göppels, father and daughter, any claims upon him? Agnes was of age and he had not given her a child. What then? "I should be a fool if I did anything to my own disadvantage which I cannot be compelled to do. I myself get nothing for nothing." Diederich was proud and glad of his excellent training. The students' corps, his military service and the atmosphere of Imperialism had educated him and made him fit. He resolved to put his well-earned principles to good use at home in Netzig, and to become a pioneer of the spirit of the times. In order to show an outward and visible sign of this resolution he went the following morning to the court hairdresser, Haby, in Mittelstrasse, and had a change made which he had more frequently noticed of late in officers and gentlemen of rank. Hitherto it had seemed to him too distinguished to be imitated. By means of a special apparatus he had the ends of his moustache turned up at right angles. When this was done he could hardly recognize himself in the glass. When no longer concealed by hair, his mouth had something tigerish and threatening about it, especially when his lips were drawn, and the points of his moustache aimed straight at his eyes, which inspired fear in Diederich himself, as though they glared from the countenance of Power itself.

Chapter 3

In order to avoid further trouble from the Göppel family, he departed at once. The heat made the railway carriage intolerable. Diederich who was alone, removed by turns his coat, waistcoat and shoes. A few stations before Netzig, people got in, two foreign-looking ladies, who seemed to be offended by the sight of Diederich's flannel shirt. He, for his part, found them repulsively elegant. In a language which he could not understand they began to complain to him, but he shrugged his shoulders and put his stockinged feet up on the seat. The ladies held their noses and shouted for help. The ticket-collector came in and then the guard himself, but Diederich showed them his second-class ticket and maintained his rights. He even gave these functionaries to understand that they had better be careful, as they could never tell to whom they were talking. When he had gained his victory and the ladies had withdrawn, another lady took their place. Diederich gave her a challenging stare, but she calmly took a sausage out of her bag and began to eat it out of her hand, smiling at him at the same time. This disarmed him, and beaming broadly he returned her overtures and spoke to her. It turned out that she was from Netzig. He told her his name and she rejoiced at the fact that they were old acquaintances. "Is that so?" Diederich looked at her searchingly: the fat, rosy face, with fleshy lips and small, impudent, pug nose, the white-blond hair, neat, smooth and carefully done, the plump youthful neck, and protruding from the half-gloves the fingers, which held the sausage and which themselves resembled little pink sausages. "No," he decided, "I do not recognize you, but you are certainly appetizing, like a freshly-scrubbed suckling pig." He put his arm around her waist and immediately received a box on the ear. "That was a good one," he said, rubbing his cheek. "Have you many more like that?" "Enough for every impudent puppy." She gave a throaty laugh and her little eyes twinkled naughtily. "You can have a piece of sausage, but nothing else." Involuntarily he compared her ability to defend herself with the helplessness of Agnes, and he said to himself: "One could marry a girl like that." In the end she herself told him her Christian name, and as he still could not guess who she was, she asked after his sisters. Suddenly he cried: "Guste Daimchen!" They both shook with laughter. "You used to give me buttons from the rags in your paper factory. I shall always be grateful to you for that. Dr. Hessling! Do you know what I used to do with those buttons? I collected them, and whenever my mother gave me money for buttons I used to buy sweets for myself."

"You are a practical person, too!" Diederich was delighted. "Then you used to climb over our garden wall, you little rogue! Most of the time you did not wear knickers, and when your dress slipped up there was a view from behind."

She shrieked; no decent man would remember such things. "Now, it must be much more interesting," added Diederich. She at once became more serious.

"Now, I am engaged to be married."

She was engaged to Wolfgang Buck! Diederich was silent and his face expressed his disappointment. Then he declared reluctantly that he knew Buck. She said cautiously: "I suppose you mean that he is rather eccentric? But the Bucks are a very distinguished family. Of course, in other families there is more money," she concluded. Feeling that this shot was directed at him, Diederich looked at her. She winked at him. He wanted to ask her something, but he had lost courage.

Just before they reached Netzig Fräulein Daimchen asked: "And what about your heart, Dr. Hessling, is it still free?"

"I have just managed to avoid an engagement." He nodded his head seriously. "Oh, you must tell me all about it," she cried, but their train was now entering the station. "I hope we'll meet again soon," said Diederich. "I can only say that a young man often comes damned near burning his fingers. A yes or no can spoil his whole life."

His two sisters were waiting at the station. When they caught sight of Guste Daimchen, they first made a wry face but then rushed up and helped to carry her luggage. As soon as they were alone with Diederich they explained their zeal. Guste had come into money and was a millionairess. So that was it! He was filled with timid respect.

The sisters related the story in detail. An elderly relative in Magdeburg had left all his money to Guste as a reward for the way she had looked after him. "And she earned it," remarked Emmi. "Towards the end, he was simply disgusting, they say." Magda added: "And, of course, you can draw your own conclusions, for Guste was in the house with him alone a whole year."

Diederich at once flushed with indignation. "A young girl should not say such things," he cried, but Magda assured him that Inge Tietz, Meta Harnisch and everyone was talking about it. "Then I command you most emphatically to contradict such talk." There was a moment's silence, then Emmi said: "Guste, you know, is already engaged." "I know that," muttered Diederich.

They met a number of acquaintances. Diederich heard them addressing him as "Doctor," beamed proudly, and walked on between Emmi and Magda, who cast admiring glances at his new style of moustache. When they reached the house, Frau Hessling received her son with open arms and shrieks like those of a drowning person being rescued at the last minute. Diederich also wept, much to his own surprise. All at once, he realized that the solemn hour of fate had come, in which he entered the room for the first time as the real head of the family, completely fitted out with the title of Doctor, and determined to guide the factory and the family according to his own well-considered views. He took the hands of his mother and sisters all together, and said in earnest tones: "I shall never forget that I am responsible before God for you."

Frau Hessling, however, was uneasy. "Are you ready, my boy?" she asked. "Our people are waiting for you." Diederich finished his beer and went downstairs ahead of his family. The yard had been swept clean and the entrance to the factory was framed with wreaths of flowers which surrounded the inscription "Welcome!" In front stood the old bookkeeper Sötbier, who said: "Well, good day, Dr. Hessling. I haven't had a chance to come up, there were still some things to do."

"On a day like this you might have left it," replied Diederich walking past him. Inside, in the rag room, he found the workers. They all stood clustered together: the twelve workmen who looked after the paper machine, the cylinder machine and the cutter, the three bookkeepers together with the women whose job it was to sort the rags. The men coughed, there was an awkward pause until several of the women pushed forward a little girl who held a bouquet of flowers in front of her and in a piping voice wished the Doctor welcome and good luck. With a gracious air Diederich accepted the flowers. Now it was his turn to clear his throat. First he turned towards his own family, then he looked sharply into the faces of his workers, one after another, even the black-bearded machinist, although this man's look made him feel uncomfortable. Then he began:

"Men and women! As you are my dependants, I will simply say to you that in the future you must put your shoulders to the wheel. I am determined to put some life into this business. Lately, as there was no master here, many of you probably thought you could take things easily. You were never more mistaken. I say this particularly for the older people who belong to my lamented father's time."

He raised his voice and spoke still more sharply and commandingly, looking all the while at old Sötbier:

"Now I have taken the rudder into my own hands. My course is set straight and I am guiding you to glorious times. Those who wish to help me are heartily welcome, but whoever opposes me in this work I will smash."

He tried to glare and the ends of his mustache rose still higher.

"There is only one master here, and I am he. I am responsible only to God and my own conscience. You can always count on my fatherly benevolence, but revolutionary desires will be shattered against my unbending will. Should I discover any connection between one of you"—

He caught the eye of the black-bearded mechanist, who looked suspicious.

—"and the Social Democratic clubs, our relationship will be severed. I regard every Social Democrat as an enemy of my business and of the Fatherland. . . . So now return to your work and consider well what I have told you."

He turned around sharply and marched off, breathing heavily. His strong words produced in him a kind of dizziness which made him incapable of recognizing any face. Disturbed and respectful, his family followed him, while the workers stared at one another in dumb amazement for quite some time before they reached for the bottles of beer which stood ready for the celebration.

Upstairs Diederich was explaining his plans to his mother and sisters. The factory would have to be enlarged, the house of their neighbor at the back would have to be purchased. The operation would have to be made competitive. A place in the sun! Did old Klüsing, who owned the Gausenfeld paper factory, imagine that he would go on forever getting all the business? . . . Finally Magda asked where he expected to get the money, but Frau Hessling cut short her impertinence. "Your brother knows all about that better than we do." Cautiously she added: "Many a girl would be happy if she could win his heart." Fearing his anger she pressed her hand to her mouth. But Diederich merely blushed. Then she had the courage to embrace him. "It would be such a terrible blow to me," she sobbed, "if my son, my dear son, went away from home. It is doubly hard for a widow. Frau Daimchen feels it too, now that her Guste is going to marry Wolfgang Buck."

"Perhaps not," said Emmi, the elder girl. "They say that Wolfgang is having an affair with an actress." Frau Hessling completely forgot to chide her daughter. "But where so much money is at stake! A million, people say!"

Diederich said contemptuously that he knew Buck, that he was not normal. "It must run in the family. The old man also married an actress."

"You can see where that leads," said Emmi. "People have been saying all sorts of things about the daughter, Frau Lauer."

"Children!" begged Frau Hessling nervously. But Diederich silenced her.

"That's all right, Mother, it is high time someone belled the cat. I take the view that the Bucks have long since become unworthy of their position in this town. They are a decadent family."

"The wife of Moritz, the eldest son," said Magda, "is nothing but a peasant. They were lately in town, and he has become quite the peasant himself." Emmi was full of indignation.

"And what about the brother of old Herr Buck? Always so elegant, and his five unmarried daughters. They have meals brought from the public soup kitchen. I know that for a fact."

"Herr Buck was the one who founded the public soup kitchen," explained Diederich. "Also the Aid Fund for Ex-Convicts and goodness knows what else. I'd like to know when he has time to look after his own business."

"I should not be surprised," said Frau Hessling, "if he hadn't very much more business left. Though, of course, I have the greatest respect for Herr Buck. He is so well thought of."

Diederich laughed bitterly. "Why? We have all been brought up to honor old Buck! The great man of Netzig! Sentenced to death in 'forty-eight!"

"But that was an historic honor, your father always used to say."

"Honor?" shouted Diederich. "When I know that anyone is against the Government that is quite enough for me. Why should high treason be an honor?"

Before the astonished women he launched into politics. These old Democrats who still pulled the strings were a positive disgrace to Netzig! Unpatriotic slackers, at odds with the Government! They were a mockery of the spirit of the time. Because old Judge Kühlemann was their representative in the Reichstag, and was a friend of the notorious Eugen Richter, business here was at a standstill and nobody got any money. Of course, there would be no railway connections or soldiers for such a radical town. No traffic and no influx of population! The gentlemen of the town administration, always from the same few families as everyone knew, awarded each other all the contracts and there was nothing left for anyone else. The Gausenfeld paper factory furnished all the supplies for the town, for Klüsing, the owner, also belonged to old Buck's gang!

Magda had something to add. "Recently the amateurs' show at the Civic Club was postponed because Herr Buck's daughter, Frau Lauer, was ill. That is simply popism."

"Nepotism, you mean," said Diederich sharply. He rolled his eyes. "And on top of it all, Herr Lauer is a Socialist. But Herr Buck had better look out! We shall keep an eye on him."

Frau Hessling raised her hands entreatingly. "My dear son, when you go to pay your calls in the town, promise me you will also go to Herr Buck's. After all, he is so influential." But Diederich promised nothing. "Other people want to see me," he exclaimed.

Nevertheless he did not sleep well that night. By seven o'clock he was down in the factory and at once made a row because the beer bottles of the day before were still lying about. "No boozing here. This is not a barroom. Surely that is in the regulations. Herr Sötbier?" "Regulations?" said the old bookkeeper. "We have none." Diederich was speechless. He shut himself up with Sötbier in the office. "No regulations? Then, of course, nothing can surprise me. What are those ridiculous orders on which you are working?" and he scattered the letters about on the desk. "It seems to be high time that I took charge. The business is going to the dogs in your hands."

"To the dogs, Master Diederich?"

"Doctor Hessling to you!" He insisted that they simply underbid all the other factories.

"We cannot do that for long," said Sötbier. "In fact we are not in a position to execute such large orders as Gausenfeld."

"And you call yourself a businessman! We'll simply install more machinery."

"That costs money," replied Sötbier.

"Then we'll borrow some! I'll bring some life into this business. Wait and see. If you don't want to back me up, I'll do it alone."

Sötbier shook his head. "Your father and I always agreed, Master Diederich. We built up this business together."

"Times have changed, and don't you forget it. I am my own manager."

"Impetuous youth," sighed Sötbier as Diederich slammed the door. He walked through the room in which the mechanical drum, beating loudly, was washing the rags in chlorine and started to enter the smaller room where the large boiler-beater was installed. In the doorway he unexpectedly met the black-bearded machinist. Diederich flinched and almost made room for him, but then elbowed him out of the way before the man could step aside. Snorting with impatience, he watched the machine at work, the cylinders turning and the knife cutting, reducing the material to fibers.

Weren't the people who attended the machine grinning at him slyly, because he had been frightened by that dark fellow? "He is an impudent dog! He must be fired!" A bestial hate arose in Diederich, the hatred of his fair flesh for the thin dark man of another race, which he would have liked to regard as inferior and which looked sinister. Diederich flared up.

"The cylinder is not in the right position, the knives are working badly!" As the men merely stared at him, he yelled: "Where is the machinist?" When the man with the black beard came along, Diederich said: "Look how this has been bungled. The cylinder is much too close to the knives and they are cutting everything to pieces. I will hold you responsible for the damage."

The man bent over the machine. "There is no damage," he said quietly, and again Diederich wondered if a smirk was not hidden by that black beard. The machinist gave him a surly mocking look, which Diederich could not stand. He stopped glaring and simply threw his arms in the air, "I hold you responsible."

"What's wrong now?" asked Sötbier, who had heard the noise. Then he explained that the fibers of the rags were not being cut too short, that they were always done in this way. The men nodded their heads in approval and the machinist stood there calmly. Diederich did not feel equal to a discussion, so he shouted: "In the future, you will kindly see that it is done differently!" and he turned away.

He reached the rag room, and he recovered his composure as he watched with an expert eye the women who were sorting the rags on the sieve plates of the long tables. One little dark-eyed woman was bold enough to smile at him from beneath her colored kerchief, but her glance met such a stony stare that she shrank back and bent over her work. Bulging sacks overflowed with brightly colored rags, the whispering women were silenced by the master's gaze, and in the warm stuffy atmosphere nothing could be heard but the gentle rattling of the blades as they came down upon the tables and cut off the buttons. But Diederich, who was examining the hot-water pipes, heard something suspicious. He looked over a heap of sacks—and started back, with blushing cheeks and quivering mustache. "Stop that now," he shouted. "Come out here!"

A young workman crawled out. "The woman, too!" shouted Diederich. "Come on!" Finally, when the girl appeared, he planted his fists on his hips. Nice goings on, indeed! Not only was the place a barroom but it was something else as well! He swore so loudly that all the workers gathered around him. "Well, Herr Sötbier, I suppose this is another example of the way things have always been done. I congratulate you on such success. These people are accustomed to wasting my time amusing themselves behind the sacks. How did this man get in here?" The young man said she was engaged to be married to him. "Married? Here, we know nothing about marriage, only about work. You are both stealing my time, for which I pay you. You are swine and thieves. I shall give you both the sack and lodge a complaint against you for indecent conduct."

He gave a challenging glance all around.

"In this place I insist upon German virtue and decency. Do you understand?" Then he caught the eye of the machinist. "And I will see that they are observed, even if you stand there and make faces," he screamed.

"I didn't make a face," said the man quietly, but Diederich could not contain himself any longer. At last, he had got something against him!

"Your conduct all along has been most suspicious. If you had been doing your duty, I should not have caught these two people."

"It is not my business to look after people," the man interrupted.

"You are very insubordinate and you have encouraged those beneath you in insubordination. You are preparing for the revolution. What's you name, anyhow?"

"Napoleon Fischer," said the man. Diederich stammered. "Nap—Well, I'm damned! Are you a Social Democrat?"

"I am."

"I thought so. You're fired."

He turned around to the others. "Let this be a lesson to you all—" And he left the room in a huff. In the yard Sötbier ran after him. "Master Diederich!" He was greatly excited, and he would not speak until the door of the private office had been closed behind him. "This won't do," said the bookkeeper. "He is a union man."

"For that very reason he is fired," replied Diederich. Sötbier explained that it would not do, because all the others would strike. Diederich could not understand this. Were they all in the Union? No. Well, then. But Sötbier explained that they were afraid of the Reds, even the older people could not be relied upon.

"I'll kick them all out," cried Diederich, "bag and baggage, every last one of them!"

"Then it would be a question whether we could get others to take their places," said Sötbier with a wan smile, looking from under his green eye-shade at his young master who was knocking the furniture about in his rage. He screamed:

"Am I master in my own factory, or not! I will show them—"

Sötbier waited until his rage had evaporated, then he said: "You need not say anything to Fischer; he won't leave us, for he knows that would cause us too much trouble."

Diederich flared up again.

"Really! So it is not necessary for me to beg him to have the kindness to stay. Napoleon the Great! I need not invite him to dinner on Sunday, I suppose? It would be too great an honor for me!"

His face was red and swollen, the room seemed to stifle him, and he threw the door open. It so happened that the machinist was just passing. Diederich gazed after him and his hatred made his senses more acute than usual. He noticed the man's thin, crooked legs, his bony shoulders, and his arms which hung forward. As the machinist spoke to the men, he could see his strong jaws working underneath his thin, black beard. How Diederich hated that mouth and those knotted hands! The black devil had long since passed and still Diederich was conscious of his odor.

"Just look, Sötbier, how his fins reach down to the ground. He will soon run on all fours and eat nuts. Just you watch, we'll trip up that ape! Napoleon! The name itself is a provocation. He had better look out for himself, for there's one thing certain, either he or I—" Diederich rolled his eyes "—will go under."

With head erect, he left the factory. Putting on a morning coat he made preparations to call on the most important people of the town. From Meisestrasse, in order to reach the house of Dr. Scheffelweis, the Mayor, in Schweinichenstrasse, he had simply to go along Kaiser Wilhelm Strasse. He wished to do so, but at the decisive moment, as if according to an arrangement he kept secret from himself, he turned aside into the Fleischhauergrube. The two steps in front of old Herr Buck's house were worn down by the feet of the entire town, and by the predeccessors of these feet. The bell-handle on the yellow glass door caused a prolonged rattling noise in the emptiness beyond. Then a door opened in the background and the old servant shuffled down the hall. But long before she could reach the outer door, the master of the house himself stepped out of his office and opened it. He seized Diederich, who bowed deeply, by the hand and dragged him in.

"My dear Hessling, I have been expecting you. I heard that you'd arrived. Welcome back to Netzig, my dear Doctor." Tears sprang into Diederich's eyes and he stammered.

"You are too kind, Herr Buck. I need hardly say, Herr Buck, that you are the first person on whom I wanted to call, and to assure that I am always—I am always—at your service," he concluded, smiling like a diligent schoolboy. Old Herr Buck still held him fast with his hand which was warm yet light and soft.

"My service"—he shoved forward a chair for Diederich—"you mean, of course, the service of your fellow citizens, who will be grateful to you. I think I can promise you that they will shortly elect you to the Town Council, for that would be a mark of respect to a family which deserves it, and then"—old Buck made a gesture of dignified generosity—"I trust you will soon give us the opportunity of seeing you appointed to the town administration."

Diederich bowed, smiling happily, as if he had already attained that honor. "I do not say," continued Herr Buck, "that the principles espoused in our town are sound in every respect"—his white beard sank on to his necktie—"but there is still room"—his beard rose again—"and God grant it may long be so, there is still room for genuine Liberals."

"I need hardly tell you that I am a Liberal," Diederich assured him.

Old Buck ran his hand over the papers on his desk. "Your lamented father often used to sit opposite me here, and particularly at the time when he was building the paper mill. To my great joy I could be of use to him then. It was a question of the stream which now flows through your yard."

Diederich said in a grave voice: "How often, Herr Buck, my father told me that he had you to thank for the stream without which we could not exist."

"You must not say that he owed it only to me, but rather to the just conditions which characterize our civic life." Looking earnestly at Diederich, the old gentleman raised his white forefinger: "But certain people and a certain party would like to make many changes as soon as they could."

Emphatically and with pathos: "The enemy is at the gate; we must stand together."

A moment passed in silence, then in lighter tones and with a slight smile, he said: "Are you not, my dear Dr. Hessling, in the same position as your father then was? Don't you want to expand your business? Have you any plans?"

"Certainly I have." With great eagerness Diederich explained what he would like to see happen. The old gentleman listened carefully, nodded, and took a pinch of snuff. . . . Finally, he said: "This much I can see; the alterations will not only be a great expense, but under certain conditions may give rise to difficulties in connection with the town-building codes, with which I, by the way, am concerned as a magistrate. Now take a look, my dear Hessling, at what I have here on my desk."

Diederich recognized an exact plan of his property and that which lay behind it. His astonished face produced a smile of satisfaction in old Buck. "I have no doubt that I can arrange things so that no complications will arise." And in reply to Diederich's profuse thanks: "We do a service to the whole community when we help one of our friends, for all except tyrants are friends of a people's party."

After these words he leaned back in his chair and folded his hands. His expression had relaxed and he nodded his head in a grandfatherly fashion. "As a child you had such lovely fair curls," he said.

Diederich understood that the official part of the conversation was over. He took the liberty of saying, "I still remember how I used to come to this house as a small boy, when I used to play soldiers with your son Wolfgang."

"Ah, yes, and now he is playing soldiers again."

"Oh, he is very popular with the officers. He told me so himself."

"I wish, my dear Hessling, that he had more of your practical disposition . . . but he will settle down once I get him married."

"I believe your son has a streak of genius in him. For that reason he is never contented with anything, and does not know whether he would like to become a general or a great man in some other field."

"Meanwhile, unfortunately, he gets into silly scrapes." The old gentleman gazed out of the window. Diederich did not dare to show his curiosity.

"Silly scrapes? I can hardly believe it. He always impressed me by his intelligence, even at school, his compositions. And his recent statement to me about the Emperor, that he would really like to be the first Labor leader. . . ."

"God save the workers from that."

"What do you mean?" Diederich was absolutely astounded.

"Because it would do them no good. It has not done the rest of us any good either."

"Yet, it is thanks to the Hohenzollerns that we have a united German Empire."

"We are not united," said old Buck, rising from his chair with unaccustomed haste. "In order to prove our unity we ought to be able to follow our individual impulses, but can we? You consider yourselves united because the curse of servility is spreading everywhere. That is what Herwegh, a survivor like myself, cried to those who were drunk with victory in the spring of 1871. What would he say now?"

Diederich's reply to this voice from another world was to stammer: "Ah, yes, you belong to Forty-Eight."

"My dear young friend, you mean that I have lost and that I am a fool. Yes, we were beaten, because we were foolish enough to believe in the people. We believed that they would achieve for themselves what they now receive from their masters at the cost of liberty. We thought of this nation as powerful, wealthy, full of understanding for its own affairs and dedicated to the future. We did not see that, without political education, of which Germany has less than any other nation, it was fated to fall victim to the powers of the past, after the first flush of freedom. Even in our time there were far too many people who pursued their own personal interests, unconcerned about the common weal, who were contented when they could fulfill the ignoble needs of a selfish life of pleasure by basking in the sun of some master's approval. Since that time their name is legion, for they no longer care about public interests. Your masters have already made you into a world power, and, while you're earning money whichever way you can, and spending whatever way you like, they will build the fleet for you— or rather, for themselves—which we ourselves at that time would have built. Our poet then knew what you are now only learning: the future of Germany will spring from the furrows which Columbus ploughed."

"So Bismarck has really accomplished something," said Diederich in quiet triumph.

"That is just the point: he has been allowed to do it! At the same time he has done it all only in fact, but nominally in the name of his master. We citizens of Forty-Eight were most honest, it seems to me, for then I myself paid the price of my own daring."

"Oh, yes, I know, you were condemned to death," said Diederich, once more intimidated.

"I was condemned because I defended the sovereignty of the National Parliament against a local, separatist power and led the people, who were acting in self-defense, to revolt. This was the nature of German unity in our hearts: a matter of conscience, the personal obligation of every individual. No! we paid no homage to any so-called creator of German unity. When, defeated and betrayed, I was waiting in this house with my last remaining friends for the King's soldiers, I was still, for better or worse, a real human being who helped to realize an ideal; I was one of many, but a human being. Where are they now?"

The old gentleman stopped and his face assumed an expression as if he were listening. Diederich felt uncomfortably warm, and thought that he ought not to remain silent any longer. He said: "The German people, thank God, is no longer the nation of poets and thinkers; it has modern and practical ends in view." The old man emerged from his thoughts and pointed to the ceiling.

"At that time the whole town thronged this house. Now it is lonelier than it has ever been. Wolfgang was the last to go. I would abandon everything, but we must respect our past, young man, even when we have been beaten."

"No doubt," said Diederich. "You're still the most powerful man in town. People always say Herr Buck owns the town."

"But I do not want that, I want it to belong to itself." He sighed deeply. "That is a long story, you will gradually learn it when you gain more insight into our administration. Every day we are more hard pressed by the Government and their Junker taskmasters. Today they want to compel us to supply light to the estate owners who pay us no taxes. Tomorrow we shall have to build roads for them. Finally they will take away our right of self-government. We are living in a beleaguered town, as you will see."

Diederich smiled with a superior air. "It cannot be as bad as all that, for the Emperor is such a modern personality."

"Hm, yes," replied old Buck. He stood up, shook his head slowly—and then decided to say nothing. He offered Diederich his hand.

"My dear Doctor, your friendship will be as precious to me as your father's was. After this conversation I have the hope that we shall be able to work together in all things."

Moved by the glance of those friendly blue eyes Diederich laid his hand upon his heart. "I am a thoroughgoing Liberal."

"Above all, I warn you against Governor von Wulckow. He is the enemy who has been sent here to the town against us. The town administration maintains only such relations with him as are absolutely unavoidable. I personally have the honor to be cut by him in the street."

"Oh!" cried Diederich, genuinely disturbed.

The old gentleman had already opened the door for him, but he still seemed to have something on his mind. "Wait a moment!" He hastened back into the library, bent down and then rose up out of the dusty depths with a small, nearly square volume. He hastily pressed it into Diederich's hands, with shy pride in his glowing face. "There, take this. A copy of my *Storm Bells*. We were also poets—back then." He gently pushed Diederich out into the street.

The Fleischhauergrube was rather steep, but that was not the only reason why Diederich was out of breath. At first he was somewhat dazed, but gradually he had the feeling of having allowed himself to be flummoxed. "An old chatterbox like that is nothing more than a scarecrow, and yet I allow myself to be impressed by him." He vaguely recalled his childhood when old Herr Buck, who had been condemned to death, inspired him with as much respect and the same fear as the policeman at the corner or the ghost in the Castle. "Am I always going to be so weak? Another man would not have allowed himself to be treated in this fashion." The fact that he had been silent, or had only feebly contradicted so many compromising speeches, might have unpleasant consequences. He prepared the most effective reply for the next occasion. "The whole thing was a trap; he wanted to catch me and render me harmless ... but I'll show him!" Diederich clenched his fist in his pocket as he marched erect along Kaiser Wilhelmstrasse. "For the present I must put up with him, but let him beware when I am the stronger!"

The Mayor's house had been newly painted, and the plate glass windows sparkled as they always had. A pretty servant received him. She took him up the stairs, passing the statue of a friendly boy holding a lamp, through an anteroom in which a small rug lay in front of almost every piece of furniture, and left him in the dining room. It was furnished with pale wood, with appetizing pictures, and here the Mayor and another gentleman sat at lunch. Dr. Scheffelweis extended a white hand to Diederich and looked at him over the edge of his pince-nez. Nevertheless, you never knew if he was looking at you, his glance was so vague, and his eyes were as colorless as his face and his scanty side-whiskers, which were cut in muttonchop fashion. Several times the Mayor attempted to talk before he finally found something which it was safe to say. "What fine scars Dr. Hessling has," he said; and turning to the other gentleman. "Don't you think so?"

The other gentlemen looked so Jewish that Diederich was at first reserved. But the Mayor introduced him: "Herr Assessor Jadassohn of the Public Prosecutor's Office." This made a respectful greeting unavoidable.

"Come and sit down," said the Mayor; "we are just beginning." He poured out some porter for Diederich and helped him to some smoked ham. "My wife and her mother have gone out, the children are at school. It's bachelor's hour! Your health!"

The Jewish gentleman from the Public Prosecutor's Office had eyes only for the servant. While she was busy at the table near him his hand disappeared. Then she left the room and he was anxious to talk of public affairs, but the Mayor would not be interrupted. "The two ladies will not be back for lunch. My mother-in-law is at the dentist's, and I know what that means; it is not an easy business for her. Meanwhile the whole house is at our disposal." He fetched a liqueur from the sideboard, sang its praises, made his guests confirm its merits, and continued to boast of his idyllic mornings, in a monotonous voice interrupted by chewing. In spite of his contentment, his expression gradually became more and more anxious, as he felt that the conversation could not continue in this fashion. After all three had been silent for the space of a minute he made up his mind.

"I suppose I may assume, Dr. Hessling—my house is not in the immediate vicinity of yours and I should think it quite natural if you had called on other gentlemen before coming to me."

Diederich was already blushing for the lie he had not yet told. "It would come out," he thought, just in time, and so he replied: "As a matter of fact I took the liberty—that is to say, my first thought, of course, was to call on you, Mr. Mayor, but my father had such a high opinion of old Herr Buck . . ."

"Quite so, quite so." The Mayor nodded emphatically. "Herr Buck is the oldest of our distinguished citizens and therefore exercises a doubtlessly legitimate influence."

"Not for much longer," said the Jewish gentleman from the Public Prosecutor's Office in an unexpectedly harsh tone, as he looked defiantly at Diederich. The Mayor had bent his head over his cheese, and Diederich, finding himself helpless, blinked. As the gentleman's look demanded a response, he mumbled something about "innate respect" and even began to cite memories of his childhood as an excuse for having gone first to Herr Buck. While he was speaking he gazed in terror at the huge, red, prominent ears of the gentleman from the Public Prosecutor's Office. The latter allowed Diederich to stammer on to the end, as if he were a defendant on the witness stand giving himself away. Finally he retorted cuttingly: "In certain circumstances respect is a habit which one must overcome."

Diederich was taken aback; he decided to laugh knowingly. The Mayor with a pale smile and a conciliatory gesture said:

"Dr. Jadassohn likes to be witty—a habit which I personally appreciate very much. In my position, of course, I am compelled to consider things objectively and without prejudice. Therefore I must admit, on the one hand. . . ."

"Let us get at once to 'on the other hand,'" demanded Jadassohn. "As a representative of the State authorities, and as a convinced supporter of the existing order, I regard Herr Buck and his comrade, Reichstag Representative Kühlemann, as revolutionaries, on account of their past record and their present opinions. That is enough for me. I do not conceal my thoughts; I consider such reserve to be un-German. Let them set up public soup kitchens by all means, but the best nourishment for the people is sound opinions. A lunatic asylum might also be very useful."

"But it must be a loyal one!" Diederich added. The Mayor made pacifying gestures. "Gentlemen!" he entreated, "gentlemen, if we must discuss the matter, then it is certainly right, with all due respect to the gentlemen named, that we confess, on the other hand—"

"On the other hand!" repeated Jadassohn sternly.

"—the deepest regret for our unfortunately most unfavorable relations with the representatives of the State administration. That said, I feel compelled to point out the unwonted harshness of Governor von Wulckow toward the city authorities—"

"Toward disloyal organizations," interjected Jadassohn. Diederich ventured: "I am a thoroughly liberal man but I must say. . . ."

"A town," explained the lawyer, "which opposes the legitimate wishes of the Government certainly cannot be surprised when the Government turns a cold shoulder on it!"

"We could travel from Berlin to Netzig," Diederich declared, "in half the time if we were on better terms with the powers that be."

The Mayor allowed them to finish their duet. He was pale and his eyes were closed behind his pince-nez. Suddenly he looked at them with a wan smile.

"Gentlemen, do not worry. I know that there are people who hold opinions more in keeping with the spirit of the times than those espoused by our town authorities. Please do not believe that it was my fault that no telegram of greeting was sent to His Majesty on the occasion of his last visit to the provinces during the maneuvers last year . . ."

"The refusal of the town administration was thoroughly un-German," Jadassohn declared emphatically.

"The national banner must be held aloft," Diederich insisted. The Mayor threw up his hands.

"I know it, gentlemen. But I am only the chairman of the town administration and must unfortunately carry out its decisions. You change the conditions! Dr. Jadassohn remembers our row with the Government about the Social Democratic teacher, Rettich. I could not reprimand the man. Herr von Wulckow knows"—the Mayor winked his eye—"that I would have done it if I could."

They looked at one another in silence for a while. Jadassohn snorted as if he had heard enough. But Diederich could not be silent any longer. "Liberalism is the harbinger of Social Democracy. Such people as Buck, Kühlemann, Eugen Richter, are making our workers impudent. My factory imposes upon me the heaviest sacrifices in work and responsibilities, and on top of that I have conflicts with my workers. Why? Because we are not united against the Red Peril, and there are certain employers with socialistic leanings, as, for example, the son-in-law of Herr Buck. Herr Lauer's workmen have a share in whatever profits the factory earns. That is immoral." Diederich glared: "It undermines law and order, and I hold that order is more necessary than ever in these tough times. Therefore, we need the strong Government of our glorious young Emperor. I declare that I stand fast by His Majesty in all circumstances. . . ." Here the two others bowed profoundly, which Diederich acknowledged with another flash of his eyes. Unlike the democratic hogwash in which the departing generation still believed, the Emperor was the representative of youth, the most out-standing personality, charmingly impulsive and a highly original thinker. "One man must be master, and master in every field!" Diederich declared that he harbored the firmest and most rigid convictions, and demanded that an end be put in Netzig, once and for all, to the old liberal nonsense. "A new age is upon us!" Jadas-sohn and the Mayor listened quietly until he had finished, Jadas-sohn's ears growing larger all the time. Then he crowed: "There *are* loyal Germans in Netzig after all!" And Diederich shouted: "We will keep an eye on those who are not loyal. It shall remain to be seen whether certain families truly deserve the social standing they have always enjoyed. Apart from old Buck, who are his sup-porters? His sons are peasants or ne'er-do-wells, his son-in-law is a Socialist, and they say his daughter. . . ."

They looked at one another. The Mayor giggled and blushed. He was bursting with delight, as he cried: "And you didn't know that Herr Buck's brother is bankrupt!"

They loudly expressed their satisfaction. That man with his five elegant daughters! The President of the Harmony Club! But, as Diederich knew, they got their meals from the soup kitchen. At this stage the Mayor poured out some more cognac and passed round the cigars. All at once he became certain that they were on the eve of a big change. "The Reichstag elections will take place in eighteen months. Between now and then you gentleman will have to work."

Diederich proposed that the three of them should there and then constitute themselves as the election committee.

Jadassohn declared that the first priority was to get in touch with Governor von Wulckow. "In the strictest confidence," added the Mayor, winking. Diederich regretted that the *Netzig Journal,* the chief newspaper in the town, was beginning to show some dangerous liberal tendencies. "A damned Semitic rag!" said Jadas-sohn. On the other hand, the loyal Government county paper had practically no influence in the town. But old Klüsing in Gausenfeld supplied paper to both. As he had invested money in the Netzig *Journal,* it did not seem improbable to Diederich that its attitude might be influenced through him. They would have to frighten him into thinking that otherwise he would lose the county paper order. "After all, there is another paper factory in Netzig," said the Mayor, grinning. Then the maid came in and announced she would have to set the table for dinner, as the mistress of the house would

soon be back—and her mother as well, she added. At the mention
of the latter, the Mayor at once jumped up. As he accompanied
his guests to the door, his head drooped, and in spite of all the
cognac, he looked quite pale. On the stairs he caught Diederich
by the sleeve. Jadassohn had remained behind, and the excited
exclamations of the maid could be heard. There was already a ring
at the door.

"My dear Doctor," whispered the Mayor, "I hope you have not
misunderstood me. In everything we discussed I have, of course,
only the interests of the town at heart. It goes without saying that
I have no intention of undertaking anything in which I am not sure
of the support of the organizations of which I have the honor to
be the chief."

He blinked earnestly, but before Diederich had collected his
thoughts, the ladies were entering the house, and the Mayor released his arm to hasten to meet them. His wife, wizened and
careworn, had scarcely time to greet the gentlemen. She had to
separate the children, who were fighting. Her mother was a head
taller and still youthful-looking, and she looked sternly at the
flushed faces of the luncheon guests. Then, with Junolike majesty,
she descended upon the Mayor, who grew visibly smaller . . . Assessor Jadassohn had already disappeared. Diederich made formal
bows which were not returned and hastened away after him. He
felt uncomfortable and looked uneasily about him in the street. He
was not listening to what Jadassohn said and suddenly he turned
back. He had to ring loudly several times, for there was a great
deal of noise inside. The Mayor's family was still standing at the
foot of the stairs, where the children were pushing one another and
screaming. A discussion was in progress. The Mayoress wanted
her husband to complain to the headmaster about a teacher who
had ill-treated her son. His mother-in-law, on the contrary, was
insisting that the teacher be promoted because his wife had the
greatest influence on the committee of the Bethlehem foundation
for fallen girls. The Mayor entreated them in turn with his hands.
At last, he got a word in.

"On the one hand. . . ."

At this point, Diederich had seized him by the arm. With many
apologies to the ladies, he took him aside and tremblingly whispered: "My dear Mr. Mayor, I am most anxious to avoid misunderstanding. I must repeat that I am a thoroughly liberal man."

Dr. Scheffelweis hastily assured him that he was no less certain of this than of his own sound Liberalism. Then he was called away and Diederich, somewhat relieved, left the house. Jadassohn awaited him with a grin.

"I suppose you got frightened. Don't worry! Nobody can ever compromise himself with the head of our town. Like God Almighty, he is always on the side of the strongest battalions. Today I just wanted to find out how far he had gone with von Wulckow. Things are not doing so badly, we can move a step forward."

"Please do not forget," said Diederich reservedly, "that my home is among the citizens of Netzig and I am naturally a Liberal."

Jadassohn gave him a sidelong glance. "A Neo-Teuton?" he asked. Diederich turned to him in astonishment, as he added: "How is my old friend Wiebel?"

"Do you know him also?"

"Do I know him? I arranged a duel with him."

Diederich seized the hand which Jadassohn held out to him and they shook hands vigorously. That settled the matter and arm in arm they went down to the *Ratskeller* to dine.

The place was empty and dimly lighted. The gas was turned on for them at the end of the room, and while they were waiting for the soup they discovered mutual friends. Fatty Delitzsch! As an eyewitness Diederich gave a circumstantial account of his tragic end. They drank the first glass of Rauenthal to his memory. It turned out that Jadassohn had also been through the February riots, and, like Diederich, he had learned to respect power. "His Majesty," said the lawyer, "showed such courage as would take your breath away. Several times I thought, by God—" He stopped and they gazed shuddering into each other's eyes. In order to banish the dreadful spectacle they raised their glasses. "Allow me," said Jadassohn. "I'm right with you," replied Diederich. "To the very good health of your family." And Diederich answered, "I shall certainly convey the compliment to them at home."

Although his food was getting cold, Jadassohn launched into an elaborate eulogy of the Emperor's character. The Philistines, the fault-finders, and the Jews might criticize him as they liked, but our glorious young Emperor is the most individual personality, charmingly impulsive and a highly original thinker. Diederich was convinced that he had already come to the same conclusion and nodded contentedly. He said to himself that a person's outward appearance was sometimes deceptive, and that the length of a man's ears did not determine his loyal German sentiments. They drained their glasses to the success of the struggle of the throne and the altar against revolution in every shape and form.

Then they got back to conditions in Netzig. They agreed that the new national spirit to which they must convert the town need have no other program than the name of His Majesty. Political parties were rubbish, as His Majesty himself had said: "I know only two parties, those who are with me and those who are against me." Those were his words and they expressed the facts. Unfortunately in Netzig the Party which was against him was still on top, but that would have to be changed, and it would be—of this Diederich was certain—by means of the Veterans' Association. Jadassohn, who was not a member, nevertheless promised to introduce Diederich to the leading people. First and foremost there was Pastor Zillich, a member of Jadassohn's students' corps and a true-born German! They would call on him as soon as they had finished. They drank his health. Diederich also drank to his captain, the captain who was initially his stern superior but who had gone on to become his best friend. "My year of military service means more to me than any other year of my life." All of a sudden, with flushed cheeks, he shouted:

"And it is such noble memories which these Democrats would like to spoil for us!"

Old Buck! Diederich could not contain his rage as he stammered: "Such a creature would prevent us from serving in the army, saying that we are slaves! Because he once took part in a revolution . . ."

"That is all over now," said Jadassohn.

"Are we all supposed to let ourselves be condemned to death on that account? If they had only chopped his head off! . . . And the Hohenzollern, they say, are no use to us!"

"Certainly not to him," said Jadassohn taking a long drink. "But I declare," continued Diederich, rolling his eyes, "that I listened to all his vicious humbug only in order to find out what type of mind he has. I call you as witness, Herr Assessor! If that old schemer ever asserts that I am his friend, and that I approve of his infamous treason to the Emperor, then I will call upon you to witness that I protested this very day."

He broke into perspiration as he thought of the affair with the Building Commission and of the favoritism he was to enjoy . . . Suddenly he threw on to the table a small book, almost square in shape, and broke into a mocking laugh.

"He goes in for poetry also!"

Jadassohn turned over the pages. *Songs of the Athletes. In Captivity. All Hail to the Republic! By the lake lay a youth, sad to see* ... "Quite so, that's what they were. Sentimentalizing about jail birds while rocking the foundations of society. Revolutionary sentimentality, subversive ideas and flabby bearing. Thank God, we are differently constituted."

"Let us hope so, indeed," said Diederich. "Our student life taught us manliness and idealism, that is enough; poetry is superfluous."

"Away with your altar candles!" declaimed Jadassohn. "That sort of thing is for my friend Zillich. Now that he has taken his nap, we can go."

They found the Pastor drinking coffee. He wanted to send his wife and daughter out of the room, but Jadassohn gallantly detained the mistress of the house. He also tried to kiss the young lady's hand, but she turned her back on him. Diederich, who was very gay, begged the ladies most urgently to stay, and they did so. He explained to them that after Berlin Netzig seemed remarkably quiet. "The ladies are rather behind the times. I give you my word of honor, *gnädiges Fräulein,* you are the first person I have seen here who could easily stroll down Unter den Linden without anyone noticing that you were from Netzig." Then he learned that she had really been once in Berlin, and had even been to Ronacher's. Diederich profited by the occasion to recall a song he had heard there, but which he could only whisper into her ear. "Our lovely ladies, pert and sweet, display it all from head to feet." As she gave him a bold glance he kissed her lightly on the neck. She looked at him beseechingly, whereupon he assured her with the utmost frankness that she was a nice little girl. With downcast eyes she fled to her mother who had been watching the entire proceedings. The Pastor was in earnest conversation with Jadassohn. He was complaining that church attendance in Netzig had fallen off terribly.

"On the third Sunday after Easter, just think of it! On the third Sunday after Easter, I had to preach to the sexton and three old ladies from the convent. Everybody else had the flu."

Jadassohn replied: "In view of the lukewarm, even hostile, attitude which the Party in power adopts toward the Church and religion, it is a wonder the three old ladies were there. Why do they not go to the Free Thought lectures given by Doctor Heuteufel?"

The Pastor shot up out of his chair. He snorted so vehemently that his beard seemed to erupt in foam, and his frock coat flapped wildly. *"Herr Assessor!"* he cried vehemently. "This man is my brother-in-law, and vengeance is mine saith the Lord. But although this person is my brother-in-law and the husband of my own sister, I can only pray to God, pray with clasped hands, that He shall strike him with the lightning of His vengeance. Otherwise, He will one day be obliged to rain fire and brimstone upon the whole of Netzig. Heuteufel gives coffee—do you understand?—free coffee to the people so that they will come to him and let him capture their souls. And then he tells them that marriage is not a sacrament, but a contract—as if I were ordering a suit of clothes." The Pastor laughed bitterly.

"Disgusting," said Diederich in a deep voice, and while Jadassohn was assuring the Pastor of the positive nature of his Christianity, Diederich began anew his amorous advances toward Käthchen, facilitating the endeavor by strategic placement of his armchair. "Fräulein Käthchen," he said, "I can assure you most seriously that to me marriage is really a sacrament." Käthchen replied:

"You ought to be ashamed of yourself, Dr. Hessling."

He turned hot all over. "Don't look at me that way!"

Käthchen sighed. "You are so frightfully designing. I am sure you are no better than Herr Assessor Jadassohn. Your sisters have told me all about your escapades in Berlin. They are my best friends."

Then they would meet again soon? Yes, at the Harmony Club. "But you needn't think that I believe anything you say. You arrived at the station with Guste Daimchen."

Diederich asked what that proved, and said that he protested against any conclusions which might be drawn from that purely accidental fact. Besides, Fräulein Daimchen was already engaged.

"Oh, her!" sneered Käthchen. "That doesn't make any difference to her, she is such a shocking flirt."

The Pastor's wife also confirmed this. That very day she had seen Guste in patent-leather shoes and lavender stockings. That promised nothing good. Käthchen's lips curled.

"And then that inheritance of hers—"

This insinuation of doubt reduced Diederich to perturbed silence. The Pastor had just admitted to Jadassohn the necessity of discussing once again more fully the position of the Christian Church in Netzig. He asked his wife for his hat and coat. It was already dark on the staircase, and as the two others went on ahead Diederich had a chance to kiss Käthchen's neck again. She said, languishingly: "Nobody in Netzig has a mustache that tickles like yours"—which flattered him at first, but immediately awoke in him painful suspicions. So he let her go and disappeared. Jadassohn was waiting for him downstairs and whispered: "Never say die! The old boy did not notice anything and the mother pretends not to." He winked provocatively.

When they had passed St. Mary's Church the three men wanted to get to the market place, but the Pastor stood still and indicated something behind him with a movement of the head. "You gentlemen doubtless know the name of the alley to the left of the church, under the arch. That dirty hole of an alley or rather a certain house in it."

"Little Berlin," said Jadassohn, for the Pastor would not move on.

"Little Berlin," he repeated, laughed painfully, and again he shouted with holy wrath, so that several people turned around: "Little Berlin . . . in the shadow of my church! Such a house! And the town administration will not listen to me. They make fun of me. But they make fun of someone else"—here the Pastor moved on again—"and He will not allow Himself to be made fun of."

Jadassohn agreed. But, while his companions were embroiled in heated discussion, Diederich saw Guste Daimchen approaching from the Rathaus. He raised his hat to her with formal politeness and she smiled disdainfully. It occurred to him that Käthchen Zillich was just as fair-haired and that she had the same small, impertinently pug nose. As a matter of fact, either girl would do. Guste, it is true, was more broadly built. "And she doesn't put up with any hanky-panky, either. She will slap your face before you know where you are." He turned round to look after Guste. From behind she looked extraordinarily round and she waddled. In that moment Diederich decided: that girl or nobody!

The other two had eventually also noticed her. "Was that not the little daughter of Frau Daimchen?" the Pastor asked, adding: "Our Bethlehem Foundation for fallen girls is still waiting for the gifts of the generous. I wonder if Fräulein Daimchen is generous? People say she has inherited a million."

Jadassohn hastened to declare that this was greatly exaggerated. Diederich contradicted him, saying that he knew the circumstances. The deceased uncle had made more money out of chicory than one would think. He was so positive that the Assessor was forced to promise to have an inquiry made by the authorities in Magdeburg. Diederich said no more, for he had achieved his purpose.

"Anyhow," said Jadassohn, "the money will go to the Bucks, that is to say, to the revolution." But Diederich insisted that he was better informed. "Fräulein Daimchen and I arrived here together," he said, by way of a feeler. "Oh, I see. May we congratulate you?" returned Jadassohn. Diederich made a deprecating movement of his shoulders. Jadassohn apologized: he had simply thought that young Buck—"Wolfgang?" queried Diederich. "I saw him in Berlin every day. He lives with an actress there."

The Pastor coughed disapprovingly. As they had reached the square on which the theater stood he looked sternly across and said: "Little Berlin, it is true, is beside my church, but it is in a dark corner at least. This den of iniquity flaunts itself on the public square, and our sons and daughters"—he pointed to the stage door where some members of the company were standing—"rub shoulders with common prostitutes."

With a grieved expression Diederich agreed that this was very sad, while Jadassohn expressed his indignation because the *Netzig Journal* had rejoiced when four illegitimate children had been mentioned in the plays of the last season, and the *Journal* had regarded this as a sign of progress!

Meanwhile they had turned into Kaiser Wilhelm Strasse and bowed to various gentlemen who were going into the Masonic Hall. When they had passed and had again put on the hats which they had so respectfully removed, Jadassohn said:

"We shall have to keep an eye on the people who take part in that Masonic humbug. His Majesty most decidedly disapproves of it."

"As far as my brother-in-law Heuteufel is concerned," declared the Pastor, "even the most dangerous sect would not surprise me."

"Well, and what about Herr Lauer?" Diederich inquired. "A man who does not hesitate to share his profits with his workmen is capable of anything."

"The worst of all," declared Jadassohn, "is Fritsche, the County Judge, who dares to show himself in that company of Jews. Imagine, one of His Majesty's judges, arm in arm with Cohn, the moneylender. Vat does dat mean, Cohn?" Jadassohn mimicked, sticking his thumb in his armpit.

Diederich continued: "Since he and Frau Lauer . . ." He stopped short and began to explain that he could easily understand why these people always won their cases in the courts. "They stick together and hatch sinister plots." Pastor Zillich muttered something about orgies which were said to be celebrated in that building, and at which unspeakable things had happened. But Jadassohn smiled significantly:

"Well, it is fortunate that Herr von Wulckow can see right into their windows." And Diederich nodded approvingly at the government building on the opposite side of the street. Next door stood the regional militia headquarters, in front of which a sentinel was marching up and down. "It does your heart good to see the glint of the rifle of one of those fine fellows," cried Diederich. "With them we can hold that gang in check."

As a matter of fact, the rifle did not shine, for it was getting dark. Groups of returning workmen were already wending their way home through the evening crowd. Jadassohn proposed that they go and have a drink at Klappsch's around the corner. It was comfortable there, for at that hour there were no customers. Klappsch was a loyal citizen, and while his daughter was bringing the beer, he expressed his warmest thanks to the Pastor for the good work which he was doing for his youngsters in the Bible class. It was true that the eldest had again stolen some sugar, but he had not been able, in consequence, to sleep at night, and had confessed his sins to God so loudly that Klappsch had heard him and had given him a good hiding. From that the talk drifted to the government officials whom Klappsch supplied with lunch. He was able to report how they spent church-time on Sundays. Jadassohn took notes, while, at the same time, his other hand disappeared behind Fräulein Klappsch. Diederich discussed with Pastor Zillich the founding of a Christian workmen's club. "Any of my men who won't join will be fired!" he promised. This prospect cheered up the Pastor. After the girl had brought several rounds of beer and cognac he found himself in the same state of hopeful determination which his two companions had attained in the course of the day.

"My brother-in-law Heuteufel," he cried, banging the table, "may preach as much as he likes about our being descended from monkeys. I shall fill up my church again in spite of him."

"Not only yours," Diederich assured him.

"Yes, there are too many churches in Netzig," the Pastor admitted. "Too few, man of God, too few," said Jadassohn sharply. He called Diederich to witness how things had developed in Berlin. There too, the churches were empty until His Majesty intervened. He had issued a command to the city authorities: "See to it that churches are built in Berlin." Then they were built, religion became fashionable again, they got customers. The Pastor, the publican, Jadassohn and Diederich were all enthusiastic about the profound piety of the monarch. Then a loud report was heard.

"That was a gun!" Jadassohn jumped up first and they all turned pale as they looked at one another. Like a flash of lightning Diederich saw in his mind's eye the bony face of Napoleon Fischer, the machinist with the black beard through which his grey skin was visible. "The revolution! It has started!" he stammered. They heard the patter of running feet, and suddenly they all seized their hats and ran out.

The people who had collected were standing in a timid semicircle, from the corner of the militia headquarters to the steps of the Masonic Hall. On the other side, where the semicircle was open, someone was lying face downwards in the middle of the street. The soldier who had previously been marching up and down so smartly was now standing motionless in the sentry box. His helmet was a little on one side and he was visibly pale. With his mouth wide open he was staring at the fallen figure, while he held his rifle by the barrel and let it drag along the ground. There was a muffled murmur from the crowd, consisting chiefly of working men and women. Suddenly a man's voice said very loudly: "Oho!" Then there was a deep silence. Diederich and Jadassohn exchanged a glance of consternation and understanding as to the critical nature of the occasion.

Down the street ran a policeman, and in front of him a girl, her dress flying in the wind, who cried while still some distance away: "There he is! The soldier fired!"

She came up, threw herself on her knees and shook the man. "Up! Do stand up!"

She waited. His feet seemed to move convulsively, but he remained on the ground, his arms and legs stretched out over the pavement. Then she cried out: "Karl!" The intensity of her scream made everybody jump.

The women joined in the crying, and several men pushed forward with clenched fists. The crowd had become denser. From between the horsedrawn vehicles, which had come to a halt, more people pressed forward. In the midst of the threatening mob the girl worked herself free, her loosened hair streaming, her face distorted with tears. It could be seen that she was screaming, but not a sound could be heard, for it was drowned in the general noise.

The solitary policeman pushed the crowd back with outstretched arms, for the people would have trodden on the prostrate figure. He shouted at them in vain, tramping on their toes, and losing his head; he began to look around wildly for help.

It came. A window was opened in the government building, an immense beard appeared, and a voice was heard, a formidable bass voice, which reached the ears of everyone above the outcry, like the rumbling of distant cannon, even when the words could not be understood.

"Wulckow," said Jadassohn. "At last."

"I forbid this!" thundered the voice. "Who dares makes this noise in front of my house?" And as it became a little quieter:

"Where is the sentry?"

Now, for the first time, most of the people noticed that the soldier had withdrawn into the sentry box, as deeply as possible so that only the barrel of his rifle projected.

"Come out, my son!" the bass voice commanded from above. "You have done your duty. He provoked you. His Majesty will reward you for your bravery. Do you understand?"

Everyone understood and grew silent, including the girl. The formidable voice boomed on:

"Disperse, or I'll have you shot!"

A moment passed and some had already begun to run. The workmen broke up into groups, lingered . . . and then went a little farther on, with downcast heads. The Governor shouted down again:

"Paschke, go and get a doctor."

Then he slammed the window. At the entrance of the building, however, there was a movement of people. Gentlemen suddenly emerged to give orders, many policemen came running up from all sides, striking out at the people who still remained, and shouting. Diederich and his companions, who had retreated around the corner, noticed some gentlemen standing on the steps of the Masonic Hall. Now Dr. Heuteufel was making his way between them. "I am a doctor," he said in a loud voice, as he quickly crossed the street and bent over the wounded man. He turned him over, opened his waistcoat and pressed his ear to his chest. At that moment there was complete silence, even the police stopped shouting. But the girl stood there, leaning forward with her shoulders hunched as if she feared the threat of a blow, and with her fist clenched to her heart as if that was the heart which had stopped beating.

Dr. Heuteufel stood up. "The man is dead," he said. Simultaneously he noticed that the girl was tottering, and he made a move to help her. But she stood erect again, looking down at the face of the dead man and said simply: "Karl." More softly: "Karl." The doctor looked round and asked: "What's to become of this girl?"

Then Jadassohn stepped forward. "I am Assessor Jadassohn of the Public Prosecutor's Office. This girl must be taken into custody. As her lover provoked the sentry, there is ground for suspicion that she took part in the offense. Inquiries will be instituted."

He made a sign to two policemen who seized the girl. Dr. Heuteufel raised his voice. "Herr Assessor, as a doctor I certify that the condition of this girl will not permit her arrest." Somebody said: "Why don't you arrest the corpse also!" But Jadassohn croaked: "Herr Lauer, I forbid all criticism of such measures as I may officially take."

Meanwhile Diederich had shown signs of great excitement. "Oh! . . . Ah! . . . Why, this is—" He was quite pale, and began again: "Gentlemen . . . Gentlemen. I am in a position to . . . I know these people, the man and the girl. My name is Dr. Hessling. Till today they were both employed in my factory. I had to discharge them on account of indecent behavior in public."

"Aha!" said Jadassohn. Pastor Zillich made a movement. "This is truly the hand of God," he remarked. Herr Lauer's face went deep red under his grey beard, his burly figure was shaking with anger.

"We can't be sure about the hand of God. What seems likely, Dr. Hessling, is that the man's outburst was provoked by his desperation over his dismissal. He had a wife and perhaps children, too."

"They were not married at all," said Diederich, indignant in his turn. "He told me so himself."

"What difference does that make?" Lauer asked. The Pastor raised his arms. "Have we sunk so low," he cried, "that it makes no difference whether God's moral law is followed or not?"

Lauer declared that it was inappropriate to argue about moral laws in the street when somebody had been shot with the connivance of the authorities. He turned to the girl and offered her employment in his workshop. Meanwhile an ambulance had come up and the dead man was raised from the ground. When they were placing him in the car the girl started out of her stupor, threw herself upon the stretcher, tore it from the grasp of the bearers before they could prevent her, and it fell to the pavement. Clasping the dead man convulsively, and with wild screams, she rolled on the ground. With great difficulty she was separated from the corpse and placed in a cab. The assistant surgeon, who had accompanied the ambulance, drove off with her.

Jadassohn advanced threateningly towards Lauer, who was moving off with Heuteufel and the other members of the Masonic Lodge. "One moment, please. You stated just now that with the connivance of the authorities—I call these gentlemen to witness that that was your expression—with the connivance of the authorities somebody had been shot here. I call upon you to answer whether this was intended as a criticism of the authorities."

"I see," replied Lauer, looking at him. "I suppose you would like to have me arrested, too?"

"At the same time," continued Jadassohn, in loud cutting tones, "I draw your attention to the fact that the conduct of a sentry, firing upon a person who molests him, was defined in authoritative quarters as praiseworthy and justifiable, a few months ago in the Lück affair. It was rewarded by marks of official distinction and approval. Be careful how you criticize the actions of the supreme authorities."

"I have not done so," said Lauer. "I have merely expressed my disapproval of the gentleman with the dangerous mustache."

"What?" asked Diederich, who was still staring at the pavement where the man had fallen, which was stained with blood. Finally he understood that it was he who had been challenged.

"His Majesty wears a mustache like that," he said firmly. "It is the German fashion. Moreover, I decline all discussion with an employer who encourages revolution."

Lauer opened his mouth in a rage, although old Buck's brother, Heuteufel, Cohn and Judge Fritzsche tried to drag him off. Jadassohn and Pastor Zillich planted themselves belligerently beside Diederich. Then a detachment of infantry arrived at a quick march and cordoned off the street, which was quite empty. The lieutenant in charge called upon the gentlemen to move on. They lost no time in obeying, but they observed that the lieutenant went up to the sentry on duty and shook his hand.

"Bravo!" said Jadassohn, and Dr. Heuteufel added: "Tomorrow, I suppose, it will be the turn of the captain, the major and the colonel to pronounce a eulogy and reward the fellow with money."

"Quite right!" said Jadassohn.

"But"—Heuteufel stood still—"gentlemen, let us understand one another. What is the sense in all that? Just because this lout of a peasant could not understand a joke. A joking reply, a good-humored laugh, and he would disarm the workman who wanted to challenge him, his comrade, a poor devil like himself; instead of that, he is ordered to shoot. And afterward come the grandiloquent phrases."

Judge Fritzsche agreed, and counseled moderation. Then Diederich, still pale and with a voice that trembled, said: "The people must learn to feel power! The life of one man is not too much to pay for the sensation of Imperial Power!" "Provided it is not *your* life," retorted Heuteufel. "Even if it were mine!" Diederich replied, placing his hand upon his heart.

Heuteufel shrugged his shoulders. While they continued on their way Diederich, who was a little behind with Pastor Zillich, tried to explain his feelings to the latter. Breathing heavily with emotion, he said: "For me, the incident has an air of grandness, something majestic, so to speak. That a person who is impertinent can be simply shot down on a public street, without trial—think of it! It brings something heroic into the dullness of civil life. It shows people what power means."

"When exercised by the Grace of God," added the Pastor.

"Of course. That's just it. That's why the thing gives me a sense of religious exaltation. From time to time one has evidence of the existence of higher things, of powers to which we are all subjected. For example, in the Berlin riots last February, when His Majesty ventured into the seething tumult with such phenomenal cold-bloodedness, I can tell you—" As the others had stopped in front of the *Ratskeller,* Diederich raised his voice. "If the Emperor on that occasion had ordered the soldiers to close off Unter den Linden, and to fire on the whole crowd of us, straight into the middle of us, I say . . ."

"You would have shouted hurrah," concluded Dr. Heuteufel.

"Would you not have done so too?" asked Diederich, attempting to glare. "I do hope that we are all inspired by national feeling!"

Herr Lauer was again on the point of replying incautiously, but was restrained. Instead, Cohn said: "I, too, am patriotic. But do we pay our army for such pranks?"

Diederich looked him up and down.

"Your army, do you say? Herr Cohn, the department store owner, has an army. Did you hear that, gentlemen?" He laughed loftily. "Up until now I have only heard of the army of His Majesty the Emperor!"

Dr. Heuteufel murmured something about the rights of the people, but in the hectoring tone of a drill sergeant Diederich declared that he had no use for a mere figurehead of an Emperor. A people without stern discipline would fall into decay. . . . By this time they had reached the cellar where Lauer and his friends were already seated. "Well, are you going to sit with us?" Heuteufel asked Diederich. "In the last analysis, I suppose, we are all liberal-minded men." Then Diederich solemnly declared: "Liberals, of course. But where great national issues are concerned I am not in favor of half-measures. In such matters there are for me only two parties, which His Majesty himself has defined: Those who are with him and those who are against him. Therefore, it is evident to me that my place is not at your table."

He made a formal bow and went over to an unoccupied table. Jadassohn and Pastor Zillich followed him. People seated in the neighborhood turned around, and a general silence ensued. In the exuberance of what he had been through Diederich conceived the idea of ordering champagne. At the other table there was whispering, then someone moved a chair. It was Fritzsche. He said good-bye, came over to Diederich's table to shake hands with him, Jadassohn, and Zillich and went out.

"He was well advised to do that," remarked Jadassohn. "He recognized in time that his position was untenable." Diederich answered: "I should have preferred a clean break with him. No one who has a clear conscience in matters of patriotism has any reason to fear those people." But Pastor Zillich seemed embarrassed. "A righteous man must suffer much," he said. "You have no idea what an intriguer Heuteufel is. God knows what atrocious story he will tell about us tomorrow." At this Diederich gave a start. Dr. Heuteufel was one of the few who knew about that shady incident in his life, when he tried to escape military service! In a mocking letter he had refused to give a certificate of ill-health. He held him in the palm of his hand and could destroy him! In his sudden terror Diederich began to fear revelations from his school days, when Dr. Heuteufel had painted his throat and accused him of being a coward. He broke into a sweat, but called all the more loudly for lobster and champagne.

The Masons at the other table had worked themselves up again over the violent death of the young workman. Just who did the military and the Junkers think they were, giving such orders to shoot? They acted as if they were in a conquered country! When the Masons had become more heated they went so far as to demand that the conduct of the State be in the hands of the civilians, who, as a matter of fact, did all the work. Lauer wanted to know in what respect the ruling caste was any better than other people. "They are not even superior in race," he declared, "they are all infested with Jews, including the various ruling families." But he added: "I mean no offense to my friend Cohn."

It was time to intervene, Diederich felt. He hastily downed another glass, then stood up, marched heavily into the middle of the room beneath the Gothic chandelier, and said sharply:

"Herr Lauer, allow me to ask whether German princes are included in the ruling families which, according to your personal opinion, are infested with Jews?"

Calmly, and in an almost friendly fashion, Lauer replied: "Why, certainly."

"Indeed," said Diederich, drawing a deep breath before delivering his final stroke. The entire restaurant was listening when he asked:

"Among these Jewish princely families in Germany do you include one which I do not need to specify?" Diederich said this with an air of triumph. He was perfectly certain that his opponent would now lose his head, stammer and crawl under the table. But he met with unexpected cynicism.

"Well, of course," said Lauer.

Now it was Diederich's turn to lose his composure; he was appalled. He looked around as if asking whether he had heard correctly. The expressions of those present assured him that he had. He muttered that the consequences of Herr Lauer's statement would reveal themselves in time, and withdrew with relative aplomb to the friendly camp. Simultaneously Jadassohn appeared again upon the scene, after having gone no one knew where.

"I was not an eyewitness of what has just happened here," he said at once. "I want to make this point absolutely clear, as it may be of the greatest importance in the later developments of the case." He then obtained an exact account of what had happened.

Diederich related the story with great heat. He claimed as his service that he had cut off the enemy's retreat. "Now we have him in the palm of our hand!" "We certainly do," confirmed Jadassohn, who had been taking notes.

An elderly gentleman with a stiff leg and a grim face approached from the entrance. He saluted both tables and prepared to join the advocates of revolution. But Jadassohn was in time to prevent him. "Major Kunze, just a word!" He talked to him in an undertone, his eyes indicating people to the right and to the left. The Major seemed to be in doubt. "Do you give me your word of honor, Dr. Jadassohn, that such a statement was actually made?" While Jadassohn was giving him his word, Herr Buck's brother came up, tall and elegant, and smiling easily, he offered a satisfactory explanation of everything to the Major. But the latter regretted that he could not see how there could be any explanation for such a statement, and his face wore an expression of the most terrible gloom. Nevertheless, he continued to look over with regret at his old *Stammtisch*. Then, at the decisive moment, Diederich lifted the champagne bottle out of the bucket. The Major saw it and decided to obey the call of duty. Jadassohn introduced: "Dr. Hessling, the manufacturer."

The two gentlemen clasped hands, each summoning to the endeavor all the strength he could muster. They gazed firmly and earnestly into each other's eyes. "Sir," said the Major, "you have behaved like a real German patriot."

Bowing and scraping, they settled their chairs in their places, presented their glasses to one another, and finally drank. Diederich immediately ordered another bottle. The Major emptied his glass as regularly as it was filled, and between drinks he assured them that he too could take his stand when it was a question of German loyalty. "Even though my King has now relieved me of active service—"

"The Major," Jadassohn explained, "was last stationed at the local militia headquarters."

"I have still got the heart of an old soldier"—striking his breast—"and I shall always oppose unpatriotic tendencies with fire and sword!" As he shouted these words his fist came down heavily upon the table. At that moment Herr Cohn tipped his hat respectfully and hastened out behind the Major's back. In order that his departure should look less like a retreat, Herr Buck's brother first went to the lavatory. "Aha!" said Jadassohn all the louder. "Major, the enemy is in flight." Pastor Zillich was still uneasy.

"Heuteufel is still there. I do not trust him."

But Diederich, who ordered a third bottle, looked round contemptuously at Lauer and Dr. Heuteufel, who were sitting alone and staring shamefacedly at their beer glasses.

"We have the power," he said, "and those gentlemen over there are well aware of it. They have already resigned themselves to the fact that the sentry fired. They now look as if they were afraid that it would be their turn next. And their turn will come!" Diederich declared that he would lodge a complaint with the Public Prosecutor against Herr Lauer because of his previous statement. "And I shall see," Jadassohn assured him, "that charges are brought. I shall personally represent the prosecution's case at the trial. You gentlemen know that I cannot be called up as a witness, since I was not present when the thing happened."

"We will clean out this town," said Diederich, and he began discussing the Veterans' Association, which every true German patriot and loyal supporter of the Emperor would have to support. The Major assumed an official air. Yes, indeed, he was on the committee of the Veterans' Association. They served their King as best they could; he was ready to nominate Diederich as a member, so that the loyal element might be strengthened; hitherto, there was no use denying it, the damned Democrats predominated even there. In the Major's opinion, the authorities were far too deferential to the status quo in Netzig. He himself, if he had been appointed commanding officer of the District, would have kept a sharp check on the Reserve officers at the elections, he guaranteed that. "But, unfortunately, my King relieved me of the opportunity, so—" In order to console him Diederich filled his glass again. While the Major was drinking, Jadassohn leaned over to Diederich and whispered: "Don't believe a word of it! He is a spineless creature and crawls before old Buck. We must make an impression on him."

Diederich proceeded to do so at once. "I may tell you that I have already made formal arrangements with Governor von Wulckow." And as the Major opened his eyes in astonishment:

"Next year, Major, there will be Reichstag elections. Then we loyal citizens will have a heavy task. The fight is already on."

"Forward," said the Major grimly. "*Prost!*"

"*Prost!*" replied Diederich. "Gentlemen, however powerful the subversive elements in the country may be, we are stronger, for we have one agitator whom our opponents have not, and that is His Majesty."

"Bravo!"

"His Majesty has issued the command to every part of his country, and therefore to Netzig, that the citizens shall at last awaken from their slumbers. That is what we want, too!"

Jadassohn, the Major and Pastor Zillich manifested their wakefulness by thumping the table, shouting their applause, and toasting one another. The Major shouted: "To us officers His Majesty said: 'These are the gentlemen upon whom I can rely!'"

"And to us," cried Pastor Zillich, "he said, 'If the Church has need of princes—'"

They abandoned all restraint, for the restaurant was quite empty. Lauer and Heuteufel had slipped away unnoticed, and the gas had been turned out under the vaulted ceiling at the end of the room.

"He also said"—Diederich puffed out his cheeks until they were fiery red and his mustache seemed to stick into his eyes, which nevertheless glared formidably—"'We stand under the emblem of commerce', and so we do. Under his exalted leadership we are determined to do business."

"And to make a career!" Jadassohn crowed. "His Majesty has said that everybody is welcome who wishes to help him. Does anybody suggest that this does not include me?" he asked in a challenging tone, his ears glowing a bloody red. The Major bellowed once more:

"My King can absolutely rely on me. He dismissed me too soon, and as an honest German citizen I am not afraid to say that to his face. He will have bitter need of me when trouble begins. I have no intention of firing off harmless crackers at club balls for the rest of my life. I was at Sedan!"

"God bless my soul, so was I!" cried a shrill piping voice out of the invisible depths, and from the shadows of the vaulted chamber in the back appeared a little old man with tousled white hair. He tottered up, his spectacles glittering, his cheeks glowing, and he shouted: "Major Kunze! Well, well, my old friend from the war, you are as well as when we were together in France. That's what I always say: 'Live well and the longer the better!'" The Major introduced him. "Professor Kühnchen, of the High School." The little man entered into lively conjectures as to how he had come to be forgotten there in the dark. Earlier he had been with some friends. "I suppose I must have dozed off a bit, and then the damned fellows left me in the lurch." His sleep had not dulled the effects of drink, and with shrill boasts he reminded the Major of their mutual achievements in the iron year. "The frank-tiroors!" he yelled, and rivulets of moisture trickled from his wrinkled, toothless mouth. "A fine pack of rabble they were! As sure as you gentlemen are looking at me, I still have a stiff finger where a frank-tiroor bit me, just because I wanted to slit his throat a bit with my sword. What a dirty trick!" He showed the finger around the table and elicited cries of admiration. Diederich's feeling of enthusiasm was frankly mixed with fear. Involuntarily he saw himself in the position of the *franc-tireur*: the fiery little man was kneeling on his chest and pointing the blade at his throat. He had to go outside for a moment.

When he returned the Major and the Professor, each trying to shout louder than the other, were telling the story of a wild battle. Neither of them could be understood. Kühnchen, however, yelled more piercingly than the other bellowed, until he had reduced him to silence and could take up his boasting undisturbed. "No, my old friend, you have a mind for detail. If you fell downstairs you wouldn't miss a step. But it was Kühnchen who set fire to that house when the frank-tiroors were inside, there's no doubt about that. I employed a ruse of war and pretended to be dead, so that the silly idiots did not notice anything. Once it was burning, of course, they had no more desire to defend their fatherland, and thought only of getting out, soofe-qui-pooh. Then you should have seen us Germans! We shot them off the wall as they tried to clamber down! They bucked like rabbits!"

Kühnchen had to interrupt his fable, he was giggling uncontrollably, while the whole table boomed with laughter.

Kühnchen recovered. "The treacherous swine had also tried to get clever with us! And the women! Upon my word, gentlemen, there is nothing can touch the French women for viciousness. They poured boiling water on our heads. Now, I ask you, was that lady-like? When the house was on fire they threw the children out of the window, and expected us to catch them. Nice, wasn't it? But foolish! On our bayonets we caught the little devils. And then the women!" Kühnchen bent his gouty fingers as if they held the butt end of a gun and looked up as if waiting to impale someone. His spectacles glittered and he continued to lie. "At last a real fat one came along. She could not get through the window frontways, so she tried if she could go backward. But you didn't reckon with Kühnchen, my child. I lost no time in getting upon the shoulders of two comrades, and with my bayonet I tickled her fat French—"

The last word was drowned in applause. The Professor added: "Every Sedan anniversary I tell the story in noble words to my class. The youngsters must learn about their heroic forebears."

They all agreed that this could only strengthen the loyal sentiments of the younger generation, and they toasted Kühnchen. In their enthusiasm no one had noticed that a newcomer had approached the table. Suddenly Jadassohn saw the modest grey figure of a man in a long Hohenzollern coat, and made a friendly sign to him. "Why, come along, Herr Nothgroschen!" In the exuberance of his spirit Diederich asked overbearingly:

"Who are you?"

The stranger bowed and scraped.

"Nothgroschen, editor of the *Netzig Journal*."

"Ah, a future patron of the soup kitchen," said Diederich, his eyes flashing. "Washed-up intellectuals, academic proletariat, a menace to us all!"

They all laughed and the editor smiled humbly.

"His Majesty has described your type," said Diederich. "Well, come and sit down."

He even poured out champagne for him, and Nothgroschen drank it gratefully. He looked around in a cool but shy manner at the company, whose self-confidence had been greatly heightened by the empty bottles which lay on the ground. They soon forgot him. He waited patiently till somebody asked him why he had turned up in the middle of the night. "I had to get out the paper," he explained with the self-assured air of a little bureaucrat. "Tomorrow morning you will want to read in the paper all about the workman who was shot."

"We know more about that than you," cried Diederich. "You have to write it up like a starving penny-a-liner."

The editor smiled apologetically and listened dutifully while they all related at the same time what had happened. When the noise subsided he continued: "As that gentleman there—"

"Dr. Hessling," said Diederich sharply.

"Nothgroschen," murmured the editor. "As you mentioned the name of the Emperor just now, it will interest these gentlemen to know that another proclamation has been made."

"I forbid such seditious faultfinding!" shouted Diederich. The editor bowed and placed his hand on his heart. "The proclamation was made by the Emperor—in a letter."

"I suppose," Diederich asked, "that it reached your desk as usual through some despicable breach of confidence." Nothgroschen extended a deprecating hand. "The Emperor himself has designated it for publication. You'll read it tomorrow in the newspapers. I have a proof here."

"Go ahead, Doctor, read it," the Major ordered. Diederich cried: "What do you mean, 'Doctor'? Have you taken a doctor's degree?" But no one was interested in anything but the letter. They snatched the proof from the editor's hand. "Hurrah!" cried Jadassohn, who could still read without much difficulty. "His Majesty has definitely identified himself with the Christian Church." Pastor Zillich rejoiced so heartily that he started to hiccough. "That's one in the eye for Heuteufel! At last that impudent scientist, hic, will get what's coming to him. These fellows dare question the doctrine of divine revelation, which I myself, hic, can hardly understand, and I have studied theology!" Professor Kühnchen waved the proof sheets in the air. "Gentlemen, if I do not make my class read that letter, and set it as a subject for composition, then my name is not Kühnchen!"

Diederich was very serious. "Hammurabi was truly an instrument of God! I would like to see anyone deny it." He glared around angrily. Nothgroschen bent his shoulders. "And Emperor Wilhelm the Great," Diederich continued, "I insist on him. If he was not an instrument of the Lord, then the Lord doesn't know what an instrument is!"

"My thoughts exactly," the Major confirmed. Fortunately nobody contradicted him, for Diederich was determined to go to extremes. Clinging to the table he pushed himself up from his chair. "What about our magnificent young Emperor?" he asked threateningly. From every side the answer came: "Personality, impulsive . . . versatile . . . an original thinker." Diederich was not satisfied.

"I move that he is also an instrument!"

The motion was passed unanimously.

"And I further move that His Majesty be informed by telegram of this resolution!"

"I second the motion!" bellowed the Major. Diederich declared: "Passed unanimously and with enthusiasm!" and flopped back into his seat. Kühnchen and Jadassohn assisted one another in drawing up the telegram. They read out what they had concocted.

"At a convivial gathering in the *Ratskeller* at Netzig—"

"At an assembly convened," corrected Diederich. They continued.

"Of loyal citizens—"

"Loyal, hic, and Christian," added Pastor Zillich.

"Are you gentlemen really serious?" asked Northgroschen in a voice of gentle entreaty. "I thought it was a joke."

Then Diederich lost his temper.

"We do not trifle with sacred things! Do you want me to prove it to you in acts as well as words, you washed-up scholar?"

As Nothgroschen's gestures indicated complete submission, Diederich calmed down immediately and said: *"Prost!"* The Major on the other hand shouted as if he would burst: "We are the gentlemen on whom His Majesty can rely!" Jadassohn begged him to be quiet and began to read:

"This assembly of loyal and Christian citizens, convened at the *Ratskeller* in Netzig, humbly pays to Your Majesty unanimous and enthusiastic homage in light of Your Majesty's Royal profession of revealed religion. We register our deepest loathing of revolution in every form, and in the courageous act of a sentry in Netzig today we greet the gratifying evidence that Your Majesty, no less than Hammurabi and Emperor Wilhelm the Great, is the instrument of Almighty God." Jadassohn gave a flattered smile when they all applauded.

"Let us sign!" cried the Major. "Or do any of the gentlemen have anything to add?" Nothgroschen cleared his throat. "Just one word, with all due modesty."

"It had better be with all due modesty!" said Diederich. The alcohol had given the editor courage, and he swayed back and forth on his seat, giggling for no reason.

"I have nothing to say against the sentry, gentlemen. In fact, I have always held that soldiers are there to shoot."

"Well, what then?"

"Yes, but how do you know that the Emperor thinks so?"

"Of course he does! Look at the Lück case."

"Precedents—hee, hee—are all very well, but we all know that the Emperor is an original thinker and—hee, hee—and impulsive. He does not like to be forestalled. If I were to write in the paper that you, Dr. Hessling, were to be appointed minister, then—hee, hee—you would certainly never be appointed."

"The perverted reasoning of a Jew," cried Jadassohn. The editor became indignant. "Every time there is a High Church festival I write a column and a half of appropriate sentiment. The sentry, however, may be accused of murder. Then we shall have put our foot in it."

A silence ensued. The Major turned pensive and laid the pencil on the table. Diederich seized it. "Are we patriotic men?" and he signed his name with vigor. Then the enthusiasm was renewed. Nothgroschen wanted to sign his name second.

"To the telegraph office!"

Diederich gave orders to have the bill sent to him the next day and they left the restaurant. Suddenly Nothgroschen was full of the wildest hopes. "If I can get the Emperor's reply it will be a real journalistic scoop."

The Major bellowed: "Now we shall see whether I am merely to continue arranging charity bazaars!"

Pastor Zillich could already see his church swarming with people and Heuteufel being stoned by the mob. Kühnchen ranted about bloodbaths in the streets of Netzig. "Does anyone dare to question my loyalty to the Emperor?" crowed Jadassohn. And Diederich: "Old Buck had better be careful! And Klüsing in Gausenfeld, too! We are awakening from our slumber!"

The gentlemen held themselves very straight, and from time to time one of them shot forward unexpectedly. They made a great noise with their sticks on the closed shutters of the shops, and sang the "Watch on the Rhine" without making the slightest effort to keep in time with one another. At the corner of the Courthouse stood a policeman, but fortunately for him he did not move. "What are you looking at, little man?" shouted Nothgroschen, who was getting quite out of hand. "We are telegraphing to the Emperor!" In front of the post office an accident befell Pastor Zillich, who had the weakest stomach. While the others endeavored to ease his plight, Diederich rang the bell and handed in the telegram. When the postal official had read it, he looked hesitatingly at Diederich, but the latter glared so fiercely that he shrank back and did his duty. Meanwhile Diederich, without any reason, continued to glare and strike an attitude as if he were the Emperor to whom an aide-de-camp had reported the heroic deed of the sentry, and the prime minister handed him the telegram of homage. Diederich felt the royal helmet on his head, he tapped the sword at his side and said: "I am very powerful!" The telegraphist thought he was making some complaint and counted his change again. Diederich took the money, went up to a desk and scribbled some lines on a piece of paper. He put it in his pocket and returned to his companions.

They had called a cab for the Pastor, and he was driving off, making tearful signs from the window as if it were a final farewell. Jadassohn turned around the corner into a side street near the theater, although the Major shouted after him that his home lay in a different direction. Soon the Major disappeared also, and alone with Nothgroschen, Diederich reached Lutherstrasse. The editor refused to go any farther when they reached the Valhalla Theater. In the middle of the night he wanted to see "The Electric Marvel," a lady who was supposed to emit sparks. Diederich had to reason earnestly with him that this was not the hour for such frivolities. For the rest, Nothgroschen forgot all about the Electric Marvel as soon as he beheld the offices of the *Netzig Journal*.

"Stop!" he shouted. "Stop the presses! The telegram of the patriotic men must be inserted . . . You'll want to see it in the newspapers tomorrow morning," he remarked to a passing watchman. Then Diederich grasped him firmly by the arm.

"Not only that telegram," he whispered sharply. "I have another one." He drew a piece of paper out of his pocket. "The night telegraphist is an old acquaintance of mine, and he gave it to me. You must promise me the utmost discretion as to its origin. Otherwise the man could lose his post."

As Nothgroschen at once promised everything, Diederich continued without looking at the paper:

"It is addressed to the regimental headquarters and is to be communicated by the colonel himself to the sentry who shot the workman. It reads as follows: 'For your valor on the field of honor against the enemy at home we are pleased to extend our approval and hereby promote you to the rank of lance corporal. . .' Here, look for yourself"—and Diederich handed the paper to the editor. But Nothgroschen did not look at it, he only stared at Diederich in blank amazement, at his adamant bearing, at his mustache pointing upward and his glaring eyes.

"It almost seems to me—" stammered Nothgroschen. "You look so very like—His. . . ."

Chapter 4

Diederich would like to have slept until the afternoon, as in the good old days of the Neo-Teutons, but the *Ratskeller* presented its bill, which was considerable enough to compel him to get up and go to the office. He felt very ill, and everything conspired to irritate him, even the family. His sisters demanded their monthly dress allowance, and, when he said he did not have it, they reproachfully contrasted him with old Sötbier, who had never failed them. Diederich dealt vehemently with this attempt at revolt. In hoarse tones that betrayed his hangover, he gave the girls to understand that they would have to accustom themselves to a different state of affairs. Sötbier, of course, had been very free with the money and had been leading the business into ruin. "If I had to pay you your shares today you'd be pretty damned surprised at how little it would amount to." As he said this, it suddenly struck him as thoroughly unreasonable that he should ever be obliged to give the two girls a share in the business. "There has to be some way around it," he thought. They, on the other hand, became more insistent. "So, we cannot pay the dressmaker, but Doctor Hessling can drink one hundred and fifty marks' worth of champagne." Diederich's wrath was terrible to behold. They were opening his letters! They were spying on him! He wasn't master in his own house, but just a clerk, a coolie, who had to toil hard for the ladies so that they might loaf about all day doing nothing! He shouted and stamped until the glasses tinkled. Frau Hessling begged plaintively for peace; their fear prompted the two sisters to answer back, but there was no stopping Diederich now that he had started. "How dare you dictate to me, you pack of silly women! How do you know whether that hundred and fifty marks is not an excellent investment of capital? Yes, a capital investment! Do you think that I would go boozing on champagne with those idiots, if I did not want to get something out of them? Here in Netzig you know nothing about how things are done, this is the modern way. It is"— he hesitated for the right phrase—"the spirit of farsighted enterprise!"

And he slammed the door behind him. Frau Hessling followed him cautiously, and when he had thrown himself down on the parlor sofa, she took his hand. "My dear son, I am with you," she said, looking at him as if she wanted to "pray from the heart". Diederich demanded a salted herring and then began to complain angrily of the difficulty of introducing the new spirit into Netzig. At least in his own home they should not thwart is efforts! "I have big things in store for you, but you must kindly leave all that to my better judgment. There can be only one master, and, of course, he must be filled with a spirit of far-seeing enterprise. Sötbier does not fit the part. I'll give the old man a little while more to potter about, then he will get the sack."

Softly Frau Hessling said she was sure that, for his mother's sake, her dear son would always do exactly what was best. Then Diederich went off to the office and wrote a letter to Büschli & Co., machinery manufacturers, of Eschweiler, in which he ordered a "New Patent Double Beater, fitted on the Maier system". He left the letter lying open on his desk and went out. When he returned Sötbier was standing at the desk, and it was evident that he was crying under his green eye-shade. His tears were falling on the letter. "You'll have to have that copied," said Diederich coldly. Then Sötbier began:

"Master Diederich, our old beater is not a Patent-Beater, but it has been around since the time when your father was just starting out. He began with that machine, and with that machine the business grew up . . ."

"Well, in my turn I wish to build up the business with my own machine," replied Diederich sharply. Sötbier entreated.

"The old one has always been good enough for us."

"Not for me."

Sötbier swore that it could produce as much as the very latest machines, which were only foisted on the market by deceptive advertisements. As Diederich remained unmoved, the old man opened the door and shouted: "Fischer! Come here a moment!" Diederich began to feel uneasy. "What do you want with that fellow? I forbid him to interfere!" But Sötbier appealed to the testimony of the machinist, who had worked in the largest factories. "Look here, Fischer, tell Dr. Hessling what our cutting machine can do." Diederich would not listen. He walked rapidly up and down, convinced that the man would jump at the opportunity to annoy him. Instead of that, Napoleon Fischer began with a generous acknowledgment of Diederich's expert knowledge, and then added every possible unfavorable comment on the old machine. From the way Napoleon Fischer was speaking, he was on the point of quitting, so dissatisfied was he with the old machine. With a snort, Diederich thanked his lucky stars for being able to retain the invaluable services of Herr Fischer. Ignoring this irony, however, the machinist explained to him all the advantages of the new Patent Two-Cylinder as set out in the prospectus, especially the ease with which it worked. "Provided I can save you work," sneered Diederich, "I have no other desire. Thanks, Fischer, you can go."

When the machinist had left, Sötbier and Diederich were each busy with their own calculations. Suddenly Sötbier asked: "Where is the money coming from to pay for it?" Diederich's face was scarlet, for he, too, had been thinking of that the whole time. "Pay for it?! Bah!" he shouted. "In the first place, I shall set a long period for delivery. Then, do you think I would buy such an expensive machine if I didn't know what I was doing? No, sir. Can't you understand that I have definite plans for the extension of the business in the near future?—But I will not discuss that today."

He left the office with a swagger, in spite of private misgivings. That fellow, Napoleon Fischer, had looked back, as he went out, with a glance which suggested that he had put one over on the boss quite nicely. "When surrounded by enemies," thought Diederich, "we show our real strength," and he held himself more erect than ever. He would smash them all right, and show them whom they were dealing with, and he decided to carry out an idea which had occurred to him when he awoke in the morning. He called on Dr. Heuteufel, but it was the hour when the latter received patients, so he had to wait. When the Doctor did see him it was in the consulting room where everything, the smell and the instruments, reminded Diederich of former unpleasant visits. Dr. Heutefel took up the newspaper from the table and said, with a short laugh: "Well, I suppose you've come to enjoy your triumph. Two successes at one blow! Your champagne-inspired greetings are mentioned— and the Emperor's telegram to the sentry leaves nothing further to be desired, from your point of view."

"What telegram?" asked Diederich. Dr. Heuteufel showed him, and Diederich read: "For your valor on the field of honor against the enemy at home we are pleased to extend our approval and hereby promote you to the rank of lance corporal!" Standing there in print it gave him the impression of complete authenticity. He was actually moved, and said with manly reserve: "Those sentiments will find an echo in the heart of every true patriot." While Heuteufel shrugged his shoulders Diederich recovered his breath. "I did not come here on that account, but in order to straighten out our relationship." "I thought that was already settled," replied Heuteufel.

"No, not at all." Diederich assured him that he desired to make an honorable peace. He was prepared to work along reasonably liberal lines, provided his strong feeling of devotion to his Emperor and country were respected. Dr. Heuteufel declared Diederich's words for empty phrases, whereupon Diederich lost his composure. This man held him in the palm of his hand, and with the help of a certain document could show him up as a coward! The mocking smile on his yellow Chinaman's face, this attitude of superiority, were a perpetual insinuation. He remained silent and allowed the sword to dangle a little longer over Diederich's head. This could not last! "I command you," said Diederich, hoarse with agitation, "to give me back my letter."

Heuteufel feigned astonishment. "What letter?" "The one I wrote you about my military service, when I was called up."

The Doctor thought back.

"Oh, I remember, when you wanted to evade service!"

"I knew you would distort my imprudent statements into something insulting to me. Once again I demand the return of the letter." Diederich stepped forward threateningly, but Heuteufel stood his ground.

"Don't bother me. I haven't got your letter any more."

"I demand your word of honor."

"I do not give that on command."

"Then I warn you of the consequences of your dishonorable conduct. Should you ever try to cause me trouble with that letter, it will be a breach of professional secrecy. I will denounce you to the Medical Council, bring proceedings against you, and use all my influence to make your further career impossible!" In the intensity of his agitation his voice dropped to a whisper. "I tell you I am prepared for the worst! Between us from now on there can be only war to the knife!"

Dr. Heuteufel looked at him curiously, and shook his head, causing the ends of his long Chinese mustache to sway. "You are hoarse," he said.

Diederich started, and stammered: "What does that matter to you?"

"Oh, nothing," said Heuteufel. "It just interests me because I always prophesied that."

"What is it? Kindly explain yourself." But Heuteufel declined. Diederich glared at him. "I must insist most emphatically upon your doing your duty as a physician!"

Heuteufel replied that he was not Diederich's doctor. Whereupon the latter's commanding air collapsed, and he begged plaintively. "Sometimes I have pains in my throat. Do you think it will get worse? Is there anything to be afraid of?"

"I advise you to consult a specialist."

"But you are the only one here! For God's sake, Doctor, do not have this on your conscience, I have a family to support."

"Then you should smoke less and drink less. You had too much last night."

"Oh, is that all?" Diederich drew himself up. "You begrudge me the champagne, and then the homage to the Emperor."

"If you suspect me of doubtful motives, you need not ask my opinion."

Diederich began to cringe again. "You might, at least, tell me whether I may develop cancer."

Heuteufel remained stern. "Well, you were always subject to scrofula and rickets as a child. You should have gone through with your military training, then you would not be so fat now."

The end of it was that the Doctor consented to examine him and decided to paint his larynx. Diederich choked, rolled his eyes in terror and clutched the Doctor's arm. Heuteufel withdrew the brush. "If you go on like that, I can do nothing," he sneered. "You haven't changed a bit."

As soon as Diederich had recovered his breath he made off as quickly as possible from this chamber of horrors. In front of the house, while his eyes were still full of tears, he ran into Assessor Jadassohn. "Well, well!" said Jadassohn. "Did the liquor disagree with you? And you went to see Heuteufel of all people?"

Diederich assured him that he had never felt better. "But that fellow certainly got my dander up! I went to him because I consider it my duty to demand a satisfactory explanation of what this man, Lauer, said yesterday. I need hardly say that the idea of meeting Lauer directly does not appeal to a man of my loyal principles."

Jadassohn proposed that they adjourn to Klappsch's beer saloon.

"As I was saying," continued Diederich when they were seated inside, "I went to him with the intention of clearing up the whole matter by attributing it to the fact that the gentleman in question was drunk. Or, at the worst, to a temporary derangement. What do you think happened? Heuteufel got impertinent, put on a superior air, and made cynical comments on our greeting to the Emperor. In fact, you will hardly believe me, but he even criticized His Majesty's telegram!"

"Well, what next?" asked Jadassohn, whose hand was busy with Fräulein Klappsch.

"There is no 'next' for me. I am finished with the gentleman for the rest of my life!" cried Diederich, in spite of his painful consciousness of the fact that he would have to return on Wednesday to have his throat painted again. Jadassohn broke in sharply: "I'm not finished with him." Diederich stared at him. "There are authorities, known as the Royal Public Prosecutor's Department, who take interest in persons like Messrs Lauer and Heuteufel." At this point he released Fräulein Klappsch and told her to disappear.

"What do you mean, exactly?" asked Diederich uneasily.

"I am thinking of taking proceedings for *lèse-majesté*."

"You?"

"Yes, me. State Attorney Feifer is away on sick leave and I am in charge. As I pointed out yesterday, immediately after the incident and in the presence of witnesses, I was not present when the offense was committed. I am not, therefore, disqualified from representing the prosecuting authorities at the trial."

"But if nobody lodges a complaint?"

Jadassohn smiled cruelly. "That, thank God, will not be necessary . . . In any case, let me remind you that yesterday you yourself offered to appear as a witness."

"I know nothing about it," said Diederich quickly.

Jadassohn clapped him on the shoulder. "I trust you will be able to remember everything when you are put on your oath." Then Diederich became indignant, and his voice was so loud that Klappsch glanced into the room discreetly.

"Herr Assessor, I am greatly astonished that my private remarks—. Obviously it is your intention to secure rapid promotion by means of a political trial, but I fail to see why I should be concerned with your career."

"And does yours concern me?" asked Jadassohn.

"I see. Then we are opponents?"

"I hope that may be avoidable."

Jadassohn then proceeded to prove that he had no reason to be afraid of the trial. All the witnesses of the incident at the *Ratskeller* would have to give the same evidence as himself, including Lauer's friends. Diederich would not have to thrust himself too much to the fore . . . Diederich replied that he had unfortunately done so already, for it was he, after all, who had had the row with Lauer. But Jadassohn comforted him. "Nobody will bother about that. The question is whether the incriminating words were in fact spoken by Herr Lauer. You will simply make your statement, like the other witnesses, but with a little discretion, if you like."

"With the utmost discretion!" Diederich assured him. Then, prompted by Jadassohn's demonic air: "Why should I be the means of landing a decent man like Lauer in jail? After all, he is a decent man. In my eyes there is no shame in professing a political opinion!"

"Especially when it is the opinion of the son-in-law of old Buck, whom you need for the moment," concluded Jadassohn—and Diederich bowed his head. This Jewish upstart was exploiting him shamelessly and he was helpless. How was anyone to believe in friendship? Again he reminded himself that everybody else was much more brutal and unscrupulous than he was himself. The problem was how to put one's foot down. He drew himself up stiffly in his chair and glared, but he preferred to leave it at that. With these officials of the Public Prosecutor's you never could tell. . . . Besides, Jadassohn had turned the conversation into other channels.

"I suppose you know that in the government offices and in the courts there are curious rumors about His Majesty's telegram to the commanding officer of the regiment? The Colonel is said to have denied that he ever received a telegram."

Although he was quaking inwardly, Diederich kept his voice in control. "But it was in the newspaper!" Jadassohn grinned ambiguously. "You can't believe everything you read in the papers." He ordered Klappsch, who again shoved his bald pate through the doorway, to bring the *Netzig Journal*. "Look here, this number is devoted exclusively to His Majesty. The leading article deals with the declaration of the His Highness concerning revealed religion. Then comes the telegram to the Colonel, then the local news of the sentry's act of heroism, and finally three anecdotes about the Imperial Family."

"They are very touching stories," remarked Klappsch, rolling his eyes.

"No doubt, they are!" Jadassohn affirmed. And Diederich: "Even that radical propagandist rag is forced to admit the importance of His Majesty."

"It is, of course, possible that, in their praiseworthy zeal, they prematurely published the telegram of His Highness—before it was dispatched." "That is out of the question," said Diederich decisively. "His Majesty's style is unmistakable." Even Klappsch could recognize it. "Well that may be . . ." admitted Jadassohn. "You never can tell, so we have issued no official denial. Although the Colonel has heard nothing, the *Netzig Journal* may have had it direct from Berlin. Wulckow sent for Nothgroschen, the editor, but the fellow refuses to make any statement. The Governor was beside himself, he came to us in person to see about invoking the law against Nothgroschen compelling witnesses to speak. Finally we decided to take no action, but to wait for a denial from Berlin— for you never can tell." When Klappsch was called into the kitchen, Jadassohn continued: "Funny, isn't it? The thing seems fishy to everybody, but no one will take any action, because in this case— in this particular case"—he emphasized these words perfidiously, and his whole bearing, even his ears, seemed perfidious—"the improbable is most likely to happen."

Diederich was paralyzed with fear. He had never dreamed of such a dark betrayal. Jadassohn noticed his dismay, became flustered, and began to squirm. "Between ourselves, you know, the man has his weaknesses." In threatening and hostile tones Diederich retorted: "Last night you were of a very different opinion." Jadassohn pleaded as his excuse the uncritical frame of mind induced by the champagne, and asked if Dr. Hessling had really taken so seriously the enthusiasm of the other gentlemen. Nobody was more critical, as a matter of fact, than Major Kunze . . . Diederich drew back his chair, and his blood ran cold, as if he had suddenly found himself in a den of thieves. With the utmost conviction he said: "I trust I can rely as implicitly upon the patriotic sentiments of the other gentlemen as my own, against which I most emphatically forbid any insinuations."

Jadassohn's voice had recovered its steely resolve. "If that implies any insinuation regarding myself, I deny it with all the scorn it deserves." He began to crow, which brought Klappsch to the door:

"I happen to be Doctor Jadassohn, one of His Majesty's judges. I am at your disposal to fight a duel whenever you want me."

Diederich could only murmur that he had not intended anything of that kind. But he called for the bill, and they parted with cold reserve.

On his way home Diederich panted with agitation. Should he not have been more cooperative with Jadassohn, in case Nothgroschen talked? Still, he was indispensable to Jadassohn in the Lauer case. At all events, it was a good thing that Diederich now knew exactly the sort of person this gentleman was. "I always thought there was something suspicious about his ears! Real patriotic feeling is incompatible with ears like that after all."

As soon as he reached the house he seized the Berlin *Lokal-Anzeiger*. There he found the anecdotes about the Emperor which would appear tomorrow in the Netzig *Journal*. Perhaps they would not appear until the day after tomorrow, for there was not room for all of them. He continued his search with trembling hands. Here it was! He was obliged to sit down. "Is there anything wrong with you, my boy?" asked Frau Hessling. Diederich was staring at the printed words which were like a fairy tale come true. There it stood, among other indubitable facts, in the only paper which was read by the Emperor himself! Within the depths of his soul he murmured, so that he himself could hardly hear it: "My telegram." He could hardly contain himself for anxious joy. Was it possible? Had he really anticipated what the Emperor would say? Was his intuition so acute? Did his brain work in unison with . . .? He was overpowered by a sense of mystic relationship . . . But there might still be a denial, he might be hurled back into his own obscurity! Diederich passed a night of anxiety, and the next morning he rushed for the *Lokal-Anzeiger*. The anecdotes. The unveiling of a monument. The speech. "From Netzig": there was the report of the recognition bestowed upon Lance Corporal Emil Pacholke for his bravery in the face of the enemy within the Reich. All the officers, led by the Colonel, had shaken his hand. He had received gifts of money. "It is well known that yesterday the Emperor telegraphed, promoting the brave soldier to the rank of lance corporal." There! Not a denial but a confirmation! He had adopted Diederich's own words and had taken action in the sense Diederich had indicated! . . . Diederich spread out the newspaper, and gazed into its mirrored reflection of himself draped in imperial ermine.

Unfortunately no word could reveal this victory and Diederich's exaltation, but his own bearing sufficed, his inflexible mien and speech, his commanding gaze. His family and his workmen were cowed into respectful silence. Even Sötbier had to admit that new vigor had entered into the business. The more clearly Diederich's dominating figure emerged, the more apelike seemed the manner in which Napoleon Fischer crept about, with his arms hanging in front of him, his eyes averted and his teeth gleaming above his scraggly black beard. He was the spirit of suppressed revolt... Now was the time to make a move in the direction of Guste Daimchen. Diederich paid her a visit.

At first Frau Daimchen received him alone, seated on the old plush-covered sofa, but attired in a brown silk dress, much beribboned. She folded her hands, red and swollen like those of a washerwoman, across her stomach so that her new rings could not escape the visitor's gaze. Out of sheer embarrassment he began to admire them, whereupon Frau Daimchen was only too glad to explain that now she and Guste need want for nothing, thank God. The only thing that worried them was whether to furnish in Old German or "Louis Kangze" style. Diederich warmly recommended Old German; he had seen it in the best houses in Berlin. But Frau Daimchen was suspicious. "Who knows whether you called on people as elegant as we are. You can't tell me. I know when people pretend they have money, when they haven't." At a loss what to reply, Diederich remained silent, while Frau Daimchen complacently drummed with her fingers on her stomach. Fortunately Guste came in, with a great rustling of petticoats. Diederich sprang gracefully from his chair, and said, with a stridently rolling "r", as he kissed her hand: *"Gnädigstes Fräulein!"* Guste laughed. "Mind you don't break anything!" But she consoled him at once. "It is easy to recognize a real gentleman. Lieutenant von Brietzen always does that, too."

"Yes, indeed," said Frau Daimchen, "all the officers visit us. Only yesterday I was saying to Guste: 'Guste,' says I, 'we could have a crest embroidered on every chair, for members of the nobility have sat on every one of them.'"

Guste made a grimace. "As far as birth is concerned, and everything else, for that matter, Netzig is awfully dull. I think we'll move to Berlin." Frau Daimchen disagreed. "We shouldn't give these Netzig people the satisfaction," she said. "Only today old Frau Harnisch nearly burst with jealousy when she saw my silk dress."

"That's mother all over," said Guste. "As long as she can brag it is all right. But I am thinking of my fiancé. Do you know that Wolfgang has passed his final examination? But what can he do here in Netzig? With our money he could amount to something in Berlin." Diederich said: "He always wanted to become a minister of State or something." With a faint sneer he added: "That's supposed to be fairly easy!"

Guste immediately bridled. "Old Herr Buck's son is a cut above the average," she said tartly. With the superior air of a man of the world Diederich explained that nowadays qualifications were demanded which could not be supplied through old Buck's influence: personality, a spirit of far-seeing enterprise, and, above all, an unimpeachable sense of patriotism. The girl no longer interrupted him, but gazed respectfully at his aggressive mustache. But his consciousness of the impression he was making carried him too far. "I have not noticed any of those qualities in Herr Wolfgang Buck," he said. "That fellow philosophizes and finds fault with everything and for the rest, he leads a pretty gay life . . . After all," he concluded, "his mother was an actress too." He stared in front of him, although he felt that Guste's threatening glance sought to catch his eye.

"What do you mean by that?" she asked. He feigned astonishment.

"I? Oh, nothing. I was only referring to the way in which rich young men live in Berlin. After all, the Bucks are a distinguished family."

"I should hope so, indeed," said Guste sharply. Frau Daimchen, who had been yawning, remembered an appointment with a dressmaker; Guste looked expectantly at Diederich, and there was nothing for him to do but to stand up and bow himself out. In view of the tension, he made no effort to kiss the ladies' hands. In the hall Guste caught up with him. "Now, will you kindly tell me what you meant about the actress?"

He opened his mouth, gasped and shut it again, blushing deeply. He had almost repeated what his sisters had told him about Wolfgang Buck. In sympathetic tones he said: "We are old friends, Fräulein Guste. . . . All I meant to say was that Buck is not a fit match for you. He has an hereditary taint, so to speak, from his mother. The old man, too, was condemned to death. What are the Bucks, in any case? Take it from me, one should never marry into a family that is on the downgrade. That is a sin against oneself," he added. But Guste had planted her hands on her hips.

"Oh, the downgrade? And you, I suppose, are on the upgrade? Because you get drunk in the *Ratskeller* and get into rows with people? The whole town is talking about you, and you try to slander a most respectable family. On the downgrade, indeed! There will be no question of the downgrade for whoever gets my money. You are jealous. Do you think I can't see that?"—and she looked at him with tears of rage in her eyes. He felt exceedingly uncomfortable and would have liked to fall on his knees and kiss her chubby little fingers, and then the tears from her eyes—but did he dare? Meanwhile she drew down her plump, rosy jowls into an expression of contempt, turned her back and slammed the door. With beating heart Diederich stood for a while on the spot, then he left, feeling very small.

He reflected that there had been no chance for him in that quarter anyhow; the matter did not concern him. For all her money, Guste was still just a silly goose—and this thought soothed him. When he heard one evening what Jadassohn had heard in the courts at Magdeburg, Diederich had his moment of triumph. Only fifty thousand marks! And with that, putting on the airs of a countess! A girl who bluffed on that scale was obviously more suitable for second-raters, like the Bucks, than for a solid, right-thinking citizen like Diederich! Käthchen Zillich would be preferable. She was like Guste in appearance, her charms were almost as irresistible, and moreover her good temper and easy manners were a recommendation. He began to go more frequently for afternoon coffee and courted her ardently. She warned him against Jadassohn, which Diederich recognized as only too well justified. She also spoke with extreme disapproval of Frau Lauer, whose conduct with Landgerichtsrat Fritzsche. . . . In the Lauer case Käthchen Zillich was the only person who wholly took Diederich's part.

This affair was assuming a threatening prospect for Diederich. Jadassohn had succeeded in getting the Public Prosecutor's Department to summon before a court of inquiry the witnesses of that night's incident. In spite of Diederich's reserve on the witness stand, the others held him responsible for bringing them into this dilemma. Cohn and Fritzsche avoided him, Herr Buck's brother forgot his natural politeness so far as to cut him dead, and Heuteufel painted his throat ferociously while refusing to talk to him in private. On the day when it became known that the court had served

Herr Lauer with a summons, Diederich's table in the *Ratskeller* was deserted. Professor Kühnchen was putting on his overcoat and Diederich had just time to seize him by the collar. But Kühnchen was in a hurry, he had to speak against the new military appropriations bill to the Liberal Voters' Association. He slipped away, and Diederich remembered bitterly that night of victory, when the blood of the enemy had flowed outside in the street and champagne inside in the restaurant. Then Kühnchen was the most militant of the patriots present. Now he was opposing the increase of our glorious army! . . . Alone and forsaken, Diederich gazed into his mug of afternoon beer. Suddenly Major Kunze appeared.

"Hello, Major," said Diederich with forced joviality, "you have been keeping very quiet lately."

"Well, that's more than can be said about you," the Major growled, as he stood in his hat and coat, looking about him as if in the middle of a snowy plain.

"Not a soul about!"

"Perhaps you will join me in a glass of wine—" ventured Diederich, but he met a speedy rebuff. "Thanks, I haven't yet got over your champagne." The Major ordered beer and sat down in silence, his expression as dark as thunderclouds. To break the terrible silence, Diederich suddenly burst out: "I say, Major, what about the Veterans' Association? I thought I should hear something of my election."

The Major looked hard at him, as if he would like to eat him alive. "Oh, really. You thought that, did you? I suppose you also thought it would be an honor for me to be mixed up in your scandal?"

"My scandal?" stuttered Diederich. "Yes, sir, yours!" thundered the Major. "Herr Lauer may have said a hasty word; that can happen, even to old soldiers who have lost a limb in the service of their King. But you led Herr Lauer, with malice aforethought, into making a rash statement. I am ready to swear that on the witness stand. I know Lauer. He was with us in France and is a member of our Veterans' Association. You, sir, who are you? How do I know whether you were ever in the army? Produce your papers!"

Diederich's hand went at once to his breast pocket. He would have stood to attention if the Major had ordered him to do so. The Major held the discharge papers at arm's length in front of him. Then he threw them down with a grim laugh. "Ah! ha! Assigned to the *Landsturm*. I thought so. Flat feet, I suppose." Diederich was pale, and trembled at every word of the Major's. He said, holding out a beseeching hand: "Major, I give you my word of honor that I have done my service. In consequence of an accident, which was entirely to my credit, I was demobilized after three months. . . ."

"We know those accidents. . . . The bill, please!"

"Otherwise I would have stayed on permanently," Diederich whined. "I was absolutely devoted to the army. You can ask my superior officers."

"Evening." The Major had put on his overcoat. "All I have to say to you, sir, is this: What business is it of a slacker when other people commit *lèse-majesté?* His Majesty has no use for slackers . . . Grützmacher," he said to the proprietor, "you should be more particular about your customers. Because of one of them who happens to frequent this place too much, Herr Lauer has been almost arrested, and I, with my stiff leg, must appear in court as a witness for the prosecution, and get myself into bad odor with everybody. The dance at the Harmony Club has been called off, I have nothing to do, and when I come here"—he again looked round as if the place were a snowy plain—"there is nobody to be seen. Except, of course, the informer!" he shouted from the steps.

"My word of honor, Major . . ." Diederich said, running after him, "it was not I who lodged the complaint; it is all a misunderstanding." But the Major had already reached the street. "At least, I rely upon your discretion!" cried Diederich after him.

He wiped his forehead. "Herr Grützmacher," he said tearfully, "you at least will agree . . ." As he ordered wine, the proprietor agreed to everything.

Diederich drank and shook his head mournfully. He could not understand these setbacks. His intentions had been pure, only the wiles of his enemies had obscured them . . . Then Judge Fritzsche turned up, and looked round hesitatingly. When he saw that Diederich was really quite alone, he came up to him. "Dr. Hessling!" he said as he shook hands. "You look as if you had just buried your best friend." Diederich murmured that there was always a lot of trouble in a big business. But he opened his heart fully when he saw the other's sympathetic expression. "I don't mind telling you, Judge, this business with Herr Lauer is damnably unpleasant for me."

"Still more so for him," said Fritzsche severely. "If it were not that he is above suspicion of flight, we should have had to arrest him today." He saw Diederich grow pale and added: "And that would have been painful even to us judges. After all, we are all human and we have to live with one another. But of course"—he steadied his pince-nez and assumed a wooden expression—"the law must be obeyed. If on that evening—I myself had already left— Lauer actually used those scandalous expressions concerning His Majesty, as stated by the prosecution, and you are the chief witness—"

"I?" Diederich started up in desperation. "I heard nothing, not a word!"

"That does not agree with your testimony before the court of inquiry."

Diederich became confused. "At first one doesn't know what to say. But now, when I think over the questionable incident, it seems to me we were all pretty merry, particularly myself."

"Particularly yourself," repeated Fritzsche.

"Yes, and I probably put leading questions to Herr Lauer. What his answers were I am no longer prepared to swear. Anyhow, the whole thing was a joke."

"Oh, I see: a joke." Fritzsche breathed more freely. "Well, what is to prevent you from simply telling the judge that?" He raised a warning finger. "Not that I have any desire to influence your testimony."

Diederich raised his voice. "I shall never forgive Jadassohn for this trick!" He described the maneuvers of this gentleman, who had purposely gone out during the scene, so that he could not be cited as a witness; who had then begun immediately to assemble evidence for the prosecution, taking advantage of the more or less irresponsible condition of those present, and binding them in advance with their testimony. "Herr Lauer and I know each other to be men of honor. What right has this Jew to force us into a quarrel?"

Fritzsche carefully explained that it was not Jadassohn's person at issue here, but rather the action being taken by the Public Prosecutor's Office. Of course, it must be admitted that Jadassohn was perhaps inclined to be overzealous. Lowering his voice he continued: "You see, that is why we do not like working with these Jewish gentlemen. A man like that never asks himself what impression it will make on the public when an educated man, an employer, is condemned for *lèse-majesté*. His radical methods take no account of material considerations."

"The radical methods of the Jew," added Diederich.

"He does not hesitate to place himself in the foreground—although I do not deny that he believes he is discharging a patriotic and a professional duty."

"What do you mean?" cried Diederich. "He's a vulgar upstart who is trafficking in our most sacred possessions!"

"That's putting it in rather strong terms"—Fritzsche smiled in satisfaction, and drew his chair nearer. "Suppose I were the judge in charge of the inquiry. There are cases in which one is justified, to a certain degree, in handing in one's resignation."

"You are a close friend of the Lauer family," said Diederich, nodding significantly. Fritzsche assumed the air of a man of the world. "But, you understand, in so doing I would definitely confirm certain rumors."

"That won't do," said Diederich, "it would be contrary to the code of honor."

"Then I have no choice but to do my duty, quietly and impartially."

"To be impartial is to be German," said Diederich.

"Especially as I may assume that the witnesses will not render my task unnecessarily difficult."

Diederich laid his hand on his heart. "Judge Fritzsche, one may be carried away when great issues are at stake. I have an impulsive nature, but I am aware that I owe an accounting to God for everything." He dropped his eyes. Then, in manly tones: "I too am susceptible to remorse." This appeared to be enough for Fritzsche, for he paid the bill. The two gentlemen shook hands solemnly and in perfect understanding.

The very next day Diederich was called before the judge in charge of the inquiry, and found himself in the presence of Fritzsche. "Thank God," he said to himself, and he made his statement in a spirit of honest impartiality. Fritzsche's only care seemed also to be the truth. Public opinion, it is true, lost none of its partiality for the accused. Predictably, this partiality found its strongest voice in the Social Democrat newspaper *Volksstimme*, reaching the point of sarcastic references to Diederich's private life, which were certainly inspired by Napoleon Fischer. But even the usually docile *Netzig Journal* chose this moment to publish a speech of Herr Lauer's to his workmen, in which the manufacturer stated that he was sharing the profits of his business with all who had cooperated in it, a quarter to the office staff and a quarter to the men. In eight years they had had the sum of one hundred thirty thousand marks to share among themselves, in addition to their salaries and wages. This produced a most favorable and widespread impression. Diederich encountered unfriendly faces. Nothgroschen, the editor, to whom he stopped to speak, actually smiled offensively and said something about social progress which could not be arrested by patriotic claptrap. The consequences to his business were particularly irritating. Orders, upon which Diederich could usually count, did not come in. Cohn, the proprietor of the department store, frankly informed him that he had given preference to the Gausenfeld paper factory for his Christmas catalogues, because he could not afford to offend his customers' sensibilities by getting mixed up in politics. Diederich now began to turn up quite early at the office in order to intercept such communications, but Sötbier was always there first, and the reproachful silence of the old manager only increased his rage. "I'll let the whole show go to the devil!" he yelled. "Then you and the rest of them will see where you find work. With my doctor's degree I can get a post as managing director tomorrow, at a salary of forty thousand marks! . . . I am sacrificing myself for you," he shouted at the men when they drank beer against the rules. "I am paying out money to keep you employed."

Toward Christmas, however, he was compelled to lay off a third of the men. Sötbier showed him by calculation that they could not otherwise meet the obligations which fell due at the beginning of the year, "since we must deduct two thousand marks as an installment on the new double-beater." He held his ground, even when Diederich seized the inkpot. In the faces of those who remained he saw a lack of confidence and respect. Whenever several of his workmen were standing together, he fancied he heard the word "informer." Napoleon Fischer's knotted, dark, hairy hands did not hang down so close to the ground, and he looked as if his cheeks actually had some color in them.

On the last Sunday in Advent—the courts had just decided on holding the public trial—Pastor Zillich preached in St. Mary's on the text: "Love your enemies." Diederich shrank at the first words. Soon he felt that the whole congregation was becoming uneasy. "Vengeance is mine, saith the Lord." Pastor Zillich addressed the words pointedly in the direction of the Hesslings' pew. Emmi and Magda sank from sight; Frau Hessling sobbed. Diederich defiantly answered the glances which sought him out. "Whosoever speaketh of vengeance, so he shall be judged!" Then everybody turned round and Diederich collapsed.

His sisters made a scene when they got home. They were being badly received in society. Young Professor Helferich no longer sat near Emmi; he had eyes only for Meta Harnisch, and she knew why. "Because you are too old for him," said Diederich. "No, because you make us unpopular!" "The five daughters of Herr Buck's brother won't speak to us any more!" cried Magda. "I'll give them five boxes on the ear," said Diederich. "That's all we need! One lawsuit is enough." Then he lost patience. "You? What business of yours are my political fights?"

"We shall be old maids because of your political rows!"

"As if you weren't already. You loll uselessly about the house while I slave for you, and into the bargain you presume to find fault and to distract me from my most sacred duties. You can shake the dust of the place off your feet! You can become nursemaids for all I care!" He slammed the door in spite of Frau Hessling's beseeching gesture.

Thus a dismal Christmas approached. The sisters refused to speak to their brother. Whenever Frau Hessling left the locked room in which she was decorating the Christmas tree, her eyes were red and swollen with tears. And on Christmas Eve, when she brought her children in, she sang all alone and with a quavering voice, "Silent Night." "This is a present from little Diederich to his dear sisters," she said, and her glance begged him not to give her the lie. Emmi and Magda thanked him with embarrassment, and he was equally embarrassed as he looked at the gifts which were supposed to have come from him. He regretted that, in spite of Sötbier's emphatic advice, he had refused the accustomed Christmas-tree celebration for the workmen in order to punish the unruly crew. Otherwise he might now be with them. Here in the family the whole mood was so artificial, a warming-over of old, dead sentiments. Only one person could have made it real, Guste, and she was not there. . . . The Veterans' Association was closed to him, and he would have found nobody in the *Ratskeller*, no friend at any rate. Diederich felt neglected, misunderstood and persecuted. How remote were the innocent days of the Neo-Teutons, when in long ranks, inspired by good will, they sang and drank beer. Now, in the rough world, sturdy university friends no longer exchanged slashes in honorable duels, but a crowd of treacherous rivals flew at one another's throats. "I do not belong to these tough times," thought Diederich as he ate the marzipan on his plate, and dreamed in the candlelight of the Christmas tree. "I am really a good-hearted fellow. Why do they drag me into horrible things like this trial, and injure me even in my business, so that, my God, I shall not be able to pay for the double-beater I ordered." A cold shiver ran through him, tears came into his eyes, and so that they might not be seen by his mother, who was watching his worried face, he crept into the dark room adjoining. Resting his arms on the piano, he buried his face in his hands and wept. Outside Emmi and Magda were quarreling about a pair of gloves, and their mother did not dare to decide to whom they had been given. Diederich sobbed. Everything had gone wrong, in politics, business and love. "What is left to me?" He opened the piano. He shivered, he felt so uncannily alone that he was afraid to make a noise. The sounds came of their own accord, his hands were unconscious of them. Folk songs, Beethoven, and drinking songs rang out in the twilight, which was thereby cozily warmed so that a comfortable drowsiness filled his brain. At one moment it seemed to him that a hand was stroking the top of his head. Was it only a dream? No, for suddenly a full glass of beer stood on the piano. His good mother! Schubert, what loyal integrity, the soul of the mother country . . . All was silent, and he did not notice it, until the clock struck: an hour had passed. "That was my Christmas," said Diederich, and he went out to join the others. He felt consoled and strengthened. As the girls were still quarreling about the gloves, he chided their lack of Christmas spirit and placed the gloves in his pocket, to exchange them for a pair for himself.

The whole Christmas season was overclouded by worry about the new machine. Six thousand marks for a New Patent Double-Beater, Maier System! He had no money in hand and, as things were, none was available. It was an incomprehensible stroke of fate, a mean-spirited opposition put up by men and circumstances that embittered Diederich. When Sötbier was not there he banged the lid of his desk and threw the letter files about the room. To the new master, who had firmly grasped the reins of the business, new opportunities would simply have to present themselves; success awaited him and events would have to shape themselves to his personality! . . . His anger was overtaken by faintheartedness, and he took precautions to ward off a catastrophe. He softened toward Sötbier; perhaps the old chap might yet be of some use. He also humbled himself before Pastor Zillich and begged him to tell the people that the sermon, which had excited so much comment, was not aimed at him. The Pastor was obviously remorseful and promised to do so, under the reproachful glance of his wife, who confirmed his promise. Then the parents left Käthchen alone with Diederich, and he felt so grateful to them in his depression that he almost proposed to her. Käthchen's consent, which hovered on her dear, plump lips, would have been a success for him, and would have brought him allies against a hostile world. But that machine which he had to find the money for! It would have swallowed up a quarter of her dowry. . . . Diederich said, with a sigh, that he would have to be getting back to the office, and Käthchen pressed her lips together without having had an opportunity of saying "yes." A decision had to be made, for the arrival of the machine was imminent. Diederich said to Sötbier: "I advise those people to deliver it punctually to the minute, otherwise I shall not hesitate to return it." But Sötbier reminded him of the custom which gave the manufacturers a few days' grace period. He insisted, in spite of Diederich's wrath. In any case, the machine arrived punctually. It had not yet been unpacked when Diederich began to fuss and fume. "It is too large. They guaranteed that it would be smaller than the old pattern. Why should I buy it when it does not even save space?" As soon as it had been installed he went over the machine with a foot-rule. "It is too big. They can't swindle me. Look at it, Sötbier; isn't it too large?" But with imperturbable accuracy Sötbier explained the errors in Diederich's measurements. Diederich retired, raging, to devise another method of attack. He sent for Napoleon Fischer. "Where is the man to adjust the new machine? Did they not send anyone with it?" Then he grew indignant. "I ordered him to come," he lied. "These people have a nice way of doing business. I should not be surprised if I have to pay twelve marks a day for this fellow, and he is conspicuous by his absence. Who will set up the damned machine for me?"

The machinist said he knew all about it. Deiderich suddenly developed the utmost cordiality towards him. "I need hardly say I would rather pay you overtime than squander good money on a stranger. After all, you are an old employee." Napoleon Fischer raised his eyebrows, but said nothing. Diederich laid his hand on his shoulder. "Look here, my man," he said confidentially, "I don't mind telling you I am disappointed in this machine. It looked different in the pictures of the prospectus. The blades of the cutter were supposed to be much wider. Where is the greater efficiency which those people promised? What do you think? Do you think the drive is strong? I am afraid the stuff will stick halfway." Napoleon Fischer looked at Diederich inquiringly, but he began to see what he was driving at. They would have to try it out, he said hesitatingly. Diederich avoided his glance, pretending to examine the machine, as he said encouragingly: "Well, all right. You will put the thing together, I will pay you an additional twenty-five per cent for overtime, and for heaven's sake, run some stuff through it at once. Then we'll see how it cuts."

"It's going to be a mess," said the mechanic, obviously seeking to conciliate Diederich, who seized his arm before he realized what he was doing. Napoleon Fischer was his friend and savior! "Come on, my good man"—his voice trembled with emotion. He took Napoleon Fischer into the house, and Frau Hessling was told to pour him out a glass of wine. Without looking at him Diederich pressed fifty marks into his hand. "I'm counting on you, Fischer," he said. "The manufacturers would take me in if it weren't for you. I have already thrown two thousand marks down the greedy gullets of those people."

"They will have to pay it all back," said the machinist obligingly. "You think that, too?" Diederich asked earnestly.

The very next day, after having spent the lunch hour at the machine, Napoleon Fischer informed his employer that the new acquisition was no good. The stuff did not move and had to be shoved on with the stirring-pole, just as in the old style of machine.

"So it is a common swindle," Diederich cried. It also required more than twenty horse power. "That is not in the contract. Do we have to accept it, Fischer?"

"We need not accept it," he decided, stroking his black-bearded chin with his knotted hand. For the first time Diederich looked him squarely in the face.

"Then you can prove to me that the machine does not fulfill the terms of purchase?"

A pale smile seemed to hover around Napoleon Fischer's sparse beard. "I can," he replied. Diederich noticed the smile and said with all the more emphasis: "I'll show those people who I am!" He wrote at once in the strongest terms to Büschli & Co. in Eschweiler. The reply came by return. They could not understand his contentions. The New Patent Beater, Maier pattern, had been installed and given a trial by several paper manufacturers, whose testimonials were enclosed. It was, therefore, out of the question for them to take it back, much less return the two thousand marks paid on account, and the balance of the agreed purchase price must be settled at once. Whereupon Diederich wrote an even sharper letter than the first and threatened proceedings. Then Büschli & Co. endeavored to pacify him, and recommended another trial. "They are afraid," said Napoleon Fischer, to whom Diederich showed the communication, and his teeth flashed. "They cannot afford a lawsuit, for their machine is not sufficiently well known." "That's right," said Diederich, "we have them at our mercy!" He was certain of victory, and therefore he refused peremptorily every compromise and their offer to reduce the price. When nothing happened for several days, however, he began to feel uncomfortable. Perhaps they were waiting for him to take legal action! Perhaps they were taking action themselves! Many times a day his uncertain glance sought Napoleon Fischer, who furtively returned the look. They no longer spoke to one another. One morning at eleven o'clock, when Diederich was having an early lunch, the servant brought in a visiting card: Friederich Kienast, Manager, Büschli & Co., Eschweiler. While Diederich was still turning it around between his fingers, the visitor entered.

He stopped at the door. "Excuse me," he said, "there must be some mistake. I have been shown in here, but I have come on a matter of business."

Diederich had recovered his presence of mind. "Very likely, but it doesn't matter. Won't you come in? I am Dr. Hessling. This is my mother and my sisters, Emmi and Magda."

The gentleman approached and bowed to the ladies. "My name is Friederich Kienast," he murmured. He was short, with a fair beard, and wore a brown morning suit of woolly material. The three ladies smiled amiably. "May I set a place for you?" Frau Hessling asked. "Of course," said Diederich, "you will have lunch with us, Herr Kienast, won't you?"

"I cannot refuse," declared the representative of Büschli & Co., rubbing his hands. Magda helped him to some kippered herring, which he praised while the first mouthful was still on his fork.

Laughing innocently, Diederich asked:

"Don't you like to have a little something to drink when you are doing business?" Herr Kienast also laughed. "I'm always sober when it comes to business." Diederich grinned. "Well, in that case we shall not quarrel." "It all depends, doesn't it?" and Kienast's jesting but challenging words were accompanied by a glance at Magda, who blushed.

Diederich filled the guest's glass with beer. "I suppose you have other business in Netzig?" "You never can tell," said Kienast evasively.

Tentatively Diederich remarked: "You won't do much business with Klüsing in Gausenfeld; he's not doing so well." As the other did not reply, Diederich thought: "They have sent him here specially about the machine; they are afraid of a lawsuit." Then he noticed that Magda and Büschli's representative were raising their glasses at the same time, and toasting each other with their eyes. Emmi and Frau Hessling looked on in rigid silence. Diederich bent his head over his plate in a fluster—but all at once he began to sing the praises of home life. "You are in luck, my dear Herr Kienast, for this lunch hour is by far the pleasantest time of the day. Coming up here, in the middle of one's work, has a humanizing effect, so to speak, and one needs it."

Kienast agreed that it was needed. To Frau Hessling's inquiry whether he was married he replied in the negative, looking, as he did so, at the top of Magda's head, for it had modestly drooped.

Diederich stood up at attention, bringing his heels together. "Herr Kienast," he said with a sharp roll of the *r*, "I am at your disposal."

"You will take a cigar, won't you Herr Kienast?" said Magda. Kienast allowed her to light it for him and hoped that he would have the pleasure of seeing the ladies again—this with a significant smile at Magda. Outside in the yard his tone changed completely. "Hm, these are small, cramped premises," he remarked in frigid tones. "You should see our works."

"In a hole like Eschweiler," replied Diederich, equally contemptuous, "that is no wonder. Just you try to pull down this block of houses!" Then he shouted in the tones of a martinet for the machinist to set the new beater in motion. As Napoleon Fischer did not come at once, Diederich stormed down upon him. "Are you deaf, sir?" But as soon as the man came in Diederich stopped shouting. In an imploring whisper, his eyes staring with anxiety, he said: "Fischer, I have been thinking things over. I am satisfied with your work, and from the first of the month your salary is raised to one hundred and eighty marks." Napoleon Fischer gave a short, understanding nod and moved away. Diederich began at once to shout. Someone had been smoking! They told him it was only his own cigar which he smelled. To the representative of Büschli & Co. he said: "Anyway, I am insured, but we must have discipline. Aren't these works fine?"

"The equipment is pretty old," retorted Herr Kienast, with a disparaging glance at the machines. "All right, my friend," sneered Diederich, "but they're as good as your beater, in any case." Ignoring Kienast's protest, he began to belittle the capacity of the domestic manufacturers. He was waiting until his trip to England before installing his new fittings. He was forging ahead at a great rate. Business had developed enormously since he took charge. "And there is still room for development." He drew on his imagination. "I now have contracts with twenty county newspapers. The Berlin orders will drive me mad . . ." Kienast interrupted him brusquely: "Then you must just have dispatched all your orders, for I don't see any finished goods about."

Diederich became indignant. "Sir! Allow me to tell you that only yesterday I sent a circular to all my smaller customers, informing them that I could promise no more deliveries until our new building was completed."

The machinist came to fetch the gentlemen. The New Patent Beater was half full, but the material still passed through it very slowly, and had to be helped by a man with the stirring-pole. Diederich held his watch in his hand. "Now, let us see. You state that in your machine the stuff takes twenty to thirty seconds to go through one cycle. I have already counted fifty. Machinist, pay out more material . . . What is wrong, it is taking ages!"

Kienast was bending over the bowl. He straightened up and smiled shrewdly. "Of course, if the valves are stopped up . . ." He gave Diederich a searching look which the other's eyes failed to meet. "I cannot say offhand what else may have been done to the machine." Diederich started up, suddenly very red. "Do you wish to insinuate that I and the machinist have—?"

"I have said nothing," replied Kienast primly.

"I must emphatically repudiate that insinuation," Diederich thundered, but it seemed to leave Kienast unimpressed. His eyes were calm and a sly grin hovered about his beard, which was brushed in a parting on his chin. If he had shaved and trained the ends of his mustache to grow upright he would have looked like Diederich! He was a force to be reckoned with! Diederich's attitude became all the more truculent. "My machinist is a Social Democrat.

The idea that he would do me a favor is absurd. Moreover, as an officer of the reserve I warn you to be careful what you say to me."

Kienast walked out into the yard. "Never mind about that, Dr. Hessling," he said calmly. "I am a sober man when it comes to business, as I told you at lunch. All I want to repeat to you is that we delivered the machine in excellent condition, and we do not propose to take it back." "We'll see about that," said Diederich. Doubtless Büschli & Co. would not consider a lawsuit particularly helpful in introducing their new merchandise. "I will give you a special testimonial in the trade papers!" Where upon Kienast retorted that blackmail would not work. And Diederich declared that the only thing to be done with a common creature who was not eligible to fight a duel was to throw him out. In the midst of this discussion Magda appeared in the doorway of the house.

She was wearing her Christmas fur coat and gave them a cheerful smile. "Are you gentlemen not finished yet?" she asked roguishly. "It is such a lovely day, I felt I must go out for a bit before dinner. By the way," she added volubly, "Mother wants to know whether Herr Kienast will be with us for supper?" As Kienast regretted that he must say no, she smiled more persuasively. "And would you refuse me, too?" Kienast gave a harsh laugh. "I would not refuse. But I don't know whether your brother . . ." Diederich snorted, and Magda looked at him beseechingly. "Herr Kienast," he managed to say, "I shall be delighted. Perhaps we may yet come to an understanding." Kienast said he hoped so, and offered gallantly to escort the young lady. "If my brother has no objection," she said with demure irony. Diederich allowed this also. Then he gazed after her in amazement as she went off with the representative of Büschli & Co. How that girl got her way when she liked!

When he came in to dinner he heard the sisters talking in sharp tones in the sitting room. Emmi was accusing Magda of behaving disgracefully.

"You shouldn't do such things." "No," cried Magda, "I suppose I must ask your permission."—"That wouldn't be such a bad idea! Besides, it's my turn!"—"Is there anything else worrying you?" And Magda burst into a mocking laugh. She stopped immediately, when Diederich entered. Diederich glanced around disapprovingly, but Frau Hessling need not have wrung her hands behind her daughters' backs. It was beneath his dignity to intervene in this feminine quarrel.

At table they spoke of their visitor. Frau Hessling praised him and said he seemed very sound. Emmi declared that such a sales-clerk might be reliable, but he had no idea how to talk to a lady. Magda indignantly asserted the contrary. As they were all waiting for Diederich's decision, he pronounced judgement. The gentleman was certainly not exactly good form. He had obviously not had a university education. "But I have come to recognize him as a first-rate man of business." Emmi could no longer contain herself.

"If Magda intends to marry that man, I declare I will have noth-ing more to do with you. He ate his stewed fruit with a knife!"

"She's a liar!" Magda broke into tears. Diederich took compas-sion on her, and said rudely to Emmi:

"You marry a reigning duke and then leave us in peace."

Then Emmi put down her knife and fork and went out.

In the evening, before the office closed, Kienast appeared. He was wearing a frock coat and his manner was more social than commercial. By tacit agreement they both refrained from speaking until old Sötbier had packed up his things. When he had retired, with a mistrustful glance, Diederich said:

"I have placed the old man on the retired list. I attend to all the more important things alone."

"Well, have you thought over our little affair?" asked Kienast.

"Have you?" returned Diederich. Kienast's eyes twinkled confidentially.

"My powers do not really extend so far, but I will take the risk. For heaven's sake, return the machine. I have no doubt some defect will be discovered in it."

Diederich understood. "You will find one," he promised. Kienast said in a matter-of-fact tone:

"In return for this concession you undertake to order all your machines from us whenever required. One moment!" he com-manded, as Diederich started to protest. "And in addition you will defray our costs and my traveling expenses to the extent of five hundred marks, which we shall deduct from your first installment."

"Oh, I say, this is sheer robbery!" Diederich's outraged sense of justice vented itself loudly. But Kienast raised his voice as well. "Dr. Hessling! . . ." With an effort Diederich controlled himself. He laid his hand on the manager's shoulder. "Let us go up to the house, the ladies are waiting." Somewhat mollified Kienast said: "So far we have understood one another perfectly." "This little difference will also be made up," Diederich assured him.

There was a festive smell in the air upstairs. Frau Hessling shone in her black satin dress. Through Magda's lace blouse more was visible than she usually displayed for the benefit of the family circle. Only Emmi's face and attire were grey and dreary. Magda showed the guest his place and seated herself on his right. They were hardly seated, and were still clearing their throats, when she began to speak, her eyes shining with feverish animation: "Now you gentlemen must have finished with your silly business." Diederich explained that they had come to a very satisfactory agreement. Büschli & Co. were thoroughly fair people.

"With such an immense business as ours," declared the manager, "Twelve hundred workmen and clerks, a whole town, with a hotel of our own for customers." He invited Diederich. "You must come and see us, you will live in style and free of charge." As Magda, beside him, was hanging on his words, he began to brag about his position, his power and privileges, the villa of which he shared one-half. "If I marry I get the other half."

Diederich laughed thunderously. "Then the simplest thing would be for you to get married. Well, good health!"

Magda dropped her eyes and Herr Kienast changed the subject. Did Diederich know why he had met his wishes so easily? "The fact is, Dr. Hessling, as soon as I saw you I knew that there would be much business to be done with you later on—even though the circumstances here at present are rather narrow," he added condescendingly. Diederich would have liked to assure him of his grandiose ideas and of the possibilities of developing his business, but Kienast would not allow his train of thought to be interrupted. His speciality was sizing up men, he said. It was especially important to see a man with whom one has to do business in his home. "If everything there is so well ordered as here—"

At this point the fragrant goose was brought in, which Frau Hessling had been anxiously awaiting. At once she acted as though they had goose very often. Herr Kienast, however, stopped a moment in silent admiration. Frau Hessling wondered if he was really gazing at the goose or, under cover of its delicious steam, at Magda's lacy blouse. Then he looked up and raised his glass. "And now to the Hessling family, to the respected mother and head of the household and her charming daughters." Magda's bosom swelled to make the charm more noticeable, and Emmi looked all the more suppressed. It was Magda's glass which Herr Kienast touched first.

Diederich answered the toast. "We are a German family. The guest we take into our home we also take to our hearts." He had tears in his eyes, while Magda blushed once more. "And even if our house is modest, our hearts are true." He wished the visitor a long life, and the latter, in turn, declared that he had always been in favor of modesty, "especially in families where there are young girls."

Frau Hessling intervened. "Isn't that so? Otherwise how would a young man have the courage to—? My daughters make all their own clothes." Herr Kienast took this as his cue to bend over Magda's blouse on the pretext of making a detailed examination.

At dessert she peeled an orange for him and in his honor took a taste of Tokay. When they went into the sitting room Diederich stopped in the doorway with his arms around his two sisters. "Yes, indeed, Herr Kienast," he said in a deep voice, "this is family happiness, Herr Kienast, look at it!" Magda nestled against his shoulder, all submission, but Emmi tried to break away from him and received a blow from the rear. "We are always like this," continued Diederich. "All day long I work for my family, and the evening sees us united here beneath the shade of the lamp. The outside world and the cliques of our so-called society we avoid as much as possible. We are satisfied with each other."

At this point Emmi succeeded in breaking loose, and she was heard slamming a door upstairs. The picture of Diederich and Magda was all the more tender, as they sat down beside the softly lighted table. Herr Kienast thoughtfully contemplated the arrival of the punch in an enormous bowl, which Frau Hessling, smiling softly, carried in. While Magda was filling the guest's glass Diederich explained how, thanks to this devotion to quiet domesticity, he was in a position to do well by his sisters when they married. "The expansion of business is to the advantage of the girls, for they are part owners of the factory, quite apart from their mere dowries. And if one of my future brothers-in-law cares to put his capital into the concern, then. . . ."

Magda, however, noticed that Herr Kienast was beginning to look worried, and changed the subject. She asked after his own people and whether he was all alone. At this his glance became tender and he moved nearer. Diederich sat on, drinking, and twiddling his thumbs. He tried several times to take part again in the conversation of Magda and their guest, but they seemed to feel that there was nobody present but themselves.

"Oh, I see you got through your year of military service all right," he said ingratiatingly, as he puzzled over the signs which Frau Hessling was making to him behind their backs. It was not until she had crept out of the room that he understood, took his glass, and went into the dark adjoining room to the piano. He ran his fingers over the keys, glided suddenly into students' songs and sang impressively to his own accompaniment: "The devil they know what freedom means . . ." When he came to the end he listened; everything was still in the next room as if they had fallen asleep, and although he would like to have filled his glass from the bowl of punch, he began again, from a sense of duty: "Here I sit, in the gloomy dungeon . . ."

In the middle of the verse a chair fell and a loud noise followed, the cause of which was not difficult to guess. In the instant Diederich had sprung into the sitting-room. "Well, well," he said, with earnest heartiness, "you seem to have serious intentions." The couple separated, and Herr Kienast answered: "I do not say that I haven't." Whereupon Diederich was deeply moved, and, his eyes gazing into those of Kienast, he shook the latter's hand, while with his disengaged hand he drew Magda toward them. "This *is* a surprise! Herr Kienast, make my dear little sister happy. You will always find in me the best of brothers, as I have been up until now, I may say."

Wiping his eyes, he shouted: "Mother! Something has happened." Frau Hessling was already standing outside the door, but so excessive was her emotion that her limbs refused to obey her. Leaning on Diederich's arm, she tottered in, fell upon Herr Kienast's neck, and dissolved into tears. Meanwhile Diederich was knocking at Emmi's bedroom door, which was locked. "Come out, Emmi; something has happened!" Finally she pulled open the door, her face flaming with rage. "What are you waking me up for? I can easily guess what has happened. Leave me out of your indecencies!" She would have slammed the door again, if Diederich had not inserted his foot. He sternly pointed out to her that, for her churlish behaviour, she deserved never to get a husband. He would not even allow her to dress, but dragged her along, in her dressing jacket, with her hair down. At the door she escaped from his grasp. "You are making us ridiculous," she hissed. She reached the engaged couple before he did, and holding her head high, she gave them a mocking glance of critical inspection. "So you were afraid to wait until the morning?" she inquired. "Of course, time has no meaning for the happy." Kienast looked at her. She was taller than Magda, and her face, now flushed, looked fuller beneath her loosened hair, which was long and thick. Kienast held her hand longer than was necessary, and when she withdrew it he turned from her to Magda in obvious doubt. Emmi gave a laugh of triumph at her sister, turned about, and, holding herself very erect, she disappeared. Meanwhile Magda had anxiously seized Kienast's arm, but Diederich came in with a glass of punch in his hand and insisted upon drinking a toast to brotherhood with his future brother-in-law.

The next morning he called for him at his hotel and asked him to come for an early glass of beer. "Please restrain your longing for the little girl until midday. Now we must have a few words as one man to another." In Klappsch's *Bierstube* he explained the situation in detail: Twenty-five thousand marks in cash on the day of the wedding—the books could be inspected at any time—and one-fourth of the business to Magda and Emmi. "So it's only one-eighth," Kienast observed. To which Diederich retorted: "Am I to slave for you people for nothing?" And an uneasy silence ensued.

Diederich restored the proper mood. "Your health, Friederich!" "Here's to you, Diederich!" replied Kienast. Then something seemed to occur to Diederich. "Of course you have an easy means of increasing your share in the business by putting your money into it. How about your savings? With a huge salary like yours!" Kienast declared that he did not object to the idea on principle, but he was still under contract with Büschli & Co. He also expected a considerable increase of salary in the course of the year, and it would be a crime to give notice now. "But if I do produce the money I must have an active hand in the business myself. Although I have every confidence in you, my dear Diederich . . ."

Diederich admitted his point, and Kienast in his turn made a suggestion.

"If you were simply to fix the dowry at fifty thousand then Magda would renounce her share in the business." To this Diederich returned an unconditional refusal. "That would be contrary to the last wishes of my late lamented father, and they are sacred to me. And given my spirit of farseeing enterprise, in a few years Magda's share may be ten times as much as the amount you now demand. I will never consent to injure my poor sister." At this the brother-in-law smirked a little. Diederich's devotion to the family

did him credit, but large ideas alone were not enough. With noticeable heat Diederich retorted that, thank heaven, he was answerable
to nobody but God for the conduct of his business. "Twenty-five-
thousand cash and one-eighth of the net profits—that is all." Kienast drummed on the table. "I am not sure that I can accept your
sister on those terms," he declared. "I will reserve my final decision
for the moment." Diederich shrugged his shoulders and they finished their beer. Kienast returned with him to lunch. Diederich had
begun to fear that he would refuse. Fortunately, Magda was even
more seductively attired than the day before—"as if she knew that
the whole game was at stake," thought Diederich, and he admired
her. By the time the sweets were brought in she had so inflamed
Kienast's ardor that he was demanding the wedding in four weeks.
"Is this your final decision?" asked Diederich teasingly. Kienast's
reply was to take the rings out of his pocket.

After lunch Frau Hessling went on tiptoe out of the room where
the engaged couple were sitting, Diederich also decided to retire.
But they fetched him to join them in a walk. "Where would you
like to go, and where are Mother and Emmi?" Emmi had refused
to come and therefore Frau Hessling stayed at home. "Otherwise,
it would give a bad impression, you know," said Magda, and Diederich agreed with her. He even brushed away a little dust which
had clung to her fur coat when she came into the factory. He
treated Magda with respect, because she had achieved success.

They went off in the direction of the town hall. It could do no
harm, you know, to let people see you. The first person, it is true,
whom they met in Meisestrasse was only Napoleon Fischer. He
bared his teeth at the couple and gave Diederich a nod and a look
which said that he knew a thing or two. Diederich blushed deeply,
and he would have stopped the man, and had a row with him in
the street. But did he dare? "It was a bad mistake to have indulged
in confidences with that shifty proletarian. Everything would have
gone all right without him. Now he creeps about the place to remind me that he has me in his power. He will try to blackmail me
yet." But, thank God, everything that had passed between himself
and the machinist had been *en tête-à-tête*. Whatever Napoleon Fischer might say about him was a libel. Diederich would simply
have him locked up. All the same, Diederich hated him because he
shared his secret, and made him perspire with fear even when the
thermometer showed twenty degrees below zero. He looked back.
Why did a brick not fall on Napoleon Fischer's head?

In Gerichtsstrasse Magda realized that their stroll had been a good idea, for Meta Harnisch and Inge Tietz were looking out from behind the shutters at Judge Harnisch's, and Magda knew for certain that their faces had betrayed great disturbance when they got a glimpse of Kienast. In Kaiser Wilhelm Strasse, unfortunately, there were very few people about that day; the only comfort was that Major Kunze and Dr. Heuteufel, who were going into the Harmony Club, stared from a distance with great curiosity. But at the corner of Schweinichenstrasse something occurred which Diederich had not anticipated; directly in front of them walked Frau Daimchen and Guste. At once Magda hastened her steps and talked with great animation. Sure enough, Guste looked around and Magda had a chance to say: "My dear Frau Daimchen, allow me to introduce my fiancé, Herr Kienast." The prospective bridegroom was looked over and seemed to come up to expectations, for Guste, who remained a few steps behind with Diederich, asked with a certain respect: "Where did you find him?" Diederich joked: "You know, every woman cannot find her man as near home as you did, but he is all the more sound." "Are you beginning that again?" cried Guste, but without resentment. She even gave Diederich a tender glance and said with a gentle sigh: "Mine is still away, goodness knows where. It makes one feel like a widow." She looked thoughtfully at Magda, who was hanging on Kienast's arm. Diederich said: "Out of sight, out of mind. There are as good fish in the sea as ever came out of it." As he said this he steered Guste close to the wall and gazed pleadingly into her eyes. And for a moment there really was a responsive smile on her dear, chubby face.

By this time, unfortunately, they had reached 77 Schweinichenstrasse, and had to say good-bye. As there was nothing to be seen beyond the Saxon Gate, they turned homewards again with Herr Kienast. Magda, who had taken her fiancés's arm, said to Diederich encouragingly: "Well, what are you thinking about?" at which he turned red and began to breathe hard. "What is there to think about?" he managed to say, and Magda laughed.

In the empty street it was rapidly growing dark when they saw someone coming toward them. "Isn't that...?" said Diederich uncertainly. The figure approached, stout, evidently still young, with a large, soft hat, fashionably dressed, and walking with his feet turned inward. "Well, if it isn't Wolfgang Buck!" He reflected disappointedly: "And Guste tried to make out that he is at the other end of the world. I must cure her of lying."

"Is that you?" Young Buck shook Diederich's hand. "Delighted to see you."—"So am I," replied Diederich, in spite of his disappointment with Guste, and he introduced his future brother-in-law to his schoolfriend. Buck congratulated the happy couple and then walked behind them with Diederich. "I am sure you were on your way to your fiancée's," Diederich remarked. "She is at home, for we have just accompanied her there." "Is that so," said Buck, shrugging his shoulders. "Well, there is always plenty of time to see her," he added indifferently. "For the present I am delighted to meet you again. Our talk in Berlin, the only one, I think, was so . . . stimulating."

Diederich now confessed to a similar happy recollection, though at the time it had merely annoyed him. This meeting had quite cheered him up. "Indeed, I still owe you a return visit, but you know how in Berlin so many things turn up. Here, at all events, one has leisure. Dull, though, isn't it? And to think that we must spend the rest of our lives here"—and Diederich pointed up to the row of bleak houses. Wolfgang Buck sniffed the air with his gently hooked nose. He seemed to taste it on his full lips and he assumed a thoughtful expression. "A lifetime in Netzig," he began slowly, "well, it all depends. People like us are not in a position to live only for excitement. In any case, there is some here." He smiled suspiciously. "That sentry created some excitement, which reached the most exalted circles."

"Oh, I see"—Diederich protruded his paunch—"you'll never stop carping, will you? I insist that I am absolutely on the side of His Majesty in that affair."

Buck swept this aside with a gesture. "Don't try that on me. I know all about him."

"I know him even better," Diederich declared. "Anyone who has stood alone with him, face to face, as I did in the Tiergarten last February, after the big riot, and has seen those eyes glaring—that truly imperial gaze—can have no doubts as to our future."

"No doubts as to the future . . . because a man's eyes glared!" Buck's mouth and jaws fell pessimistically. Diederich snorted impatiently. "Of course, I know, you do not believe in any personality of this era. Otherwise you would have become a Lassalle or a Bismarck."

"In the end I may indulge in some such luxury. Why not? Just as well as he . . . even if I am less favored by external circumstances."

His voice became more animated and assured. "What matters personally to each of us is not that we should really change the world very much, but that we should create in ourselves the feeling that we are causing changes. That only requires talent, and the Emperor has plenty."

Diederich was looking about uneasily. "Here we are alone, more or less, for the company in front of us has more important matters to discuss, yet I do not think—"

"You really believe that I have something against the Emperor, don't you? I do not dislike him any more than I dislike myself. In his place I would have taken Lance Corporal Lück and our Netzig sentry just as seriously. Would power truly be power if it were not threatened? Only when there is a revolt is it aware of itself. What would become of the Emperor if he had to admit to himself that the Social Democrats do not aim at him, but, at most, at a somewhat more practical distribution of profits?"

"Aha!" cried Diederich.

"Don't you see? That would seem to you an outrage, and to him also. To move along, beside the main current of events, to be caught up in their development instead of being the leader—would that be tolerable? . . . To have unlimited power and to be incapable, at the same time, of arousing even hatred except through words and gestures! What, after all, do the fault-finders seize upon? Has anything tangible happened? Even the Lück affair was only another gesture. When the hand of authority ceases to act, everything is as before; only the actor and his audience have had a thrill. And that, my dear Hessling, is the only thing that matters to any of us today. The man himself, about whom we are speaking, would be most astonished, believe me, if the war, whose specter he is constantly conjuring up, or the revolution, which he has imagined a hundred times, were really to happen."

"You won't have to wait long for that," cried Diederich. "And then you will see how all loyal patriots will rally faithfully and steadfastly to their Emperor!" "No doubt." Buck was shrugging his shoulders more frequently. "That is the traditional sequence, as he himself has prescribed it. You people allow him to prescribe phrases for you, and never was opinion so well drilled as now. But deeds? My excellent contemporary, our age is not prepared for deeds. In order to exercise one's capacity to experience it is necessary, first of all, to live, and deeds are dangerous to life."

Diederich drew himself up. "Are you trying to associate the accusation of cowardice with—?" "I have expressed no moral judgement. I have mentioned a circumstance inherent in the history of our times which concerns us all. For the rest, we are not responsible. The time for action is finished for the actor on the stage, for he has played his part. What more can reality demand of him? I suppose you do not know whom history will designate as the representative type of the era?"

"The Emperor!" said Diederich.

"No," Buck replied. "The actor."

At this Diederich burst into such a roar of laughter that the engaged couple in front started away from each other and turned around. But they had reached the Theaterplatz, an icy wind was blowing across it, and they went on.

"Why, of course," Diederich burst out. "I might have guessed where you got such crazy notions. You are connected with the theater." He slapped Buck on the shoulder. "Have you finally gone on the stage yourself?" Buck's eyes took on a troubled expression. He shook off the hand that slapped him with a movement which Diederich found unfriendly. "I? Not at all," said Buck, and after they had reached Gerichtsstrasse in uneasy silence: "So you do not know why I am in Netzig?"

"Presumably because of your fiancée."

"That is part of it, but it is chiefly because I have undertaken the defense of my brother-in-law, Lauer."

"You are . . .? In the Lauer case . . .?" It took Diederich's breath away and he came to a standstill.

"Well, why not?" said Buck, shrugging his shoulders. "Does that surprise you? I have recently been admitted to practice at the Netzig County Court. Did my father not tell you about it?"

"I rarely see your father . . . I don't go out much. Business cares . . . My sister's engagement . . ." Diederich began to stammer incoherently. "Then you must often . . . Perhaps you are settled here altogether?"

"Only temporarily—I imagine."

Diederich pulled himself together. "I must say, I have often failed to understand you properly, but never so completely as today when we have been walking halfway through Netzig together."

Buck winked at him. "Because in the trial tomorrow I am counsel for the accused and you are the chief witness for the prosecution? That is just chance. The situation might just as well have been reversed."

"I beg your pardon!" cried Diederich indignantly. "Every man in his right place. If you have no respect for your profession—"

"Respect? What do you mean? I am delighted to act for the defense. I do not deny it. I'm going to go all out and give the people something for their money. I shall have some unpleasant things to say to you, Dr. Hessling, but I trust you will take everything in good part. It is all part of my effect."

Diederich was frightened. "Pardon me, are you familiar with my sworn statement? It is by no means unfavorable to Lauer."

"Let that be my worry." There was a threatening touch of irony in Buck's attitude.

By this time they had reached Meisestrasse. "The trial!" thought Diederich breathlessly. He had completely forgotten it in the excitement of the last few days. Now he felt as if he were going to have both legs amputated within the next twenty-four hours. So Guste, the treacherous creature, had purposely said nothing to him about her fiancé. He was to get the shock at the last moment! . . . Diederich took leave of Buck before they got to the house. He hoped that Kienast had not noticed anything! Buck proposed that they go to some café. "You don't seem too anxious to get back to your future wife," said Diederich. "At this moment I'd much sooner have a cognac." Diederich laughed derisively. "You always seem to want one." So that Kienast should not notice anything, he turned back again with Buck. "You see," he began abruptly, "the problem of my fiancée is another of the problems which I put to Fate." And as Diederich asked, "What do you mean?" he continued: "If I really become a lawyer in Netzig, then Guste Daimchen will be in her right place in my home. But do I know how things will turn out? In view of other . . . circumstances which may come into my life, I have someone else in Berlin . . ."

"I heard something about an actress." Diederich blushed for Buck, who so cynically admitted this. "That is to say," he stammered, "I may have been mistaken."

"So you know," Buck concluded. "Now the situation is this. For the present I am involved there and cannot look after Guste as I should. Would you not like to take the poor girl under your wing a bit?" he asked calmly and innocently.

"You want me to—"

"Keep the pot stirred, so to speak, in which I have left some sausage and cabbage simmering . . . while I am busy elsewhere. After all, we're good friends, aren't we? . . ."

"Thanks," said Diederich coldly. "Not quite such good friends as all that. Give somebody else the job. I take a more serious view of life." He turned and left him.

Apart from Buck's immorality, his undignified familiarity outraged Diederich, especially after they had just proved themselves opponents once more in both theory and practice. An insufferable person! One would never figure him out. "What does he have up his sleeve for me tomorrow?" Diederich wondered.

At home he relieved his feelings. "A fellow as spineless as a jellyfish, and with such intellectual conceit! God preserve our home from such an all-consuming lack of principle, the sure sign of decadence in any family!" He checked to make sure that Kienast really did have to leave that night. "Magda will have nothing alarming to write to you," he said, out of the blue, and laughed. "So far as I am concerned, there may be fire and slaughter in the town, I'll stick to my office and my family."

Kienast had hardly left when he confronted Frau Hessling. "Well, where is the summons for me to appear in court tomorrow?" She had to admit that she had intercepted the ominous letter. "I didn't want it to spoil your Christmas, my dear son." But Diederich would hear of no excuses. "Dear son, be damned! I suppose it is for love of me that the food gets worse and worse, except when we have guests, while you waste the housekeeping money on folderol. Do you think you can make me believe that Magda made that lace blouse herself? Tell that to the fool Kienast!" Magda protested against the insult to her fiancé, but it was no good. "You had best hold your tongue! Your fur coat is half stolen. You women are in league with the servant. When I send her for wine, she brings cheap stuff, and you pocket the difference . . ."

The three women were outraged, and Diederich shouted all the louder. Emmi declared that he was angry only because he was going to make a fool of himself the next day before the whole town. All Diederich could do in reply was to hurl a plate on to the ground. Magda stood up, went out, shouting over her shoulder: "Thank the Lord, I don't need you any more!" At once Diederich ran after her. "You had better mind what you are saying. If you have got a husband at last, you have only me to thank and the sacrifices I am making. Your intended haggled over your dowry in a way that was positively shameful. Anyway, you are nothing but a make-weight!"

At this juncture, he received a resounding slap in the face and before he could recover his breath Magda was in her room, and had locked the door. In stunned silence Diederich rubbed his cheek. Then his indignation boiled up again, but a kind of satisfaction ensued. The crisis was over.

During the night he had quite made up his mind to appear in court rather late, and to show by his whole demeanor how little the whole thing affected him. But he could not bring himself to carry out this resolution. When he entered the particular courtroom which had been specified, an entirely different case was still being heard. Jadassohn, who presented an uncommonly sinister appearance in his black gown, was just engaged in demanding two years in the reformatory for a poor young lad who was scarcely more than a child. The judge granted only one, it is true, but the youthful convict broke out into such a fit of wailing that Diederich, himself in a state of great anxiety, felt ill out of sheer compassion. He went outside and entered a lavatory, although a notice on the door read: "For members of the Bar only." Immediately after him Jadassohn appeared. When he saw Diederich he wanted to retreat, but the latter at once asked what sort of place a reformatory was, and what a pimp like that would do there. "As if we could be bothered with those details!" was Jadassohn's only reply, as he disappeared. Diederich's insides contracted even more at the thought of the ghastly abyss that yawned between Jadassohn, representing Authority, and himself, and he had ventured too near its treacherous cogwheels. He had acted with the most pious intentions in an excess of zeal for Authority. However, now he would have to take himself in hand, lest he be seized and mashed to a pulp. He would have to kneel and cringe in the hope of escaping. Lucky the man who lived in the obscurity of private life! Diederich vowed to pursue in the future only his own insignificant but shrewdly perceived advantage.

People were now standing outside in the corridor: some of the common herd and some of the élite. The five Buck girls, dressed up as if the trial of their brother-in-law, Lauer, were the greatest honor for the family, were chattering in a group with Käthchen Zillich, her mother and the wife of Mayor Scheffelweis. The

Mayor, however, could not get rid of his mother-in-law, and from the glances which she darted at Herr Buck's brother and his friends, Cohn and Heuteufel, it was evident that she had set him against the Bucks' cause. Major Kunze, in uniform, was standing near them with a grim scowl, and declined to talk. Just then Pastor Zillich and Professor Kühnchen appeared, but when they saw the big group they remained in the shelter of a pillar. The gray figure of Nothgroschen, the editor, moved unnoticed from one group to another. Diederich looked in vain for someone to whom he could attach himself. Now he regretted that he had forbidden his own family to come. He stood in the shadow, behind a turn in the corridor, and cautiously peered out. Suddenly he drew back. Guste Daimchen and her mother! She was immediately surrounded by Buck's daughters, as a valuable reinforcement to their party. At the same moment a door opened in the background, and Wolfgang Buck emerged, in cap and gown, and wearing patent-leather shoes which turned noticeably inward. He smiled brightly, as though at a reception, shook hands with everyone and kissed his fiancée. Everything would go beautifully, he assured them. The Public Prosecutor was well disposed and so was he. Then he went up to the witnesses whom he had called and whispered to them. At that instant everybody stopped talking, for at the head of the stairs the accused, Herr Lauer, appeared and with him was his wife. The Mayoress fell upon her neck. How brave she was! "Not at all," she answered in a deep resonant voice, "we have nothing to reproach ourselves with, have we, Karl?" Lauer said: "Certainly not, Judith." Just then Judge Fritzsche passed, and there was silence. When he and old Buck's daughters exchanged bows, people winked at each other, and the Mayor's mother-in-law muttered something half aloud, but her meaning could be easily read in her eyes.

Diederich had been discovered in his sheltered post by Wolfgang Buck, who dragged him forward and led him up to his sister. "My dear Judith, I wonder if you know our honorable enemy, Dr. Hessling? Today he will destroy us." But Frau Lauer neither laughed nor returned Diederich's bow. She simply stared at him with ruthless curiosity. It was hard to meet those somber eyes, and still harder because she was so beautiful. Diederich felt the blood rushing to his face, his glance wandered, and he stammered. "Your brother likes to joke. As a matter of fact, there must be some mistake. . . ." The eyebrows met in that pale face, the corners of the mouth drooped expressively, and Judith Lauer turned her back on Diederich.

A court servant came along and Wolfgang went into the courtroom beside his brother-in-law, Lauer. As the door did not open very wide, the whole crowd pushed through in haste, and the better-class people got in ahead of the common herd. The petticoats of the five Buck sisters rustled furiously in the struggle. Diederich was the last to get in, and had to sit down on the bench provided for witnesses beside Major Kunze, who at once moved away from him. The President of the court, Herr Sprezius, looking like an old, worm-eaten vulture, declared from his lofty eminence the session open, called upon the witnesses to stand up and warned them of the sacredness of their oath—whereupon Diederich assumed the expression he used to assume in Sunday school. Judge Harnisch was putting his papers in order and looked in the audience for his daughter. More attention was paid to old Judge Kühlemann, who had left his sickroom to take his place on the bench to the left of the President. People thought he did not look well. The Mayor's mother-in-law professed to know that he intended to resign his seat in the Reichstag—and where would all his money go if he died? To the other witnesses Pastor Zillich expressed the hope that he would leave his millions for the erection of a church, but Professor Kühnchen doubted this in a penetrating whisper. "He'll not separate himself from the money even when he's dead. He has always believed in getting what was his, and if possible what belonged to others, as well. . . ." Then the Judge ordered the witnesses to leave the courtroom.

As there was no room for them to wait in, they found themselves again in the corridor. Messrs. Heuteufel, Cohn, and Buck, junior, annexed a window sill. Beneath the ferocious gaze of the Major, Diederich reflected painfully: "Now the defendant is being heard. If I only knew what he is saying! I would like him to be acquitted just as much as his friends wish it." Diederich tried in vain to convince Pastor Zillich of his softened mood, and claimed that he had always said the whole affair was trumped up. Zillich turned away in embarrassment, and Kühnchen went off, whistling through his teeth: "Just you wait, my boy, we'll cook your goose." The silent oppression of general dislike weighed upon Diederich. At length, the usher appeared. "Dr. Hessling!"

Diederich pulled himself together in order to pass before the spectators in a manner worthy of a gentleman. He stared fixedly in front of him; he felt just then that Frau Lauer was looking at him. He breathed hard and swerved a little to one side. To the left, beside the junior counsel who was regarding his fingernails, stood Jadassohn, erect and menacing. The light from the window behind him shone through his prominent ears, which glowed a bloody red, and his expression demanded such slavish submission from Diederich that the latter was compelled to avert his glance. To the right, in front of the accused and somewhat lower he saw Wolfgang Buck sitting carelessly, his fists resting on his plump thighs, from which his gown had fallen. He looked as clever and as cheerful as though he represented the spirit of Light. Justice Sprezius administered the oath to Diederich, saying only two words at a time, with great condescension. Diederich swore dutifully; then he was asked to describe the sequence of events that evening in the *Ratskeller*. He began:

"We were a lively party. At the other table were Messrs. . . ."

As he had already come to a full stop, there was laughter in court. Sprezius jumped up, snapped his vulture's beak and threatened to have the room cleared. "Is that all you remember?" he asked testily. Diederich begged him to take into consideration that, in consequence of business and other cares, the facts had meanwhile become a little obscured in his memory. "Then, to refresh your memory, I will read out your sworn statement before the examining magistrate"—and the Judge had the affidavit handed up to him. From this document Diederich learned to his disagreeable surprise that he had made the definite charge, in the presence of the examining judge, Justice Fritzsche of the County Court, that the accused was guilty of a serious libel on His Majesty the Emperor. What had he to say to this? "That may be," he stammered, "but there were a number of gentlemen there. Whether it was the accused who said it . . ." Sprezius leaned forward over his desk. "Think back. Remember you are on your oath. Other witnesses will testify that you went up to the accused alone and had with him the conversation in question." "Was I the one who did that?" asked Diederich, blushing crimson, and the whole court rocked with laughter. Even Jadassohn's face was pulled into a sneer of contempt. Sprezius had opened his mouth to let himself go, but Wolfgang stood up. His soft features, by a visible effort, assumed an energetic look, and he asked Diederich: "I suppose you were distinctly under the influence of liquor that evening?" Immediately the presiding judge and the Public Prosecutor fell upon him. "I appeal that the question be disallowed!" cried Jadassohn shrilly. "Counsel for the defense will submit the question to me," croaked Sprezius. "Whether I put it to the witness or not is for me to decide." Diederich observed with astonishment that both had found a determined adversary. Wolfgang remained on his feet. In the ringing tones of an orator he demurred against the stand taken by the presiding judge, which was prejudicial to the rights of the defense. He moved that the court make a ruling as to whether the right of cross-examining witnesses directly was not conferred upon him by the rules of criminal procedure. Sprezius snapped his beak in vain. He had no alternative but to withdraw into the consulting room with the four judges. Buck looked around in triumph. His cousins moved their hands as if applauding. But in the meantime his father had also come in, and people noticed that old Buck made a sign of disapproval to his son. The accused, for his part, shook his counsel's hand, his apoplectic face expressing angry excitement. Diederich, who was exposed to the gaze of all, struck an attitude and surveyed the scene. But, alas, Guste Daimchen avoided his glance! Old Buck was the only one who gave him a friendly nod. He was pleased with Diederich's testimony. He even forced his way out of the crowded auditorium in order to proffer his soft, white hand to Diederich. "Many thanks, dear friend," he said. "You have treated the matter as it deserved." In his loneliness Diederich felt tears in his eyes because of so much kindness from the great man. Only after Herr Buck had gone back to his seat did it dawn on Diederich that he was doing old Buck's dirty work! And the son, Wolfgang, too, was by no means the weakling Diederich had imagined. Probably he had indulged in those political debates in order to use them against Diederich now. Loyalty, true German loyalty, did not exist any more. Nobody could be trusted. "How long am I to stand here and be gaped at from all sides?"

Fortunately the judges were returning. Old Kühlemann exchanged a glance of regret with old Buck, and Sprezius, with remarkable self-control, read out the decision. Whether counsel for the defense had the right to cross-examine witnesses remained undecided, for the question itself: was the witness intoxicated on that occasion? was ruled out as irrelevant. Then the Judge asked whether the prosecution had any question to put to the witness. "Not just now," said Jadassohn with disdain, "but I move that the witness not be dismissed for the present," and Diederich was allowed to sit down. "I further move that Dr. Fritzsche, the examining judge, be called upon to give evidence as to the nature of the witness Hessling's earlier attitude toward the defendant." Diederich started. The public all turned toward Judith Lauer. Even the junior members of the bar present looked in her direction . . . Jadassohn's request was granted.

Then Pastor Zillich was called, took the oath, and proceeded to give his account of the fateful evening. He declared that it had been a day of confusion, and his conscience as a Christian had been sorely troubled, for that afternoon blood had been spilled in the streets of Netzig, even though it was for patriotic reasons. "That has nothing to do with the case," Sprezius ruled—and at that moment Governor von Wulckow entered the courtroom, dressed in hunting clothes, with great, muddy boots. Everyone turned around, the presiding judge bowed from the bench, and Pastor Zillich trembled. The Judge and the Public Prosecutor harassed him alternately. Jadassohn even said in tones of dreadful insinuation: "Reverend sir, I need hardly remind you, as a minister of God's word, of the sanctity of the oath you have taken." Then Zillich collapsed, and admitted that he had certainly heard the expression alleged to have been employed by the defendant. The latter jumped up and struck his fist on the seat. "I never mentioned the name of the Emperor at all! I took care not to!" His counsel quieted him with a reassuring gesture and said: "We shall produce evidence to prove that only the provocative intention of the witness, Dr. Hessling, caused the accused to make the statements which have here been misrepresented." For the present he would ask the President to ask the witness, Pastor Zillich, whether he had not preached a sermon which was specifically directed against the witness Hessling's inflammatory accusations. Pastor Zillich stammered that he had only counselled peace in general and done his duty as a servant of the Church. Then Buck asked another question. "Has the witness Zillich not a particular interest in maintaining good relations with the chief witness for the prosecution, Dr. Hessling, because his daughter—" Jadassohn at once intervened: he protested against that question. Sprezius ruled it out and in the audience there was a disapproving murmur of women's voices. The Governor leant over the seat and said to old Buck in an audible voice: "Your son is putting his foot in it!"

Meanwhile Kühnchen was called to the witness stand. The little old man stormed into the room, his glasses glittering, and he was hardly across the threshold when he began to shout out his name,

address and profession. He rattled off the form of the oath before
it was read to him, but after that he could not be induced to say
anything, except that the tide of national enthusiasm was running
high on that evening. First, the sentry's glorious deed! Then His
Majesty's magnificent letter with its profession of positive Christianity! "What of the row with the defendant? Well, gentlemen, I
know nothin' about it. I just happened to doze off at that moment."
"But afterwards the matter was discussed," the Judge insisted.
"Not by me," cried Kühnchen. "All the same, I spoke about our
glorious deeds in 1870. The frank-tiroors! My stiff finger is where
a frank-tiroor bit me, just because I wanted to give him a little jab
in the throat with my sword. A low trick for the fellow to play!"
Kühnchen tried to submit his finger to the bench's inspection.
"That will do!" croaked Sprezius and he threatened again to have
the court cleared.

Major Kunze stepped up stiffly, as if he were walking on stilts,
and he repeated the oath in a tone as though it were the deadliest
insult directed against Sprezius. Then he declared briefly that he
had nothing to do with the whole drunken affair; that he had
arrived at the *Ratskeller* afterwards. "All I can say is that Dr.
Hessling's conduct savors to me of the informer."

But for some time the atmosphere of the room had savored of
something else. Nobody knew where the smell came from, and the
members of the public suspected one another. With their handkerchiefs to their mouths they moved discreetly a little bit away from
each other. The presiding judge sniffed the air, and old Kühlemann,
whose chin had long since sunk on his breast, stirred uneasily in
his sleep.

When Sprezius argued that the gentlemen who had reported the
circumstances to him at the time were all loyal patriots, the Major
simply replied that he did not care, that Dr. Hessling was a person
quite unknown to him. Then, however, Jadassohn intervened. His
ears glowed and in a voice which cut like a knife he said: "Witness,
I ask you if the defendant is not in fact known to you. Will you
deny that you borrowed a hundred marks from him a week ago?"
The whole courtroom was silent with horror, and everyone stared
at the Major in uniform, who stood there searching for an answer.
Jadassohn's boldness was making an impression. He lost no time
in pressing his advantage home and succeeded in dragging out of
Kunze that the indignation of the loyal citizens at Lauer's statements was genuine, and that he himself shared it. Without a doubt,

the defendant had meant His Majesty—Here Wolfgang Buck could not resist the opportunity to say: "Since the President considers it unnecessary to censure the Public Prosecutor when he insults his own witnesses, my client and I can hardly complain, I suppose." Sprezius snapped at him at once. "Counsel for the defense will permit me to censure or not, as I think fit." Unruffled, Buck retorted: "That is just the point I wish to establish. So far as the charge itself is concerned, we assert, and we have witnesses to prove, that there was no reference to the Emperor." "I took care not to!" interjected the defendant. Buck continued. "Should the accusation be proven, however, then I move that the publisher of the *Almanach de Gotha* be called as an expert witness to state which German princes are of Jewish blood." Whereupon he sat down again, pleased at the sensational murmur which swept the court. "An outrage!" said a formidable bass voice. Sprezius was on the point of breaking forth, but looked just in time to see who it was. Wulckow! It even aroused Kühlemann, who had been asleep. The judges consulted together and the presiding judge announced that the motion of the counsel for the defense could not be admitted, as the truth of the libel was not the question before the court. The mere expression of disrespect was sufficient to establish guilt. Buck was beaten, and his plump cheeks puckered like those of a sad child. People tittered and the Mayor's mother-in-law laughed outright. In his seat among the witnesses, Diederich was grateful to her. Listening anxiously he felt that public opinion was veering around quietly to the side of those who were more clever and powerful. He exchanged glances with Jadassohn.

Nothgroschen, the editor, was called. He suddenly appeared, a gray, inconspicuous figure, and began to function like a machine, like a commissioner for oaths. Everyone who knew him was surprised. He had never seemed so sure of himself. He knew everything, made the gravest allegations against the accused, and spoke fluently, as if he were reciting a leading article. The only difference was that the Judge gave him his cue at the end of every paragraph with a word of encouragement, as if to a model pupil. Buck, who had recovered, raised the point against him that the *Netzig Journal* had championed Lauer. "Ours is a liberal—that is, an impartial paper," declared the editor. "We reflect public opinion. Since here and now opinion is unfavorable to the defendant—" He must have informed himself as to this outside in the corridor! Buck began in ironical tones: "I beg to draw attention to the curious conception of his oath which this witness betrays." But Nothgroschen could not be browbeaten. "I am a journalist," he explained. "I appeal to the presiding judge to protect me from the insults of counsel on the opposite side." Sprezius did not hesitate and he allowed the editor to retire with flying colors.

It struck twelve, and Jadassohn drew the President's attention to the fact that Dr. Fritzsche, the examining judge, was at the disposal of the court. He was called, and scarcely had he appeared at the door when all eyes glanced back and forth from him to Judith Lauer. She had become even paler, and her somber gaze, which followed him as he approached the judge, was intensified. Her eyes had an insistent, silent appeal, but Fritzsche avoided them. He looked unwell, but he walked with an air of determination. Diederich decided that of his two habitual expressions Fritzsche had chosen the more matter-of-fact for this occasion.

What were his impressions of the witness Hessling during the preliminary inquiry? The witness had made his statement absolutely freely and independently, in the form of a narrative still colored by his recent experiences. The reliability of the witness, which Fritzsche had an opportunity of testing by means of his further inquiries, was beyond all question. That the witness today should not longer have distinct recollections could be explained by the excitement of the moment . . . And the accused? At this question a pin might have been heard falling in court. Fritzsche swallowed a lump in his throat. The defendant also had made a rather favorable impression upon him, in spite of the many damaging circumstances.

"In a conflict of testimonies would you hold that the defendant was capable of the crime with which he is charged?" asked Sprezius.

Fritzsche replied: "The defendant is an educated gentleman. He would have taken care not to use specifically insulting words."

"That is what the defendant says himself," remarked the Judge severely. Fritzsche began to talk more rapidly. By reason of his civil activities the accused was accustomed to associate authority with progressive inclinations. He obviously regarded himself as more enlightened and more entitled to criticize than most other people. It was, therefore, conceivable that in a state of exasperation—and he felt exasperated by the shooting of the workman by the sentry— he may have given such expression to his political opinions as would suggest an offensive intention, although outwardly free from reproach.

The presiding judge and the Public Prosecutor gave a visible sigh of relief. Justices Harnisch and Kühlemann glanced at the public, which stirred with agitation. The junior counsel sitting to the left again examined his nails; his colleague on the right, however, a thoughtful-looking young man, observed the accused, who was directly in front of him. The hands of the defendant clenched the rail of the seat, and his bulging brown eyes were turned toward his wife. She was looking steadily at Fritzsche, with parted lips, as if in a dream, and her expression was one of suffering, weakness and shame. The Mayor's mother-in-law said distinctly: "And she has two children at home!" Suddenly Lauer seemed to notice the whispering all around him, all these glances which turned away when they met his own. He crumpled up, and his face paled so abruptly that the young barrister moved anxiously in his chair.

Diederich, who was feeling better and better, was probably the only person who still followed the dialogue between the presiding and examining judges. Poor Fritzsche! At first the affair could not have been more painful to anyone, even to Diederich, than to him, and had he not influenced Diederich's statement in a manner which was almost a violation of professional ethics? In affidavit form, however, Diederich's testimony was very damaging, and Fritzsche's own evidence even more so. He had not been any less ruthless than Jadassohn. His close relations with the Lauer household had not made him falter in the task before him: the defense of Power. Nothing from the realm of human affairs could persist in the face of Power. What a lesson for Diederich! Even Wolfgang Buck admitted it after his own fashion. He looked up at Fritzsche with an expression of nausea on his face.

As the examining judge made his way toward the exit with a bearing that clearly revealed his unease, the whispering grew louder. The Mayor's mother-in-law pointed her lorgnette at Frau Lauer and said: "A nice crowd!" Nobody contradicted her, for people had begun to abandon the Lauers to their fate. Guste Daimchen bit her lip and Käthchen Zillich gave Diederich a quick look from under her eyelashes. Dr. Scheffelweis bent over to the head of the Buck family, pressed his hand, and said sweetly: "I hope, my dear friend and supporter, that all may yet be well."

The judge gave an order to the usher. "Bring in the witness Cohn!" The witnesses for the defense were to have their turn! The

Judge sniffed: "There is a most unpleasant smell here," he remarked. "Krecke, open that window over there!" He gazed searchingly at the poorer public, which was sitting closely packed in the upper galleries. On the other hand, there was plenty of room in the lower seats, and most of all in the vicinity of Governor von Wulckow in his sweat-soaked hunting jacket... The icy draft through the open window caused complaints among the out-of-town journalists, who were sitting stowed away in the rear. But Sprezius merely snapped his beak at them, and they retracted into their overcoat collars.

Jadassohn looked at the witness with an air of conscious victory. Sprezius allowed him to speak for a while, then Jadassohn cleared his throat and he held up a document in his hand. "You have been the proprietor since 1889 of the shop bearing your name?" Then, without warning: "Do you admit that at that time one of the people who supplied you with goods, a certain Lehmann, committed suicide by shooting himself on the premises of your business?" With fiendish satisfaction he looked at Cohn, for the effect of his words was extraordinary. Cohn began to fidget and to gasp for air. "The old libel!" he screamed. "He didn't do it on my account! He was unhappily married! People broke me once before with that story and now the man is starting in again!" Counsel for the defense also protested. Sprezius snapped at Cohn. The Public Prosecutor was not to be referred to as a "man," and the witness would be fined fifty marks for contempt of court because of the expression "libel". That settled Cohn. Herr Buck's brother was called. He was asked pointblank by Jadassohn: "Your business is notoriously failing: what are your means of livelihood?" At this there was such a murmur of protest that Sprezius quickly intervened. "Does counsel for the prosecution really think this question pertinent?"

But Jadassohn was worthy of the occasion. "The prosecution is interested in establishing the fact that the witness is financially dependent upon his relations, and particularly upon his brother-in-law, the accused. The reliability of his testimony can be measured by that." Tall and elegant, Herr Buck stood there with bowed head. "That is all," said Jadassohn, and Sprezius dismissed this witness. Then the crowd saw his five daughters huddled together on their seat like a herd of lambs in a storm. The poorer section of the audience in the upper galleries laughed in a hostile way. Sprezius amiably called for silence and ordered Heuteufel to the witness stand.

When Heuteufel raised his hand to swear Jadassohn thrust forward his own with a dramatic effort.

"First I must ask the witness one question. Does he admit that he approved of the expressions which constitute the crime of *lèse-majesté*, and even improved upon them?" Heuteufel replied: "I admit nothing." Whereupon, Jadassohn confronted him with his statement at the preliminary hearing, and said in a loud voice: "I appeal for a ruling that this witness not be allowed to take the oath, because he is suspected of complicity in the crime." Still more sharply: "The opinions of the witness cannot be ignored by this court. He is one of those people whom His Majesty the Emperor has rightly called men without a fatherland. Furthermore, at regular meetings, which he calls *Sunday services for free men,* he is actively engaged in spreading the crassest atheism, which is sufficient to define his attitude towards a Christian monarch." Jadassohn's ears glowed with a fire which in itself was a profession of faith. Wolfgang Buck stood up, smiled skeptically and said they all knew that the religious convictions of counsel for the prosecution were monastic in their severity, and that nobody could expect him to give any credence to a non-Christian. The court, however, would think differently and refuse the appeal of the prosecution. Then Jadassohn rose in his wrath. For contempt of his person he demanded that counsel for the defense be fined one hundred marks. The judges withdrew for consultation. Immediately an animated discussion broke out in the courtroom. Dr. Heuteufel put his hands in his pockets and looked Jadassohn up and down slowly and deliberately. Deprived of the protection of the bench, the latter was panic-stricken and cowered against the wall. It was Diederich who came to his rescue, for he had an important communication to make to him. . . . Soon the judges returned. They had decided to proceed for the time being without administering the oath to Heuteufel. For contempt of the Public Prosecutor counsel for the defense was fined eighty marks.

When the hearing was resumed counsel for the defense intervened to ask the witness what was his opinion, as an intimate friend of the defendant, of his domestic life. Heuteufel made a move, there was a rustle of excitement among the public, who understood. Would Sprezius allow the question? He had already opened his mouth to refuse, but understood just in time that a sensation should be encouraged. Thereupon Heuteufel praised the model conditions which prevailed in Lauer's household. Jadassohn absorbed the witness's words, trembling with impatience. Finally he had an opportunity of asking his question in tones of unspeakable triumph. "Will the witness state with what kind of women he himself is familiar so that we can judge his attitude towards family life? Does he not frequent a certain establishment known in the vernacular as 'Little Berlin'?" As Jadassohn spoke he made sure that the ladies in the audience, and the judges also, were showing signs of disgust. The chief witness for the defense was ruined! Heuteufel tried to answer: "You probably know that better than anyone else. We have run into each other there a number of times." But that only resulted in a fine of fifty marks being imposed by Sprezius. Finally the Judge decided: "The witness must remain in court. He is required for further elucidation of the facts of the case." Heuteufel declared: "I, for my part, have a sufficiently lucid picture of the type of operation being run here, and I would prefer to leave." At once his fine of fifty marks was raised to one hundred. Wolfgang Buck looked about uneasily. His lips seemed to taste the mood of the court. He drew them back as if that mood were expressed in the curious odor which was again noticeable since the window was closed. Buck realized that the sympathies which had accompanied him here had been dulled and destroyed, that his ammunition had been wasted. And the yawning faces drawn with hunger, the impatience of the judges who were eyeing the clock, all boded him no good. He jumped up to save what could still be rescued! He assumed an energetic tone as he moved that witnesses be called for the afternoon session. "Since the Public Prosecutor has adopted the method of casting systematically into doubt the credibility of our witnesses, we are prepared to prove the good name of the accused by means of the most prominent citizens of Netzig. His Honor, Mayor Scheffelweis, himself will testify to the services which the accused has rendered the city. Governor von Wulckow cannot refuse to acknowledge his sense of civic and patriotic duty."

"Well, I never!" said the formidable basso from the empty space behind. Buck steadied his voice.

"As for the social virtues of the defendant, all his employees will vouch for them."

Buck was panting audibly as he sat down. Jadassohn remarked icily: "My learned friend for the defense is asking for a plebiscite." The judges consulted in whispers, and Sprezius announced that the court could only allow counsel's motion insofar as it related to

Mayor Scheffelweis's testimony. As the latter was present he was called at once.

He worked his way out of his seat. His wife and mother-in-law held him firmly on both sides and gave him hurried instructions which must have been contradictory, for the Mayor reached the witness stand visibly perturbed. What attitude did the defendant display in the civic life of the community? Dr. Scheffelweis was able to report favorably. For example, the defendant had voted at the board meetings of the Town Council for the restoration of the famous old presbytery where was preserved the hair which Dr. Martin Luther had, as was well known, pulled from the Devil's tail. True, he had supported the building of "secular Sunday schools," and had undoubtedly given offense in so doing. Then, the accused was universally esteemed in business circles; the social reforms which he had introduced into his own factory were generally admired—although it must be added that there had also been objections to them, because they increased the demands of the workers to an unlimited degree and thus perhaps brought nearer the day of revolution. "Would you consider the defendant capable of the crime with which he is charged?" asked counsel for the defense. "In one sense," Scheffelweis replied, "certainly not." "But in another sense?" queried counsel for the prosecution. The witness replied: "In another sense, yes, certainly."

After this answer the Mayor was allowed to retire. His two ladies received him, each equally dissatisfied. The presiding judge was preparing to adjourn the session when Jadassohn cleared his throat. He moved that the witness, Dr. Hessling, be heard again, as he wished to add to his testimony. Sprezius blinked his eyelids peevishly and the public, who were just scrambling out of their seats, grumbled audibly. But Diederich had already stepped forward confidently, and had begun to speak in a clear voice. After mature consideration he had come to the conclusion, he said, that he could strengthen the substance of his testimony at the preliminary hearing. He repeated it, but in stronger and more detailed form. He began with the shooting of the workman and retailed the critical comments made by Lauer and Heuteufel. The audience, now forgetting their earlier desire to leave, followed the clash of opinions along the bloodstained Kaiser Wilhelm Strasse as far as the *Ratskeller,* watched the hostile ranks lining up for the decisive battle, and saw Diederich spring forward under the gothic chandelier with drawn sword, so to speak, and challenge the accused to mortal combat.

"Then, gentlemen, I will not deny it, I challenged him! Would he say the incriminating word? He did, gentlemen, and I challenged him. In so doing I only did my duty, and I would do so again today, even though I should suffer greater social and financial losses than I have had to bear of late. Unselfish idealism, gentlemen, is the privilege of a German, and he will defend his ideals, even though his courage falters at times in the face of the multitude of his enemies. When I previously hesitated in my statement, it was not, as the examining judge so charitably assumed, because my memory was confused. I am not afraid to confess that I hesitated because of a perhaps pardonable dread of the great struggle which I would have to undertake. But I am undertaking it, for none less than His Majesty our noble Emperor demands it of me . . ." Diederich went on fluently, with a swing to his phrases which took the crowd's breath away. Jadassohn felt that the witness was beginning to regard the effect of his own peroration as a foregone conclusion, and looked anxiously at the presiding judge. Sprezius, however, had no intention of interrupting Diederich. With motionless vulture's beak and unblinking eyelids, he watched Diederich's grim face in which the eyes glared threateningly. Even old Kühlemann listened with gaping mouth. Wolfgang Buck leaned forward in his chair and gazed up at Diederich, with the excited interest of an expert, his glance betraying a hostile joy. That was a mob oration! A sure hit! A winner! "Let our citizens," cried Diederich, "awaken from the slumber in which they have so long been lulled, and no longer leave to the State and its instruments alone the fight against the revolutionary elements, but let them do their own part! That is His Majesty's command. Gentlemen, can I hesitate? Revolution is raising its head; a gang of people unworthy of the name of Germans dares to drag in the dust the sacred person of the Emperor . . ." Somebody laughed among the poorer members of the audience. Sprezius snapped his beak and threatened to fine the person who laughed. Jadassohn sighed. Now it was frankly no longer possible for Sprezius to interrupt the witness.

In Netzig, unfortunately, the imperial call to battle had awakened only a feeble response! Here people were closing their eyes and ears to the danger, and clinging to the antiquated views of narrow-minded democracy and humanity which paved the way for the unpatriotic enemies of the divine world order. Here they did not yet understand virile national sentiment and far-seeing Imperialism. "The task of modern thinkers is to win even Netzig to the new spirit, as defined by our glorious young Emperor, who has appointed every true patriot, whether he be aristocrat or commoner, to be the instrument of his exalted purpose." And Diederich concluded: "Therefore, gentlemen, I was justified in firmly challenging the defendant when he began to criticize. I have acted without personal malice, for the sake of the cause. To be impartial is to be German! I for my part"—he glared across at Lauer—"stand by my actions, for they spring from an exemplary life, which rests upon honor in the home and knows neither untruth nor immorality!"

There was a great sensation in court. Diederich was swept off his feet by the noble sentiments he had expressed, and, intoxicated by his success, he continued to glare at the accused. Suddenly Diederich shrank back, for the accused was helping himself up by the rail of his seat, trembling and shaking. His eyes were wild and bloodshot and his jaws moved convulsively, as if he had had a stroke. "Oh!" cried the women's voices, shivering with expectation. But the defendant had only time to utter a few hoarse imprecations against Diederich; his counsel had taken him by the arm and was speaking to him in insistent tones. Meanwhile the presiding Judge announced that the Public Prosecutor would begin his address at four o'clock, and disappeared with his colleagues. Half-dazed, Diederich found himself suddenly surrounded by Kühnchen, Zillich and Nothgroschen, who were congratulating him. Strangers shook him by the hand and assured him that a verdict of guilty was absolutely certain, that Lauer might as well prepare to leave. Major Kunze reminded the victorious Diederich that there had never been a difference of opinion between them. In the corridor old Buck passed quite close to Diederich, who was just then surrounded by a crowd of women. Buck was putting on his black gloves and he looked the young man full in the face as he did so. He did not respond to Diederich's involuntary salute, but looked at him with a sad, searching glance, so sad that Diederich, in the midst of his triumph, looked after him unhappily.

All of a sudden he became aware that the five Buck girls had the audacity to pay him compliments. They fluttered about him with rustling skirts and inquired why he had not brought his sisters to this thrilling trial. He looked these five over-dressed geese up and down, and explained sternly and brusquely that there were things which were to be taken more seriously than a theatrical performance. They walked off in blank amazement. The corridor began to empty; the last to appear was Guste Daimchen. She made a movement in Diederich's direction, but Wolfgang Buck approached her, smiling as if nothing had happened, and with him were the defendant and his wife. Guste quickly glanced at Diederich, appealing to his tender emotions. He stepped back behind a pillar and with beating heart allowed the vanquished to pass.

As he turned to go, Governor von Wulckow came out of one of the offices. Hat in hand, Diederich took up his position and at the right moment clicked his heels together and stood at attention. And Wulckow actually stopped! "Well, well!" he rumbled from the depths of his beard, clapping Diederich on the shoulder. "You carried the day. Most excellent sentiments. You'll hear from me again." He went off in his muddy boots, his paunch quivering in his sweaty riding breeches, and left behind him, as penetrating as ever, that odor of brutal masculinity which had permeated everything that happened in the courtroom.

Downstairs at the entrance door the Mayor still lingered with his wife and mother-in-law. Both women were nagging him, and he was trying to reconcile their wishes, a hopeless expression on his pale face.

At home Diederich's family had already heard everything. The three women had waited in the vestibule for the end of the hearing, and had asked Meta Harnisch to tell them what happened. Weeping silently Frau Hessling embraced her son. The sisters looked on feeling rather small, for only yesterday they had had nothing but contempt for Diederich and his role in the whole affair, which had now turned out so brilliantly. But in the happy oblivion of victory Diederich ordered wine for dinner, and assured them that this day would assure their social position in Netzig for all time. "The five Buck girls will be careful not to cut you in the street. They may consider themselves lucky if you return their greeting." Lauer's conviction, he explained, was nothing but a mere formality now; his fate had already been decided, as had been Diederich's irresistible advance! "Naturally"—he nodded into his glass—"even while faithfully discharging my duty I might have made a wrong move, and then, my dears, let's make no mistake about it, it would have been all over with me and with Magda's marriage, too!" As Magda turned pale he touched her arm. "Now we have come through very nicely," he said, raising his glass with manly resolve. "How well things have turned out under God's guidance!" He ordered the two girls to make themselves pretty and come along with him. Frau Hessling begged to be excused, she was afraid of the excitement. On this occasion Diederich could afford to wait, and his sisters could take as long to dress as they liked. By the time they arrived everyone was in the courtroom, but they were not the same people. All the Buck family was missing, and also Guste Daimchen, Heuteufel, Cohn, the whole Masonic Lodge and the Independent Voters' Association. They admitted their defeat! The whole town knew it and crowded in to witness their annihilation. The poorer people had moved up into the front seats. Those belonging to the vanquished clique who were still in attendance, Kühnchen and Kunze, took care that everyone should read their unimpeachable sentiments in their faces. There were a few suspicious-looking figures scattered about as well: young men with a tired, soulful air, together with several loud young women, with unnaturally radiant complexions, and they all exchanged greetings with Wolfgang Buck. The State Theater! Buck had actually dared to invite them to hear his oration.

Every time anyone entered Lauer turned his head anxiously. He was expecting his wife! "If he imagines that she will come again!" thought Diederich. But there she came, even paler than in the morning, greeted her husband with an imploring look, and sat down quietly at the end of a row of seats, her eyes staring fixedly in front of her at the Bench, proud and silent, as if awaiting Destiny . . . The judges had entered the courtroom, the presiding justice opened the session and called upon counsel for the prosecution to speak.

Jadassohn launched forth at once with extreme vehemence; after a few sentences his effects were exhausted and he lost his grip on the audience. The theatrical people smiled at one another contemptuously. Jadassohn noticed this and began to swing his arms until his gown whirled about him; his voice rose to a shriek and his ears glowed. The painted ladies fell on the rails of their seat in paroxysms of uncontrollable giggling. "Is Sprezius blind?" asked the Mayor's mother-in-law. But the Bench was fast asleep. Diederich inwardly rejoiced. This was his revenge on Jadassohn, who could think of nothing to say that Diederich himself had not said earlier. It was all over, as Wulckow knew; and Sprezius knew it, therefore he slept with his eyes open. Jadassohn knew it best of all, and the noisier he became the more ineffective he was. When he finally called for a penalty of two years' imprisonment, all the people he had bored disagreed with him, even the judges, as it seemed. Old Kühlemann gave a snore and awoke with a start. Sprezius blinked his eyes several times to rouse himself, and then called upon counsel for the defense.

Wolfgang Buck stood up slowly. His curious friends in the audience gave a murmur of applause and Buck calmly waited until they had finished, in spite of Sprezius's threatening beak. Then he declared lightly, as if it would be all over in two minutes, that the evidence had shown the defendant in a thoroughly favorable light. Counsel for the prosecution was wrong in his view that any value could be ascribed to the testimony of witnesses who had been intimidated by ruthless attacks upon their own private lives. Or rather, it had the value of proving incontrovertibly the innocence of the defendant, since so many truthful men could only be blackmailed into—of course he was not allowed to continue. When the judge had calmed down, Buck imperturbably continued. Even if they accepted as proven that the defendant had really uttered the expression with which he was charged, then the notion of indictability could not be applied to the action in question, for the witness Hessling had publicly admitted that deliberately and with malice aforethought he had provoked the defendant. He would suggest that the witness Hessling, with provocative intention, was really guilty of incitement to commit an offence, which he had carried out with involuntary cooperation of the accused and by taking deliberate advantage of his agitated state. Counsel recommended the witness Hessling for further questioning by the Public Prosecutor. Everyone turned toward Diederich, who began to feel uncomfortably warm. But the deprecatory air of the judge restored his courage.

Buck made his voice tender and warm. No, he did not wish any ill to the witness Hessling, whom he regarded as the victim of one more exalted. "Why are the charges of *lèse-majesté* proliferating in these times? You might say: as a result of such occurrences as the shooting of the workman. I answer: No. They are proliferating as a result of the speeches which are made in connection with such occurrences." Sprezius's head shot up, he sharpened his beak, but then drew back. Buck refused to be intimidated, and made his voice strong and virile.

"Threats and exaggerated claims on the one side provoke rebuffs on the other. The principle, he who is not with me is against me, draws too sharp a line between sycophants and calumniators."

Then Sprezius snapped, "Counsel for the defense cannot be permitted to criticize the words of His Majesty in this place. If he continues to do so the court will impose a fine."

"I accept the ruling," said Buck, and the words assumed in his mouth ever more contour and weight. "I will speak then not of the ruler, but of the loyal subject, whom he has molded: not of Wilhelm II but of Diederich Hessling. You have seen what he is like! An average man, with a commonplace mind, the creature of circumstance and opportunity, without courage so long as things were going badly for him here, and tremendously self-important as soon as they had turned in his favor."

Diederich fumed in his seat. Why did Sprezius not protect him? It was his duty! He allowed a loyal patriot to be treated with contempt at a public hearing—and by whom? By counsel for the defense, the professional champion of subversive tendencies! There was something rotten in the State! He began to boil with rage as he looked at Buck. There was the enemy, his antithesis. There was only one thing to do: smash him! That insulting humanity in Buck's fat profile! One could feel his patronizing affection for the words he formed to describe Diederich.

"At all times," said Buck, "there have been many thousands like him, men who looked after their business and developed political opinions. What is added, and makes of him a new type, is solely the gesture: the swaggering manner, the aggressiveness of an alleged personality, the craving for effect at any price, even at the expense of others. Those who differ in opinion are to be branded enemies of their country, even if they were to constitute two-thirds of the nation. Class interests, no doubt, but hulled in a cloak of romantic lie. Romantic prostration at the feet of a master who confers just enough of his power upon his subjects to enable them to keep the lesser men at bay. And as neither sovereign nor slave exists, neither in law nor in fact, public life takes on the aspect of bad comedy. Opinion appears in costume, speeches fall as from the lips of crusaders who turn out to be nothing more than manufacturers of tin, or paper, and the pasteboard sword is drawn for an idea such as majesty, which nobody can experience outside fairy tales. Majesty! . . ."

Buck repeated the word, rolling it on his tongue, and some of his listeners tasted it along with him. The theater people, who were clearly more interested in the words than their meaning, cupped their hands to their ears and murmured approvingly. For the others

Buck's language was too refined, and they were put off by his avoidance of dialect. Sprezius, however, sat bolt upright in his chair and gave a predatory screech:

"For the last time I must warn counsel not to bring the person of the Emperor into the discussion."

There was a sensation among the audience. When Buck began again to speak, someone tried to applaud. Sprezius snapped his beak just in time. It was one of the conspicuous young women.

"The presiding judge was the first to mention the person of the Monarch. But, now that it has been mentioned, I may be permitted, with all due respect, to observe that the extent to which his person so perfectly expresses and represents the tendencies of Germany at this moment has taken on an almost venerable aspect. You will not interrupt me when I say that the Emperor is a great artist. Can I say more? We know nothing loftier. . . . And for that very reason it should not be allowed that every contemporary mediocrity may ape him. Amidst the splendor of the throne one might allow his undoubtedly unique personality full play; he may make speeches without arousing in us any expectation of more than mere words; he may flash and dazzle; he may provoke the hatred of imaginary rebels and the applause of the gallery, which despite this enthusiasm never loses sight of its own bourgeois realities. . . ."

Diederich trembled, and all eyes and mouths were open in tense excitement, as if Buck were walking on a tightrope between two towers. Would he fall? Sprezius held his beak in readiness to pounce, but not a trace of irony could be seen in the expression of the speaker, into which a suggestion of embittered enthusiasm had crept. Suddenly the corners of his mouth dropped and all the color seemed to leave his face. "But a paper manufacturer in Netzig?" he queried. He had not tumbled, and was once more on solid ground! Everybody turned to look at Diederich, and even smiled. Emmi and Magda also smiled. Buck had secured his effect, and Diederich admitted to himself sadly that their conversation yesterday in the street had been the dress rehearsal for this. He cowered under the open scorn of the speaker.

"Nowadays papermakers have ambitions; they aspire to a role for which they were never created. Let us hoot them off the stage! They have no talent. The aesthetic level of our public life, which has been so gloriously raised since the advent of Wilhelm II, has nothing to gain from the cooperation of such persons as the witness Hessling. . . . And the moral level, gentlemen, rises and falls with the aesthetic. Fraudulent ideals bring evil manners in their train; political swindle follows on the heels of swindle in civil life."

Buck had made his voice stern. Now, for the first time, he struck a note of pathos.

"I do not restrict myself, gentlemen, to the mechanical doctrine so dear to the so-called revolutionary party. The example of a great man can effect more changes in the world than all the social legislation. But beware, if the example be misunderstood! Then it may happen that a new type of man may arise, who sees in severity and repression not the sad transition to humane conditions, but the aim of life itself. Weak and pacifistic by nature, he strives to appear a man of iron because, in his conception, Bismarck was such a man. Invoking without justification one higher than himself he becomes noisy and dangerous. Without a doubt the victories of his vanity will serve commercial ends. First his travesty of opinion brings a man to prison for *lèse-majesté*. Afterward he reaps his profit." Buck extended his arms as if his gown were to enfold the whole world, and he had the intense expression of a leader of men. He let fly with everything he had.

"You, gentlemen, wield sovereign power. Your sovereignty is first and most powerful. The fate of the individual is in your hands. You can send him back into the realm of life or you can bring about his moral death—a thing no prince can do. But a generation is created by your approval or condemnation. Thus your power extends to our future. Upon you rests the tremendous responsibility whether, in the future, men like the defendant shall fill the prisons, while the governing class is composed of creatures like the witness Hessling. Choose between them! Make your choice between selfish ambition and courageous action, between comedy and truth! Between a man who will sacrifice a victim to raise himself and one who will make sacrifices to advance the welfare of others. The defendant has done what few have dared; he has divested himself of his privileges; to those beneath him he has granted equal rights, comfort and the joy of hope. Can one who so respects his neighbor as himself be guilty of disrespect for the person of the Emperor?"

The audience drew a deep breath. With transformed feelings they gazed at the accused, who sat with forehead resting on his hand, and at his wife, who stared fixedly in front of her. Several people sobbed. Even the presiding judge was subdued. He had stopped blinking and sat there with wide-open eyes, as if Buck had

captivated him. Old Kühlemann nodded respectfully and Jadassohn began to twitch in spite of himself.

But Buck spoiled his effect by allowing his excitement to carry
him away. "The citizens are awake!" he shouted. "True patriotism!
The quiet deed of one Lauer strengthens it more than a hundred
resounding monologues, even though spoken by a crowned artist!"

Sprezius immediately began to blink again, and everybody
looked at him. He had remembered the true state of affairs and
resolved not to fall into the trap a second time. Jadassohn grinned,
and in court there was a feeling that counsel for the defense had
overplayed his part. Amidst general uneasiness the judge allowed
him to end his eulogy of the accused.

When Buck sat down the actors tried to applaud, but Sprezius
did not even snap at them. He merely gave them a bored glance
and asked if the prosecution wished to reply. Jadassohn declined
contemptuously and the Bench quickly withdrew. "It won't take
long to reach a verdict," said Diederich, shrugging his shoulders—
although he was still terribly perturbed by Buck's speech. "Thank
Heaven!" said the Mayor's mother-in-law. "And to think that five
minutes ago those people were getting the best of it." She pointed
at Lauer, who was wiping his face, and at Buck whom the actors
were actually congratulating.

By this time the judges had returned and Sprezius was pro-
nouncing the sentence: six months' imprisonment—which seemed
to everyone the most natural conclusion. In addition the accused
was divested of the public offices which he held.

The presiding judge based the verdict on the fact that libelous
intention was not essential to the establishment of guilt. Therefore
the question of provocation had no bearing upon the case. On the
contrary, the fact that the accused had dared to speak in that fashion in the presence of loyal citizens must weigh against him. The
defendant's plea that he had not meant the Emperor was held by
the court to be untenable. "In view of the political sympathies
of the listeners, and the known antimonarchical tendencies of the
defendant, they could not but conclude that his utterances were
directed against the Emperor. When the accused professes to have
taken good care not to libel His Majesty, he merely proves his
desire, not to avoid *lèse-majesté*, but to avoid its judicial
consequences."

Everybody saw the force of this, and found that Lauer's conduct
was understandable, but not quite honest. The accused was at once

arrested, and when the crowd had witnessed this final incident it broke up, making unfavorable comments about him. Now it was all over with Lauer, for what would become of his business during his six months in confinement? As a result of the sentence he was no longer a town councillor. In the future he could neither help nor harm anyone. For the Buck clique, which talked so big, it was a well-deserved lesson. People turned to look for the prisoner's wife, but she had disappeared.

"She didn't even shake hands with him! A nice state of affairs!"

But in the days that followed things happened which gave rise to even harsher judgements. Judith Lauer had packed her trunk immediately and gone off to the South. To the South!—while her husband was in prison, with a sentry marching beneath his barred window. And . . . a remarkable coincidence!

Judge Fritzsche suddenly took leave. A card from him, posted in Genoa, reached Dr. Heuteufel, who showed it round, probably in order to make people forget his own conduct. It was hardly necessary to pump the Lauer servants and the poor, forsaken children. People knew exactly what to think. The scandal grew to such dimensions that the *Netzig Journal* intervened with a warning to the upper ten not to encourage revolutionary tendencies by shameless profligacy. In a second article Nothgroschen set forth the foolishness of overpraising such reforms as Lauer had introduced into his factory. What did the workers get out of profit sharing? On an average, according to Lauer's own showing, hardly eighty marks a year. That might have been given to them in the form of a Christmas present. But then, of course, it would no longer be a demonstration against the existing social order! Then the antimonarchical views of the manufacturer, as established by the court, would derive no advantage! And if Herr Lauer had counted on the gratitude of the workers, he could now learn better, provided, Nothgroschen added, that he was allowed to read the Social Democratic newspaper in prison: this paper had accused him of having endangered the existence of several hundred working-class families by his irresponsible remarks about the Emperor. The *Netzig Journal* took account of the changed circumstances in another very significant way. The manager, Tietz, went to Hessling's factory for a portion of his paper supply. They were printing more papers, and Gausenfeld, he said, had more orders than could be filled. Diederich thought at once that old Klüsing himself was behind this move. He held a stake in the newspaper, and nothing happened there without his consent. If he surrendered something it was obviously because he was afraid he would otherwise lose even more. The local papers! The government contracts! He was afraid of Wulckow, that was it. The old man must have heard, although he now rarely came into town, that Diederich had attracted the Governor's attention by his testimony. The old paper spider, back there in his web, which covered the whole province and more, felt in danger and was uneasy. "He wants to buy me off with the *Netzig Journal!* But he won't get off as cheaply as that, not in these tough times! If he only knew what plans I have! Wait until I have Wulckow behind me—I'll simply take over his entire business!" Diederich said these words aloud and struck the desk so that Sötbier jumped up in alarm. "Beware of undue excitement," Diederich mocked, "at your age, Sötbier. I admit that in former years you did a good deal for the firm. But that was a bad business to return the cylinder machine. You undermined my courage, and now I could use the machine for the *Netzig Journal.* You had better take a rest. You are losing your touch."

Among the results which the trial brought Diederich was a letter from Major Kunze. The latter wished to clear up a regrettable misunderstanding and informed him that there was now no obstacle to Dr. Hessling's admission to the Veterans' Association. Deeply moved by his triumph Diederich's impulse was to clasp the two hands of the old soldier. Fortunately, he made inquiries, and discovered that Governor von Wulckow was responsible for the letter! The Governor had honored the club with a visit and expressed his amazement at not finding Dr. Hessling there. Then Diederich realized what a power he was, and acted accordingly. To the Major's private letter he replied with an official communication to the Club, and requested that two members of the committee should call on him, Major Kunze and Professor Kühnchen. And they came. Diederich received them in his office, between business calls which he had purposely arranged for the same hour, and he dictated to them the form of an address, the public acknowledgement of which he made a condition of accepting their flattering invitation. In it he had them assure him that he had upheld his loyalty, as a German and to the Emperor, with brilliant fearlessness and in the face of slander and calumny. That his action had made it possible to deal a decisive blow to the unpatriotic element in Netzig. That Diederich had emerged, a pure and true-blue German, from a struggle waged at great personal loss.

At the ceremony marking Diederich's admission to the Association Kunze read the address, while Diederich, with tears in his voice, confessed his unworthiness to receive such praise. If patriotism was gaining ground in Netzig, they should thank, after God, one higher than himself, whose gracious commands he executed in joyful obedience. . . . They were all moved, even Kunze and Kühnchen. It was a great evening. Diederich presented the club with a cup . . . and he made a speech in which he touched upon the difficulties which the new military appropriations bill was meeting in the Reichstag. "Our sharp sword alone," cried Diederich, "assures our place in the world, and it is the business of His Majesty the Emperor to keep it sharp. When the Emperor commands, it will fly from its sheath! Those politicians in the Reichstag who object to this had better take care that they are not the first to feel it! You cannot fool with His Majesty, gentlemen, I can tell you that." Diederich glared and nodded weightily, as if he knew more than he could tell. At that moment he had a real inspiration. "Recently in the provincial legislature of Brandenburg the Emperor made his attitude to the Reichstag clear. He said: 'If these chaps refuse me my soldiers, I'll clear out the whole Reichstag!'"

The phrase aroused enthusiasm, and by the time Diederich had replied to everyone who toasted him, he could not have said whether the words were his own or the Emperor's. . . . A stream of raw power flowed from the words and thrilled through his being, as though these words had been genuine. The next day the phrase appeared in the *Netzig Journal* and the same evening in the *Lokal-Anzeiger*. The radical papers demanded an official denial, but none was forthcoming.

Chapter 5

Such feelings of exaltation were still swelling in Diederich's breast when Emmi and Magda received an invitation to tea one afternoon from Frau von Wulckow. It could only be in connection with the play which the Governor's wife was having produced as the next event of the Harmony Club. Emmi and Magda were to have parts. They returned home flushed with pleasure. Frau von

Wulckow had been exceedingly charming, with her own hands she had put cake after cake on their plates. Inge Tietz was furious! Some officers were going to take part in the play! Special costumes would be required; if Diederich thought they could do with their fifty marks . . . But Diederich gave them unlimited credit. None of the things they bought were fine enough in his opinion. The sitting room was strewn with ribbons and artificial flowers and the girls were bewildered by Diederich's interruptions and advice. Then a visitor called; it was Guste Daimchen.

"I haven't yet properly congratulated the happy bride," she said, trying to smile with a patronizing air, but her eyes roved anxiously over the flowers and ribbons. "I suppose these are for the silly play?" she inquired. "Wolfgang heard about it. He says it is awfully silly." Magda replied: "He could hardly tell you anything else, since you are not acting in it." And Diederich declared: "That is just his way of excusing himself because, on his account, you are not invited to the Wulckows'." Guste gave a contemptuous laugh. "We can do without the Wulckows, but anyway we are going to the Club dance." Diederich asked: "Don't you think it would be better to wait until people have forgotten the trial?" He looked at her sympathetically. "Dear Fräulein Guste, we are old friends. You will allow me to warn you that your relations with the Bucks are not exactly a help to you in society just now." Guste's eyes flinched and it was evident that she herself had already arrived at the same conclusion. "Thank Heaven," said Magda, "my Kienast is not like that." To which Emmi retorted: "But Herr Buck is more interesting. I cried at his speech the other day. It was like being at the theater." "Why, of course!" cried Guste, taking courage. "Only yesterday he made me a present of this bag." She held up the gilt bag, at which Emmi and Magda had been glancing for some time. Magda said snappishly: "I suppose he earned a lot from that case. Kienast and I believe in economy." But Guste had had her revenge. "Well, I won't disturb you any longer," she concluded.

Diederich accompanied her downstairs. "I'll see you home, if you are a good girl," he said, "but I must first look in at the factory. They will be breaking off work in a moment." "But I can go with you," suggested Guste. In order to impress her he led the way to the big paper machine. "I am sure you have never seen anything like that before." He began self-importantly to explain to her the system of tanks, rollers and cylinders, through which the material passed the whole length of the room, first wet, then drier and drier, until at the end of the machine great rolls of finished paper came out. Guste shook her head. "My word! What a noise it makes! And the heat here!"

Not yet satisfied with the impression he was making, Diederich found an excuse to shout at the workers, and when Napoleon Fischer came up, he was blamed for everything. Both shouted over the noise of the machine and Guste could not understand a word. But in secret fear Diederich saw beneath that straggly beard the peculiar grin which was a reminder of Fischer's complicity in the affair of the double beater, and was an open defiance of all authority. The more violent Diederich became the calmer Fischer remained. That calm was rebellion! Trembling and fuming Diederich opened the door of the packing room and allowed Guste to enter. "That fellow is a Social Democrat!" he declared. "A chap like that is capable of setting fire to this place. But I will not dismiss him, just for that reason! We'll see who is the stronger. I'll attend to the Social Democrats!" Guste gazed at him admiringly, as he continued: "I am sure you would never have guessed what dangerous posts people like myself must hold. Fearless and true, that's my motto. You see, I am defending our most sacred national possessions just as the Emperor does. That requires more courage than making fine speeches in court."

Guste admitted it, with a pious expression on her face. "It is cooler here," she remarked, "after coming out of that inferno next door. The women in here should consider themselves lucky." "They?" queried Diederich. "They couldn't be better off!" He led Guste up to the table. One of the women was sorting the sheets, another checked them, and a third counted them up to five hundred. It was all done with incredible speed. The sheets flew one after another uninterruptedly, as though of their own accord, and without resisting the busy hands, which seemed to merge into the endless stream of paper that passed over them. Hands and arms, the woman herself, her eyes, her brain, her heart. All of these had come into being and lived so that the sheets might fly . . . Guste yawned—while Diederich railed against the shameless negligence of the women who were working on piecework. He was about to intervene because they passed a sheet from which the corner was torn off, when Guste said rather spitefully: "You needn't imagine that Käthchen Zillich cares particularly for you . . . at least no more than for certain other people," she added. And her only reply to his bewildered question as to what she meant was to give a suggestive smile. "But you must tell me," he repeated. Whereupon Guste assumed her patronizing air. "I am speaking only for your own good. I suppose you haven't noticed anything? For instance, with Herr Jadassohn? But that's the sort of girl Käthchen Zillich is." Here Guste laughed loudly, because Diederich looked so crestfallen. She moved on and he followed her. "With Jadassohn?" he asked anxiously. Then the noise of the machines stopped, the bell rang to signal the end of the shift, and the employees were already disappearing across the yard. Diederich shrugged his shoulders. "What Fräulein Zillich does leaves me cold," he said. "At most I am sorry for the old pastor, if that's the sort of person she is. Are you quite sure of it?" Guste looked away. "You can find that out for yourself!" Then Diederich felt flattered, and smiled.

"Leave the gas on," he shouted to the machinist, who was passing. "I'll turn it off myself." The doors of the rag room were just then opened wide to let the workers out. "Oh!" cried Guste, "how romantic it looks in there." Back there in the shadow she had caught a glimpse of gray hills splashed with many bright patches, and above these what seemed to be a forest of branches. "Ah," she said, as she drew nearer, "it is so dark here I thought. . . . But they are only heaps of rags and hot water pipes . . ." She made a grimace. Diederich drove off the women who were resting on the sacks, in disregard of the factory rules. Several were knitting, although they had hardly ceased work. Others were eating. "No doubt you find this very comfortable!" he snorted. "Cadging heat at my expense!" They got up slowly, in silence, without a sign of resistance, and passing the strange lady, at whom they all turned to look with dull curiosity, they tramped out in their men's boots, heavy as a herd of cattle and enveloped in the odor in which they lived. Diederich kept a sharp watch on each of them until they were outside. "Fischer!" he suddenly shouted. "What has that fat one hidden under her skirts?" With his ambiguous grin the machinist answered: "That's only because she is expecting a certain event." Whereupon Diederich turned away dissatisfied and explained to Guste: "I thought I had caught one of them. They steal rags, you know, to make children's clothes." And when Guste turned up her nose: "They're too good for working-class brats."

With the tips of her glove Guste lifted one of the pieces from the floor. Immediately Diederich seized her wrist and kissed her hand greedily at the opening in her glove. She gave a frightened look around. "Oh, I see, they are all gone." She laughed confi-

dently. "I guessed what you really wanted to do in the factory."
Diederich looked at her defiantly. "Well, and what about yourself?
Why did you come here at all today? You must have come to the
conclusion that I was not, after all, such an impossible person. Of
course, your Wolfgang—it is not everybody who can make such
an ass of himself as he did in court the other day." To which Guste
retorted indignantly: "Just you keep your mouth shut. You will
never be half the man he is." But her eyes spoke differently, as
Diederich noticed. He laughed excitedly. "How anxious he is to
have you! Do you know how he regards you? As a pot of sausage
and cabbage which I am to keep stirred for him!" Guste could
have killed him. "You're a liar!" she said. But Diederich was in
good form. "All that worries him is that there is not enough sausage and cabbage in the pot. At first, of course, he also believed
you had come into a million. But you can't get a man of that
type for fifty thousand marks." Then Guste's rage boiled over. She
looked so dangerous that Diederich shrank back. "Fifty thousand!
Are you crazy? Why must I listen to such talk? I, who have three-
hundred-fifty thousand in the bank in gilt-edged securities. Fifty
thousand! Whoever insults me by spreading such stories is in danger of an action for libel!" She had tears in her eyes, and Diederich
stammered apologies. "You needn't bother," said Guste, and she
used her handkerchief. "Wolfgang knows exactly how I am situ-
ated. But you believed the lie yourself. That's why you were so
cheeky!" she cried. Her rosy cushions of fat quivered with rage,
and her little snub nose had turned quite pale. He recovered his
presence of mind. "That shows you that I like you even without
money," he pointed out. She bit her lips. "Who knows?" she said,
looking at him from under her eyelashes, pouting and uncertain.
"Even fifty thousand is a lot of money for people like you."

He felt a pause was in order. She took the powder puff from her
golden handbag and sat down. "I must say, your behavior has
given me quite a flush!" But she laughed again. "Have you perhaps
anything else to show me in your so-called factory?" He nodded
significantly. "Do you know where you're sitting right now?"
"Well, on a sack of rags, I should think." "But what a sack of rags!
In this corner, behind the sacks here, I once caught a worker and
a girl just as they were—well, you understand. I fired them both,
of course; and that evening, yes indeed, on that very evening,"—
he raised his index finger, and his eyes radiated an exalted thrill—
"they shot the fellow dead, and the girl went mad." Guste sprang

up. "Was that—? My God, that was the worker who provoked the sentry. . .? You mean here, behind the sacks, they—?" Her eyes scanned the sacks, as though she were looking for traces of blood. She had fled to Diederich's side. Suddenly they looked into each other's eyes: through both pairs moved the same unfathomable thrill—a thrill of vice or a thrill of the supernal. They breathed audibly upon each other. Guste closed her eyes for the space of a second: the two of them then plumped down onto the sacks, rolled with entwined limbs down into the dark space behind, flailed about, gasped and panted as though they were drowning.

Guste was the first to emerge into the light. She kicked her foot, on which he was trying to hold fast, into his face and jumped out with a clatter and a thud. When Diederich had managed to catch up with her, they stood there and panted. Guste's bosom and Diederich's paunch were working violently. She was the first to regain her speech. "You'll have to try that with someone else! What am I doing here?" With increasing bitterness: "I've told you, it's three-hundred-fifty thousand!" Diederich moved his hand in a gesture which conceded his impropriety. But Guste cried out: "Just look at me! Am I supposed to walk through town like this?" He flinched anew and laughed helplessly. She stamped her foot. "Haven't you got a brush?" He obediently set off to look for one; Guste called after him: "Don't you dare let your sisters find out about this! Otherwise the whole town will be talking about me tomorrow!" He went only as far as the office. When he returned, Guste was sitting on the sack again, her face in her hands, and tears trickled from between her dear, fat little fingers. Diederich stopped, heard her whimpering, and all at once he began to cry as well. He brushed her clothes with a consoling hand. "But nothing happened," he repeated. Guste stood up. "That'll be the day"—and she regarded him with irony. Diederich plucked up courage at this. "Of course, your fiancé doesn't need to find out," he remarked. And Guste, biting her lip: "So what if he does!"

Taken aback by her reply, he brushed on in silence; first her, then himself, while Guste smoothed her clothes. "Come on, let's go!" she said. "I won't be inspecting another paper factory any time soon." He peered beneath the brim of her hat. "Who knows?" he countered. "I stopped believing five minutes ago that you still love your Buck." Guste quickly answered: "Oh yes I do!" And without a pause she asked: "What's this stuff here?"

He explained: "That's the sand trap; we flush the rags through the trough, and the buttons and things are left behind, as you can see. The people haven't bothered to clean up again, of course." She poked about in the clutter with the point of her umbrella; he added: "We reclaim enough odds and ends in a year to fill several sacks."—"And what is that there?" asked Guste and quickly reached out toward some glittering object. Diederich's eyes opened wide. "A diamond stud!" She held it in the light so that it sparkled. "And it's a real diamond! If you find things like this now and then, your business can't be all that bad!" Diederich said doubtfully: "I'll have to turn that in, of course!" She laughed. "To whom? The leavings belong to you, don't they?" "Well yes, but not the diamonds. I'm sure we'll be able to find out who delivered that." Guste looked up at him. "You're quite a fool, aren't you?" she said. "I am not!" he retorted with conviction, "I am a man of honor!" Her only reply was a shrug of her shoulders. Slowly she pulled off her left glove and placed the diamond over her little finger. "This must be made into a ring!" she exclaimed as though with sudden inspiration; she sank into a reverie as she regarded her hand, and sighed: "Well, we'll let someone else find it!"— and abruptly threw the stud back into the rags. "Are you crazy?" Diederich bent down, and not finding it right away, dropped huffing and puffing to his knees. In his haste he started flinging rags left and right. "Thank God!" He held up the diamond, but Guste did not take it. "If it were up to me, I would say that the first worker who finds it tomorrow deserves it. He'll pocket it, believe me. He won't be so stupid."—"Neither will I," declared Diederich. "The stone would most likely have been thrown away. Things being as they are, I needn't consider it incorrect—" He placed the diamond over her finger again. "And even if it were incorrect, it becomes you so well." Guste exclaimed with surprise: "What do you mean? You want to give it to me?" He stammered: "Well you found it. It looks like I have to." Guste rejoiced. "That will be my most beautiful ring!"—"Why?" asked Diederich, full of anxious hope. Guste said evasively: "After all. . . ." And with a sudden look: "Because it didn't cost anything, you know?" At this, Diederich blushed, and they looked into each others' twinkling eyes.—"Oh, good Lord!" Guste exclaimed suddenly. "It must be terribly late. Seven o'clock already? What will I tell my mother. . . ? I know, I'll tell her I found the diamond at a ragman's, and he thought it was a fake and only charged me fifty pfennigs for it."

She opened her golden handbag and dropped in the stud. "*Adieu* then. . . . But look at you! You must tie your tie at least." She was already doing it as she spoke. He felt her warm hands under his chin; her thick, moist lips moved quite close. He suddenly felt hot, and he held his breath. "There we go," said Guste, and she made a move to go, this time in earnest. "I'm just turning off the gas," he called after her. "Wait for me."—"I'm waiting," she answered from outside; but when he stepped out into the yard, she was gone. Bewildered, he locked up the factory and spoke aloud: "Tell me, is that instinct or scheming?" He shook his head in apprehension at the eternal riddle of femininity embodied in Guste.

Perhaps, Diederich said to himself, things were developing with Guste, but the progress was admittedly slow. The events connected with the trial had made an impression on her, but that was not enough. Also, he heard nothing more from Wulckow. After such promising steps had been taken by the Governor at the Veterans' Association, Diederich confidently expected further developments, an approach, a mark of friendship, he did not know exactly what. Perhaps it would happen at the Harmony Club ball. Otherwise, why had his sisters been given parts in the play given by the Governor's wife? But it was all coming together much too slowly for one with Diederich's zest for action. It was a time of stress and unrest. He overflowed with hopes, plans, and prospects. As each day came around he wanted to seize everything at one stroke. And at the end of each day he found himself empty-handed. Diederich was possessed by a desire for movement. Several times he did not turn up at his *Stammtisch,* but went out walking aimlessly in the country, a thing he never did as a rule. He turned his back on the center of the town, tramped with energetic steps to the end of the empty Meisestrasse in the evenings, covered the whole length of Gäbbel-chenstrasse, with its suburban inns, where drivers were yoking or unyoking their carts, and passed in front of the jail. Up there under the guard of a soldier and a barred window, sat Herr Lauer, who had never dreamt this would happen to him. "Pride goes before a fall," Diederich reflected. "As a man sows, so shall he reap." And although he was hardly a stranger to the events which had brought the manufacturer to jail, Lauer now appeared to him as an uncanny creature, bearing the mark of Cain. Once he fancied he saw a figure in the prison yard. It was dark at the time, but perhaps. . . ? A shudder ran through Diederich and he hurried away.

Beyond the city gate lay the country road to the hill on which stood Schweinichen Castle, where once upon a time little Diederich had shared with Frau Hessling the delightful thrill of the Castle ghost. That childishness was now far behind him. Now he preferred every time to turn sharply, on the other side of the gate, into the road leading to Gausenfeld paper factory. He had not intended to do so, and he hesitated, for he would not like anyone to have caught him on this road. But he could not resist. The big paper factory drew him like a forbidden paradise. He simply had to go a few steps nearer to it, walk around it, peer over the walls . . . One evening Diederich was disturbed in this occupation by voices which were quite close in the dark. He had barely time to crouch down in the ditch. While the people, probably employees of the factory who had stayed late, were passing his hiding place, Diederich squeezed his eyes shut, partly out of fear and partly because it seemed to him their covetous gleam might have betrayed him.

His heart was still beating fast when he returned to the city gate, and he looked around for a glass of beer. In the corner of the gateway stood the "Green Angel," one of the least reputable inns in town, crooked with age, dirty and notoriously squalid. At that moment a woman's figure disappeared into the arched entrance. Seized with a desire for adventure Diederich hastened after her. As she passed through the reddish light of a stable lantern she tried to hide her face, which was already veiled, with her muff. But Diederich had recognized her. "Good evening, Fräulein Zillich!" "Good evening, Dr. Hessling." There they both stood with their mouths open. Käthchen Zillich was the first to speak, and she murmured something about children who lived in the house, and whom she was to take to her father's Sunday school. Diederich began to talk, but she continued to chatter, faster and faster. No, as a matter of fact the children did not live there, but their parents frequented this bar, and they were not to know anything about the Sunday school, for they were Social Democrats . . . She blathered on, and Diederich, who had only thought at first of his own guilty conscience, began to realize that Käthchen was in an even more compromising position. He did not, therefore, trouble to explain his presence in the "Green Angel." He simply proposed that they wait for the children in the inn. Käthchen nervously refused to have anything to drink, but a sense of his own power caused Diederich to order beer for her as well. "Your health!" he said, and his ironical look was a reminder that they had almost become engaged at their last meeting in the cozy sitting room of the manse. Beneath her veil Käthchen blushed and paled by turns and spilled her beer. Every now and then she fluttered up helplessly from her chair and tried to go, but Diederich had edged her into the corner behind the table and planted his bulk in front of her. "The children should be here any moment," he said amiably. Instead it was Jadassohn who came. He entered suddenly and stood as if he had been struck dumb. The two others did not move either. "So it's true after all!" thought Diederich. Jadassohn seemed to come to a similar conclusion. Neither of the men could think of a thing to say. Käthchen began again to talk about children and Sunday school. Her voice was beseeching and she was almost in tears. Jadassohn listened to her disapprovingly, and even remarked that some tales were too involved for him—and he gave Diederich an inquisitorial glance.

"Actually," Diederich interposed, "It's very simple. Fräulein Zillich is looking for children here and we two are going to help her."

"Whether she will end up with one is another matter," added Jadassohn smartly. "And from whom," retorted Käthchen.

The men sat down their glasses in front of them. Käthchen had stopped crying and, throwing back her veil, she looked from one to the other, with remarkably bright eyes. An open, frank tone had crept into her voice. "Well, now that you are both here," she said by way of explanation, as she took a cigarette from Jadassohn's case. Then she suddenly drank off the glass of cognac which was in front of Diederich. Now it was the latter's turn to struggle for composure. This other side of Käthchen did not seem unfamiliar to Jadassohn. The two of them continued to exchange double entendres until Diederich grew indignant with Käthchen. "This time I am seeing you in your true colors!" he cried, striking the table. Käthchen at once resumed her most ladylike expression. "I do not understand what you mean, Dr. Hessling." Jadassohn continued: "I presume you do not intend any insinuation against the lady's honor!" Diederich stammered: "I only meant that I like Fräulein Zillich much better when she is like this." He rolled his eyes helplessly. "Recently, when we nearly became engaged, she did not appeal to me half as much." Then Käthchen laughed out loud; a laughter straight from the heart, which Diederich had also never heard before. He began to feel warm and joined in her mirth,

Jadassohn following, and all three rocked with laughter and called for more cognac.

"Well, now I must be off," said Käthchen, "otherwise Papa will get home before me. He has been paying sick calls, and then he always distributes pictures like these." She pulled two colored pictures out of her leather bag. "There are some for you." Jadassohn received Magdalene the sinner, and Diederich the lamb with the shepherd. He was not satisfied. "I want a sinful woman too." Käthchen searched but could not find another. "You'll have to be content with a sheep," she decided, and they set off, Käthchen in the middle hanging on their arms. Making wide curves, all three staggered jerkily along the dimly lighted Gäbbelchen Street, singing a hymn which Käthchen had started. When they came to a corner she said she would have to hurry and disappeared down a side street. "Good-bye, sheep!" she shouted to Diederich, who struggled in vain to follow her. Jadassohn held him tight, and suddenly began in authoritative tones to convince Diederich that this meeting had been a joke and mere chance. "I wish to make it perfectly clear that there is absolutely no ground for misunderstanding."

"I had no intention of drawing improper conclusions," said Diederich.

"And if I," continued Jadassohn, "had the privilege of being considered by the Zillich family as a possible member of that family, this accidental occurrence would not hold me back. I owe it to my sense of honor to tell you this."

Diederich replied: "I thoroughly appreciate the correctness of your conduct." Then the gentlemen clicked their heels together, shook hands and parted.

Käthchen and Jadassohn had exchanged a sign on parting, and Diederich was certain they would meet again immediately at the "Green Angel." He loosened his overcoat and a feeling of pride filled him because he had uncovered a malicious trap and had got out of it with all the rules of his code intact. He felt a certain respect and sympathy for Jadassohn. He too would have acted similarly. Men understood one another. But what a woman! That other side of Käthchen, the pastor's daughter whose face had unsuspectedly revealed the loose woman! This insidious two-faced creature, so remote from the simple integrity which lay at the root of his own character! He shuddered as if he had looked into an abyss. He buttoned up his coat again. He realized that outside the bourgeois world there were other worlds apart from that in which Herr Lauer now lived.

He was fuming as he sat down to supper. His voice was so threatening that the three women maintained silence. Frau Hessling plucked up courage. "Don't you like your supper, my dear child?" Instead of answering Diederich barked at his sisters. "I forbid you to have anything more to do with Käthchen Zillich!" As they stared at him, he blushed and exclaimed angrily: "She is a depraved woman!" But they merely pursed their lips and did not seem particularly astonished by the terrible intimations into which he clumsily launched. "I suppose you are talking about Jadassohn?" Magda asked finally, with the utmost calm. Diederich started. So they knew all about it; they were co-conspirators, all the women probably were. Guste Daimchen, too! She had once begun to talk about it. He had to wipe the perspiration from his brow. Magda said: "If you by any chance had serious intentions concerning Käthchen, you certainly never asked us." At this Diederich, to keep himself in countenance, banged the table so that they all screeched. In strident tones, he forbade such insinuations. He hoped that there were still a few decent girls left. Frau Hessling pleaded, trembling: "You have only to look at your own sisters, my dear son." And Diederich really looked at them and glared. For the first time he thought, not without fear, of what these female creatures, who were his sisters, might have been up to during their lives. . . . "Confound it all," he decided, pulling himself up stiffly, "the reins will simply have to be held more tightly over you. When I marry, my wife will know who is the master!" As the girls smiled at one another, he gave a start, for he remembered Guste Daimchen; were they thinking of Guste when they smiled? He could trust nobody. He could see Guste in front of him, with her white-blonde hair and plump, rosy cheeks. Her fleshy lips were parted and she was sticking out her tongue at him. That was what Käthchen Zillich had done when she shouted, "Good-bye, sheep!" And Guste, who was very similar to her in type, would have looked just like that, if she were half-drunk and had her tongue out!

Magda was saying: "Käthchen is awfully silly, but it is understandable when you have waited so long for a man and none comes."

Emmi at once interposed. "To whom are you referring, please? If Käthchen had been content with any old Kienast she would not have to wait any more either."

Conscious of her superior position Magda did not reply, but her breast heaved.

"Anyway," said Emmi, rising and throwing her napkin down, "how can you believe so easily what the men say about Käthchen? It is disgusting. Are we all to remain defenseless against their gossip?" In high dudgeon she sat down in a corner and began to read. Magda simply shrugged her shoulders, while Diederich sought anxiously and in vain for a transition which would enable him to ask if Guste Daimchen also . . . With such a long engagement? "There are situations," he declared, "where it is no longer just gossip." Then Emmi flung away her book.

"Well, what about it? Käthchen does what she thinks fit. We girls have just as much right as you men to live our own lives! You may consider yourselves lucky if you can get us at all afterward!"

Diederich stood up. "I will not listen to such talk in my house," he said seriously, and he glared at Magda until she stopped laughing.

Frau Hessling brought him his cigar. "I know my little Diedel will never marry anyone like that"—she stroked him consolingly. He replied with great emphasis: "Mother, I cannot imagine that a true German man ever did so."

She began to flatter him: "Oh, they are not all idealists like my dear son. Many think more materially and if there is money they are willing to accept some gossip." Under his commanding glance she continued to chatter nervously. "For instance, Daimchen. God knows, he is dead now, and it can't make any difference to him, but at the time there was a great deal of talk." Now all three children looked at her inquiringly. "Well, yes," she continued timidly, "that affair between Frau Daimchen and Herr Buck; Guste was born too soon."

After this statement Frau Hessling had to take refuge behind the screen in front of the stove, for the three of them thronged about her at once. "What a sensation," cried Magda and Emmi together. "How did it happen?" Diederich, in his turn, thundered against this women's tittle-tattle. "Well, we had to listen to your men's gossip," cried the girls, as they tried to shove him away from the screen. Wringing her hands the mother looked on at the struggle. "Children, I didn't say anything! Everyone said so at the time, though, and Herr Buck gave Frau Daimchen her dowry."

"So that's the reason," said Magda. "That's the sort of rich uncles they have in the Daimchen family! That's where the gilt bags come from!"

Diederich defended Guste's inheritance. "It comes from Magdeburg!"

"And the husband?" Emmi asked. "Does he come from Magdeburg, too?"

Suddenly they all fell silent and looked at each other, stunned. Then Emmi went quietly back to the sofa and took up her book again. Magda began to clear the table. Diederich went up to the screen behind which Frau Hessling was hidden. "Now, mother, do you see where it leads when people don't watch what they say? You don't mean to tell me that Wolfgang Buck is marrying his own sister?" A tearful voice answered: "My dear child, I can't help it. I had long since forgotten the old story, and it's not even certain whether it is true or not. No living soul knows anything about it." Raising her head from her book Emmi interjected: "Old Herr Buck must know where he gets the money for his son." And into the tablecloth which she was folding Magda said: "Strange things do happen." Then Diederich raised his arms, so if to appeal to Heaven. Just in time he suppressed the feeling of horror which threatened to overcome him. "Have I fallen into a den of thieves and murderers?" he asked in matter-of-fact tones, as he strode with rigid bearing toward the door. There he turned. "Of course, I cannot prevent you from hawking your remarkable wisdom about the town. You can spread this tale, but as far as I am concerned, I will declare that I have nothing more to do with you. I'll put a notice to that effect in the papers!" With that, he went out.

He avoided the *Ratskeller,* and at Klappsch's he reflected upon a world in which such horrors prevailed. The code of honor of his students' corps was obviously inadequate to meet such circumstances. Whoever wished to extract from the Bucks their shameful booty must not shrink from stern measures. "With mailed fist," he pronounced gravely into his beer. As he clapped the lid for a fourth glass, it sounded like the rattle of swords. . . . After a while his stern demeanor relaxed; scruples presented themselves. His intervention would assuredly result in the whole town pointing a finger of scorn at Guste Daimchen. No man of the slightest honor could then marry such a girl. Diederich's deepest feelings made him feel sure of this; his deeply grounded belief in manliness and idealism. What a shame! What a pity when one remembered Guste's three-hundred-fifty-thousand marks, which were now without a master and without a purpose. The opportunity would have been favorable to provide them with both. . . . Diederich rejected the thought with scorn. He was only doing his duty! A crime must be prevented. The woman would then see what her place was in the struggles of men. What did he care for any of these creatures who, for their part, as Diederich had learned by experience, were capable of every treason. Only a fifth glass was now required and he had reached a decision.

At breakfast he showed great interest in the finery his sisters would be wearing to the Harmony Club Ball. Only two days left, and nothing was ready! It had been so difficult lately to arrange an appointment with their dressmaker; she now sewed for the Bucks, the Tietzes, the Harnisches, for everybody. The seamstress's sudden and widespread popularity seemed to fill Diederich with downright admiration. He offered to call on her himself and bring her back, cost what it may. He succeeded, but not without considerable coaxing. He thereupon tucked into his early lunch so noiselessly that the conversation in the adjoining living room was not disturbed. Just then the dressmaker was dropping one insinuation after another about a scandal destined to overshadow everything else that had ever happened in the town. The sisters seemed to have no idea of what the dressmaker was talking about, and when names were finally mentioned they put on a display of shock and disbelief. Frau Hessling deplored the loudest that Fräulein Gehritz could even think of such a thing. The dressmaker asserted in reply that everyone in town knew about it already. She had just come from an appointment with the Mayor's wife, Frau Scheffelweis, whose mother had all but demanded that her son-in-law intervene! It cost her nevertheless considerable effort to convince the women. Diederich had actually expected things to happen the other way around. He was quite pleased with his family. But had the walls indeed had ears? One was tempted to believe that a rumor, once having broken out in a closed room, had wafted out with the smoke of the fireplace and drifted over the entire town.

He was anything but reassured, however. He told himself that the healthy instincts of the working classes were under certain circumstances a factor to be condoned and even utilized. Up until lunchtime, he made every effort to avoid Napoleon Fischer. But just as the bell was ringing to announce the noontime break, a piercing scream rang out from the vicinity of the supercalender, and Diederich and the machinist, who burst in at the same time, managed to extract the arm of a young working girl, which had been caught and crushed by one of the steel rollers. The arm dripped with black blood. Diederich dispatched someone immediately to phone the municipal hospital. In the meantime, Diederich remained at the girl's side, as sickened as he was by the sight of the arm, while a makeshift bandage was applied. The girl watched, whispering quietly, her eyes soft with horror like those of a wounded young animal. Diederich's benevolent attempts to ascertain her domestic situation met with a blank, uncomprehending stare. Napoleon Fischer answered for her. Her father had run off, her mother was bedridden; the girl provided for herself and her two younger siblings. She was only fourteen years old.—One would never have guessed all that by looking at her, Diederich remarked. Anyway, the workers had been warned often enough about the machine. "She has only herself to blame for the accident, I am under no obligation to do anything. Well," his voice took on a milder tone, "come along, Fischer."

In the office, he poured out two glasses of cognac. "We can really use it, after that shock. . . Give me your honest opinion, Fischer, do you think I'll have to pay? The safety devices on the machine are certainly more than sufficient, don't you think?" And as the machinist shrugged his shoulders: "Are you saying I can take my chances if the case comes to trial? No, I'm not going to let things come to that; I'll pay up front."

Napoleon Fischer bared his large yellow teeth in an uncomprehending grin, and Diederich continued: "Yes, that's the kind of man I am. I suppose you thought only Herr Lauer could do that? As far as he is concerned, I'm sure you've learned a thing or two about his sympathy for the workers from your own party newspaper. I for one don't get myself locked up for *lèse majesté* and rob my workers of their livelihood; I look to more practical means to give voice to my social conscience." He made a solemn pause. "And that is why I have decided to pay the girl her wages throughout the entire time she is in the hospital. How much does she make, anyway?" he asked quickly.

"One mark fifty" said Napoleon Fischer.

"Hm, let's see. . . if she's laid up for eight weeks. . . Of course, I won't be able to keep up the payments forever."

"She's only fourteen," said Napoleon Fischer from below. "She can sue." Diederich gasped.

Napoleon Fischer broke once more into his inscrutable grin and looked at his employer's fist, which the latter held anxiously clenched in his pocket. Diederich pulled it out. "Now make sure the people know about my magnanimous decision! I don't suppose that squares with your ideas about me now, does it? I'm sure you'd rather tell each other about the dirty tricks of the capitalists. You've probably been making eulogies to Herr Buck in your party meetings."

Napoleon Fischer wore once more his uncomprehending expression, to which Diederich paid no attention. "I consider it a pretty unpleasant business," he continued, "when someone lets his son marry the very girl with whose mother he had an affair, and before the birth of the daughter at that. . . . But—"

Napoleon Fischer's face began to work.

"But!" Diederich repeated emphatically. "I would be very much opposed if my people were to start spreading nasty rumors to that effect, and if you, Fischer, were perhaps to agitate the workers against the municipal authorities because an official in the town administration had done something which can be proven by no one." He swung his fist indignantly through the air. "People have been saying that it was I who instigated the trail against Lauer. I deny any responsibility in the affair, and my people should keep their mouths shut."

His voice took on a more intimate note and he leaned closer. "Yes, and since I'm quite aware of the influence you yield, Fischer. . . ."

Suddenly his hand was open, and upon the palm lay three large gold pieces.

Napoleon Fischer saw them, and his face broke into a grimace as though he were staring the Devil in the face. "No!" he cried, "Never! I cannot betray my convictions! Not for all the mammon in the world!"

His eyes were red and he screeched. Diederich shrank back; never before had he gazed from such proximity into the face of the Revolution. "The truth must come to light!" screeched Napoleon Fischer. "We proletarians will see to that. You will never be able to prevent it, Dr. Hessling! The scandalous deeds of the propertied classes. . . ."

Diederich quickly proffered him another cognac. "Fischer," he said insistently, "I am offering you the money so that my name not be mentioned in connection with the affair." But Napoleon Fischer made a gesture of refusal; lofty pride began to shine from his face.

"Dr. Hessling, we do not force our people to reveal their sources. That is not the way we operate. Anyone who supplies us with agitatory material has nothing to fear."

"Then everything is in order," Diederich said with relief. "I've always known, Fischer, that you were a great politician. And for that reason, getting back to the subject of the girl—that is, the worker who had the accident—. I have done you a favor just now, in passing on the information about the filthy scandal of the Buck family. . ."

Napoleon Fischer broke out in a flattered grin. Since you say that I am a great politician, Dr. Hessling. . . I won't say another word about worker's compensation claims. Intimate details from the upper crust are more important to us than—"

"—than some girl," Diederich finished. "Always thinking like a politician, aren't you?"

"Always," affirmed Napoleon Fischer. "Good-bye, Dr. Hessling."—He withdrew—while Diederich acknowledged that proletarian politics had their advantages. He dropped the three gold pieces back into his pocket.

On the evening of the following day all the mirrors in the house had been brought into the sitting room. Emmi, Magda and Inge Tietz were twisting and turning in front of them until their necks ached. Then they sat down nervously on the edge of a chair. "Good heavens, isn't it time to go?" But Diederich was determined not to arrive early, as he had at Lauer's trial. The impression one made went to the devil when one arrived too early. When they finally started Inge Tietz apologized again to Frau Hessling for taking her place in the carriage. Once more Fraud Hessling repeated: "Don't worry about it, it's a pleasure. An old woman like me is too frail for something so grand. Have a good time, children!" With tears in her eyes she embraced her daughters, who repelled her coldly. They knew that all their mother was afraid of was that the only subject of conversation at the party would be the horrible, scandalous story about Frau Daimchen and Herr Buck for which she herself was responsible.

In the carriage Inge began at once to talk about it again. "What about the Bucks and the Daimchens? I wonder if they will really have the infernal cheek to show up?" Magda replied calmly: "They must come, otherwise they would be admitting that it is true." "Well, even if it is," said Emmi. "It is their own affair. I am not going to get excited about it." "Nor I," added Diederich. "The first I heard of it was from you tonight, Fräulein Tietz."

At this Fräulein Tietz lost her temper. The scandal could not be taken so lightly. Did he mean to imply that she had invented the whole story? "The Bucks have long since had egg on their faces from the affair; their own servants know about it." "I see," said Diederich. "Servants' gossip," while he returned the nudge which Magda gave him with her knee. Then they had to get out and go down the steps which connected the new section of Kaiser Wilhelm Strasse with the lower level of the old Riekestrasse. Diederich cursed, for it was beginning to rain and their dancing shoes were getting wet. In front of the place where the ball was being held, working people had gathered and indulged in hostile comment. Why hadn't this old rubbish heap been torn down when that quarter of the town was levelled up? The historic Concert Hall had to be preserved at all costs—as if the town could not afford to build a modern first-class entertainment hall in a central location. In this old hall everything was musty. At the entrance the ladies always giggled because there was a statue of Friendship clothed in nothing more substantial than a wig. "Be careful," said Diederich on the stairs, "or we'll fall through." The two slender curves of the stairway stretched out like the skinny arms of an old man. The reddish brown of the woodwork had faded, but at the top, where they met, there smiled from the banisters the white marble face of a pigtailed mayor from days gone by, who had left all this to the city, and whose name had been Buck. Diederich sullenly ignored him as he passed.

In the long mirrored gallery all was quiet. A solitary lady was standing in the background and seemed to be peering into the entertainment hall through a door opened to a crack. Suddenly the girls were seized with horror: the play had begun! Magda ran through the gallery and burst into tears. Then the lady turned around and put her finger to her lips. It was Frau von Wulckow, the authoress. She smiled excitedly and whispered: "It's going splendidly. They like my play. You are just in time, Fräulein Hessling; go now and change your clothes." Of course! Emmi and Magda did not appear until the second act. Diederich had also lost his head. While his sisters hurried off through the anterooms to the dressing rooms with Inge Tietz, who was to help them, he introduced himself to the Governor's wife and stood there not knowing what to do. "You can't go in now," she said, "it would

disturb people." Diederich stammered his apologies and then rolled
his eyes, and thus caught a glimpse of his mysteriously pale reflection between the painted vines that framed the half-blind mirrors.
The pale yellow varnish of the walls was shot through with erratic
cracks, and the colors of the faces and the flowers died away upon
the panels. . . . Frau von Wulckow shut a little door, through which
somebody seemed to enter, a shepherdess with a beribboned staff.
She shut the door very carefully, so that the performance would
not be disturbed, but a little cloud of dust arose, as if it were
powder from the hair of the painted shepherdess.

"This building is so romantic," whispered Frau von Wulckow.
"Don't you think so, Dr. Hessling? When one looks at oneself in
the mirror here, one fancies one is wearing a crinoline." At this
Diederich, more and more bewildered, looked at her evening gown.
Her bare shoulders were hollow and rather stooped, her hair a
Slavic white-blonde, and she wore a pince-nez.

"You fit these surroundings perfectly, Madame . . . Countess,"
he corrected, and he was rewarded with a smile for this bold flat-
tery. Not everyone would have reminded Frau von Wulckow so
diplomatically that before her marriage she had been a countess
Züsewitz by birth!

"As a matter of fact," she said, "it is hard to believe that in its
time this building was erected not for aristocrats, but only for the
good citizens of Netzig." She smiled indulgently.

"Yes, that is funny," confirmed Diederich, bowing and scraping.
"But today, only a countess such as yourself can truly feel at
home here."

"I am sure you have a feeling for the beautiful," Frau von Wulckow hazarded, and as Diederich admitted it, she declared he must
not miss the first act altogether, but must look through the crack
in the door. For some time she had been showing obvious signs of
impatience, and with her fan she pointed in the direction of the
stage. "Major Kunze will go off in a moment. He is not very good,
but it can't be helped, he is on the Club committee, and was the
first to point out to these people the artistic significance of my
work." While Diederich had no trouble in recognizing the Major,
who had not changed his appearance in the least, the authoress
with lightning fluency gave him a synopsis of what had gone before.
The young peasant girl, with whom Kunze was speaking, was his
natural daughter, that is, the daughter of a Count, and for that
reason the play was called "The Secret Countess." As gruff as ever,

he was just explaining the circumstances to her. He was also telling her of his intention to marry her to a poor cousin and leave her one-half of his possessions. On that account, after he had gone, there was great rejoicing on the part of the girl and her foster mother, the good wife of the tenant-farmer.

"Who is that dreadful person?" asked Diederich, without thinking. Frau von Wulckow looked astonished.

"She's the one from the Municipal Theater who always plays the comical old lady. We had nobody else who could play the part, but my niece rather likes acting with her."

Diederich started in horror, for it was the niece he had referred to as a dreadful person. "Your niece is absolutely charming," he hastened to assure her and smiled delightedly at the fat, red face, which seemed to rest directly on the shoulders—and they were Wulckow's shoulders! "And she has plenty of talent, too," he added to be on the safe side. Frau von Wulckow whispered: "Just watch"—and Jadassohn came out from the wings. What a surprise! His clothes were freshly pressed and with his fashionably cut morning coat he wore an immense ascot, upon which a red stone of imposing dimensions glittered. But however bright its glow, Jadassohn's ears glowed even more brightly. As his head was closely cropped and very flat, his ears stood out and illuminated his grandeur like two lamps. He swung his yellow-gloved hands about as if he were pleading for a sentence of many years' imprisonment. As a matter of fact, he was saying the most terrible things to the niece, who seemed thunderstruck, and to the comic lady who was bawling. . . . Frau von Wulckow whispered: "He is a bad character."

"I should say he is," said Diederich with conviction.

"Do you know my play?"

"Oh, I see. No. But I can guess what he wants to do."

The situation was that Jadassohn, who was the son and heir of the old Count Kunze, had been eavesdropping, and was not at all disposed to share with the niece the possessions with which God had endowed him. He demanded imperiously that she clear out, otherwise he would have her arrested as a fraudulent legatee and have Kunze declared non compos mentis.

"What a cad," said Diederich. "After all, she is his sister." The authoress explained to him:

"That is true, but, on the other hand, he is right in wanting to entail the estates. He is working for the good of the whole family, even though the individual must suffer. Of course, that is tragic for the secret countess."

"When you look at it properly—" Diederich was delighted. This aristocratic standpoint suited him perfectly, because he felt disinclined to give Magda a share in the business when she married.

"Countess, your play is excellent," he said, with deep conviction. But just then Frau von Wulckow anxiously seized his arm. There was a noise among the audience; chairs were scraped and people were sniggering and blowing their noses. "He is overdoing it," groaned the authoress. "I've told him time and again."

Jadassohn was acting outrageously. He had cornered the niece, together with the comical old lady, behind a table, and filled the whole stage with noisy demonstrations of his aristocratic personality. The more hostile the audience became, the more aggressively did he act his part. Now they were actually hissing. Several people had even turned toward the door behind which Frau von Wulckow was trembling, and were hissing. Perhaps it was only because the door was squeaking—but the authoress drew back, lost her glasses, and in helpless horror clawed the air, until Diederich restored them to her. He tried to console her. "This doesn't matter. Jadassohn goes off very soon, doesn't he?" He was listening through the closed door. "Yes, thank Heaven!" she cried, while her teeth chattered. "Now he has finished. Now my niece flees with the comical old lady and then Kunze returns, you see, with the Lieutenant."

"Is there a lieutenant in the play also?" asked Diederich, clearly impressed.

"Yes, that is to say, he is still at school; he is the son of Judge Sprezius. He is the poor relation, you see, whom the old Count wishes his daughter to marry. He promises the old man that he will search the whole world for the secret countess."

"Very naturally," said Diederich. "It is in his own interest to do so."

"You will see, he is a noble character."

"But Jadassohn, Countess. If you will allow me to say so, you should not have given him a part," said Diederich reproachfully and with secret satisfaction. "If only because of his ears."

Frau von Wulckow replied glumly:

"I did not think that they would be so visible on the stage. Do you think it will be a failure?"

"Countess!" Diederich laid his hand on his heart. "A play like 'The Secret Countess' cannot be spoiled so easily!"

"Isn't that so? In the theater it is artistic significance that counts."

"Certainly. But it must be admitted that ears like that have a great deal of influence." Diederich looked doubtful.

Frau von Wulckow cried pleadingly:

"And the second act is so much better. It takes place in the house of an upstart manufacturer, where the secret countess is engaged as housemaid. They have a music teacher, a vulgar person, who has even kissed one of the daughters, and he now proposes to the countess, but she naturally rejects him. A music teacher! How could she?"

Diederich agreed that it was out of the question.

"But now you will see how tragic it becomes. The daughter who allowed the music teacher to kiss her becomes engaged to a lieutenant at a dance, and when the lieutenant comes to the house, it is the same lieutenant who—"

"Good heavens, Countess!" Diederich stretched out his hands in self-defense, quite excited by so many complications. "How do you think of such things?"

The authoress smiled passionately.

"Yes, it is that which is most interesting. Afterwards one doesn't know how it happens. It is worked out so mysteriously in one's mind! Sometimes I think I must have inherited the gift."

"Have you had so many authors in your respected family?"

"Not exactly. But if my great ancestor had not won the battle of Kröchenwerda, who knows if I should have written 'The Secret Countess'? In the end, it is always a question of bloodline."

Diederich bowed and scraped when he heard the name of the battle and did not dare to continue the subject.

"Now the curtain ought to fall any moment," said Frau von Wulckow. "Do you hear anything?"

He could hear nothing. The authoress alone was oblivious of the door and the walls. "Now the lieutenant is vowing eternal fidelity to the distant countess," she whispered. "Now"—and all the blood drained from her face. Immediately it flowed back with a rush. People were applauding, not vigorously but still it was applause. The door was opened from inside. In the background the curtain had risen again, and when young Sprezius and the Wulckows' niece came forward, the applause was more animated.

Suddenly Jadassohn shot out from the wings, planted himself in front of the pair and looked as if he would take all the applause for himself—whereupon the audience hissed. Frau von Wulckow turned away indignantly. To Mayor Scheffelweis's mother-in-law and to Frau Harnisch, who were congratulating her, she declared: "Herr Jadassohn is impossible as Public Prosecutor. I shall tell my husband so."

The ladies at once began to spread the news of this verdict, to great effect. The gallery of mirrors was suddenly filled with knots of people criticizing Jadassohn's ears. "The play is well written, but Jadassohn's ears . . ." But when it became known that he would not appear in the second act, people were disappointed. Wolfgang Buck, with Guste Daimchen, came up to Diederich. "Have you heard the latest?" he asked. "Jadassohn is to issue a writ and confiscate his own ears." Diederich answered coldly: "I do not make jokes about another's misfortune," and as he said this he carefully watched the glances being cast upon Buck and his companion. Faces everywhere came to life at the sight of this couple. Jadassohn was forgotten. From the doorway the high-pitched voice of Professor Kühnchen was heard above the din saying something that sounded like "infernal outrage." When Frau Zillich laid her hand entreatingly upon his arm he turned in their direction, and could be heard distinctly: "It is an absolute outrage!"

Guste looked around and her eyes narrowed. "There they are talking about it too," she said mysteriously.

"About what?" stammered Diederich.

"Oh, we know all about that. And I also know who began it."

Diederich broke into a perspiration. "What on earth is wrong with you?" asked Guste. Buck, who was eyeing the refreshment room through a side door, said calmly:

"Hessling is a cautious politician; he does not like to hear that while on the one hand the Mayor is a devoted husband, he cannot, on the other hand, refuse his mother-in-law anything."

Diederich blushed a deep crimson. "That is an awfully low blow! How could anyone think of anything so low?"

Guste giggled violently, but Buck remained unmoved. "In the first place, it appears to be a fact, since Her Ladyship caught the two of them by surprise and told a friend about it. But in any case, it was self-evident."

Guste remarked: "Well, Dr. Hessling, you would never have guessed such a thing, of course." As she said this she gave her fiancé a tender smile. Diederich glared. "Aha!" he said severely. "I believe I've heard enough!" And he turned on his heels. So they themselves were inventing scandals, and about the Mayor at that! Diederich felt he could hold his head high. He made for Kühnchen's group, which was steering towards the refreshment room, leaving behind a wake of moral indignation. The Mayor's mother-in-law, purple in the face, swore that "this crew" would in future see her house only from the outside. Several of the ladies seconded the resolution, in spite of the misgivings expressed by the department store owner Herr Cohn, who, in the absence of further information, doubted the whole story, because a moral lapse of that kind by a tried old Liberal like Herr Buck seemed inconceivable. Professor Kühnchen, on the other hand, was of the opinion that radicalism, when taken too far, posed a threat to the very moral fiber of the community. Even Dr. Heuteufel, although he had instituted the freethought Sunday celebrations, remarked that old Buck had never lacked a sense of family, of nepotism, he might say. "You can all easily recall cases in point. That he should now try to marry his illegitimate with his legitimate offspring, in order to keep the money in the family, I should diagnose medically as the senile manifestation of a natural tendency hitherto repressed." At this the ladies looked shocked and the Pastor's wife sent Käthchen to the cloakroom to fetch her handkerchief.

On her way Käthchen passed Guste Daimchen, but Käthchen bowed her head and did not speak to her. Guste seemed crushed. In the refreshment room people noticed this and expressions of disapproval were mixed with sympathy. Guste was now to learn what it meant to defy public morality. It might have been remembered in her favor that she perhaps had been deceived and influenced for evil. But Frau Daimchen knew the exact circumstances and she had been warned! The Mayor's mother-in-law described her visit to Guste's mother, and her vain efforts, by pointed allusion, to wring a confession from the hardened old lady, whose youthful dream would doubtless be realized by a legitimate connection with the Buck family! . . .

"Well, but what about Herr Buck, barrister-at-law?" screeched Kühnchen. As a matter of fact, who did he think believed that he was not fully acquainted with this new scandal connected with his family? Was he not aware of the offenses of the Lauer household? And yet he did not hesitate to wash the dirty linen of his sister and his brother-in-law in a public courtroom, simply so that he would be talked about. Dr. Heuteufel, who wanted to justify after the fact his own attitude during the trial, declared: "That man is no defense attorney, he is a comedian!" When Diederich raised the point that Buck, after all, had definite, if arguable, views in politics and morals he was told: "You, Dr. Hessling, are his friend. That you should defend him is to your credit, but you cannot convince us." Whereupon Diederich retired with a worried look, but not without a glance at the editor, Nothgroschen, who was modestly chewing a ham sandwich and was listening to everything.

All of a sudden there was dead silence, for in the room near the stage old Herr Buck could be seen surrounded by a group of young girls. Apparently he was explaining the paintings on the walls, the life of former times, the faded gaiety of which enveloped the whole room, with the periphery of the town as it used to be, with meadows and gardens long since vanished, and all the people who were once the reveling masters of this festive house, and were now banished into the depths of old memories by the generation which was reveling at this very moment . . . It actually seemed as if the old man and the girls were now imitating the figures. Just above them was a picture of the town gate, and a gentleman in his wig and chain of office was coming out, the same man who stood in marble at the head of the stairs. In the lovely wood full of flowers, which may very well have stood where the Gausenfeld paper factory now was, bright children were dancing toward him, throwing a wreath about him, with which they tried to turn him around. The glow of rosy little clouds fell upon his happy face. Old Buck was at this moment smiling just as happily, as he let himself be dragged hither and thither by the girls, who had encircled him like a living wreath. His lightheartedness was incomprehensible, and a downright irritation. Had he stifled his conscience to such a degree that his illegitimate daughter. . . .

"*Our* daughters are not illegitimate children," said Frau Cohn. "My Sidonie arm-in-arm with Guste Daimchen! . . ."

Buck and his young friends did not notice that they were standing at the end of a space cleared of people. A hostile crowd had formed a solid wall; eyes were gleaming and anger rose. "That family has been on top far too long! One of them is now safe in jail. The turn of number two will soon come!" . . . "He's quite the pied piper, isn't he?" someone grumbled; and from another corner: "I can't stand by and watch this any longer!" Two ladies impetuously broke out of the throng and quickly crossed the empty space.

The wife of Councillor Harnisch, rolling along in her red satin train, met Frau Cohn, in yellow, exactly at their common goal. With the same gesture the one seized her Sidonie and the other her Meta, and with obvious satisfaction they returned to their own group. "I nearly fainted," said Frau Zillich, when Käthchen fortunately turned up.

Good humor was restored and people joked about the old sinner, comparing him with the Count in Frau von Wulckow's play. Guste, of course, was not a secret countess; but one could sympathize with the characters in a story, in deference to the wife of the Governor. Besides, in the play, conditions were tolerable, for the countess was only going to marry her cousin, whereas Guste . . . !

Old Buck looked puzzled when he became aware that there was nobody near him except his prospective daughter-in-law and one of his nieces. Indeed, he was obviously embarrassed by the curious glances which were cast at him in his isolation. This was noticed and commented upon and even Diederich began to wonder if there wasn't, after all, some truth in the scandal his mother and sisters were spreading. He himself had become frightened, since he saw this phantom, which he himself had conjured forth, take tangible shape and become more and more threatening. This time it was not a mere nobody like Lauer. It was old Herr Buck, the most venerable figure of Diederich's childhood, the great man of the town, and the personification of its civic virtues—the man who had been condemned to death in Forty-Eight! In his own heart Diederich felt a revulsion against what he had begun. Besides, it was folly; it would take more than this gossip to smash the old man. But if it ever came out who had started it, then Diederich would have to be prepared to see everyone turn against him . . . At all events, he had aimed a stroke and it had not missed. Now it was no longer merely the family which was crumbling and which burdened the old man: the brother on the verge of bankruptcy, the son-in-law in jail, the daughter away on a trip with her lover, and the two sons, one degraded to the level of a peasant, and the other suspect on account of his life and opinions. Now the position of old Buck himself was beginning to be shaken, for the first time. Down with him so that Diederich might rise! Nevertheless, Diederich was frightened to the very pit of his stomach. He got up to inspect the anterooms.

Running to resume his place—the bell was ringing for the second act—he ran into the Mayor's mother-in-law, who for a different reason was in every bit of a hurry as he was. She came just in time to prevent her son-in-law, who was being steered by his wife, from approaching Buck senior and shielding him with his authority. "To hide such a scandal with your authority as mayor!" She was hoarse with agitation. The Mayor's wife, however, maintained in her shrill little voice that the Bucks were the most distinguished people here, after all; just yesterday Milli Buck had given her a marvelous dress pattern. With clandestine blows, each drove him to her own side; he agreed with each by turns, his pale side-whiskers flying left and right and his rabbitlike eyes twitching. Passers-by nudged each other and repeated as a joke, in whispers, what Diederich had learned from Wolfgang Buck. In the middle of such important proceedings he forgot his stomachache, stopped in his tracks and executed a defiant bow. The Mayor mustered his composure, took leave of his ladies, and gave Diederich his hand. "My dear Dr. Hessling, what a pleasure to see you, the festivities are quite a success, wouldn't you say?"

But Diederich showed not the slightest inclination to indulge the empty cordiality so loved by Dr. Scheffelweis. He drew himself up like Destiny itself and glared. "Your Honor, I feel I would not be justified in keeping you in the dark about certain things which—"

"Which. . . ?" asked Dr. Scheffelweis, having turned quite pale.

"Which have been occurring," replied Diederich, not without severity. The Mayor pleaded for mercy. "But I already know. It's that terribly unfortunate affair concerning our esteemed—that is to say, that filthy scandal with old Buck," he whispered ingratiatingly. Diederich remained cold.

"There's more. Don't deceive yourself, Your Honor; it involves you."

"Young man, I must ask you. . ."

"I place myself at your disposal, Your Honor."

Dr. Scheffelweis was mistaken if he hoped that he could pass up this cup more easily with resistance than with entreaties! He was in Diederich's hand; the mirrored gallery had emptied; the two ladies, too, disappeared into the crowd.

"Buck and his comrades are mounting a counteroffensive," Diederich commented matter-of-factly. They've been unmasked and now they're getting revenge."

"On me?" The Major jumped.

"Slander, I repeat: vicious slander is being spread about you. No one in his right mind would believe it, but in these times of political struggle—"

Rather than finishing his sentence, he shrugged his shoulders. Dr. Scheffelweis had become visibly smaller. He wanted to look at Diederich, but was compelled to avert his gaze. At this, Diederich took on the voice of the Court.

"Your Honor! Surely you remember our initial conference at your house, with Assessor Jadassohn. At that time, I informed you of the new spirit which would be taking our city by storm. The flabby democratic attitude has proved its impotence! Nowadays one must be strictly national! You were warned!"

Dr. Scheffelweis attempted to explain himself.

"Deep down, I've always been on your side, my dear friend. All the more since I am a particular admirer of His Majesty. Our splendid young Emperor is such an original thinker. . . impulsive . . . and. . . ."

"The most personal personality," added Diederich sharply.

The Mayor repeated: "Personality. . . . But I, who must always look to both sides of every issue, even today I can only repeat: you try and change the facts!"

"And my trial? I thoroughly smashed the enemies of His Majesty!"

"I did not impede you in any way. I even congratulated you."

"Not to my knowledge."

"Silently, at least."

"Nowadays one must come to a decision openly, Your Honor. His Majesty has said it himself: Anyone who is not for me is against me! It is time our citizens awakened from their slumber and lent their hands to the battle against the revolutionary elements!"

At this, Dr. Scheffelweis lowered his eyes. Diederich drew himself up all the more imperiously.

"But where does that leave Your Honor?" he asked, and his question reverberated in the threatening silence until Dr. Scheffelweis decided it was time to venture a friendly squint. He was not actually able to bring forth any words; the sight of Diederich—with glaring eyes, bristling, blond, and bloated—left him dumbstruck. His mind aflutter, he thought: "On the one hand—on the other hand"—squinting all the while at the embodiment of the new generation that knew what it wanted, at the representative of the tough times to come!

Diederich, the corners of his mouth turned down, accepted the homage. He savored one of the moments in which he signified more than himself, in which he acted in the spirit of one higher than himself. The Mayor was taller than he, but Diederich looked down upon him as though he were perched upon a throne. "The Town Council elections are coming up: everything will depend on you," he intoned tersely, as though issuing a reprieve. "The Lauer trial has turned the tide of public opinion. People are afraid of me. Whoever who wants to help me is welcome; anyone who opposes me——"

Dr. Scheffelweis did not wait for the rest. "I agree with you completely. Friends of Herr Buck must not be elected any more."

"That lies in your very own interest. People of unsound opinions are undermining your good reputation, Your Honor! Would you be able to survive today if those of sound opinions were no longer to speak out against this scandalous libel?" There was a pause, during which Dr. Scheffelweis trembled, and then Diederich repeated reassuringly: "Everything will depend on you alone."—The Mayor mumbled: "With all due respect to your energy and your sound views—"

"My unimpeachable views!"

"Yes, quite. . . . But you are a political hotspur, my young friend. This town is not yet ready for you. How will you cope with the situation here?"

Instead of answering, Diederich took a sudden step backward and began bowing and scraping. In the doorway stood Wulckow.

He came up, his paunch swinging with majestic elasticity from side to side, laid his black-bristled paw on the shoulder of Dr. Scheffelweis and said in stentorian tones: "Well, my little Mayor, all alone here? I suppose your town councillors have thrown you out?" Dr. Scheffelweis answered with a feeble laugh. But Diederich looked around anxiously at the door of the large room, which was still open. He went up in front of Wulckow, so that the latter could not be seen from the other room, and whispered something in his ear, with the result that the Governor turned away and adjusted his clothing. Then he said to Deiderich: "'Pon my soul, you really are very serviceable, Doctor."

Diederich felt flattered and smiled. "Your appreciation, Governor, makes me happy."

Wulckow graciously remarked: "No doubt there are a lot of other things you can tell me. We must talk things over some time." He thrust forward his face, liver-spotted and with high Slavic cheekbones, and stared at Diederich from the depths of his Mongolian eyes, which were full of warm-blooded, impish violence. He stared until Diederich became breathless from sheer nervousness. This result seemed to satisfy Wulckow. He brushed his beard in front of the mirror, but immediately pressed it down on his shirt front, for he carried his head like a bull. "Well, let's go! It looks like this racket is about to start up again." With Diederich and the Mayor on either side he set out energetically to disturb the performance. Then a piping voice from the refreshment room was heard: "Good Heavens, Otto dear!" "Oh, there she is," growled Wulckow, as he went to meet his wife. "I might have guessed. When things come to a head she is always afraid. More dash, my dear Frieda!"

"Gracious, Otto darling, I am so horribly frightened."

Turning to the two other gentlemen, she chatted easily, even if her voice betrayed a tremble. "I know one ought to go into the battle with a more joyful heart."

"Especially," said Diederich, not missing a beat, "when it is already won," and he made a chivalrous bow. Frau von Wulckow tapped him with her fan.

"Dr. Hessling kept me company out here during the first act. He has a remarkable aesthetic sense and even gives one useful hints." "I have noticed that myself," said Wulckow, while Diederich kept bowing alternately to him and to his wife, overflowing with gratitude. "We should just stay right here near the buffet," the Governor added.

"That was also my plan of campaign," confided Frau von Wulckow, "the more so as I have now discovered that there is a little door which opens into the large room. In this way we can enjoy the isolation from what is happening, which I need, and yet keep in touch with things."

"My little Mayor," said Wulckow, smacking his lips, "you ought to get some of that lobster salad." He pulled Dr. Scheffelweis's ear, and added: "In that matter of the Labor Exchange, the Town Council has again cut a very poor figure."

The Mayor was eating obediently and listening obediently, while Diederich stood beside Frau von Wulckow and peered out at the stage. There Magda Hessling was having a music lesson and the teacher, a black-haired virtuoso, was giving her passionate kisses, which she did not appear to resent particularly. "It's a good thing Kienast is not here," thought Diederich, but even on his own account he felt offended, and he remarked:

"Don't you think, Countess, that the music teacher's acting is too realistic?"

Taken aback, the authoress answered: "That was precisely my intention."

"I only meant . . ." Diederich stammered, and then he started, for on the stage Frau Hessling appeared in the doorway, or a lady who looked like her. Emmi came in too and the two women were crying and screaming. Wulckow was obliged to raise his voice:

"Oh, no, Mayor. You won't be able to use old Buck as your scapegoat this time. Even if he did manage to push through the municipal Labor Exchange, the important thing now is how it is used. That is your responsibility."

Dr. Scheffelweis tried to speak but on the stage Magda shouted that she had no intention of marrying the man, the servant-girl was good enough for him. The authoress remarked:

"She should say that in a much more vulgar way. They are only *parvenus*."

Diederich smiled in agreement, although he was terribly humiliated by such a state of affairs in a home on the stage that was like his own. In his own mind he thought Emmi was quite right when she declared there must be no scandal and sent for the servant. But when the latter appeared, hang it all, it was the Secret Countess! In the silence brought about by her entrance, Wulckow's bass voice boomed out:

"Don't come to me with your eyewash about social responsibilities! I suppose you find it socially responsible to lead our agriculture into ruin?"

Several people in the audience turned around; the authoress whispered anxiously: "Otto, for heaven's sake!"

"What's the matter?" He stepped into the doorway. "Let's hear them hiss now!"

No one hissed. He turned once more to the Mayor:

"With your Labor Exchange, you're going to draw away all the workers from those of us with estates in the East, that much is certain. And furthermore, you even have workers' representatives in your miserable Labor Exchange—and you hook people up with jobs in agriculture on top of it all. So what are you paving the way for? For the coalition of agricultural workers. Do you see, my little Mayor?" His paw fell onto Dr. Scheffelweis's pliant shoulder. "We're on to your tricks. We won't tolerate them!"

On the stage the Wulckows' niece then addressed herself to the public, as the manufacturer's family was not supposed to hear her:

"What! I, the daughter of a count, am to marry a music teacher? Never, even if they should promise me a trousseau. Others may debase themselves for money, but I know what I owe to my noble birth!"

At this there was applause. Frau Harnisch and Frau Tietz were observed wiping away the tears which the Countess's nobility of mind had provoked. But their tears flowed again when the niece said:

"But, alas, where shall I, as a servant, find one so well born as myself?"

The Mayor must have dared to retort, for Wulckow rumbled: "I will not allow myself to be bled dry for the sake of lowering the unemployment rate. My money is my money."

Diederich could not not restrain himself from thanking him with a bow. But the authoress as well correctly inferred the bow as referring to herself.

"I know," she said, herself moved, "I did a good job with that scene."

"That is art that speaks to the heart," Diederich declared. As Magda and Emmi slammed the piano and the door shut, he added: "And highly dramatic as well." Hereupon he spoke to the other side:

"Next week two Town Council members will be elected to take the places of Lauer and Buck junior. It's a good thing he's going of his own accord." Wulckow said: "Then just make sure that decent people are elected. They say you have good connections to the *Netzig Journal.*"

Diederich lowered his voice to a confidential whisper: "I'm holding back for the time being. It's better for the national cause."

"Well, well, would you look at that," said Wulckow, and indeed he looked at Diederich, with a penetrating gaze. "I suppose you want to run for the post yourself?" he asked.

"I would make the sacrifice. Our municipal legislative bodies have too few members who are reliable in a national sense. . . ."

"And what will you do when you're elected?"

"Make sure that the Labor Exchange is put out of commission."

"Ah yes," said Wulckow, "as a nationally minded man."

"As an officer," said the Lieutenant on the stage, "I cannot, my dear Magda, allow this girl to be badly treated, even if she is only a poor servant."

The Lieutenant who had already appeared in the first act, the poor cousin who was to marry the Secret Countess, was Magda's fiancé! The audience was trembling with excitement. Even the authoress noticed it. "Inventiveness is one of my strongest points," she said to Diederich, who was indeed amazed. But Dr. Scheffelweis had no time to abandon himself to the emotions of the drama. He saw the danger he was in.

"No one," he asserted, "would more enthusiastically embrace a spirit—" Wulckow interrupted him.

"We've heard that before, my little Mayor. You're good at enthusiastic embraces when they don't cost anything."

Diederich added: "But to draw a sharp line between the loyal ones and the revolution!"

The Mayor raised his arms in a pleading gesture. "Gentlemen! Do not misunderstand me, I am prepared to take any and all necessary measures. But such a sharp line will do no good at all, for here it will mean merely that almost all of those who do not vote Liberal will vote Social Democrat."

Wulckow gave an angry grunt, whereupon he fetched himself a sausage from the buffet. Diederich was the one to express absolute confidence.

"If favorable election results don't come by themselves, they'll just have to be created!"

"But how?" asked Wulckow.

The Wulckow's niece, on the other hand, was shouting to the public:

"Surely he must see that I am a Countess, he who comes from the same noble lineage!"

"Oh, Countess," said Diederich, "I am just dying to know whether he will recognize their relationship."

"Of course," replied the authoress. "They recognize each other because of their finer manners." Indeed, the Lieutenant and the niece were exchanging glances, because Emmi, Magda, and Frau Hessling were eating cheese with a knife. Diederich was openmouthed. The vulgar demeanor of the manufacturer's family evoked the greatest amusement in the audience. The Buck girls, Frau Cohn, and Guste Daimchen were all delighted. Even Wulckow became interested. He licked the grease from his fingers and said to his wife: "You're out of the woods, Frieda: they're laughing."

Indeed, the authoress had brightened up considerably. Her dazed eyes glittered behind her pince-nez, she sighed, her bosom swelled, and restlessness drove her from her chair. She leaned cautiously out of the doorway to the buffet room; immediately a number of people turned around to face her with unconcealed curiosity, and the Mayor's mother-in-law made a sign to her. Frau von Wulckow called feverishly over shoulder:

"Gentlemen, the battle is won!"

"If only it would happen so quickly with us," said her husband. "So then, Doctor, how do you intend to rein in the Netzigers?"

"Your Excellency!" Diederich pressed his hand to his heart. "Netzig will become loyal to the Emperor. I guarantee it with all that I am and all that I have!"

"I'm glad to hear it," said Wulckow.

"For we have an agitator," Diederich continued, "whom I would like to characterize as first-class; yes indeed, first-class," he repeated, encompassing with the word all that is great; "and that agitator is His Majesty himself!"

Dr. Scheffelweis quickly collected his wits. "The most personal personality," he ventured. "Original. Impulsive."

"Hm," said Wulckow. He planted his fists on his knees and stared between them at the floor, in the attitude of a troubled cannibal. All at once, the other two realized that he was leering at them from below.

"Gentlemen"—he hesitated again—, "well, I've got something to tell you. I think the *Reichstag* is about to be dissolved."

Diederich and Dr. Scheffelweis thrust their heads forward, they whispered: "Your Excellency knows—?"

"The Minister of War was on a hunting trip with me recently, at the estate of my cousin's, Herr von Quitzin."

Diedrich bowed. He stammered something, even he did not know what. He had predicted it! Back then, at his initiation into the Veterans' Association, he had recounted His Majesty's speech—and had he merely recounted it? It had contained expressly the phrase "I'll clear out the whole *Reichstag*!" And now it was to happen, just as if he himself were performing the action. A mystical thrill shot through him. Meanwhile, Wulckow was saying:

"Eugen Richter and his consorts no longer suit us. If they don't accept the military appropriations bill, it's over,"—and Wulckow wiped his mouth with his fist, as if the feeding frenzy were about to begin.

Diederich regained his composure, "That is—that is a most far-seeing attitude! That is most certainly the personal initiative of His Majesty himself!" Dr. Scheffelweis had turned quite pale. "That means that *Reichstag* elections will be held again? And I was so glad that we had our tried and true representatives in office. . ." He received a deeper shock. "That is, of course, Kühlemann is also a friend of His Honor Judge. . ."

"A grumbler!" Diederich snorted. "A man without a fatherland!" He rolled his eyes. "Your Excellency! This time, it is all over in Netzig for those people. Just wait until I am on the Town Council, Your Honor!"—"What do you propose to do then?" asked Wulckow. Diederich did not know. Fortunately, an incident occurred inside the auditorium; chairs were moved about, and someone had opened the large door. It was Kühlemann himself. The old man dragged his heavy, ailing bulk rapidly through the mirrored gallery. The people standing about the buffet remarked that his condition had deteriorated even more since the trial.

"He would rather have acquitted Lauer, the other judges outvoted him," said Diederich. Dr. Scheffelweis observed: "It seems that kidneystones lead in the end to dissolution." To which Wulckow quipped: "Well, then in the *Reichstag* we are his kidneystones."

The Mayor laughed obligingly. But Diederich opened his eyes wide. He leaned close to the Governor's ear and whispered:

"His will!"

"What about it?"

"He has made the town his beneficiary," Dr. Scheffelweis explained with an air of importance. "We will probably use the money to build a foundling hospital."

"That's what you're going to build?" Diederich sneered. "You couldn't come up with a more national purpose?"

"Ah yes, I see." Wulckow nodded to Diederich approvingly. "How big a bundle has he got?"

"At least a half a million," said the Mayor, and he declared: "I would be most happy if it were at all possible to—"

"No problem whatsoever," Diederich replied.

But then a laugh was heard of a very different kind. It was quite unrestrained and clearly expressed delight in someone's misfortune. The authoress retreated precipitately behind the buffet. She looked as if she would like to creep into the sideboard. "Gracious heavens," she whispered, "all is lost!" Her husband stood sternly at the door and said: "What's going on here!" but even this could not check the laughter. Magda had said to the Countess: "Hurry up, now, you silly country lout, and see that the Lieutenant gets his coffee." Another voice corrected, "tea." Magda repeated, "coffee," the other insisted and so did Magda. The public saw there was a misunderstanding between her and the prompter. Happily the Lieutenant intervened, clicked his spurs and said: "I'll take both"—whereupon the laughter took on a more well-meaning note. But the authoress was raging. "The public! It is and always will be a beast!" she snarled.

"Something can always go wrong," said Wulckow and winked at Diederich.

Diederich replied, just as significantly: "Not when there is mutual understanding, Your Excellency."

Hereupon he felt it advantageous to devote himself entirely to the authoress and her work. Even if the Mayor were to betray his friends and commit himself to all of Wulckow's wishes for the sake of the elections!

"My sister is a goose," said Diederich. "I shall tell her what I think of her afterwards."

Frau von Wulckow smiled deprecatingly. "The poor thing, she is doing her best. But the arrogance and ingratitude of the crowd is really intolerable. Only a moment ago my play had edified them and roused them to an enthusiasm for ideals."

"Countess," said Diederich with conviction, "you are not the only one to have this bitter experience. It is the same everywhere in public life." He was thinking of the general exaltation at the time of his clash with the man who insulted His Majesty, and of the trials which he subsequently suffered. "In the end the good cause triumphs," he said firmly.

"Isn't that so?" she agreed with a smile which seemed to break forth from the clouds. "The Good, the True, the Beautiful."

She held out her slender hand. "I believe, my friend, that we understand one another." Conscious of the occasion, Diederich boldly pressed it to his lips, and bowed. He placed his hand on his heart and declared from the depths of his soul: "You can trust me, Countess. . . ."

The niece and young Sprezius were now alone, had recognized one another as humiliated countess and poor cousin, knew now that they were destined for one another, and reveled together in visions of future splendor, when they would be illuminated, under a golden canopy, together with others similarly distinguished, in humble pride, by the sun of majesty. . . . Just then, Diederich heard the authoress heave a deep sigh.

"To you I can confess," she sighed. "I really do miss the Court. When one has belonged, as I have, to the Court nobility from birth—. And now—"

Diederich saw two tears pearl up behind her pince-nez. He was so deeply shaken by the view afforded him into the tragedy of the great ones that he stood at attention. "Countess!" he breathed incredulously. "So the secret countess is actually—" He faltered in his shock.

At this point, the Mayor's feeble voice was divulging to the Governor that Kühlemann would not be running again in the upcoming election and that the Liberals planned to nominate Dr. Heuteufel. He and Wulckow agreed that countermeasures had to be taken before anyone began to suspect that the *Reichstag* would be dissolved. . . .

Diederich ventured once more, delicately:

"But Countess, it will all turn out well, won't it? They'll be united in the end, won't they?"

Frau von Wulckow, with tact and composure, curtailed the familiarity with which she had expressed her feelings. In a light, breezy tone she explained:

"Well, my dear Dr. Hessling, what can one do? It's that confounded money problem! I just don't see how the young couple can ever be happy together."

"They could sue, couldn't they?" cried Diederich, his sense of justice offended. But Frau von Wulckow wrinkled her nose contemptuously. "Fi donc! That would only result in the young Count, Jadassohn, that is, having his father legally incapacitated. In the third act, which you are about to see, he threatens the Lieutenant that he will do just that in a scene which I believe has turned out quite well. How could the Lieutenant ever answer for such a thing? And to chop up the family inheritance like that? Perhaps that would do in your circles. But among us certain things are simply not possible."

Diederich bowed. "Up there with you there prevail notions which are naturally beyond our judgement. And beyond that of the courts as well," he added. The authoress smiled indulgently.

"Do you see? The Lieutenant renounces the Secret Countess, quite correctly, and marries the manufacturer's daughter."

"Magda?"

"Indeed. And the Secret Countess marries the piano teacher. That is what the powers that be demand, my dear Dr. Hessling, powers to whom *we*"—her voice took on a somewhat darker tone—"simply have to submit."

Diederich still harbored a doubt, but he did not express it. The Lieutenant should have married the Secret Countess even without money; this would have gratified deeply Diederich's soft and idyllic heart. But alas! These tough times thought differently.

The curtain fell, the audience slowly extricated itself from the grip of its emotion and then expressed its feelings all the more deeply by applauding the servant-girl and the Lieutenant who, it was unfortunately evident, would have to bear still longer with the cruel fate of not being received at Court.

"What a truly wretched fate!" sighed Frau Harnisch and Frau Cohn.

At the buffet, Wulckow said, at the close of his deliberations with the Mayor:

"We'll give that motley crew a lesson in sound opinions!"

Then he let his paw drop heavily onto Diederich's shoulder. "Well, little Doctor, has my wife invited you to tea yet?"

"By all means, and do come soon!" The Governor's wife held out her hand for a kiss, and Diederich took his leave in high spirits. Wulckow himself wanted to see him again! Together with Diederich he wanted to conquer Netzig!

While the Governor's wife was holding a reception in the mirrored gallery and receiving congratulations, Diederich tried to drum up enthusiasm for the play. Heuteufel, Cohn, Harnisch and several gentlemen made his task difficult, for they let it be understood, though cautiously, that they considered the play ridiculous. Diederich had to give them hints about the absolutely first-rate third act, in order to shut them up. He dictated a detailed account of what the authoress had told him to Nothgroschen, who had to leave, as the paper was going to press. "If you write any nonsense, you damned penny-a-liner, I'll box your ears with that rag of yours!" Nothgroschen thanked him and took his leave. Professor Kühnchen, who was listening, buttonholed Diederich and screeched: "I say, old man, there's one thing you forgot to tell our gossip-monger." The editor, hearing himself mentioned, returned, and Kühnchen continued: "I mean that the magnificent story by our honored hostess has been anticipated, and by no less a person than our old master Goethe in his *Natural Daughter*. Now, that is the highest praise that can be given to the authoress!"

Diederich had his doubts about the appropriateness of Kühnchen's discovery, but did not think it necessary to mention them. The little old man was already fighting his way through the throng, his hair billowing wildly, and he could be seen stopping in front of Frau von Wulckow, scraping a leg and explaining to her the result of his researches into comparative literature. The rebuff he experienced could not have been foreseen, even by Diederich. The authoress said in icy tones: "There must be some mistake in what you say, Professor. Is the *Natural Daughter* by Goethe at all?" she asked, turning up her nose suspiciously. Kühnchen assured her that it was, but in vain.

"In any case, you have read a novel by me, in the magazine, *The Beloved Home,* and that is what I have now dramatized. My stories are all original work. You gentlemen"—she looked round—"will certainly deny any malicious rumors to the contrary."

There upon Kühnchen was dismissed, and withdrew gasping. In a tone of condescending sympathy Diederich reminded him of Nothgroschen, who had gone off with his dangerous information, and Kühnchen tore after him to prevent the worst.

When Diederich turned around again, the scene in the room had altered. Not only the Governor's wife, but old Buck was holding a reception. It was amazing what one was learning about these people. They could not bear the idea that they had previously given free rein to their instincts. With expressions protesting innocence, one person after another came up to the old gentleman, and tried to look as if they had done nothing. So great, even after such cataclysmic upheavals, was the power of that which has always prevailed, of that which has been held in esteem since time immemorial! Diederich himself found it advisable not to remain too noticeably out of step with the majority. After he had made sure that Wulckow had gone, he went up to pay his compliments to Buck. The old man was sitting alone in an armchair which had been placed for him up in front near the stage. He let his white hand hang over the arm in a curiously tender attitude and looked up at Diederich.

"There you are, my dear Hessling. I have often regretted that you never came"—he said it so simply and considerately that Diederich felt tears again coming immediately to his eyes. He gave him his hand and was glad when Herr Buck held it a little longer than was necessary. He began to stammer something about business troubles and "to tell the honest truth"—for he was suddenly seized with a strong desire for truth—about misgivings and fears.

"It is fine of you," said the old man, "not to let me guess that, but to confess it. You are young and are probably affected by the impulses which men's minds follow nowadays. I will not give in to the intolerance of old age."

Diederich's eyes were downcast, for he understood that this was forgiveness for the trial which had taken away the civic honors of the old man's son-in-law. He felt uncomfortable in the face of such mildness—and such an open lack of regard. The old man, however, continued:

"I respect a fight and know too much to hate anyone who is against my friends." At this Diederich, seized with fear lest this should lead too far, took refuge in denial. He hardly knew himself . . . you get into things. . . . The old man made it easy for him. "I know, you are seeking and have not yet found yourself."

His white curly beard was sunk in his silk neckerchief. When he raised his head Diederich saw that something new was coming.— "You haven't bought the house behind yours after all," he said. "I suppose you have changed your plans?"

Diederich thought: "He knows everything," and feared that his most secret plans had been laid bare.

Herr Buck smiled slyly and yet kindly. "Perhaps you will shortly be moving the site of your factory, and then making your extensions. I can imagine you would like to sell the site and are waiting for a certain opportunity—of which I, too, am taking account," he added, and with a glance at Diederich: "The town is thinking of erecting a foundling hospital."

"Old cur!" thought Diederich. "He's speculating on the death of his best friend!" At the same time, however, he was struck by the inspiration of what he could suggest to Wulckow so that they might conquer Netzig! . . . He gasped.

"Not at all, Herr Buck. I will not surrender the family property."

Then the old man took his hand again. "I will not tempt you," he said. "Your family feeling does you credit."

"Silly ass!" thought Diederich.

"Then we must look for another site. Indeed, you will perhaps help us. We do not want to discourage any man's unselfish desire to serve the community, my dear Hessling, even though he seems momentarily to be working in the wrong direction."

He stood up.

"If you run for the Town Council I will support you."

Diederich stared, unable to understand him. The old man's eyes were blue and deep, and he was offering Diederich the public office of which Diederich had deprived his son-in-law. He did not know whether to spit in disgust, or crawl away in shame. He decided it was preferable to click his heels and politely tender his thanks.

"You see," the old man resumed, "a sense of public service bridges the gap between young and old, and extends even beyond to those who are no longer with us."

He moved his hands in a semicircle towards the walls where the people of former times, faded but full of gaiety, seemed to step out of their painted background. He smiled at the young girls in their hoop skirts, and also at one of his nieces and Meta Harnisch, who were passing. When he turned his face towards the old Mayor, who was coming through the city gate, amidst flowers and children, Diederich noticed the similarity between them. Old Buck pointed out one portrait and then another from the painted assembly.

"I have heard a great deal about that man. I used to know that lady. Doesn't the clergyman look like Pastor Zillich? No, there can never be any serious estrangement among the citizens of this town. For a long time past we have been jointly pledged to good will and our common progress, beginning with those who bequeathed to us this Harmony Club."

"Some harmony!" thought Diederich, as he looked about for an excuse to get away. The old gentleman, as usual, had made a transition from business to sentimental nonsense. "There he goes playing the poet again," Diederich thought.

Just then Guste Daimchen and Inge Tietz passed; Guste had taken her arm and Inge was bragging about her experiences behind the scenes. "We were awfully frightened when they kept on saying: 'tea, coffee, tea.'" Guste declared, "Next time Wolfgang will write a much finer play and I'll have a part." At this Inge disengaged her arm and assumed an expression of meek dissent. "Oh, you will, will you?" she said, and Guste's fat face at once lost its harmless air of enthusiasm. "Why not, may I ask?" she said with whining indignance. "What on earth is wrong with you again?"

Diederich, who could have told her, turned back hastily to old Buck, who prattled on. "The same friends, nowadays as in former times, and the same enemies are here as well. But that one has almost faded out, the armored knight, the children's bogy there in the niche near the gate. Don Antonio Manrique, a cruel cavalry general, who pillaged poor Netzig in the Thirty Years' War, where would even the faintest echo of his fame be, if Riekestrasse had not been named after him? . . He was another of those who did not like our desire for freedom and thought he could destroy us."

Suddenly a silent chuckle shook the old man. He took Diederich's hand.

"Don't you think he looks like our Herr von Wulckow?"

At this, Diederich's face took on a more solemn air, but the old man did not notice it. Now that he had once started, other things occurred to him. He motioned to Diederich to follow him behind an arrangement of plants, and showed him two figures on the wall, a young shepherd, whose arms were opened longingly, and on the other side of the brook a shepherdess, who was preparing to jump across. Herr Buck whispered: "What do you think? Do you believe they will meet? Very few people know that now, but I still remember." He looked round to make sure he was not being watched, then suddenly he opened a little door which nobody would ever have discovered. The shepherdess on the door moved towards her lover. A little more, and she would lie in his arms in the dark behind the door . . . The old man pointed to the room which he had revealed. "This is called the cabinet of love." The light of a lantern from some courtyard streamed through the uncurtained window, lit up the mirror and the spindle-legged sofa. Herr Buck drew a long breath of the musty air that wafted out after who knows how many years. He gave a forlorn smile and then shut the little door.

Diederich, who was not much interested in any of this, observed the approach of something that promised to be much more exciting. It was Judge Fritzsche who had arrived. His leave was probably over, he was back from the south, and he had put in an appearance, though rather late, and also without Judith Lauer, whose holiday would last as long as her husband was in prison. He wound his way self-consciously through the crowd, there was a great deal of whispering, and everyone whom he greeted stole a glance at old Herr Buck. Fritzsche doubtless realized that, under the circumstances, he would have to do something. He plucked up his courage and went ahead. The old man, who was still unaware of his presence, suddenly found Fritzsche in front of him. He turned completely white. Diederich was frightened and stretched out his arms, but nothing happened, the old man had regained his composure. He stood there, holding himself so stiffly erect that his back was hollow, and looked calmly and steadily at the man who had run off with his daughter.

"Back so soon, Judge?" he asked in a loud tone.

Fritzsche tried to laugh genially. "The weather was nicer down south, Herr Buck. And the art!"

"We have only a pale reflection of it here," and without taking his eyes off Fritzsche he motioned towards the walls. His demeanor made an impression on most of those who were watching eagerly for a sign of weakness. He maintained his bearing and upheld his public dignity in a situation where a lack of restraint would have been understandable. He stood for the old eminence, he alone represented his ruined family, and his following, which was conspicuously absent. In that moment he gained the sympathy of many new followers who replaced the many he had lost . . . Diederich heard him saying, in clear, formal tones: "I succeeded in having our modern street plan altered in order to save this house and these paintings. They may only have the value of descriptive records. But a picture which lends permanence to its own times and manners may hope for permanence itself." Then Diederich retreated; for he was ashamed on Fritzsche's account.

The Mayor's mother-in-law asked him what old Buck had said about "The Secret Countess." Diederich thought back, and had to confess that he had not mentioned the play at all. Both were disappointed.

Meanwhile he noticed that Käthchen Zillich was casting derisive glances his way, and she was the last one who should be allowing herself such liberties. "Well, Fräulein Käthchen," he said quite loudly, "What do you think of 'The Green Angel?'" She answered even more loudly: "'The Green Angel?' Would that be you?" And she laughed in his face. "You should really be more careful," he retorted, with furrowed brow. "I almost feel it is my duty to bring this to the attention of your father."

"Papa!" Käthchen called out immediately. Diederich started. Fortunately, Pastor Zillich had heard nothing.

"Of course I told my papa right away about our little excursion recently. What does it matter? It was only you."

She was going too far. Diederich gasped. "Yes, and for lovers of beautiful ears, Jadassohn was there as well." As he saw that this had hit home, he added: "Next time in 'The Green Angel' we'll paint them green, that'll be a lark."

"Fine, if you think it's the ears that matter." With this, Käthchen's face betrayed such boundless contempt that Diederich was determined to proceed with all the means at his disposal. They were standing by the arrangement of plants. "What do you think?" he asked. "Will the shepherdess jump across the brook and make the shepherd happy?"

"Sheep," she said. Diederich ignored the barb, walked up and felt around on the wall. He found the door. "Do you see? She jumps."

Käthchen came closer, her curiosity getting the better of her, and stuck her head into the secret room. Just one push and she was completely inside. Diederich slammed the door and fell wordlessly upon Käthchen, panting wildly.

"Let me out, I'll scratch!" she cried out and wanted to scream. But she had to laugh, which rendered her helpless and brought her closer and closer to the sofa. The struggle with her bared arms and shoulders drove him completely out of his senses. "That's right," he panted, "now you're going to get it. With each step he gained he repeated: "Now you're going to get it. Am I still a sheep? Aha, when you think a girl is decent, and you have upright intentions, then you're a sheep. Now you're going to get it." With one last effort he threw her down. "Ouch," she said, choking with laughter. "What am I going to get then?"

Suddenly her attempts to defend herself became serious. She struggled free; the stripe of gaslight let in by the bare window illuminated her disarray, and her face, swollen from her efforts, had turned toward the door. He turned his head: there stood Guste Daimchen. She stared at them aghast, Käthchen's eyes popped out of her head, and Diederich, kneeling on the sofa, craned his neck. . . . Finally, Guste pulled the door closed and walked resolutely up to Käthchen.

"You vulgar little tramp!" she said from her innermost depths.

"You're one yourself!" said Käthchen, quickly regaining her composure. Guste could only gasp for air. Her eyes, helpless and so outraged that they filled with a moist shimmer, turned from Käthchen to Diederich. He spoke: "Fräulein Guste, I assure you, this is all in jest," but his plea was ill received. Guste burst out: "I know you, this doesn't surprise me a bit."

"So, you know him," Käthchen sneered. She stood up, as Guste moved in even closer. Diederich, for his part, seized the opportunity to draw himself up with dignity and step back to let the ladies take care of the matter between themselves.

"The very thought of having to watch such a thing!" Guste cried out, and Käthchen: "You didn't see anything at all! Why were you even watching in the first place?"

Diederich, too, began to find this peculiar, especially since Guste had nothing to say. Käthchen had clearly gained the upper hand. She threw back her head and said: "I find it particularly strange coming from you. From someone with as much egg on your face as you do."

Guste's face registered immediate and deep alarm. "Me?" she asked slowly. "What have I done?"

Käthchen immediately turned coy—while Diederich was seized with anxiety.

"I'm sure you know quite well yourself. It's too embarrassing for me to even talk about."

"I don't know anything," whined Guste.

"Well, that's the limit; who would have thought it?" said Käthchen and turned up her nose. Guste lost her patience. "This is going too far! What's the matter with all of you?"

Diederich suggested: "I really think it would be better if we left this place right now." But Guste stamped her foot.

"I'm not going to take one step until I know. All evening long they've been staring at me as though I had swallowed a dead fish."

Käthchen turned away. "Well, there you have it. Just be glad they don't throw you out along with your half brother Wolfgang."

"With whom? . . . My half brother. . . . What do you mean 'half brother'?"

In a deep silence, Guste panted softly, her eyes darting about distractedly. All at once she understood. "Of all the low-down, dirty tricks!" she cried out in dismay. A smile of relish spread over Käthchen's face. Diederich for his part parried, denying any complicity in the affair. Guste extended her finger toward Käthchen. "You girls cooked this up, didn't you! You're envious of my money!"

"Humph!" said Käthchen. "We can do without your money if that's what comes along with it."

"It's not true!" Guste screamed. Suddenly, she fell forward onto the sofa and began to whimper. "Oh God, oh God, what have we got ourselves into?"

"That shouldn't be too hard to figure out," said Käthchen, without a trace of pity.

Guste's sobs became louder and louder; Diederich touched her shoulder. "Fräulein Guste, you don't want the people to come now, do you?" He tried to think of something to console her. "One can never tell about these things. You don't look alike."

But the consolation only served to provoke Guste. She jumped up and took the offensive. "You—you're quite a proper little number yourself," she hissed at Käthchen. "I'm going to tell everyone what I saw you doing!"

"And you really think they'll believe you? No one would believe anything coming from a hussy like you. Everyone knows I'm an upright girl."

"Upright! Smooth out your dress at least!"

"The only thing more vulgar than you—"

"Is you!"

At this, both girls started in shock, broke off, and maintained their face-off in silence, hate and fear in their fat faces which so resembled each other; their bosoms thrust forward, their shoulders raised, their arms planted in their hips, they looked as though their fragrant ball dresses were about to burst from their bodies. Guste undertook yet another thrust: "I'm going to tell!"

Käthchen dropped her last scruple. "Then you'd better make it quick, before I beat you to it and tell everyone that I was the one who opened the door and caught the two of you."

Since at this Guste could only flutter her eyelids, Käthchen sobered immediately; she added: "Well, I owe it to myself, don't I? I mean, it hardly matters any more with you."

But Diederich's eyes had met Guste's; they reached a silent understanding with her and then wandered downwards until they came to rest on the diamond gracing her little finger, the diamond they together had pulled out of the rags. Diederich gave a chivalrous smile and Guste, blushing deeply, came so close that she seemed to be leaning on him. Käthchen tiptoed to the door. His head bowed over Guste's shoulder, Diederich said softly: "Your fiancé has left you by yourself for quite some time, hasn't he?"—"Oh, him," she retorted. He lowered his face a little more and pressed it into her shoulder. She did not stir. "Pity," he said and withdrew so unexpectedly that Guste lost her balance. She realized all of a sudden that her circumstances had changed considerably. Her money was no longer trump, it had become devalued, a man like Diederich was worth more. Her face immediately assumed the expression of a dog. Diederich said evenly: "In your fiancé's place, I would go about things quite differently."

Käthchen pulled the door closed again with the utmost cautiousness and returned, her finger to her lips.

"Do you know what? The play has started again—quite some time ago, I think."

"Oh, God!" said Guste, and Diederich:

"Well, then it looks like we're sitting in the trap."

He searched the walls for an exit; he even moved the sofa. Since none was to be found, he became indignant.

"This is indeed a trap! And for the sake of this old dump Herr Buck rearranged the entire street plan! He'll see me tear it down before long! Just wait until I'm elected to the Town Council!"

Käthchen tittered. "Why are you blustering so? It's so nice and cozy here. Now we can do whatever we want." And she jumped over the sofa. Guste pulled herself together and tried to jump over as well. She did not quite make it, however, and Diederich caught her. Käthchen too, came over and put her arm in his. He winked to each in turn. "So what are we going to do?" Käthchen said: "That would depend on you, wouldn't it? After all, the three of us have gotten to know each other quite well."—"And besides, what have we got to lose?" asked Guste. At that, they all burst out laughing.

But Käthchen gave a cry of dismay. "Goodness gracious! In this mirror I look just like my dead grandmother!"

"It's all black."

"And there are things written all over it."

They brought their faces up close to read, in the dim gaslight, the slogans and pet names inscribed together with the dates of bygone years within the outlines of entwined hearts, on scratched-in vases, cupids, and even over graves. "Look what's written on this urn down here. Well, I never!" said Käthchen. "'Only now shall we suffer' . . . Why? Because they were in here? They must have been mad."

"We're not mad," Diederich asserted. "Fräulein Guste, you've got a diamond, haven't you?" He drew three hearts, added an inscription, and had the girls try to figure out his work. As they turned away screeching, he asked proudly: "Why do you think they call this the Cabinet of Love?"

Suddenly, Guste cried out in alarm. "Someone is watching here!"
A ghostly pale head was peering out from behind the mirror! . . .
Käthchen was already at the door. "Come back," Diederich called
out. "It's only painted."
One side of the mirror had detached itself from the wall, and it
could be turned around even more: the entire figure emerged.
"It's the shepherdess that's jumping over the brook outside!"
"Now she has it all behind her, said Diederich, for the shepherd-
ess was sitting there and crying. On the reverse side of the mirror,
however, the shepherd was departing.
"And that is the way out!" Diederich pointed to an illuminated
crack, he felt about, and the painted tableau opened.
"This is the exit, when one has it behind him," he noted, and
led the way. Following on his heels, Käthchen remarked mockingly:
"I haven't anything behind me at all."
And Guste, woebegone: "Neither have I."

Diederich ignored this; he realized that they were in one of the
small salons behind the buffet. He quickly made his way to the
mirrored gallery and mingled inconspicuously with the crowd
which was beginning to empty out from the auditorium. Everyone
was deeply affected by the tragic fate of the Secret Countess, who
had married the piano teacher after all. Frau Harnisch, Frau Cohn
and the Mayor's mother-in-law emerged, their eyes red with tears.
Jadassohn, who had washed off his greasepaint and come to receive
congratulations, was not well received by the ladies. "It is your
fault, Dr. Jadassohn, that this happened! After all, she was your
own sister."—"I beg your pardon, ladies," and Jadassohn proceeded to defend his attitude as the legitimate heir to the Count's
possessions. Then Meta Harnisch said:
"Well, you did not have to look so arrogant in the process."
Immediately everyone looked at his ears and sniggered. Jadassohn,
who kept crowing in vain asking what the matter was, was taken
aside by Diederich. With the sweet throb of revenge in his heart
Diederich led him right up to where the Governor's wife was saying
goodbye to Major Kunze, with the liveliest expressions of thanks
for his efforts on behalf of her play. As soon as she saw Jadassohn
she turned her back on him. Jadassohn stood as if rooted to the
spot. Diederich did not lead him any further. "What's wrong?" he
asked disingenuously. "Oh, of course, Frau von Wulckow. You

have annoyed her. You are not to be made Public Prosecutor. Your ears were too prominent."

Whatever Diederich may have expected, Jadassohn's monstrous grimace was a surprise! Where was the high-spirited dash to which he had dedicated his life? "I say I shall," was all he could say, quite softly, yet it sounded for all the world like an anguished wail. Then he began to move, dancing about as he spoke: "You may laugh, my friend! You do not know what an asset your face is. If I only had your face I'd be a Cabinet Minister in ten years."

"Come, come!" said Diederich. "You don't even need the whole face, only the ears," he added.

"Will you sell them to me?" asked Jadassohn, with a look that frightened Diederich. "Is that possible?" he asked uncertainly. With a cynical laugh Jadassohn went up to Heuteufel. "You *are* an ear specialist, aren't you, Doctor—?"

Heuteufel explained to him that, as a matter of fact, operations were performed, though so far only in Paris, whereby the size of the ears could be reduced by one-half. "Why remove the lot?" he queried. "You can keep half of them." Jadassohn had recovered himself. "That's a good joke. I'll tell it in court, you old rascal!" he said, digging Heuteufel in the ribs.

Meanwhile Diederich had gone off to meet his sisters, who had changed into their ball dresses and were coming out of the dressing room. They were greeted with applause and gave their impressions of what had happened on the stage. "Tea—coffee: Heavens, wasn't that exciting!" said Magda. As their brother, Diederich also received congratulations. He got between them, and Magda at once linked her arm in his, but he had to hold Emmi tightly. "Stop this play-acting," she hissed. Between nods and smiles he snorted at her: "I know you had only a small part, but consider yourself lucky to have a part at all. Look at Magda!" Magda nestled willingly against him and seemed ready to represent a picture of a happy united family as long as he liked. "My dear little sister," he said, with tender respect, "you have been a success. But I can assure you so have I." He even began to pay her compliments. "You look stunning tonight. You are almost too nice for Kienast." When the Governor's wife nodded to them graciously on her way out, everyone turned to face the threesome with the most devoted expressions. The auditorium had been cleared, and behind a group of palms a polonaise was struck up. Diederich bowed to Magda with the utmost correctness and conducted her triumphantly to the dance, right behind Major Kunze, who was leading. Thus they passed Guste Daimchen, who was sitting out. She was beside hunchbacked Fräulein Kühnchen, and she looked after them as if she had been slapped. The sight of her moved Diederich as uncannily as that of Herr Lauer in prison.

"Poor Guste!" said Magda. Diederich frowned. "Yes, that is what happens."

"But, as a matter of fact. . ." Magda smiled with downcast eyes, "happens when?"

"That doesn't matter, my child, it has happened now."

"Diedel, you should ask her for a waltz afterwards."

"I can't. A man must remember what he owes to himself."

With that, he left the auditorium. Young Sprezius, now no longer a lieutenant, but a schoolboy again, was just inviting hunchbacked Fräulein Kühnchen to dance. He was doubtless thinking of her father, his schoolmaster. Guste Daimchen was left alone . . . Diederich took a turn through the anterooms, where the elderly gentlemen were playing cards. When he surprised Käthchen Zillich behind a door with an actor, she made a face at him. He reached the refreshment room, and there was Wolfgang, sitting at a little table sketching the mothers who were waiting around the dance floor.

"Very talented," said Diederich. "Have you drawn your future bride yet?"

"In this connection she does not interest me," retorted Buck so phlegmatically that Diederich began to doubt whether his escapades with Guste in the cabinet of love would have interested her fiancé at all.

"I can never make you out," said he disappointedly.

"I can always make you out," replied Buck. "I would like to have drawn you that time in court, when you were delivering your great monologue."

"Your speech was enough for me. It was an attempt, though fortunately ineffective, to bring myself and my actions into discredit with the public, and to make me seem contemptible."

Diederich glared, which Buck noticed with astonishment. "Apparently you are offended. And I made such a good speech." He moved his head and gave a pensive, delighted smile. "Won't you split a bottle of champagne with me?" he asked.

Diederich began: "Are you really the person I ought to—" But he gave in. "The decision of the court established the fact that your accusations were directed, not only against me, but against all right-thinking patriots. So I regard the matter as settled."

"I suppose that means we'll order Heidsieck!" said Buck. He insisted on Diederich's clinking glasses with him. "You must admit, my dear Hessling, that nobody has ever occupied themselves as thoroughly with you as I did. Now I don't mind telling you that your role in court interested me much more than my own. Afterward, when I got home, I imitated you in front of the mirror."

"My role? You mean, I suppose, my convictions. I know, of course, that you regard actors as the representative men of today."

"I said that in reference to . . . someone else. But surely you see how much closer I am to the observation. . . . If I had not to defend the washerwoman tomorrow, who is accused of having stolen a pair of drawers from Wulckow's, I might perhaps play Hamlet. *Prost!*"

"*Prost!* You do not need to have any convictions for that!"

"Good Lord, I have convictions. But always the same ones? So you would advise me to go on the stage?" asked Buck. Diederich had opened his mouth to advise him to do so, when Guste entered. Diederich blushed, for Buck's question had made him think of her. Buck mused: "Meanwhile, the pot in which my meal is cooking is boiling over, and it's such a tasty dish." But Guste crept up softly from behind, pressed her hands over his eyes, and asked: "Guess who?" "There it is," replied Buck, giving her a playful slap.

"You gentlemen are having an interesting talk, I suppose? Shall I leave you?" asked Guste. Diederich hastened to get her a chair, but he would have preferred to be alone with Buck. The feverish brightness of Guste's eyes boded no good. She talked more freely than usual.

"You get on wonderfully together, if only you were not so formal."

"That is mutual respect," said Buck. Diederich was taken aback, and then he made a remark which astonished himself. "The fact is, every time I leave your fiancé I could throttle him, but when we next meet I am glad." He drew himself up. "If I were not already a loyal citizen he would make me one."

"And if I were," said Buck, smiling, "he would cure me of it. That is the charm of it."

But Guste obviously had other worries. She was pale and she gulped.

"Now I'll tell you something, Wolfgang. Will you bet you will keel over?"

"Herr Rose, some of your Hennessy!" Buck called out. While he mixed cognac and champagne, Diederich seized Guste's arm and as the noise of the dance music was very loud, he whispered entreatingly: "Don't do anything foolish." She laughed derisively. "Dr. Hessling is afraid! He thinks it's a vulgar story, but I find it terribly funny." She laughed loudly. "What do you think? They say your father and my mother . . . you understand, and therefore we are supposedly . . . you know!"

Buck moved his head slowly, and then his lips curled. "So what if we are?" Guste stopped laughing.

"What do you mean, 'so what'?"

"I mean if the Netzig people believe such a thing, it must be a common occurrence among them, and therefore it doesn't matter."

"Soft words butter no parsnips," said Guste decisively. Diederich then felt it his duty to enter a protest.

"To err is human, but nobody can defy public opinion with impunity."

"He always thinks he is too good for the world," said Guste. And Diederich: "These are tough times. He that does not defend himself must suffer the consequences." Then Guste cried, full of painful enthusiasm:

"Dr. Hessling is not like you! He defended me. I have proof, I know it, from Meta Harnisch, because in the end she had to tell me what she knew. He was the only person of them all who took my part. He, in your place, would tell the people what he thought of them when they gossip about me!"

Diederich confirmed this with a nod of his head, but Buck kept twisting his glass and looking at his reflection in it. Suddenly he put it down.

"How do you know I, too, wouldn't like to give them a piece of my mind—to take one of them down, without choosing particularly, for they are all about equally mean and stupid?" As he said this he shut his eyes. Guste shrugged her bare shoulders.

"That's what you say, but they are not so stupid, they know what they want . . . The stupider they are the cleverer," she concluded challengingly, and Diederich nodded ironically. Then Buck looked at him with eyes which suddenly seemed to be those of a madman. His trembling fists fumbled convulsively about his neck; his voice was hoarse. "If I could only—if I had only one of them by the scruff of the neck, the one that I knew had started the whole thing, that embodied in himself all the hateful and evil qualities of the rest; if—if I could get hold of the one who was the personification of all that is inhuman and subhuman—!" Diederich turned as white as his shirtfront as he edged from his chair and slowly drew back, step by step. Guste shrieked and shrank back to the wall in panic. "It's the cognac!" Diederich shouted to her . . . But Buck's glance, which radiated malice as it wavered between them, suddenly relaxed. He blinked, and then his eyes twinkled merrily.

"Unfortunately I am accustomed to this mixture," he explained. "It was only to show you that we too can play that game."

Diederich sat down again noisily. "You are nothing but a comedian after all," he said indignantly.

"Do you really think so?" Buck asked, and his eyes twinkled even more brightly. Guste turned up her nose. "Well, I hope you'll continue to enjoy yourselves," she said, preparing to leave them. But Judge Fritzsche had come in, and he bowed to her and also to Buck, and asked if he would allow him to have the pleasure of dancing the cotillion with his fiancée. He was exceedingly polite, almost entreating. Buck frowned and did not answer, but in the meantime Guste had taken Fritzsche's arm.

Buck looked after them, a heavy furrow between his eyebrows, and oblivious of everything. "Yes, indeed," thought Diederich, "it is not pleasant, my friend, to meet a man who has been off on a pleasure trip with your sister, and then he takes your fiancée away from the table, and you can do nothing, for that would only increase the scandal, because your engagement in itself is a scandal . . ."

Rousing himself with a start, Buck said: "Do you know it is only now that I really feel as if I'd like to marry Fräulein Daimchen. I regarded the matter as . . . well, not exactly sensational, but the inhabitants of Netzig have made it into quite a racy little affair."

This effect left Diederich thunderstruck. "Well, if that's what you think," he managed to say.

"Why not? You and I, though at opposite poles, are introducing in Netzig the advanced tendencies of the moral-free age. We are stirring things up. The spirit of the times still sneaks about the streets here in carpet slippers."

"We'll put spurs on it," declared Diederich.

"*Prost!*"

"*Prost!* But they'll be *my* spurs"—Diederich glared. "Your skepticism and your flabby point of view are out of date. The intellect"—he breathed heavily—"is of no use today. National deeds"—he banged his fist on the table—"will win the future!"

To this Buck retorted with a pitying smile: "The future? That's just where you are wrong. National deeds have died out over the course of a century. What we are experiencing, and shall experience for some time to come, is the spasmodic twitching and the odor of their corpse. It will not sweeten the air."

"From you I did not expect anything better than that you should drag what is most sacred into the dust!"

"Sacred! Inviolable! Why not call it eternal and have done with it! Except in the realm of the ideal, your kind of nationalism will never, never revive again. Formerly, it may have been possible, in that dark period of history which had not yet experienced the likes of you. But now you are here and the world has moved on to its goal. Conceit and hatred among nations, that is the end and you cannot avoid it."

"We are living in tough times," Diederich declared seriously.

"Not so much tough as ossified . . . I am not sure that the people who lived during the Thirty Years' War believed in the immutability of their by no means easy circumstances. And I am convinced that the tyranny of the Rococo age was seen by those subject to it as something surmountable. Otherwise, they would never have made the Revolution. Where, in those chambers of history which we can still enter in spirit, is there an age which would have declared itself permanent, and prided itself before eternity on its miserable limitations, which would have superstitiously censured everyone who did not wholly identify himself with it? The lot of you are filled more with horror than hate when confronted by a lack of red-blooded patriotism! But the men without a fatherland are on your tracks. Do you see them there in the ballroom?

Diederich turned around so suddenly that he spilled his champagne. Had Napoleon Fischer and his comrades forced their way in? . . . Buck laughed inwardly. "Don't get excited. I mean merely the silent folk on the walls. Why do they look so gay? . . . What gives them the right to flowered paths, light footsteps and harmony? Ah, friends!" Over the heads of the dancers Buck motioned with his glass. "You friends of humanity, and of every future good, your generous hearts did not know the sordid selfishness of nationalistic clannishness. You citizens of the world, return! Even among us there are still some who wait for you!"

He emptied his glass and Diederich noticed with contempt that he was weeping. Then he looked very sly. "You, my contemporaries, do not know, I am sure, what sort of a sash the old Mayor is wearing, as he smiles his rosy smile there in the midst of officials and shepherdesses. The colors have faded, and you doubtless think they are yours? But it is the French tricolor. Then the colors were new, and they did not belong to any country, but heralded the universal dawn. To wear them was to wear the best badge of opinion. It was, as you would say, most correct. *Prost!*"

But Diederich had surreptitiously drawn away his chair and was looking about to see if anyone was listening. "You're drunk," he murmured, and in order to save the situation he shouted: "Herr Rose, another bottle!" Thereupon he drew up his chair again and struck a most authoritative attitude. "You seem to forget that we have had a Bismarck since then!"

"Not only one," said Buck. "On all sides Europe is being driven along this road to national ruin. Let us suppose it could not have been avoided. Better times will come again. But did you follow your Bismarck as long as he was in the right? You allowed yourselves to be pulled along; you lived in a state of conflict with him. But now, when you should have moved beyond him, you cling to his powerless shadow! Your national metabolism is depressingly slow. By the time you have grasped the fact that a great man is among you, he has ceased to be great!"

"You will come to know him soon enough," Diederich assured him. "Blood and iron are still the most effective remedy! Might before right!" His face became swollen and red at the utterance of this credo. But Buck also became excited.

"Might! Might will not allow itself to be carried eternally on the bayonet's point like a skewered sausage. Nowadays the real power is peace. Play your comedy of force! Brag about your imaginary enemies at home and abroad! Fortunately, deeds are forbidden to you."

"Forbidden?" Diederich snorted as if he were about to erupt in fire. "His Majesty has said: We would rather leave our eighteen army corps and forty-two million inhabitants dead on the field . . ."

"Than that the German eagle—" cried Buck impetuously, and then even more wildly: "No parliamentary resolutions! The army is our only tower of strength."

Diederich would not be outdone. "You are called upon, in the first place, to defend me against my domestic and foreign enemies."

"To ward off a host of miserable traitors," yelled Buck. "A mob of people—"

Diederich concluded the sentence: "—unworthy to bear the name of Germans!"

Then both in chorus: "Shoot down your brothers and relatives!"

Some of the dancers, who had come for refreshments, were attracted by the shouting, and fetched their womenfolk to contemplate this spectacle of heroic intoxication. Even the card players put their heads in the doorway, and everyone was astounded at the sight of Diederich and his partner, rolling in their chairs, clutching the table and hurling strong words at each other, with glassy eyes and snarling teeth.

"There is one enemy and he is my enemy!"

"There is one master in my kingdom and I will endure no other!"

"I can be very unpleasant!"

They tried to shout one another down.

"False humanitarianism."

"Enemies of the Fatherland and of the divine order of the world!"

"They must be exterminated to the last man."

A bottle crashed against the wall.

"I will smash!"

"German dust . . . from their shoes . . . glorious days!"

Just then an apparition with blindfolded eyes glided through the spectators. It was Guste Daimchen looking for a partner in a game of blind-man's buff. She came up behind Diederich and touched him, trying to make him stand up. He stiffened and repeated threateningly: "Glorious days!" She pulled down the blindfold, stared at him anxiously and went to get his sisters. Buck also saw that it was time to stop. He lent a discreet, supporting hand to his friend as he escorted him out, but he could not prevent Diederich from turning at the door to the gaping crowd of dancers, and drawing himself up haughtily, though his eyes were too glassy to glare.

"I will smash!"

Then he was taken downstairs and put into the carriage.

When he came into the living room toward midday, with a terrible headache, he was astonished to see Emmi march out indignantly. But Magda made a few cautious allusions and then he remembered what the matter was. "Did I really do that? Well, I admit there were ladies present. There are more ways than one for a true-born German to prove himself. With ladies it is different . . . In such cases, of course, one must lose no time in setting the matter to rights in the frankest and most correct fashion."

Although he could hardly see straight he knew perfectly well what had to be done. While a two-horse Victoria was being sent for, he put on his frock coat, white tie and silk hat. Then he handed the coachman the list which Magda had drawn up, and drove off. At each house he asked to see the ladies and disturbed many of them at lunch. Without being quite sure whether he was addressing Frau Harnisch, Frau Daimchen or Frau Tietz, he reeled off a statement in his hoarse voice of "the morning after":

"I frankly confess . . . as a German gentleman, in the presence of ladies . . . in the fullest and most correct fashion. . . ."

By half-past one he was back, and sat down to lunch with a sigh of relief: "The matter is settled."

That afternoon he had a more difficult task before him. He sent for Napoleon Fischer to come up to the house. "Herr Fischer," he said, offering him a chair, "I am receiving you here, instead of in the office, because our affairs are no concern of Herr Sötbier's. It is a political matter, I ought to explain."

Napoleon Fischer nodded as if he had already guessed that. He now seemed to be accustomed to these confidential conversations. At Diederich's first nod he at once took a cigar, and he even crossed his legs. Diederich was far less sure of himself: he was breathing hard. Then he decided, without beating about the bush, to go straight to the point with brutal frankness. That is what Bismarck had done.

"The fact is I want to get a seat on the Town Council," he explained, "and for that I will need you."

The machinist glanced up at him. "And I you," he said, "for I also want to be a municipal councillor."

"What! Come now! I was prepared for most things . . ."

"I suppose you had another couple of twenty-mark pieces ready?"—and the proletarian bared his yellow teeth. He no longer concealed his grin and Diederich saw that it was not going to be as easy to deal with electoral politics as it was with a mangled worker. "I may tell you, Doctor," Napoleon began, "my party is sure of one of the two seats. The Liberals will probably get the other. If you want to kick them out, you will need us."

"I am with you so far," said Diederich. "It is true, I have the support of old Buck as well. But his people might not trust me sufficiently to elect me if I went forward as a Liberal. It is safer to come to an understanding with you Social Democrats."

"And I have a very good idea how that can he arranged," declared Napoleon. "Because for a long time I have had my eye on you, wondering whether you would not soon be entering the political arena."

Napoleon began to blow smoke rings, he felt so elated.

"Your trial, Dr. Hessling, and then that business with the Veterans Association, and so on, that was all excellent as an advertisement. But a politician must always ask: How many votes will I get?"

Napoleon was giving him the benefit of his experience! When he referred to "patriotic hullabaloo" Diederich tried to protest, but Napoleon shut him up.

"What do you mean? In my party we have a certain respect for patriotic hullabaloo. It is easier to do business with the lot of you than with the Liberals. Soon the few remaining middle-class Democrats will all be able to fit into one cab and drive off."

"And then we'll finish off these few," cried Diederich. The allies laughed for joy. Diederich got a bottle of beer.

"*But,*" intoned the Social Democrat, as he stated his terms: a trade union hall, which the town was to help the party to build . . . Diederich jumped up from his chair. "And you have the cheek to demand that of a true patriot?"

The other remained cool and ironical. "If we do not help the true patriot to be elected, where will that leave the true patriot?" In spite of his pleas and threats, Diederich finally had to sign a paper, pledging himself not only to vote for the hall, but to get the support of the councillors with whom he had influence. After that he bluntly declared the conference over and took the beer bottle out of the machinist's hand. But Napoleon Fischer had a twinkle in his eye. Dr. Hessling ought to be thankful that he was dealing with him and not with Rille, the proprietor of the Social Democrats' beer hall. Rille was trying to get into the running himself and would not have agreed to such a compromise. Opinion was divided within the party. Diederich therefore would have good reason to do something on behalf of Fischer's candidacy in the press where he had influence. "If strangers, like Rille, for example, were to poke their noses into your affairs, Doctor, I am sure you would not like it. Between the two of us it is quite different. We have already turned a few tricks together."

With this he left Diederich to his own feelings.

"Turned a few tricks together!" Diederich thought, and thrills of fear crossed inside him with surges of rage. This cur dared to say such a thing to him; his own coolie, whom he could throw out onto the street any time he wanted! That is to say, this would unfortunately not do, for they had indeed turned a few tricks together. The double beater! The mangled worker! One shared secret entailed another, and another; Diederich and his prole now depended on one another not only within the firm, but politically as well. Diederich would have much preferred to ally himself with Rille, the proprietor of the party beer hall, but then he would have to worry about Napoleon Fischer taking revenge and bringing everything to light. Diederich saw no alternative but to take sides with him, no less, against Rille. "But"—he shook his fist at the ceiling—"we'll meet again. Even if it takes ten years, the day of reckoning will come!"

After this he was obliged to pay a visit to old Herr Buck and listen with devotion to his sanctimonious, literary drivel. For this he was rewarded with the candidacy for the Liberal party. . . . In the *Netzig Journal,* which in a warmly-disposed article endorsed Herr Doctor Hessling as a man, a citizen, and a politician, the candidacy of the laborer Fischer was sharply opposed in another article which appeared, albeit in smaller print, just below Diederich's endorsement. The Social Democratic Party counted within its ranks more than enough entrepreneurs; regrettably so, it might be added. It should certainly have been able to find a way to spare the bourgeois City Councilmen the necessity of rubbing elbows with a common laborer. What if Herr Doctor Hessling were to meet his own machinist within the bosom of the municipal assembly?

This invective aired by the bourgeois newspaper resulted in complete accord among the Social Democrats; even Rille saw no alternative but to endorse Napoleon—who went on to carry the day. Diederich received only half of the votes from the party that nominated him, but he was saved by the Social Democrats. The two victors were initiated together into the assembly. The Mayor Dr. Scheffelweis congratulated them, remarking that on the one hand the active middle-class citizen, on the other hand the upward-striving laborer. . . . And in the very next session Diederich plunged into the deliberations. The matter under discussion was the laying of sewers in Gäbbelchenstrasse. A considerable number of the old houses located on this street at the edge of town were still equipped, hardly to the credit of the town, with cesspools, whose vapors at times engulfed the entire vicinity. And this at the close of the nineteenth century! At the time of his visit to The Green Angel, Diederich himself had made this observation. Thus did he counter most emphatically the financial reservations expressed by the representative of the town administration. A matter so requisite to the town's cultural honor cannot yield to such petty concerns. "Germanness means culture!" Diederich exclaimed. "Gentlemen! This sentiment was expressed by no less a person than His Majesty the Emperor! And on another occasion His Majesty spoke the words: This filthy rot must come to an end. Wherever deeds are accomplished in a far-seeing manner the exalted example of His Majesty lights the way, and for this reason, gentlemen—"

"Hurrah!" called out a voice from the left, and Diederich encountered the grin of Napoleon Fischer. Diederich drew himself up and glared. "Quite correct!" he replied stridently. "I can think of no better way to close. His Majesty the Emperor, hurrah, hurrah, hurrah!"

Astonished silence—but when the Social Democrats laughed, a number of voices from the right called out "hurrah." Dr. Heuteufel interposed the question of whether the curious context into which Dr. Hessling had brought the person of the Emperor did not actually represent a case of *lèse-majesté*. But the chairman was quick to ring his bell. The debate, however, was continued in the press. The Social Democratic newspaper *Volksstimme* maintained that Herr Hessling was bringing to the Town Council the spirit of the most repugnant toadyism, whereas the *Netzig Journal* characterized his speech as the refreshing deed of a guileless patriot. But not until it was reported in the Berlin *Lokal-Anzeiger* did the weighty import of the incident become apparent. The paper read by his Majesty had nothing but praise for the courageous stand taken by the Town Councillor Dr. Hessling from Netzig. The paper observed with satisfaction that the new, determined national spirit, heartily endorsed by the Emperor, was now making progress in the provinces. The Emperor's admonition was being heeded, the citizens were awakening from their slumber, the separation of the populace into the camps of those for him and those against him was now being effected. "It is our sincere wish that many upright representatives of our cities and towns might follow the example of Dr. Hessling!"

Diederich had been carrying around in his heart this issue of the *Lokal-Anzeiger* for a week when he crept one quiet morning hour through the streets of Netzig, avoiding Kaiser Wilhelm Strasse, and through the rear entrance of Klappsch's Beer Hall, where he found company: Napoleon Fischer and the party publican Rille. Although the establishment was empty, the three moved into a corner in the very back. Fräulein Klappsch was sent away as soon as she had brought their beer, and Klappsch himself, who was listening at the door, could hear only whispering. He tried to make use of the service hatch through which he would pass the beer glasses on busy nights, but Rille, who was on to this ploy, slammed it shut in his face. The proprietor did manage to notice that Dr. Hessling had jumped up and seemed to be about to leave. As a true patriot, he would never condone such a thing! . . . Later, however, Fräulein Klappsch, who had been called to bring the check, insisted she had seen a piece of paper bearing the signatures of all three.

That afternoon Emmi and Magda were invited to tea at Frau von Wulckow's, and Diederich accompanied them. With their chins in the air the three of them marched along Kaiser Wilhelm Strasse, and Diederich raised his hat very calmly to the gentlemen on the steps of the Freemasons' Lodge, who stared in amazement as he entered the Governor's Palace. He greeted the sentry with a genial wave of his hand. In the cloak room they met several officers and their wives, to whom the Fräuleins Hessling were already well known. Clicking his spurs, Lieutenant von Brietzen helped Emmi off with her coat, and she thanked him over her shoulder like a countess. She nudged Diederich with her foot to draw his attention to the shaky ground on which they were treading. After they had given precedence to Herr von Brietzen on entering the drawing room, had bowed and scraped ecstatically to the Governor's wife, and had been introduced to everybody—what a task it was, as dangerous as it was honorable, to sit on a little chair, squeezed in among the ladies' dresses to balance one's teacup while passing around plates, and to offer the cakes with a respectful smile! And while eating it was necessary to utter a dulcet word about the successful performance of *The Secret Countess,* one of manly recognition for the far-seeing administrative ability of the Governor, and a weighty one about revolution and patriotism—and, into the bargain, to feed the Wulckows' dog which was begging! This was not like the unpretentious gatherings in the *Ratskeller* and of the Veterans' Association. One had to gaze with a strained smile into the watery eyes of Captain von Köckeritz, whose bald pate was white, but whose face from the middle of his forehead down was a fiery red, and who talked about the parade ground. And if one were already breaking into a sweat from anxiety lest the question be raised whether one had served in the army, there came the unexpected relief that the lady at one's side, who combed her white-blond hair flat over the top of her head, and whose nose was sunburned, began to talk about horses . . . This time Diederich was saved by Emmi with the aid of Herr von Brietzen, with whom she seemed to be on very familiar terms. Emmi joined easily in the conversation about horses, used technical terms, and even went so far as to draw on her imagination about cross-country rides which she said she had taken on the estate of an aunt. When the Lieutenant offered to go out riding with her, she pleaded poor Frau Hessling as an excuse, who would not allow it. Diederich could hardly recognize Emmi. Her uncanny talents left Magda altogether in the shade, even if the latter had succeeded in capturing a fiancé. As on the occasion when he returned from The Green Angel, Diederich reflected uneasily on the unaccountable ways which, when you were out of sight, a girl would . . . Then he noticed that he had not been listening to a question of Frau von Wulckow, and that everyone had stopped talking so that he might reply. He gazed around helplessly, looking for assistance, but his eyes only met the gaze of the forbidding portrait of a man, pale and unbending, in a red hussar's uniform, with his hand on his hip, his mustache curling up to his eyes, who glared coldly over his shoulder! Diederich was trembling and nearly choked on his tea. Herr von Brietzen had to clap him on the back.

Now a lady who had previously done nothing but eat was going to sing. The guests drew together in the music room. Diederich stood at the door and was glancing surreptitiously at his watch, when the Governor's wife gave a little cough behind him. "I know my dear Dr. Hessling, that you cannot sacrifice your valuable time on our frivolous, our all-too-frivolous conversation. My husband is expecting you, come along." With her finger to her lips she led him along a passage and through an empty anteroom. She knocked very gently. As there was no reply, she looked anxiously at Diederich, who also felt uncomfortable. "Otto, dearest." she cried, nestling tenderly against the closed door. After they had listened for a while the terrible bass voice was heard inside. "Dearest Otto is not here! Tell those idiots to drink their tea without him!" "He is so dreadfully busy," whispered Frau von Wulckow, turning a little paler. "His health is being undermined by the subversive elements . . . Now, unfortunately, I must return to my guests, but the servant will announce you." And she disappeared.

Diederich waited in vain many long minutes for the servant. Then the dog came out, went past Diederich full of immense contempt and scratched at the door. Immediately the voice within shouted: "Schnaps, come in here!"—whereupon the Great Dane raised the latch. As it forgot to shut the door again Diederich took the liberty of creeping in behind the dog. Herr von Wulckow was sitting at his desk, in a cloud of smoke, with his enormous back turned towards the intruder.

"Good day, sir," said Diederich, with an awkward bow. "Hello, have you learned to babble, too, Schnaps?" asked Wulckow, without looking around. He folded up a document and slowly lit a fresh cigar. "Here it comes," thought Diederich, but Wulckow began to write something else. Only the dog took any notice of Diederich. It obviously found the visitor out of place here and its contempt turned to hostility. Showing its teeth it sniffed at Diederich's trousers, and almost went farther than mere sniffing. Diederich hopped as quietly as possible from one leg to the other, and the dog growled threateningly but softly, knowing well that otherwise its master would intervene. Finally Diederich succeeded in interposing a chair between himself and the enemy, and clinging to this he twisted about, now quickly, now slowly, always on the lookout for Schnaps's flank attacks. Once he noticed Wulckow turning his head a little and he fancied he saw him grin. At length the dog grew tired of the game, and went to its master to be stroked. Encamped near Wulckow's chair, it measured Diederich with the bold gaze of a hunter, as he mopped up his perspiration.

"Vulgar beast!" Diederich thought—and suddenly he boiled over inside. Outrage and the thick smoke took his breath away; he thought to himself with suppressed fuming: "Who am I to stand here and take this rot? My lowest machinist would never stand for the likes of this from me. I am a doctor. I am a Town Councillor! This uncivilized boor needs me far more than I need him!" Everything he had experienced this afternoon assumed the nastiest air. He had been mocked, that bounder of a lieutenant had clapped him on the back! These uniformed cretins and blueblooded geese had chatted on about their stupid affairs the whole time and left him sitting there like a fool! "And who pays these impudent beggars? We do!" Sound opinions and feelings, it all collapsed at once within Diederich's breast, and from the rubble flared up wildly the raging fires of hate. "Slave drivers! Sable rattlers! Stuck-up bunch of louts. . . . Just see if we don't put an end to the whole pack of them some day—!" His fists clenched involuntarily, in a fit of mute rage he saw everything topple and disintegrate: the gentlemen of the government, army, civil service, all assemblages of power and indeed, Power itself! The Power which tramples over us and whose hooves we kiss! Against which we are impotent, for we all love it! Which we have in our blood, for in our blood is submission. We are an atom of that Power, a minuscule molecule of something it has spit out. . . . There, from the wall, from behind blue clouds, its pale countenance looked down with an iron gaze, iron, bristling, with glaring eyes: but Diederich, in wild self-forgetfulness, raised his fist.

Just then, the Wulckows' dog growled, but from underneath the Governor there came a thundering report, a long, rolling, resonant tattoo—and Diederich started in shock. He did not understand what had come over him. The edifice of order, erected once again within his breast, trembled only softly now. The Governor had important affairs of state to attend to. One simply had to wait until one was noticed, after which one had to give assurance of one's sound opinions and keep an eye open for good business opportunities. . . .

"Well, my little Doctor." said Herr von Wulckow, turning around his chair, "what is the matter with you? You are becoming a real statesman. Won't you take this seat of honor?"

"If I may be so bold," stammered Diederich. "I have been able to do a number of things for the national cause."

Wulckow blew an enormous volume of smoke into his face, then he came quite close to him with his hot-blooded, cynical eyes beneath their Mongolian lids. "To start with, my little Doctor, you have succeeded in getting into the Town Council. We won't go into how you managed to do that. At all events, it will help you, for I understand your business is in a pretty bad way." Wulckow laughed boisterously as Diederich winced. "That's all right. You are the man for me. What do you think I have been writing here?" The huge sheet was hidden by the paw which he placed upon it.

"I have asked the Minister for a little something for a certain Dr. Hessling in recognition of his services on behalf of loyal patriotic opinion in Netzig ... I am sure you never thought I could be as nice as that," he added, for Diederich kept bowing from his chair, looking dazzled and seized with sudden shyness. "I can hardly say," he murmured, " ... my modest services ..."

"It is the first step that counts," said Wulckow. "This is only a little encouragement. Your attitude in the Lauer trial was pretty good. The antimonarchical press was beside itself after you cheered the Emperor during the sewer debate. In three different places in the country complaints of *lèse-majesté* have been raised as a result. We must, therefore, show you some mark of our appreciation."

Diederich cried: "My highest reward is the fact that the *Lokal-Anzeiger* brought my humble name to the attention of His Gracious Majesty himself!"

"Well, now, won't you take a cigar?" Wulckow concluded, and Diederich understood that they were coming down to business. Already a doubt had arisen in the midst of his elation as to whether Wulckow's condescension had not some special motive. He said, as a feeler:

"The town, I am pretty sure, will sanction its quota for the railway line to Ratzenhausen."

Wulckow thrust his head forward. "So much the better for you. Otherwise we have a much more inexpensive scheme, in which Netzig will not be involved at all. So see that those people learn sense. On that condition you will have the privilege of furnishing your light to the Quitzin estates."

"The Town Administration doesn't want that." Diederich pleaded with his hands for consideration. "The town loses on the transaction, and Herr von Quitzin pays no taxes to us ... But now I am a Municipal Councillor, and as a loyal patriot ..."

"I must insist on that, otherwise my cousin, Herr von Quitzin, will simply install his own electric plant. He can get that cheap, as you may imagine; two Cabinet Ministers come to his place for hunting. Then he will undersell you here in Netzig itself."

Diederich straightened himself up. "Sir, I am determined, I am determined, despite all hostile attacks, to hold aloft the national banner in Netzig." Then, in softer tones: "In any case we can get rid of one enemy, indeed a particularly bad one, old Klüsing the paper manufacturer in Gausenfeld."

"That fellow?" Wulckow smiled contemptuously. "He eats out of my hand. He supplies paper to the official newspapers of the district."

"Do you know whether he does not supply even more to the bad papers? On that score, with all due respect, I am probably better informed."

"The *Netzig Journal* has become more reliable from the national standpoint."

"That is true"—Diederich nodded impressively—"since the day when old Klüsing allowed me to supply part of the paper. Gausenfeld was supposed to be too busy with other orders. Of course, he was really afraid that I would become interested in a rival sheet on the national side. And perhaps he was also afraid"—a significant pause—"that the Governor might prefer to order the paper for the official Press from a patriotic firm." "So you now supply the *Netzig Journal?*"

"Never will I so betray my patriotic convictions as to supply a paper which has Liberal money behind it."

"Hm. Very well." Wulckow rested his hands on his thighs. "You needn't say anything more. You want the whole contract for the *Netzig Journal.* You also want the official newspapers in the district. Probably also the supplies of paper for Government use. Anything else?"

To which Diederich replied in practical tones:

"I, sir, am not like Klüsing. I have no truck with revolution. If you, sir, as President of the Bible Society, will give me your support, I may say that it can only be to the advantage of the national cause."

"Hm. Very well," repeated Wulckow, and winked. Diederich played his trump card.

"Under Klüsing, sir, Gausenfeld is a breeding ground of revolution. Among his eight hundred workmen there is not one who ever votes for anyone but a Social Democrat." "Well, and what about your men?"

Diederich struck his chest. "God is my witness that I would rather shut the shop today, and go into poverty with my family, than keep one single man in my employment whom I knew to be unpatriotic."

"Most excellent sentiments," said Wulckow. Diederich looked at him with candid eyes. "I only take people who have been in the army. Forty of them served in the war. I no longer employ youths since that affair with the workman whom the sentry laid low on the field of honor, as His Majesty was pleased to state, after the fellow and his girl, behind my rags—"

Wulckow interrupted: "That's your worry, my little man."

Diederich did not allow his plan to be spoiled. "There shall be no revolution hatched in my rags. In yours, I mean in politics, it is different. There we can use the revolution so that out of the rags of Liberalism, white patriotic paper may come." He looked exceedingly profound, but Wulckow did not seem impressed. His smile was terrible.

"My boy, I wasn't born yesterday. Let me hear what you have worked out with your machinist."

When he saw Diederich giving ground, Wulckow continued: "He is also one of your old soldiers, Mr. Councillor?"

Diederich gulped, but saw there was no use beating about the bush. "Your Excellency." He spoke with determination at first, but his voice became quick and nervous. "The man wants to go into the Reichstag, and from the national standpoint he is better than Heuteufel. In the first place, many Liberals will turn patriotic out of fear, and in the second, if Napoleon Fischer is elected, we shall be given a monument to Emperor Wilhelm in Netzig. I have it in writing."

He spread out the paper in front of the Governor. Wulckow read it, then he stood up, kicked away his chair, and walked up and down the room, smoking like a chimney. "So Kühlemann snuffs out, and with his half-million the town will build, not a foundling hospital, but a monument to Emperor Wilhelm." He stood still. "Mind, my friend, in your own interest, if Netzig afterward has a Social Democrat in the Reichstag, but no statue of William the Great, then I'll teach you a lesson. I'll smash you to pulp. I'll break you so small that they won't even admit you to the foundling hospital!"

Diederich and his chair had both retreated against the wall. "Everything I am, my whole future, is staked on the national cause. The uncertainty of human affairs may affect me. . . ."

"Then, God help you!"

"Suppose Kühlemann recovers from his kidney stones?"

"You are responsible! My head is also at stake!" Wulckow dropped heavily into his chair, and smoked furiously. When the clouds had dispersed he had cheered up again. "What I told you the night of the play still holds. This parliament will not last long.

Lay the groundwork. Help me against Buck and I'll help you against Klüsing."

"Your Excellency!" Wulckow's smile filled Diederich with a great wave of hope. He could not contain himself. "If you would let him know on the quiet that you contemplated taking away the contracts from him! He will not make a row about it, you need not fear, but he will take measures accordingly. Perhaps he would negotiate—"

"With his successor." Wulckow concluded. Then it was Diederich's turn to jump up and walk up and down the room. "If you only knew, sir . . . Gausenfeld is a machine of a thousand horsepower, so to speak, and there it stands rusting away, because the current is lacking. I mean, the current of the modern farsighted spirit!"

"You have that, apparently," insinuated Wulckow.

"In the service of the national cause," Diederich assured him. He returned to his chair. "The Emperor Wilhelm Monument Committee will be most happy if we succeed in inducing you to have the kindness to signify your esteemed interest by accepting the position of honorary chairman."

"Done!" said Wulckow.

"The Committee will duly acknowledge the disinterested services of its honorary chairman."

"Be a little more explicit!" There was an ominous note in Wulckow's voice, but in his excitement Diederich failed to notice it.

"This idea has already given rise to certain discussions in committee. There is a desire to erect the monument on the most frequented site, and to surround it with a public park, so that the indissoluble bond between the ruler and his people may be strikingly allegorized. For that reason we had our eye on a rather large piece of property in the center of town. The adjoining houses are also available. It is in Meisestrasse."

"Oh, really? Meisestrasse." Wulckow's frown betokened a storm. Diederich was frightened, but he could not back out now.

"It occurred to us that, before the town looks into the matter more closely, we should secure the property in question, and thus anticipate undesirable speculations. Our honorary chairman, of course, would have the first right . . . "

At this word Diederich retreated and the storm broke. "Sir! What do you take me for! Am I your business agent! This is intolerable: it is unbelievable! A damned tradesman has the cheek to presume that the representative of His Majesty the Emperor will take a hand in his dirty deals!"

The room reverberated with Wulckow's superhuman bellowing. He advanced with his powerful body heat and his personal scent towards Diederich, who shrank back. The dog, too, had stood up and taken the offensive, barking furiously. At once the room was filled with terror and turmoil.

"You are guilty of insulting a Government official, sir!" Wulckow screamed, and Diederich, who was feeling behind his back for the door, could only wonder whether the dog or his master would be the first to seize him by the throat. His terrified glance strayed until it was held by the pale face on the wall which glared down threateningly at him. Now Power had caught him by the throat! He had dared to tread with Power on equal footing. That had proved his undoing. It broke upon him with all the terror of a cataclysm. . . . The door behind the desk opened and someone in a police uniform entered. The demoralized Diederich was no longer capable of astonishment. The presence of the uniform suggested another fearful thought to Wulckow. "I could have you arrested this moment, you contemptible upstart, for attempted bribery of an official, bribery of the authorities, the highest authority in the district! I'll put you in jail and ruin you for life!"

This last judgement had nowhere near the same effect upon the gentleman from the police as it did upon Diederich. He laid the document which he had brought upon the table and disappeared. For the rest, Wulckow also turned around suddenly and lit his cigar again. Diederich no longer existed for him. Even Schnaps ignored him. Then Diederich ventured to fold his hands.

"Your Excellency," he whispered shakily, "allow me, sir, to assure you; there is, if I may say so, a regrettable misunderstanding. With my well-known patriotic sentiments I would never . . . How could I?"

He waited, but nobody took any notice of him.

"If I were thinking of my own advantage," he resumed, a little more confidently, "instead of always having the national interest in view, I would not be here today, but at Herr Buck's. Herr Buck, I ought to tell you, proposed that I should sell my property to the town for the Liberal foundling hospital. But I repelled the suggestion with indignation, and came straight to you. Better, I said, the Monument to Emperor Wilhelm the Great in the heart, than the foundling hospital in the pocket, said I, and I say it now with no uncertain voice!"

As Diederich actually did raise his voice, Wulckow turned to him. "Are you still here?" he asked. And Diederich, again in mortal fear: "Your Excellency . . ."

"What are you waiting for? I do not know you at all. Have never had anything to do with you."

"Your Excellency, in the national interest—"

"I don't deal with real estate speculators. Sell your plot of ground and good luck to you. Afterwards we can do business."

Diederich turned pale and felt as if he were being crushed against the wall. "In that case, do our conditions still hold good? The decoration? The hint to Klüsing? The honorary chairmanship?"

Wulckow made a wry face. "Well and good. But you must sell at once."

Diederich gasped for breath. "I will make the sacrifice," he declared. "The noblest possession of a loyal patriot, my fidelity to the Emperor, must stand above all suspicion."

"Hm," said Wulckow, as Diederich withdrew, proud of his exit, though disturbed by the discovery that the Governor did not tolerate him as an ally with any greater favor than he tolerated his machinist. In the drawing room he found Emmi and Magda alone, turning over the pages of a magnificent-looking volume. The visitors had all gone and Frau von Wulckow had left them, because she had to dress for a soiree given by the wife of Colonel von Haffke. "My conference with the Governor passed off quite satisfactorily for both of us," Diederich remarked. And when they were in the street, he added: "You can see what it is like when two honorable men negotiate. In the business world today that is now very rare, there are so many Jews."

Emmi was also greatly excited and announced that she would take riding lessons. "If I give you the money," said Diederich, but only for form's sake, for he was proud of Emmi. "Has Lieutenant von Brietzen no sisters?" he asked. "You ought to make their acquaintance and get us invited to Frau von Haffke's next soiree." The Colonel passed just at that moment. Diederich stared after him for a long time. "I know," he said, "one shouldn't turn around, but he represents, after all, what is highest in the land. It draws you irresistibly."

Diederich's understanding with Wulckow, however, had only increased his troubles. The definite obligation to sell his house promised nothing more in return than hopes and prospects: vague prospects and hopes that were too bold. . . .

It was freezing. On Sunday Diederich went to the park, where it was already growing dark, and on a lonely path he met Wolfgang Buck.

"I have made up my mind." Buck declared. "I am going on the stage."

"And what about your social position? And your marriage?"

"I have tried my best, but the theater is preferable. There is less comedy, you know, people are more genuine. The women are also more beautiful."

"That is no attitude," replied Diederich. But Buck was in earnest. "I must say the rumor about Guste and me amused me. On the other hand, silly as it is, the rumor exists. The girl is unhappy and I cannot compromise her any longer." Diederich gave him a look of scorn, for he had the impression that Buck was using the rumor as a pretext to escape. "No doubt," he said sternly, "you understand what you are doing. Now, of course, it will not be easy for her to find a husband. It would take a hell of a lot of chivalry to marry her."

Buck admitted this. "It would be a special satisfaction," he said significantly, "for a really modern, far-seeing man to raise a girl up to his own level, under such circumstances, and to stand up for her. Here, where there is also money, nobility of mind would doubtless carry the day in the end. Remember God's judgment in *Lohengrin*."

"What do you mean, *Lohengrin*?"

Buck did not answer. As they had reached the Saxon Gate he became uneasy. "Will you come in with me?" he asked. "In where?" "Just here, 77 Schweinichenstrasse. I must tell her. Perhaps you could . . ." Then Diederich whistled through his teeth. "You are really . . . You haven't said anything to her yet? You spread it all over town first? That's your affair, my dear fellow, just leave me out of it. I am not in the habit of breaking off the engagements of other men's fiancées."

"Make an exception," begged Buck. "I cannot stand scenes."

"I have principles," said Diederich. Buck turned into the street. "You need not say anything. You need only play a silent part, as moral support."

"Moral?" Diederich queried.

"As the spokesman, so to speak, of the fatal rumor."

"Just what do you mean by that?"

"I am only joking. Come on. Here we are."

Feeling disturbed by Buck's last allusion, Diederich accompanied him without another word.

Frau Daimchen was out, and Guste sent word to them to wait. Buck went to find out what was keeping her. Finally she came, but she was alone. "Wasn't Wolfgang here, too?" she asked.

Buck had left!

"I don't understand this," said Diederich. "He had something very urgent to tell you."

Guste blushed. Diederich turned towards the door. "Then I had better be going as well."

"What on earth did he want?" she inquired. "It doesn't often happen that he wants anything. And why did he bring you with him?"

"I don't understand that either. In fact, I may say that I decidedly object to his bringing witnesses in such a matter. It is not my fault. Good-bye."

The more embarrassed he looked the more insistent she became.

"I must decline," he confessed finally, "to burn my fingers in the affairs of a third person, especially when the third party runs away and evades his most earnest obligations."

With eyes wide open Guste watched each word singly as it fell from Diederich's lips. When the last was uttered she remained motionless for a moment, and then buried her face in her hands. She was sobbing and he could see her swollen cheeks and the tears trickling between her fingers. She had no handkerchief, and Diederich, affected by her sorrow, lent her his. "After all," he said, "he is not such a great loss." But then Guste arose in her wrath. "You dare say that! It was you who always attacked him. That he should send you of all people seems to me more than strange."

"Kindly explain what you mean." demanded Diederich. "You must have known just as well as I, my dear young lady, what to expect from the gentleman in question. When a man's opinions are limp everything else in him is equally so."

As she looked him up and down mockingly, he continued, all the more severely: "I told you beforehand what would happen."

"Because you wanted it to happen." she replied venomously. And Diederich said ironically: "He himself appointed me to keep his pot stirred. And if the pot had not been wrapped in a brown cloth, he would long since have let it boil over."

Then it burst from Guste, in spite of herself: "If you only knew. It is that which I cannot forgive: *everything* was indifferent to him, even my money!"

Diederich was staggered. "One shouldn't have anything to do with such people." he said primly. "They have no backbone, and are as slippery as eels." He nodded his head earnestly. "The person who is indifferent to money does not understand life."

She gave a feeble laugh. "In that case, you understand it wonderfully."

"Let us hope so," he replied. She came closer to him and smiled at him through the last of her tears.

"Well, you have been right all along. What am I to do now?" She turned down the corners of her mouth. "Anyway. I never loved him. I was only waiting for an opportunity to get rid of him. Now he shows what a cad he is by going off himself! . . . Let us get on without him," she added with an alluring glance. But Diederich merely took back his handkerchief, and seemed to have no wish for anything more. Guste realized that his thinking was every bit as strict as it was that time in the Cabinet of Love, and her behavior was consequently all the meeker.

"You are no doubt referring to the position in which I have been placed."

He declined to be drawn. "I did not say anything." Guste complained softly: "If people say dreadful things about me I cannot help it."

"Neither can I."

Guste bowed her head. "Ah, yes, I suppose I shall have to resign myself to it. A person like me does not deserve to be married to a really fine man with a serious view of life." As she said this she peered at him from under her eyelashes to see the effect.

Diederich became flustered. "It is possible"—he began and he paused. Guste held her breath. "Let us suppose," he said with sharp emphasis, "that someone, on the contrary, takes a most earnest view of life, looks at things in a far-seeing modern fashion, as fully conscious of his responsibilities to himself and his future children as to his Emperor and country, and undertakes to protect the defenseless woman and to raise her up to his own level."

Guste's expression had become meeker and meeker. She pressed her palms together, and looked at him, with her head to one side, fervently entreating him. This did not seem to be enough—he obviously demanded something quite unusual, so Guste fell plump upon her knees—then Diederich graciously approached her. "So shall it be," he said, his eyes flashing.

At this point Frau Daimchen entered. "Hello," she said, "what has happened?" With great presence of mind Guste replied: "Oh, mother, we are looking for my ring." Whereupon Frau Daimchen also got down on the ground. Diederich did not wish to be out of it. After they had all crawled about for a while in silence, Guste cried: "Here it is!" She stood up and said in resolute tones: "In case you don't know, mother, I have changed my mind." Frau Daimchen, still out of breath, did not understand at first. Guste and Diederich united their efforts in making the matter clear to her. In the end she admitted that she herself had thought the same thing because of the way people were talking: "In any case, Wolfgang was a bit of a wet blanket, except when he had had something to drink. But the family—you have to admit, the Hesslings just don't quite match up."

Diederich said she would see, and announced that nothing could be really settled until the practical side of the question had been discussed. They had to produce documentary evidence of Guste's dowry, and then he insisted upon joint ownership of the property—and then, whatever he did with the money afterwards, nobody would be able to interfere! Every time they opposed him he took hold of the door handle, and each time Guste remonstrated with her mother in a beseeching whisper: "Do you want the whole town to be wagging their jaws tomorrow because I have got rid of one man and lost the other?"

When everything was settled Diederich became genial. He stayed to supper with the ladies, and without waiting for their answer, he was on the point of sending the servants for champagne to celebrate the engagement, Frau Daimchen was offended at this, for of course she had some in the house, the officers who came to see them expected it. "The truth is you have more luck than cunning, for Lieutenant von Brietzen could also have had Guste." At this Diederich laughed good-humoredly. Things were going swimmingly. He had the money and Emmi had Lieutenant von Brietzen! . . . They grew very jolly. After the second bottle the happy couple were rolling up against one another on their chairs, their legs intertwined up to the knees, and Diederich's hand was busy. Frau Daimchen sat twiddling her thumbs. Suddenly a thundering report was heard for which Diederich at once accepted full responsibility, saying that it was the custom in aristocratic circles, that he was a frequent guest of the Wulckows.

What a surprise when Netzig learned the strange turn the affair had taken! To the inquiries of his congratulating friends Diederich replied that he was quite undecided what he would do with his wife's million and a half. Perhaps he would move to Berlin, the ideal location for far-seeing endeavors. In any case he thought he would sell his factory if an opportunity offered. "The paper industry is going through a crisis anyhow: this little piece of property buried in the middle of Netzig is quite inadequate to my circumstances."

At home there was joy and sunshine. The girls received increased pocket money, and Diederich allowed his mother as many embraces and tender scenes as her heart desired. He even accepted her blessing with good grace. Every time Guste came she appeared as a good fairy, with her arms full of flowers, sweets and silver bags. By her side it seemed to Diederich he was walking along a flower-strewn path. The heavenly days passed quickly, with purchases, champagne breakfasts and visits by the engaged couple, who sat inside the carriage busily absorbed in one another, while the box seat was occupied by a footman hired for the occasion.

Lady Fortune, who had of late been toying capriciously with their existence, led them one evening to a production of *Lohengrin*. Both of their mothers had to agree to stay home; the engaged couple had made up their minds to disregard propriety and sit alone in a proscenium box. The wide, red plush sofa against the wall, where one could sit and not be seen, was caved-in and spotted, which lent it a charmingly dubious air. Guste claimed to know that this box actually belonged to the officers, who received visits here from actresses!

"We've put the actresses safely behind us," Diederich declared, and he hinted that until recently, with a certain lady from the theater, whose name of course he could not mention, he had—. Gustes feverish questions were interrupted in time by the conductor's tapping. They took their seats.

"Hänisch has become even flabbier," Guste remarked at once, nodding down towards the conductor. Upon Diederich he made a highly artistic yet unhealthy impression. He kept time with all his limbs, with straggly locks of black hair flying about his large gray face, upon which pendulous sacks of fat jiggled in unison, while rhythmic undulations could be seen under his coat and trousers. The orchestra was in full swing, but Diederich nevertheless made it clear that he set no store by overtures. Guste remarked that this was nothing compared to the productions of *Lohengrin* put on in Berlin! The curtain rose, and already she was giggling disparagingly. "Heavens, look at Ortrud! She's wearing a dressing gown and a corset!" Diederich was paying more attention to the King under the oak tree, by all appearances the most prominent personality. His bearing did not give a particularly dashing impression; Wulckow made decidedly better use of his bass voice and beard. His words, however, were perfectly sound from a national point of view. "To defend the Empire's honor, in the East and in the West." Bravo! Every time he sang the word "German" he thrust his hand upward, and the music, for its part, substantiated the sentiment. In other respects as well the music underscored vigorously what one was supposed to hear. Vigorous, that was the word. Diederich wished he had had such music when he gave his speech in the sewer debate. The sight of the herald, on the other hand, put him in a melancholy mood, for he bore an uncanny resemblance to Fatty Delitzsch in all his bygone beery guilelessness. This discovery prompted Diederich to take a closer look at the faces of the other vassals, and he found Neo-Teutons everywhere. Their paunches and beards had grown considerably, and they had clad themselves against the tough times in plate armor. It also seemed that not all of them had attained favorable positions in life; the noblemen looked like mid-level public servants of the middle ages, with leathery faces and knock-knees, and those of lesser birth looked even less dashing, but relations with them would most certainly have been carried out in the most impeccable form. Indeed, Diederich noticed from the very beginning that he felt quite at home in this opera. Shields and swords, lots of clanking armor, patriotic sentiments, "Ha!" and "Hail!" and upraised banners and the German Oak Tree. It nearly made one want to play along.

The feminine half of Brabant society, however, left much to be desired. Guste posed derisive questions: now which is the one with whom he—? "Maybe that nanny goat there in the off-the-shoulder dress? Or the fat cow with the gold hoops between her horns?" And Diederich was on the verge of deciding that the black-haired lady with the corset was the one for him when he noticed in time that she was the very one who did not appear in an irreproachable light in the whole affair. Her husband Telramund seemed at first to have a passable sense of form, but a highly unsavory bit of gossip entered the picture here as well. Alas! German loyalty was threatened even here, where it appeared in all its glory, by the Jewish machinations of the dark-haired race. Elsa's appearance removed all doubt as to which side could truly be characterized by the notion of class. The worthy King need not have handled the matter with such objectivity; Elsa's decidedly Germanic cast, her flowing blond hair, the deportment so becoming of her race offered from the beginning certain guarantees. Diederich caught her eye, she looked up, she smiled sweetly. At this point he reached for the opera glass, but Guste snatched it away. "So it's Merée, isn't it?" she hissed, and as he smiled suggestively: "You certainly have fine tastes, I can consider myself flattered. That scrawny little Jew!"—"Jew?"—"Merée, of course, everyone knows her name is Meseritz, and she's forty years old."—He sheepishly took the glass that Guste offered him with a smirk, and saw for himself. Oh well, the world of appearances. Disappointed, Diederich settled back in his seat. Nevertheless, he could not prevent Elsa's chaste presentiment of feminine sensuality from touching him every bit as deeply as it did the King and the noblemen. He, too, deemed the ordeal a superbly practical solution; it insured that no one would be compromised. That the noblemen would never agree to take part in such shady business was of course quite predictable. One had to expect something extraordinary. The music did its part; it prepared one, so to speak, for whatever might come. Diederich's mouth hung open and his eyes shone with such vacuous rapture that Guste had to suppress convulsions of laughter. Now he was ready, everyone was ready, and Lohengrin could make his appearance. He came, he sparkled, he sent away the enchanted swan, he sparkled even more entrancingly. Vassals, noblemen, and King all succumbed to the same astonishment that befell Diederich. Higher powers did not exist for nothing . . . Indeed, the highest power of all was embodied here, glaring enchantingly. Be it the helmet of the swan or that of the eagle: Elsa knew very well why she fell plump upon her knees before him. Diederich, for his part, glared at Guste, who immediately swallowed her laughter. She too had learned what it was like to be the subject of everyone's gossip and to be rid of the first one and not to be able to show one's face anywhere and to really have no choice but to leave town: but then the hero and savior appeared and ignored all the gossip and offered his hand in spite of it all! "So shall it be!" said Diederich and nodded down toward the kneeling Elsa—while Guste, with downcast eyes, sank against his shoulder in contrite submission.

The subsequent events could be counted on one's fingers.

Telramund brought himself into sheer disgrace. No one undertook the slightest action against the powers-that-be. Toward their representative, Lohengrin, even the King behaved at best like one of the more prominent territorial sovereigns. He joined in the chorus of voices singing the hymn of victory to his superior. The stronghold of sound opinions was extolled with fervor, and the revolutionaries were admonished to shake the German dust from their slippers.

The second act—Guste, in quiet devotion, was still eating one praline after another—illustrated in an edifying manner the contrast between the splendid festivities being celebrated without a trace of discord by those of sound opinion in the elegantly illuminated halls of the palace, and the two dark insurgents reclining in abject squalor on the cobblestones. "Arouse thyself, o comrade in disgrace!" Diederich was certain he himself had uttered this at some fitting opportunity. He associated Ortrud with certain personal memories: a vulgar little tramp, what more could one say? But something moved in him when she beguiled her man and wrapped him around her finger. He dreamed. . . . Ortrud had a definite edge on Elsa, the silly goose, with whom she did what she pleased; she had that certain something possessed by all assertive and severe women. Elsa, to be sure, was a woman one could marry. He stole a glance at Guste. "There can be joy without regret," remarked Elsa, and Diederich to Guste: "I should certainly hope so."

The well-rested noblemen and vassals were then informed by Fatty Delitzsch that, by the grace of God, they now had a new sovereign. Only yesterday they had stood by Telramund, loyal and true; today they were true and loyal subjects of Lohengrin. They allowed themselves no opinion and swallowed everything placed before them. "We'll bring the *Reichstag* around to that point before long," Diederich vowed.

When Ortrud wanted to enter the cathedral ahead of Elsa, however, Guste was incensed. "That really isn't necessary, I hate it when she does that. Especially since she hasn't anything left, and just on general principle."—"Jewish impudence," Diederich muttered. Furthermore, he could not help but find it imprudent, to put it mildly, of Lohengrin to place it so clearly within Elsa's power to determine whether or not he should divulge his name and thereby place the whole deal at risk. One ought never to give women such power. Why would one want to? The last thing he needed to do was to prove to the vassals that he, in spite of the grumbler Telramund, had clean hands and a clean scutcheon: their patriotic opinions were marred not by the least bit of wariness.

Guste promised him that in the third act would come the loveliest part, but she would simply have to have more pralines. When these had been duly procured, the strains of the Wedding March began to swell, and Diederich sang along. The vassals in the wedding procession suffered a considerable loss of dash appearing without their armor and banners; Lohengrin, too, would have been better off not showing up in a doublet. At the sight of him Diederich was inspired anew with a sense for the value of a uniform. Happily, the ladies had made their exit, with their voices like sour milk. But the King! He simply could not tear himself away from the presence of the newlywed couple; he tried to ingratiate himself with them and seemed to have no greater wish than to stay on as a spectator. Diederich, who had found the King far too conciliatory all along, now simply called him a nincompoop.

Finally he found the door, and Lohengrin and Elsa on the sofa busied themselves with "the bliss that only God bestows." At first, their embraces involved only the upper body; the lower parts sat as far from one another as possible. The more they sang, however, the closer they sidled up to each other—whereby their faces turned frequently toward Hähnisch. Hähnisch and his orchestra seemed to fan the flame of their passion: it was understandable, for Diederich and Guste as well in their quiet box panted softly and cast each other burning glances. Their feelings were swept along in the wake of the enchanting tones that Hähnisch teased forth with flailing limbs, and their hands followed in turn. Diederich let his slide down between Guste's seat and her back, he encircled her below and murmured in rapture: "The first time I saw that, I said to myself, she's the one!"

But just then they were wrenched from this magical spell by an incident which seemed destined to occupy Netzig's art lovers for quite some time hence. Lohengrin showed his undershirt! He was just striking up "Do you not breathe the same sweet scents as I," when there it came, out of the back of his doublet, which had popped open. Until a visibly perturbed Elsa managed to button him up again, the audience stirred with restless agitation, only to succumb once more to the magical spell. Guste, to be sure, who had choked on a praline, was struck with a thought. "How long has he been wearing that undershirt? And anyway, he hasn't got anything with him, the swan swam off with all his luggage!" Diederich reprimanded her sternly for having dared to think. "You're every bit the silly goose that Elsa is," he declared. For Elsa was on the verge of spoiling everything because she could not keep herself from asking Lohengrin about his political secrets. The revolution was utterly crushed, for Telramund's cowardly assassination attempt failed by the grace of God; but the women, as Diederich had to admit to himself, had an even greater subversive potential when one did not keep a tight rein on them.

After the transfiguration scene, this became clear beyond all doubt. Oak tree, banners, all the patriotic accoutrements were there again, and "For German soil the German sword, thus is the Empire's power restored:" bravo! But Lohengrin really did seem determined to withdraw from public life. "Doubt was cast upon me from all sides," he too could rightfully say. He raised his voice in accusation against the dead Telramund and the unconscious Elsa. Since neither of them contradicted him, he would most certainly have been vindicated in the end, but what was more, he did indeed stand at the top of the ranking. For now he revealed himself. The very mention of his name threw the assembly, who had never heard of him before, into riotous commotion. The vassals were beside themselves with excitement; they seemed to have been prepared for anything but the fact that his name was Lohengrin. With all the more fervor they entreated their beloved sovereign to refrain just this once from the fateful step of abdication. But Lohengrin remained hoarse and unapproachable. Besides, the swan was waiting. One last bit of impudence on the part of Ortrud turned out to be her undoing, to the general satisfaction of all present. Unfortunately, Elsa herself sank to the battlefield immediately thereafter. Upon all of this Lohengrin turned his back and departed, drawn not by the disenchanted swan, but by a muscular dove. His place was taken by the young, newly arrived Gottfried, who became the third sovereign in so many days to whom the nobles and vassals, loyal and worthy as ever, knelt down and paid homage.

"That's what comes of it all," remarked Diederich, helping Guste into her coat. All of these catastrophes, which were the fundamental emanations of Power itself, had left him feeling edified and deeply satisfied. "That's what comes of what?" Guste demanded to know, feeling contentious. "Just because she wants to know who he is? She has every right to ask that, it's a matter of common decency."—"There is a higher meaning to it all," Diederich explained to her with severity. "The business with the Grail, that's supposed to mean that the highest sovereign is responsible, after God, only to his own conscience. And we in turn are responsible to him. When the interest of His Majesty is at stake, I don't care what the circumstances are; I'm not saying anything, but if it comes down to it,—" He indicated with a gesture that he too, if he were to find himself in such a predicament, would sacrifice Guste without a second thought. This incensed Guste. "Why that's murder! Why should I have to pay with my life just because Lohengrin is an apathetic old sheep? Elsa couldn't even get a rise out of him on their wedding night!" And with that, Guste turned up her nose, just as she had done when she walked out of the Cabinet of Love, where nothing had happened either.

The couple made up on the way home. "This is the art we need!" cried Diederich. "This is German art!" For here, he felt, all patriotic demands were fulfilled, in the words as well as in the music. Rebellion was tantamount to crime in this world. The existing, the legitimate were celebrated with splendor; the highest value was placed on nobility and on the grace of God; and the masses, a chorus perpetually surprised by the events which transpired, surged willingly into battle against the enemies of their lords. The warlike underpinnings and the mystical spires, both of these were thus maintained. Furthermore, it struck a familiar and reassuring chord that in this world the man was the one more richly endowed with beauty and favor. "I feel my heart begin to melt, when I behold this delightful man," as the men sang together with the King. Thus was the music, for its part, full of manly bliss, heroic in its luxuriance and patriotic even in its ardor. Who could resist? A thousand performances of such an opera, and there would be no one left who was not nationally disposed! Diederich pronounced: "The theater is one of my weapons as well!" A *lèse-majesté* trial would be hard put to rouse the citizens so thoroughly from their slumber. "I may have sent Lauer to prison, but I take my hat off to the man who wrote *Lohengrin*." He proposed a telegram of approval to Wagner. Guste had to explain to him that this was no longer possible. Having once embarked on such a lofty flight of thought, Diederich began to expound upon art in general. There existed among the various arts an order of precedence. "The highest is music, and for this reason it is the German Art. And then comes drama."

"Why?" asked Guste.

"Because it can be set to music sometimes, and because you don't have to read it, and, well,—"

"And what comes after that?"

"Portraiture, of course, because of the portraits of the Emperors. The rest isn't so important."

"And the novel?"

"That's no art. At least not a German art, thank God. The name alone tells you that."

Then came the wedding day; for they were both in a hurry, Guste because of the people in the town, Diederich for political reasons. In order to make a bigger splash it had been arranged that Magda and Kienast should be married on the same day. Kienast had arrived and Diederich kept looking at him uneasily, for he had shaved off his beard, turned up the points of his mustache and already learned to glare. In the negotiations over Magda's share in the business he displayed a truly terrifying business sense. Not without anxiety over the ultimate outcome of the whole affair, though determined to fulfill his duty to himself completely, Diederich now found himself absorbed in his account books quite often ... Even on his wedding morning he was sitting in his office, in full dress, when a visiting card was presented: Karnauke, First Lieutenant, Retired. "What on earth could he want, Sötbier?" The old bookkeeper did not know either. "Well, it doesn't matter. I can't refuse to see an officer," and Diederich went himself to the door.

In the doorway, however, he met a gentleman who held himself unusually stiffly, in a greenish summer overcoat, which was dripping and was buttoned tightly around his neck. A pool of water formed at once underneath his pointed patent leather shoes, and the rain fell from his green Tyrolese hat, which, curiously, he had not removed. "First let us get dried a bit," said the gentleman, moving towards the stove before Diederich could speak. "For sale, what? In a bit of a bind, what?" At first Diederich did not grasp his meaning: then he glanced uneasily at Sötbier. The old fellow had resumed his letter. "You must have made a mistake in the number of the house, Lieutenant," said Diederich in a conciliatory tone, but it was no use. "Bosh, I know exactly what I'm doing. No nonsense. Superior orders. Sell and keep your mouth shut, or God help you."

These speech mannerisms were too blatant. Diederich could no longer ignore the fact that, in spite of his military past, the incredible stiffness of the gentleman's bearing was not natural, and that his eyes were glassy. Just as Diederich came to this conclusion the gentleman took off his little green hat and shook the water out of it on to Diederich's shirt-front. This resulted in a protest from Diederich which the gentleman took in very bad part. "I am at your disposal," he snarled. "Herren von Quitzin and von Wulckow will call upon you as my seconds." He wiinked with difficulty at these words, and Diederich, upon whom an awful suspicion was dawning, forgot his anger, his sole thought being to get the Lieutenant out through the door. "We'll talk outside," he whispered to him, and to Sötbier, on the other side: "The man is helplessly drunk. I'll have to see how I can get rid of him." But Sötbier's lips were pressed together, his brow wrinkled, and this time he did not return to his letter. The gentleman went straight out into the rain; Diederich following him. "No offense meant; we can talk things over." It was not until he too was soaked that he succeeded in piloting the gentleman back into the building. Through the empty machine room the Lieutenant yelled: "A glass of brandy; I'll buy everything, including the brandy." Although the workmen had the day off, on account of the wedding, Diederich looked around anxiously. He opened the little room where the sacks of chlorine were kept, and got the gentleman inside with a desperate shove. The stench was awful. The gentleman sneezed several times, and then said: "My name is Karnauke. Why do you stink so?"

"Who is backing you?" asked Diederich. This also irritated the gentleman. "What do you mean to insinuate? . . . Oh, I see, I'll buy the whole show." Following Diederich's glance he gazed at his dripping, light summer coat.

"Temporarily embarrassed financially," he growled. "Am acting for honorable parties. Genuine offer."

"How much are you commissioned to offer?"

"A hundred and twenty for the lot."

Diederich grew dismayed and angry by turns. The land alone was worth two hundred thousand. The Lieutenant insisted: "A hundred and twenty for the lot."

"Nothing doing"—Diederich made an incautious move toward the door, whereupon the gentleman lunged for him. Diederich had to struggle, fell on to a sack of chlorine, and the gentleman fell on top of him.

"Get up," gasped Diederich. "we'll be bleached here." The Lieutenant howled aloud as if it already burnt through his clothes—then he suddenly resumed his stiff demeanor. He winked. "Governor von Wulckow will be nasty; if you don't sell, he'll do nothing for you. Cousin Quitzin is extending his property hereabouts. He's counting on your meeting his wishes. A hundred and twenty for the lot." Diederich turned whiter than if he had remained in the chlorine, and tried to say: "One hundred and fifty"—but his voice failed him. It was too much for an honorable man! Wulckow, bristling with honor as a civil servant, incorruptible as the Last Judgment! . . . Disconsolately he once again regarded the figure of this Karnauke, First Lieutenant, Retired. That was the man Wulckow sent; he put himself in the hands of such a person! Couldn't they have negotiated the deal discreetly between themselves, with all due precautions and with mutual respect? But these Junkers could only spring at your throat: they could not yet understand that business is business. "Just go on ahead to the notary's," whispered Diederich. "I'll follow you." He showed him out, but when he himself was on the point of leaving, old Sötbier was standing there, with his lips still drawn into a tight line. "What do you want?" Diederich was exhausted.

"Young master," began the old man in a hollow voice. "I can no longer be responsible for what you are now planning to do."

"You're not asked to be." Diederich recovered his composure. "I am the best judge of what I am doing." The old man raised his hands in dismay.

"You do not know, Master Diederich! It is the life-work of your lamented father and myself that I am defending. Your present success has been made possible by the diligence and the quality work with which we built up this business. If you buy expensive machinery at one time and decline contracts the next, that is a zigzag course that will bring the business to ruin. And now you are selling the old house."

"You were listening at the keyhole. If anything happens without your knowledge, you cannot stand the idea. Mind you don't catch cold here," Diederich sneered.

"You must not sell it!" moaned Sötbier. "I cannot look on and see the son and heir of my old master undermining the solid foundations of the firm and playing the big politician."

Diederich gave him a pitying look. "In your time, Sötbier, far-seeing endeavors were unknown. Nowadays people take risks. Push is the main thing. Later you will see why it was a good idea to sell the house."

"Yes, you will see that later, too. Perhaps when you are bankrupt, or when your brother-in-law, Herr Kienast, begins a lawsuit against you. You have arranged things to the disadvantage of your sisters and your mother! If I were to tell Herr Kienast certain things—if it weren't for the reverence in which I hold your father's memory I could get you into quite a bit of trouble!"

The old man was beside himself. He was screaming and tears of passion brimmed over his red eyelids. Diederich went up to him and held his clenched fist under his nose: "Just you try it! I will simply prove that you have been robbing the firm and always did. Do you imagine I haven't taken precautions?"

The old man also raised his trembling fist. They fumed at one another. Sötbier's bloodshot eyes were rolling. Diederich glared. Then the old fellow drew back. "No, this cannot happen. I was always a faithful servant of the old master. My conscience commands me to give my faithful services to his successors as long as possible."

"That would suit you very well," said Diederich harshly and coldly. "Consider yourself lucky that I don't fire you on the spot. You may send in your resignation, it is accepted." And he marched off.

At the notary's he asked that the purchaser in the deed of sale be described as "unknown." Karnauke grinned. "Unknown—that's a good one. Don't we know Herr von Quitzin?" At this the notary also smiled. "I see," he said, "Herr von Quitzin is expanding. For a long time he owned only the tiny Rooster Tavern in Meisestrasse. But he is also in negotiation for the two pieces of property behind yours, Dr. Hessling. Then he will be on the borders of the park and will have room for immense buildings."

Diederich began to tremble again. In a whisper he begged the notary to be discreet as long as possible. Then he said goodbye, as he had no time to lose. "I know," said the Lieutenant, holding him back. "Day of joy. Luncheon at the Hotel Reichshof. I'm ready." He opened his green overcoat and pointed to his crumpled dress-suit. Diederich looked at him in horror, tried to put him off, but the Lieutenant again threatened him with his backers.

The bride had been waiting for a long time, and the two mothers were drying her tears amidst the knowing smiles of the other ladies present. This bridegroom had bolted as well! Magda and Kienast were furious, and messengers were running between Schweinichen- strasse and Meisestrasse . . . At last Diederich came, though he was wearing his old dress suit. He did not even attempt any explana- tion. At the civil ceremony and in the church he gave a bewildered impression. Everyone said that no blessing could rest upon a union brought about under such circumstances. Pastor Zillich even men- tioned in his sermon that earthly possessions did not endure. His disappointment was comprehensible. Käthchen did not show up at all.

At the wedding luncheon Diederich sat in silence, obviously thinking about other things. He even kept forgetting to eat and stared into space. Lieutenant Karnauke alone had the ability to arouse his attention. Admittedly, the Lieutenant did his best. No sooner had the soup been removed than he proposed a toast to the bride, making allusions for which the assembled guests were not quite ready, judging from the amount of wine that had thus far been consumed. Diederich was disturbed by certain other refer- ences of Karnauke's, which were accompanied by winks in his direction and which unfortunately roused Kienast's suspicions. The moment arrived which Diederich had foreseen with beating heart. Kienast stood up and asked him for a word in private. . . . Just then the Lieutenant tapped energetically on his glass, and jumped smartly from his seat. The festive clamor broke off abruptly. A blue ribbon could be seen hanging from Karnauke's fingers, and beneath it hung a cross, on which the gold rim sparkled . . . Oohs and ahs and uproar and congratulations! Diederich stretched out his two hands, a nearly unbearable joy flowed from his heart to his throat, and he began to speak involuntarily, before he knew what he was saying: "His Majesty . . . unprecedented graciousness . . . modest services . . . unshakable loyalty." He bowed and scraped, and as Karnauke handed him the cross, he laid his hands on his heart, closed his eyes and sank back, as if another stood before him: the majestic donor himself.

Basking in the sun of imperial approval Diederich felt that this was his rescue, this his victory. Wulckow had kept his pact. Author- ity kept its pact with Diederich! The Order of the Crown, fourth class, glittered. It was an event, foreshadowing the Wilhelm the Great monument and Gausenfeld, business and glory!

It was time to break up. Kienast was moved and intimidated. Diederich flung him a few general remarks about the glorious days which he would enjoy, and the great things which were in store for him and the whole family—and then Diederich left with Guste.

They got into a first-class carriage. He gave the porter three marks and pulled down the blinds. Carried on the wings of happiness, his desire for action suffered no relaxation. Guste could never have expected so amorous a temperament. "You are not like Lohengrin after all," she said. As she closed her eyes and began to sink back, Diederich got up again. Like a man of iron he stood before her, his order hanging on his breast; a man of iron with eyes aglare. "Before we go any further," he said in martial tones, "let us think of His Majesty, our Gracious Emperor. We must keep before us the higher aim of doing honor to His Majesty, and of giving him capable soldiers."

"Oh!" cried Guste, carried away into loftier splendors by the sparkling ornament on his breast. "Is it... really... you... my Diederich!"

Chapter 6

Herr and Frau Dr. Hessling from Netzig gazed mutely at one another in the lift of the hotel in Zurich, for they were being taken up to the fourth floor. This was the result of the quick, discreet glance with which the clerk at the desk had appraised them. Diederich obediently filled out the form for visitors, but when the waiter had withdrawn, he gave vent to his indignation at the way things were done here, and about Zurich in general. His invectives grew louder and finally took shape in the resolve to write to Baedeker. As this reprisal seemed a little too intangible he turned on Guste. It was all the fault of her hat. Guste, in turn, blamed his Hohenzollern coat.

Thus they descended to lunch, both red with anger. At the door they stopped, and sniffed superciliously as they met the gaze of the hotel guests. Diederich in his dinner jacket, and Guste wearing a hat with ribbons, feathers and a buckle, which certainly entitled her to the best floor in the hotel. Their earlier acquaintance, the waiter, conducted them in triumph to their seats.

That night they became reconciled to both Zurich and the hotel. In the first place their room on the fourth floor may not have been distinguished, but it certainly was cheap. And then, just opposite the twin beds of the married couple there hung an almost life-size picture of an odalisque, whose brownish body reclined voluptuously on a pillow, her hands under her head, and her dark eyes full of languishing desire. The figure was cut off in the middle by the frame, a fact that moved them to joking comment. The next day they went about with eyelids heavy as lead, ate enormous meals, and wondered what would have happened if the odalisque had been entirely visible instead of being cut off from the waist. They were both so tired that they missed the train and returned in the evening, as soon as possible, to their inexpensive and exhausting room. There was no saying when this sort of existence might have ended, if Diederich's heavy eyes had not caught sight of an announcement in the newspaper that the Emperor was on his way to Rome to visit the King of Italy.

He roused himself in a flash. With elastic stride he went from the hall-porter to the office, and from the office to the lift, and though Guste wailed that she was dizzy, the trunks were made ready, and Diederich dragged Guste off. "Oh, why," she complained, "must we leave a place where the bed is so comfortable?" But Diederich had only a mocking look for the odalisque as they left. "Have a good time, my dear young lady!"

For a long time he could not sleep for excitement. Guste snored peaceably on his shoulder, while Diederich, hurtling through the night, remembered how at that very moment, on another line, the Emperor himself was hurtling towards the same goal. The Emperor and Diederich were having a race! And, as Diederich had more than once been privileged to utter thoughts which in some mystic way seemed to coincide with those of His Highness, perhaps at that hour His Majesty knew of Diederich, knew that his loyal subject was crossing the Alps by his side, in order to show these cowardly Latins what loyalty to Emperor and country means. He glared at the sleepers on the opposite seat, small, dark people, whose faces seemed haggard in their sleep. They would see what Germanic valor was!

Passengers got out in the early morning at Milan, and at Florence, about noon, to Diederich's astonishment. Without any no-

264 · Heinrich Mann

ticeable success he endeavored to impress upon those who remained what a great event awaited them in Rome. Two Americans showed themselves somewhat more receptive, at which Diederich exclaimed triumphantly: "Ah, I am sure you also envy us our Emperor." Then the Americans looked at one another in a mute query that remained unanswered.

Before they reached Rome Diederich's excitement grew into a feverish desire for action. With his finger in a phrase book he ran after the employees on the train, trying to find out who would arrive first, his Emperor or he. His enthusiasm had infected Guste. "Diedel!" she cried, "I feel like throwing my veil on the ground for him to walk on and flinging the roses from my hat at him!" "What if he sees you and you make an impression on him?" asked Diederich, with a feverish smile. Guste's bosom began to heave and she dropped her eyes. Diederich, who was panting, broke the fearful tension. "My manly honor is sacred. I must insist. But in such a case . . ." and he concluded with a brief gesture.

Then they arrived, but very differently from how they had imagined. In the greatest confusion the passengers were pushed by officials out of the station, over to the edge of a broad square and into the streets behind it, which were immediately closed off again. With unshakable enthusiasm Diederich broke through the barriers. Guste, who stretched out her arm in horror, was left standing there with all the hand luggage, while he stormed blindly forward. He had reached the middle of the square, and two soldiers with plumed helmets were running after him so that the tails of their gaily colored dress tunics flapped in the breeze. Then several gentlemen walked down the sloping entrance to the station, and almost simultaneously Diederich saw a carriage driving toward him. He waved his hat and bawled so loudly that the gentlemen in the carriage interrupted their conversation. The one on the right leaned forward and—they were face to face, Diederich and his Emperor! The Emperor smiled coldly and critically with the corners of his eyes, and the corners of his mouth dropped slightly. Diederich ran along beside the carriage for a stretch, with bulging eyes, waving his hat and shouting all the while. For a few seconds, while a crowd of strangers in the background applauded, the Emperor and his loyal subject were alone together, in the middle of the empty square, beneath the glaring blue sky.

The carriage had already disappeared along the streets hung with bunting and the cheers were fading in the distance, when Diederich heaved a great sigh, closed his eyes, and put on his hat.

Guste was beckoning to him frantically, and the people who were still standing around applauded, their faces beaming with cheerful good nature. Even the soldiers who had previously followed him were now laughing. One of them showed his sympathy by calling a cab. As he drove off Diederich saluted the crowd. "They are like children," he said to his wife. "But correspondingly undisciplined." he added, and he admitted: "That could not have happened in Berlin ... When I think of the crowd in Unter den Linden, I remember that order was much more sharply maintained." He tidied himself before they drove up to the hotel. Thanks to his manner, they were given a room on the second floor.

The early morning sun saw Diederich once more in the streets. "The Emperor is an early riser," he had informed Guste, who only grunted from the pillows. In any case she would be of no use to him in his task. With his finger in a guidebook he arrived in front of the Quirinal, and took up his position. The quiet square gleamed bright gold under the oblique rays of the sun. The stark and massive bulk of the palace stood out against the empty sky—and opposite stood Diederich, awaiting His Majesty, the Order of the Crown, fourth class, on his protruding chest. A herd of goats tripped up the steps from the city, and disappeared behind the fountain and the statues of giant horse-tamers. Diederich did not look around. Two hours went by, more people began to pass, a sentry had come out of his box, in one of the portals a gatekeeper was moving about, and several persons went in and out. Diederich became restless. He approached the façade and slowed his pace as he passed by, peering anxiously inside. On his third pass the gatekeeper touched his hat hesitantly. When Diederich stopped and returned his salute, he became more confidential. "Everything is in order," he said behind his hand, and Diederich acknowledged the report with an air of understanding. It seemed to him only natural that he should be informed of the Emperor's welfare. His questions, when the Emperor would be going out and where, were answered without hesitation. The gatekeeper himself came up with the suggestion that in order to accompany the Emperor Diederich would need a carriage, and he sent for one. Meanwhile a little knot of curious onlookers had formed, and then the gatekeeper stepped to one side. Behind an outrider, in an open carriage, came the blond ruler of the North, beneath his flashing eagle-helmet. Diederich's hat was in the air and he shouted in Italian, with the precision of a pistol shot: "Long live the Emperor!" And obligingly the knot of people shouted with him. In a jump Diederich had got into his one-horse carriage, which stood ready, and was off in pursuit, urging the coachman with hoarse cries and an ample tip. And indeed, now he stopped, for the imperial carriage was only just coming up. When the Emperor got out there was another little knot of people, and again Diederich shouted in Italian ... Watch must be kept in front of the house where the Emperor lingers! With chest extended and flashing eyes: let him beware who ventures too near! In ten minutes the little group had re-formed, the carriage drove out through the gate, Diederich shouted: "Long live the Emperor!" and the shout was echoed by the crowd, as the company rushed wildly back to the Quirinal. Guard was mounted. The Emperor in a shako. Another visit, another return, another uniform, and again Diederich, and again an enthusiastic reception. So it went, and never had Diederich known such a glorious life. His friend the gatekeeper kept him reliably informed as to the Emperor's movements. It also happened that an official would salute and give him a message which he condescendingly received, or that another would ask for instructions—which Diederich then gave in general terms, but in a commanding voice. The sun rose higher and higher. In front of the marble squares of the façade, behind which his Emperor was holding conversations covering the whole orbit of the world, Diederich suffered hunger and thirst without flinching. Although he held himself firmly erect, he felt, nevertheless, as if his paunch were sinking to the pavement under the burden of noon, and his Order of the Crown, fourth class, were melting on his chest ... The coachman, whose visits to the nearest tavern were becoming more frequent, was finally impressed by the German's heroic sense of duty and brought him back some wine. With a new fire in their veins the pair took up the next race. The imperial horses ran quickly: in order to get there before them, it was necessary to plunge through side streets that looked like canals, where the few pedestrians shrank back in terror against the walls. Or they had to get out and clamber madly up flights of steps. But Diederich appeared punctually at the head of his little crowd, watched for the seventh uniform emerging from the carriage and shouted. Then the Emperor turned his head and smiled. He recognized him, his loyal subject! The one who shouted, who was always on the spot, like a devoted retainer. Diederich flew on the wings of elation, basking in His Highness's attention. He glared at the people, whose faces wore an expression of cheerful good nature.

Only when the gatekeeper assured him that His Majesty was now at lunch did Diederich allow himself to think of Guste. "What a sight you are!" she cried, drawing back against the wall, when she beheld him. He was as red as a tomato, soaked with perspiration, and his eyes were as bright and wild as those of an ancient Germanic warrior on a foray through the Latin territories. "This is a great day for the national cause!" he replied furiously. "His Majesty and I are making moral conquests!" How fine he looked! Guste forgot her fright and her annoyance at the long wait. She came up with her arms affectionately outstretched and clung to him humbly.

Diederich, however, would hardly allow himself the brief hour for lunch. He knew that the Emperor rested after eating. Then it was his duty to mount guard under his windows and not to budge. He did not budge, and the result showed how right he had been. For he had not been eighty minutes at his post opposite the portal of the palace, when a suspicious looking individual, taking advantage of the brief absence of the gatekeeper, slipped in, hid behind a pillar, and in the dark shadow harbored plans which could be nothing less than calamitous. But he had not reckoned with Diederich! With a warlike cry the latter could be seen thundering across the square like a storm. Startled spectators rushed after him, the guard hurried up, in the gateway servants were running about—and everyone admired Diederich as he dragged some man forward, wildly struggling, who had hidden himself. The two of them flailed about so frantically that not even the armed guards could get near. Suddenly Diederich's opponent, who had succeeded in freeing his right arm, was seen swinging a box. A breathless second—then the panic-stricken crowd rushed yelling to the gate. A bomb! He is going to throw it! . . . He had thrown it! In expectation of the explosion, those nearest threw themselves on the ground, whimpering in advance. But Diederich, his face, shoulders and chest all white, stood there and sneezed. There was a strong smell of peppermint. The boldest returned and investigated him with their noses. A soldier, with waving plumes, gingerly dipped his moistened finger into it, and tasted it. Diederich grasped the situation and explained it to the crowd, whose expression of cheerful good humor returned, for he himself was no longer in doubt that he was covered with tooth powder. Nevertheless, he remained heedful of the danger that the Emperor, thanks to his vigilance, had perhaps escaped. The bomb-thrower—absolutely in vain—tried to sidestep him and make his getaway. Diederich's iron fist delivered him to the police. The latter ascertained that the man was a German, and asked Diederich to question him. In spite of the tooth powder which covered him, he undertook this duty with the utmost dignity. The answers of the man, who, significantly enough, was an artist, had no particular political color, but their abysmal lack of respect and moral sense betrayed only too clearly revolutionary tendencies. Therefore Diederich strongly urged that he be arrested. The police led him off, and they did not forget to salute Diederich, who had only just time to get himself brushed off by his friend the gatekeeper. For the Emperor was announced, and Diederich's personal service began again.

This service led him hither and thither without pause into the night and led him at last to the German embassy, where His Majesty was holding a reception. One of His Highness's longer visits provided Diederich with the opportunity to revive his spirits at a nearby tavern. He climbed up onto a chair in front of the door and addressed the populace in a speech, borne aloft by patriotic spirit, which drove home to this unruly mob the merits of strict discipline and an emperor who was no puppet. . . . They saw him, bathed in the red glow of the flames which blazed in open basins in front of the palace of the German Empire, standing on his chair, his mouth bracketed by its adornment of angular facial hair and working furiously, they saw him glare and stiffen as though cast in iron—all of which apparently sufficed for them to understand him, for they jubilated, applauded, and hailed the Emperor every time Diederich hailed him. With a gravity that was not without an aspect of threat, Diederich accepted the foreign homage on behalf of his sovereign and of the terrible power of his sovereign; upon which he climbed down from the chair and returned to his wine. Several of his countrymen, hardly less animated than he, toasted him and returned his toasts in the traditional German manner. One of them opened up an evening newspaper with a huge portrait of the Emperor and read the account of an incident brought about by a German in the portal of the Quirinal. It was only through the presence of mind demonstrated by an official in the personal service of the Emperor that the incident did not come to anything more dire; the article also included a picture of this official. Diederich stared in recognition. Even if the likeness was at most of a general nature and the name was badly garbled, the mustache and the breadth of the face tallied. Thus did Diederich see the Emperor and himself united on the same newspaper page: the Emperor, together with his subject, presented to the world for admiration. It was too much. His eyes glistening moistly, Diederich drew himself up and began to sing "The Sentry on the Rhine." The wine, which was so cheap, and the enthusiasm, which received fresh nourishment again and again, had brought about a considerable detriment to Diederich's deportment by the time he received the message that the Emperor was leaving the embassy. He nevertheless did everything within his power to fulfill his duty. He zigzagged down the Capitol, stumbled, and rolled down the steps. His drinking companions caught up with him in the narrow street below; he was standing with his face to the wall . . . Blazing torches, hoofbeats: the Emperor! The others reeled after the carriage; but Diederich, his sense of form could not help him now, slipped and fell where he stood. Two municipal watchmen found him, propped up against the wall, sitting in a puddle. They recognized the official in the personal service of the German Emperor, and fearing the worst, they bent down over him. But in the next moment they looked at one another and burst out in raucous merriment. The personal official was not dead, thank heavens, for he was snoring; and the puddle in which he was sitting was not blood.

The following evening at the gala performance at the theater the Emperor looked more serious than usual. Diederich noticed it, and said to Guste: "Now I know why I spent our good money coming here. Just watch, this will be an historic occasion!" His premonition did not deceive him. The evening papers were seen in the theater, and it was learned that the Emperor was going away that night, that he had dissolved the Reichstag! Diederich, no less serious than the Emperor, explained the significance of the event to everyone near him. The revolutionaries had dared to vote against the military appropriations bill! The patriotic parties were entering upon a life-and-death struggle for their Emperor! He himself was returning home by the next train, he assured them, and they hastened to tell him at what hour it left . . . The one person who was dissatisfied was Guste.

"When one has arrived in a new place, at last, and thank God, one has the money and can afford it, why should I, after moping two days in the hotel, start back at once, just because of—" She threw a glance of such disgust at the royal box that Diederich had to intervene with the utmost severity. Guste answered loudly, everyone around them cried *Sh!* and when Diederich turned around to glare defiantly at the objectors, he and Guste found themselves compelled to leave well before their train was to depart. "That rabble has no manners," he remarked, snorting furiously, when they got outside. "What's so good about this place anyway, I'd like to know? The weather is all right, I suppose. . . Well, at least have a look at all this old stuff lying about," he commanded. Browbeaten back into submission, Guste whined, "I *am* enjoying it." Then they departed at a respectful distance behind the Emperor's train. Guste had forgotten her sponges and brushes in their haste and at every station she wanted to get out. Diederich had to remind her ceaselessly of the national cause, in order to induce her to wait for thirty-six hours. When they finally arrived in Netzig, however, her first thought was for the sponges. Of course, they had arrived on a Sunday! Fortunately, the Lion Pharmacy, at least, was open. While Diederich was waiting in the station for the luggage Guste went over to it. When she did not return, he went after her.

The door of the apothecary's was half-open, and three youths were peering in and laughing. Diederich looked over their shoulders and was amazed, for inside his old university friend, Gottlieb Hornung, was marching up and down behind the counter, with folded arms and his face set in a scowl. Guste was just saying: "Now I'd really like to know when I am going to get my toothbrush." Then Gottlieb Hornung stepped forward from behind the counter, with arms still crossed, and turned his scowl upon Guste. "You cannot fail," he began oratorically, "to have noticed by my expression that I have neither the will nor the power to sell you a toothbrush." Guste drew back and said: "Really! But you have a whole showcase full." Gottlieb Hornung smiled demonically. "My uncle upstairs"—he jerked up his head and pointed with his chin to the ceiling, above which his employer doubtless resided—"my uncle can sell here what he likes. That does not concern me. I did not study for three years and belong to a swagger students' corps in order to come here and sell toothbrushes." "What are you here for, then?" asked Guste, visibly intimidated. Then Hornung replied with majestic emphasis: "I am here to attend exclusively to prescriptions!" Guste must have felt that she was beaten, for she turned to go. Then something else occurred to her: "I suppose it is the same with sponges?" "Just the same," Hornung assured her. This was obviously what Guste had been waiting for, and now she lost her temper properly. She stuck out her chest and was going to give him a piece of her mind. Diederich had just time to intervene.

He agreed with his friend that the dignity of the Neo-Teutons should be preserved and their banner held aloft. But if anyone wanted a sponge he could, after all, take it himself and deposit the amount—which Diederich proceeded to do. Gottlieb Hornung, meanwhile, moved to one side and began to whistle, as if he were quite alone. Then Diederich expressed his interest in what his friend had been doing since they last met. Unfortunately, it was a story of many mishaps, for as Hornung never wanted to sell sponges and toothbrushes, he had already been dismissed by five apothecaries. Nevertheless he was determined to stand by his convictions, at the risk of losing his present situation. "Take a look— there's a real Neo-Teuton for you!" said Diederich to Guste, who took a good look at him.

In his turn, Diederich was not slow to relate all his experiences and achievements. He drew attention to his medal, turned Guste around in front of Hornung, and mentioned the size of her fortune. The Emperor, whose enemies and slanderers were behind lock and key, thanks to Diederich, had recently escaped grave personal danger in Rome, also thanks to Diederich. In order to avoid panic in the courts of Europe and on the Stock Exchange, the press had spoken only of a silly tooth powder trick played by a half-wit. "But between ourselves, I have reason to believe that it was a widespread plot. You will understand, Hornung, that the national interest commands the utmost discretion for I am sure you, too, are a loyal patriot." Of course, Hornung was, and so Diederich could unburden himself about the highly important task which had compelled him suddenly to return from his honeymoon. It was a question of pushing through the national candidates in Netzig! They must not underestimate the difficulties. Netzig was a stronghold of Liberalism, and revolution was undermining the foundations. . . . At this stage Guste threatened to drive off home with the luggage. Diederich could only invite his friend urgently to come to see him that very evening, as he had pressing matters to talk over with him. As he got into the cab he saw one of the young rascals, who had waited outside, going inside the shop and asking for a toothbrush. Diederich reflected that Gottlieb Hornung, because of the aristocratic tendency which so hindered him in the sale of sponges and toothbrushes, might be an invaluable ally in the fight against democracy. But this was the least of his immediate cares. He only gave Frau Hessling a brief opportunity to shed a few tears; then she was ordered to return to the top floor, formerly reserved for the servant and the wet laundry, and where Diederich had now banished his mother and Emmi. With the soot from his journey still in his beard he walked by way of the back streets to Governor von Wulckow's, whereupon he sent with no less discretion for Napoleon Fischer, and in the meantime had taken steps to arrange without delay a meeting with Kunze, Kühnchen, and Zillich.—All of this was rendered more difficult because it was a Sunday afternoon; the Major could be dragged only with the greatest difficulty from his game of nine-pins, the Pastor had to be interrupted as he was preparing to go out on a family excursion with Käthchen and Jadassohn, and the professor was in the hands of his two boarders, who had already got him half drunk. Finally they were all united in the club room of the Veterans' Association, and Diederich explained to them, without further loss of time, that they would have to run a national candidate. And, as things were, there could be no question of anyone but Major Kunze. "Hurrah!" cried Kühnchen, at once, but the Major's expression threatened a storm. Did they take him for a fool? he snarled. Did they think he was anxious to put his foot in it? "A national candidate in Netzig—I have no doubts as to what will happen to him! If everything else were as certain as his defeat!" Diederich would not hear of this. "We have the Veterans' Association, you must take that into account, gentlemen. The Veterans' Association is an invaluable basis of operations. From that point we can strike out in a straight line, so to speak, to the Emperor Wilhelm Monument: there the battle will be won." "Hurrah!" cried Kühnchen again, but the other two wanted to know what all this talk was about a monument. Diederich initiated them into his idea, but preferred to gloss over the fact that it was the result of a pact between himself and Napoleon Fischer. The Liberal foundling hospital was not popular, so much he confided, and many voters would be drawn to the national cause if they were promised an Emperor Wilhelm Monument out of the Kühlemann bequest. In the first place, this would create more employment, and then it would bring business to the town, for the unveiling of such a monument drew people from far and wide. Netzig had a prospect of losing its bad reputation as a democratic swamp and of basking in the sun of official favor. At this Diederich remembered his pact with Wulckow, which he also preferred to leave unmentioned. To the man who has achieved and secured so much for us all"—he pointed with a flourish to Kunze—"our dear old town will one day certainly erect a monument. He and Emperor

Wilhelm the Great will face each other—" "And stick out our tongues," concluded the Major, whose skepticism was unshaken. "If you believe that the people of Netzig are only waiting for the great man to lead them, with fifes and drums, into the national camp, why do you not play the part of that great man yourself?" And his eyes looked squarely into Diederich's. But the latter only returned his gaze all the more virtuously and laid his hand on his heart. "Major, my well-known devotion to my Emperor and country has already imposed upon me trials more severe than a candidacy to the Reichstag, and I think I may say I have stood the test! And in doing so I was not afraid, as a pioneer in a good cause, to draw upon myself all the hatred of ill-disposed people, thereby making it impossible for me to reap the fruit of my sacrifice. Netzig would not vote for me, but it will vote for my cause. Therefore, I withdraw, for it is characteristic of a German to be practical, and I leave you, Major, without envy, the joys and the honor!"

The assembly stirred with emotion; Kühnchen's "bravos" sounded tearful, the Pastor nodded solemnly, and Kunze stared under the table, visibly shaken. Diederich felt relieved, and virtuous; he had allowed his heart to speak, and it had expressed loyalty, sacrifice, and manly idealism. Diederich's blond-bristled hand reached across the table and the Major's brown-bristled one clasped it, hesitantly yet firmly.

After the hearts of all four had spoken, however, reason spoke up. The Major inquired whether Diederich was prepared to compensate him for the losses, intangible as well as material, that threatened him if he were to enter the lists against the candidate of the Liberal gang and be defeated. "Look here"—he pointed his finger at Diederich, who could not immediately find words to counter this directness—"the national cause does not seem all that kosher to you either, and knowing you, Dr. Hessling, the fact that you insist on bringing me into it is connected with some chicanery or other on your part, which a bluff old soldier like myself cannot, thank God, understand." At this, Diederich hastened to promise the bluff old soldier a decoration, and as he gave a hint of his understanding with Wulckow, the national candidate was finally won over completely. . . . Meanwhile Pastor Zillich had given serious thought to whether his position in the town would permit of his being chairman of the national camp's election committee. Was he to introduce dissension among his flock? His own brother-in-law, Heuteufel, was the Liberal candidate! Of course, if a church were to be built instead of a monument! "Truly, the house of God is more necessary than ever, and my beloved St. Mary's is so neglected by the town that one of these days it will fall on the heads of myself and my Christians." Without hesitation Diederich guaranteed all the necessary repairs. The only condition he made was that the Pastor ensure that all positions of trust in the new party were kept free of any persons for whom even certain mannerisms gave rise to legitimate doubt as to the genuineness of their national sentiments. "Without wishing to interfere in family matters," Diederich added, looking hard at Käthchen's father, who had clearly understood, for he remained silent ... But Kühnchen, who had long since ceased to shout *hurrah,* also presented himself. The two others had only kept him in his seat by force while they were speaking. They had scarcely released him when he stormed into the debate. Where would national sentiment necessarily have its roots, above all? Among the youth! But how could that be, when the headmaster of the high school was a friend of Herr Buck's? "I could talk myself hoarse about our glorious deeds back in 1870." In short, Kühnchen wanted to be appointed headmaster, and Diederich magnanimously granted his request.

After the political standpoint had thus been established on the healthy foundation of common interests, the gentlemen could give themselves over in good conscience to that enthusiasm which, as Pastor Zillich explained, came directly from God and bestowed the requisite benediction upon even the best of causes, and so they repaired to the *Ratskeller.*

In the gray of dawn, as the four gentlemen were returning home, they found posted between the white campaign placards of Heuteufel's and the red ones of Comrade Fischer's the broadsides bordered in black, white, and red which hailed Major Kunze as the candidate of "The Emperor's Party." Diederich planted himself in front of them as firmly as he could and read with a vigorous tenor voice: "Those men without a fatherland from the dissolved *Reichstag* have dared to deny our glorious Emperor the means he requires to maintain the greatness of the Empire ... Let us prove ourselves worthy of the great Monarch and smash his enemies! Our only program: the Emperor! Those for me and those against me: Revolution and the Emperor's Party!" Kühnchen, Zillich, and Kunze affirmed all of this with clamorous cries, and as a number of workers on their way to the factory stopped in astonishment, Diederich turned around and elucidated to them the national manifesto.

"People!" he cried. "You don't know how lucky you are to be Germans. For the whole world envies us our Emperor; I can personally attest to this after my travels abroad." At this, Kühnchen beat a tattoo on the billboard with his fist, and the four gentlemen shouted "hurrah" while the workers looked on. "Do you want your Emperor to present you with colonies?" Diederich asked them. "Well, then. You'll just have to sharpen his sword for him, won't you! Don't even think of voting for any men without a fatherland, I won't stand for it! The only one to vote for is the candidate of the Emperor, Herr Major Kunze, otherwise there is no telling what will become of our status in the world, and it may very well happen that you will go home every two weeks with twenty marks less in your pockets!" At this, the workers exchanged mute glances and then trudged on towards the factory.

But the gentlemen lost no time either. Kunze himself, on stiff legs, set about the task of driving home the standpoint to the members of the Veterans' Association. "If those fellows believe," he declared, "that they will be able to belong to free unions in the future! We'll drive the liberalism out of them! Let me tell you, starting today it's going to be a different tune altogether!" Pastor Zillich made a similar promise of action in the Christian organizations, while Kühnchen anticipated ecstatically the fresh enthusiasm of his senior class, who were to dash about the town on their bicycles and drum up voters. The most feverish sense of duty, however, was the one that seized Diederich. He disdained all rest; to his wife, who lay in bed and greeted him with remonstrations, he retorted with eyes aglare: "My Emperor has beaten upon his sword, and when my Emperor beats upon his sword, then there are no more conjugal duties. Is that understood?" Thereupon Guste turned over in a huff and piled up the feather bed, filled with her posterior charms, like a tower between herself and the disobliging Diederich. Diederich suppressed the regret that threatened to seize him and promptly penned an admonition against the Liberal foundling hospital. The *Netzig Journal* printed it as well, even though it had printed a thoroughly favorable recommendation of the foundling hospital from the quill of Dr. Heuteufel just two days before. For, as the editor Nothgroschen added, the organ of the educated bourgeoisie owed it to its subscribers above all to apply the touchstone of its cultural conscience to every new idea as it emerged. This is just what Diederich did, and in an utterly devastating fashion at that. For whom was such a foundling hospital intended above all? For illegitimate children. So what did it foster? Vice. Is that what we really needed? Hardly; "for we have not sunk to the unfortunate level of the French, thank God, who due to the consequences of their democratic licentiousness are clearly on their way out. Let them celebrate illegitimate births; that is the only way they will ever have enough soldiers. We, however, have not reached such a state of decay; we enjoy an inexhaustible birth rate! We are the salt of the earth!" And Diederich worked out for the subscribers of the *Netzig Journal* how long it would take them and their fellow countrymen to reach the hundred-million mark, and how long it would take, at most, until the entire earth was German.

These were the preparations that the national committee considered necessary for the first election meeting of the "Emperor's Party." It was to take place at Klappsch's, who had patriotically thrown open his rooms. In the midst of green wreaths flaming mottoes were set. "The Will of the Emperor is the Supreme Command." "You have only one Enemy, and that is My Enemy." "Leave the Social Democrats to Me." "Mine is the Right Course." "Citizens, awaken from your Slumbers!"—The awakening was helped along by Klappsch and his daughter, who kept them constantly supplied with fresh beer, without being as particular as usual about the amount each guest consumed. Thus everyone was in a good mood to receive Kunze when he was introduced by the chairman, Pastor Zillich. Diederich, however, from behind the cloud of smoke in which the committee sat, made the unpleasant discovery that Heuteufel, Cohn and some of their followers had also gained admission. He took Gottlieb Hornung to task, for the latter was supposed to be watching the door. But he would not listen, for he was irritated; he had had enough trouble trying to get people to attend. Thanks to his efforts, there were now so many contractors for the Emperor Wilhelm Monument that the town would never be able to pay them, not even if old Kühlemann were to die and leave his money three times over! Hornung's hands were swollen from shaking those of all the newly converted patriots! The demands they had placed on him were quite unreasonable; that he should associate with mere chemists was the least of his grievances. But Gottlieb Hornung protested against this democratic lack of respect for rank. The proprietor of the Lion Pharmacy had just given him notice to leave, but he was more determined than ever to sell neither toothbrushes nor sponges . . . Meanwhile Kunze was stammering through his speech. For in spite of his dark scowl,

Diederich could clearly see that the Major was not at all sure of what he wanted to say, and that he was more flustered by the election campaign than he would have been in a really grave crisis. He was saying: "The army, gentlemen, is our one pillar of strength," but as a heckler in Heuteufel's neighborhood shouted: "It is already crumbling!" Kunze immediately lost his head, and added: "But who will pay for it? The citizens." At this the people near Heuteufel shouted bravo. Thereby forced into a false position, Kunze began to explain: "Therefore, we are all pillars of support, on that we must insist, and woe to the monarch who—" "Hear! Hear!" replied the Liberal voters, and the credulous patriots cheered along with them. The Major wiped the perspiration from his brow. In spite of himself his speech was developing as if it had been addressed to a Liberal meeting. From behind Diederich kept pulling his coattails and begged him to stop, but Kunze was unable to do so. He could not make a transition to the electoral slogan of the Emperor's Party. Finally he lost patience, turned suddenly very red, and with unexpected ferocity, he yelled: "Stamp them out root and branch! Hurrah!" The Veterans' Association thundered its applause. Wherever people were not applauding, Klappsch or his daughter hastened in with beer, at a sign from Diederich.

Dr. Heuteufel at once asked permission to take part in the discussion, but Gottlieb Hornung got in before him. Diederich, for his part, preferred to remain in the background, behind the cloud of smoke that enveloped the platform. He had promised Hornung ten marks and the latter was not in a position to refuse. Gnashing his teeth he stepped over to the edge of the platform and began to clarify the gallant Major's speech, asserting his meaning to have been that the army, for which we are prepared to make any sacrifice, was our bulwark against the turbid flood of democracy. "Democracy is the philosophy of the half-educated," said the pharmacist. "It has been defeated by science." Someone shouted: "Hear! Hear!" It was the chemist who had wanted to associate with him. "There will always be masters and slaves," decreed Gottlieb Hornung, "for it is the same in nature. It is the one great truth, for each of us must have a superior whom we can fear, and an inferior to frighten. What would become of us otherwise? If every nobody believes that he is somebody in his own right, and that we are all equals! Woe to the nation whose traditional and honorable social forms are dissolved in the mishmash of democracy, which allows the disintegrating element of personality to get the upper hand!" Here Gottlieb Hornung folded his arms and thrust forward his head. "I," he cried, "who have been a member of a crack students' corps and know what it is to shed my blood gladly for the colors—I refuse to sell toothbrushes!"

"Or sponges either?" asked a voice.

"Or sponges either!" said Hornung decisively. "I emphatically forbid anyone else to ask that of me. People should always know with what sort of a person they are dealing. Honor to whom honor is due. And in that sense we give our votes to the one candidate who will allow the Emperor as many soldiers as he wants. Either we have an Emperor or we have not!"

Then Gottlieb Hornung stepped back and gazed with pugnaciously protruding jaw and furrowed brow at the applauding audience. The Veterans' Association would not be deprived of the opportunity to march past him and Kunze with upraised beer glasses. Kunze received handshakes. Hornung stood there with iron bearing—and Diederich could not but feel rather bitterly that these two second-rate personalities had all the advantage of a situation which he had created. He had to allow them the popular approval of the moment, for he knew better than these two simpletons where it was all going to lead. Since the national candidate's sole reason for existence was to procure reinforcements for Napoleon Fischer, it was wiser for Diederich not to go forward himself. But Heuteufel was anxious to draw Diederich out. Pastor Zillich, the chairman, could no longer refuse to allow Heuteufel to take the floor. The latter began at once to talk about the foundling hospital; it was a matter of humanity and social conscience. What was the Emperor Wilhelm Monument? A speculation, and vanity was the least discreditable factor exploited by the speculators ... The contractors in the rear listened in embarrassed silence from which here and there muffled murmuring arose. Diederich was trembling. "There are people," Heuteufel declared, "who do not mind another hundred million for the army, for they know they can get some of it back to their own profit." Then Diederich jumped up. "I wish to say a word!" With cries of "Bravo!" "Ha, ha!" "Sit down," the feelings of the contractors exploded forth. They yelled until Heuteufel made way for Diederich.

Diederich waited for some time before the storm of patriotic indignation had subsided. Then he began: "Gentlemen!" "Bravo!" shouted the contractors and Diederich had to wait again, in that atmosphere of like-minded natures in which he breathed so easily.

When they allowed him to speak he gave expression to the general indignation that the previous speaker had dared to cast suspicions upon the loyal sentiments of the meeting. "An outrage!" cried the contractors. "This only proves," said Diederich, "how opportune has been the founding of the 'Emperor's Party.' The Emperor himself has commanded all those to join hands who, whether aristocrats or commoners, wish to free him from the pestilence of revolution. That is our purpose, and therefore our loyal and patriotic sentiments are far above the suspicious of those who themselves are nothing but the harbingers of revolt!" Before the applause could break out, Heuteufel said in a very loud tone: "Wait—I propose a second ballot!" Although the contractors immediately drowned the rest with the thunder of their hands, Diederich sensed so much danger in these words that he hastened to change the subject. The foundling hospital was a less treacherous subject. What? A matter of social conscience, they said? It was an encouragement to vice! "We Germans leave such things to the French, a decadent people!" Diederich had only to recite the article he had sent to the *Netzig Journal*. Pastor Zillich's Young Men's Christian Association and the Christian Shop-Assistants' Association applauded every word. "The Teuton is chaste," cried Diederich, "that is why we won in the year 1870!" Now it was the turn of the Veterans' Association to give the noisiest sign of enthusiasm. Kühnchen jumped up behind the chairman's table, waved his cigar and screeched: "We'll soon smash 'em again!" Diederich raised himself on his toes. "Gentlemen," he shouted with effort into the tide of national emotion, "the Emperor Wilhelm Monument shall be a mark of reverence for the noble grandfather whom we all, I think I may say, worship almost as a saint, and also a pledge to the noble grandson, our magnificent young Emperor, that we shall ever remain as we are, pure, liberty-loving, truthful, brave and loyal!"

The contractors could no longer be restrained. They floated in oblivious rapture in the realm of the ideal. Diederich, too, was no longer aware of any worldly consideration, neither his pact with Wulckow, nor his conspiracy with Napoleon Fischer, nor his vague intentions concerning the second ballot. Pure enthusiasm seized his soul and catapulted it into dizzying flight. It took him a little while before he was able to resume his yelling. "We roundly reject and banish within their proper bounds all charges brought by those who want nothing more than to soften us with their false humanity!"—"So where do you keep your real humanity?" asked Heuteufel's voice, goading thereby the national sentiments of the assembly to such a frenzy that Diederich's words could be heard only intermittently. He declared that what he wanted was not eternal peace, for that was a mere dream and not a particularly pleasant one at that. What he wanted was a spartan regimen of racial hygiene. Imbeciles and perverts were to be subjected to a surgical procedure to prevent them from breeding. At this point, Heuteufel and his cohorts left the assembly. He called back from the doorway: "You'll castrate the revolution as well!" Diederich answered: "We certainly will if you keep up your grumbling!" "We will!" repeated voices from all sides. At once, the entire crowd was on its feet, calling out *Prost!*, whooping, and making a raucous display of its elation. Diederich, with waves of adulation crashing about him, reeling under the onslaught of loyal German hands all striving to shake his, and patriotic beer glasses reaching out to clink with him, looked from his podium out into the room, which appeared larger and higher to his smoke-fogged gaze. From the highest of these tobacco-smoke clouds, the commandments of his Sovereign emerged, glowing mystically: "The Will of the King!" "My Enemy!" "My Course!" He wanted to shout these out to the roaring masses—but he clutched at his throat, and not a sound came forth: Diederich had lost his voice. Full of worry, he looked about for Heuteufel, who had unfortunately left. "I shouldn't have provoked him so much. Heaven help me when he paints my throat!"

Heuteufel's worst revenge was forbidding Diederich to leave the house. Outside, the battle raged with increasing vehemence, and everyone appeared in the newspaper, for everyone was talking: even Pastor Zillich; indeed, even the editor Nothgroschen, not to mention Kühnchen, who talked everywhere at once. Diederich, in his salon, newly furnished in Old German, could only gurgle mutely. From the estrade by the window, three bronze statues in two-thirds life-size watched him: the Emperor, the Empress, and the Trumpeter of Säckingen. He had bought them on sale at Cohn's; although Cohn had stopped ordering Hessling paper and still lacked the proper national sentiments, Diederich simply could not do without them. Guste reproached him for them whenever he found one of her hats too expensive.

Guste had begun to be peevish of late, and to have fits of nausea, during which Frau Hessling had to take care of her in the bedroom.

As soon as she felt better she would remind the old lady that everything in the house had been bought with her money. Frau Hessling parried by describing the marriage with her Diedel as a true act of mercy for Guste in the peculiar circumstances of her position at the time. This exchange ended with Guste fuming, her cheeks swollen and red, while Frau Hessling shed tears. Diederich was the one to profit by all of this, for afterwards each of them was as affectionate as possible toward him, with the object, which he did not suspect, of bringing him on to her side.

As far as Emmi was concerned, she simply slammed the door as she always did and went up to her room, which had a slanted ceiling. Guste kept wondering how she could drive her even out of that room. Where were they to dry the washing when it rained? If Emmi couldn't get a husband, because she had no money, they would simply have to marry her to someone beneath her socially, some honest tradesman. But, as a matter of fact, Emmi acted as though she were the most elegant member of the family, for she visited the von Brietzens . . . It was this that embittered Guste most. Emmi was often invited by the von Brietzen daughters, although they had never set foot in her house. Their brother, the Lieutenant, would at least have owed Guste a visit for the suppers her mother had given, but he condescended to visit only the second story of the Hesslings' house. His attentions had become quite blatant . . . Her social success, however, did not prevent Emmi from having days of the utmost depression. Then she would not even leave her room for meals, which the family was wont to take together. Once Guste went up to her, out of pity and sheer boredom, but when Emmi saw her she shut her eyes, and lay there, pale and motionless, in her flowing morning wrap. Getting no answer, Guste tried to exchange confidences about Diederich and about her own condition. Then Emmi's rigid face contracted suddenly, she turned on one of her arms and with the other pointed violently to the door. Guste did not fail to express her indignation. Emmi jumped up impetuously, and gave her most clearly to understand that she wished to be alone. By the time old Frau Hessling came up it was already decided that the two families would in future have their meals apart. Diederich, to whom Guste came crying, was disturbed by these women's quarrels. Fortunately he had an idea which promised immediate peace. Since he had got some of his voice back, he went to Emmi and announced that he had decided to send her away to stay awhile in Eschweiler with Magda. To his amazement, she declined to go. As he kept insisting, she was on the point of flaring up, but she was suddenly seized as if by some fear, and began to beg softly and entreatingly to be allowed to stay. Diederich, touched by an ill-defined emotion, looked helplessly around the room and then retreated.

The following day Emmi appeared at lunch as if nothing had happened; her cheeks were freshly rouged and she was in the best of humors. Guste, who was all the more reserved, kept exchanging glances with Diederich. Thinking he understood, he raised his glass to Emmi, and said teasingly: "*Prost,* Frau von Brietzen." Emmi turned deadly pale. "Don't make an ass of yourself," she cried angrily, throwing down her napkin and banging the door after her. "Well!" growled Diederich, but Guste merely shrugged her shoulders. It was only after old Frau Hessling had gone that she gave Diederich a curious glance and asked: "Do you really think . . . ?" He winced inwardly, but looked inquiring. "I mean," Guste explained, "that the Lieutenant might at least greet me in the street. Today he went out of his way to avoid me." Diederich thought this was all nonsense. Guste replied: "If I am only imagining it, then I am imagining other things as well, because at night I have many times heard something creeping through the house, and today Minna said—" Guste got no farther. "Aha," Diederich fumed, "you are hobnobbing with the servants! Mother always used to do that. All I can tell you is that I won't have it. I alone watch over the honor of my family, and do not need either Minna's assistance or yours. If you don't agree with me, then the pair of you know where the door is through which you came!" Naturally, Guste could only duck and cringe in the face of this virile attitude, but she smiled slyly after him as he went out.

For his part, Diederich was happy at having disposed of the matter by his firm procedure. He could not allow his life to become any more complicated than it was. His hoarseness, which had unfortunately kept him out of the struggle for three days, had not been overlooked by the enemy. In fact, Napoleon Fischer had told him only that morning that the "Emperor's Party" was getting too strong for him, and had been agitating too strongly against the Social Democrats lately. Under these circumstances . . . In order to quiet him Diederich had to promise to carry out his bargain that very day, and ask the town councillors to sanction the Social Democratic Trade Union Hall . . . So, although his throat was not quite well, he went to the meeting—and there he discovered that the motion concerning the Trade Union Hall had just been introduced by Messrs. Cohn and company! The Liberals voted for it, and it went through as smoothly as if it had been the most ordinary measure. Diederich, who wanted to launch into a scathing denunciation of the betrayal of the national cause perpetrated by Cohn and his comrades, could only bark hoarsely. This clever trick had once more robbed him of his voice. No sooner had he got home than he sent for Napoleon Fischer.

"You're fired!" Diederich bellowed. The machinist grinned ambiguously. "All right," said he, preparing to go.

"Stop!" shouted Diederich. "Don't think you are going to get off as easily as that. If you start cutting deals with the Liberals, then you may be sure I will make our agreement public! I'll show you!"

"Politics is politics," Napoleon remarked with a shrug, and as Diederich could not even bellow any more in the face of such cynicism, Napoleon Fischer stepped confidentially nearer, and almost clapped Diederich on the shoulder. "Dr. Hessling," he said amiably, "don't be like that. The two of us—yes, I need only say the two of us . . ." His grin was so full of threats that Diederich shuddered. He quickly offered Napoleon Fischer a cigar. Fischer smoked and said:

"If one of us two were to begin talking where would the other stop? Am I right, Dr. Hessling? But we are not a pair of old chatterboxes who have to blab everything immediately, like Herr Buck for example."

"What do you mean?" asked Diederich in a whisper, as he fell into one fright after another. The machinist feigned astonishment. "Don't you know? Herr Buck goes about everywhere saying that you do not really mean all that patriotic stuff. You simply want to get Gausenfeld cheap, and you think you will get it cheaper if Klüsing is frightened about certain contracts because he is not a patriot."

"Is that what he says?" asked Diederich, turned to stone.

"That's what he says," Fischer repeated. "And he also says he will do you a favor and speak a word on your behalf to Klüsing. That should calm you down a bit, he says."

Diederich regained his senses. "Fischer," he said with a short bark, "you watch what happens. You will see old Buck standing in the gutter begging. That's what you'll see. I'll make sure of it, Fischer. Good-bye."

Napoleon Fischer had left, but Diederich went on barking to himself and stomping about the room for quite some time thereafter. That scoundrel! Posing as a man of honor! Behind all the resistance he had encountered stood old Buck, Diederich had suspected as much all along! The motion introduced by Cohn and his cohorts had been his doing—and now this scandalous character assassination with Gausenfeld. Diederich's entire inner being rebelled, he was scandalized in the incorruptibility of his patriotic sentiments. "And how does he know about it?" he thought with angry dismay. "Has Wulckow sold me out? I suppose they all think I'm playing a double game here?" For Kunze and the others had made a noticeably cooler impression on him today. So they no longer felt it necessary to clue him in on what was going on? Diederich did not belong to the committee; he had brought to the cause the sacrifice of his personal ambition. But did that mean he was not the actual founder of the "Emperor's Party?" . . . Treachery was everywhere, intrigues, malevolent distrust—and nowhere simply German loyalty.

Since he was unable to raise his voice above a bark, he could only watch helplessly at the next electoral assembly, as Zillich—the personal interest in which he acted was quite clear—allowed Jadassohn to speak, and as Jadassohn reaped thunderous applause when he railed against the men without a fatherland who would vote for Napoleon Fischer. Diederich pitied this highly unstatesmanlike display and was made thereby keenly aware of his superiority to Jadassohn. On the other hand, it was becoming more and more evident that the more Jadassohn allowed himself to be swept along by his success, the louder swelled the sounds of approval among certain members of the audience, who in no way gave the impression of being true patriots, but who quite clearly belonged to the ranks of Cohn and Heuteufel. They had appeared in suspiciously large numbers—and Diederich, overwrought perhaps by the traps which surrounded him, saw as the source of this maneuver as well his arch enemy, the hidden hand of Evil: old Buck.

Old Buck had blue eyes, a benevolent smile, and he was the most treacherous dog of all the ones beleaguering those of sound opinion. The thought of old Buck held Diederich in thrall, even in his dreams. The next evening, under the light of the lamp, he was so busy with imaginary moves against old Buck that he did not hear the family when they spoke to him. He was particularly embittered because he had looked upon the old man as a toothless old chatterbox, and now he was showing his teeth. After all his humanitarian phrase-making it now seemed an impertinent challenge to Diederich that he did not simply allow himself to be gobbled up. The hypocritical gentleness with which he pretended he had forgiven Diederich the ruin of his son-in-law! Why had he protected him? Got him on to the Town Council? Only so that Diederich might compromise himself and be more easily caught. The old man's question at that time, whether Diederich wanted to sell his property to the town, now appeared as the most dangerous trap. Diederich felt as if his game had been seen through the whole time. He now felt as if old Buck had been present, invisible in the clouds of smoke, at his secret interview with Governor von Wulckow. When Diederich had crept along to Gausenfeld one dark winter's night, and had hidden in the ditch, shutting his gleaming eyes, old Buck had passed above and peered down at him. . . . In his imagination Diederich saw the old gentleman stooping down and stretching out his soft white hand to help him out of the ditch. The kindness in his face was simply mockery, it was more unbearable than anything else. He thought he could make Diederich docile, and with his tricks bring him back like the prodigal son. But they would see which of them would end by eating husks.

"What is the matter my dear child?" asked Frau Hessling, for Diederich had groaned aloud from hate and fear. He gave a start. At that moment Emmi was walking across the room: it seemed to Diederich that she had already done so several times. She went to the window, put her head outside, sighed as if there was nobody present, and walked back. Guste looked after her, and as Emmi passed in front of Diederich, Guste's mocking look included them both. This startled Diederich more than ever, for this was the revolutionary smile which he had learned to recognize in Napoleon Fischer. Guste was smiling in the same way. He wrinkled his brow in terror and shouted sharply: "What are you smirking about?" Immediately Guste cringed back into her darning, but Emmi stood still and gazed at him with those dumbstruck eyes she now sometimes had. "What's wrong with you?" he asked, as she remained silent. "Whom are you looking for in the street?" She merely shrugged her shoulders, but her face remained motionless. "Well?" he repeated more softly, for her look, her demeanor, which seemed curiously indifferent and therefore superior, made it difficult for him to be loud. Finally she decided to speak.

"It was possible that the two Fräulein von Brietzens might have come."

"So late at night?" asked Diederich. Then Guste said: "Because we are accustomed to that honor. And anyhow, they went away yesterday with their mamma. If they do not even say goodbye to people, because they do not even know them, all one has to do is to go past their villa to know that they are gone."

"What?" said Emmi.

"Why, certainly!" Beaming with triumph Guste told her the whole story. "The Lieutenant will soon follow them. He has been transferred." She paused, and looked up. "He has had himself transferred."

"You're a liar!" cried Emmi. She had swayed and was visibly holding herself erect. With her head high she turned and let the curtain fall behind her. There was silence in the room. Old Frau Hessling on the sofa folded her hands. Guste looked defiantly at Diederich, who bustled about fuming. When he reached the door again he gave a start. Through the opening he caught a glimpse of Emmi who was sitting, or rather huddled up in a chair in the dining room as if she had been tied up and thrown there. She quivered, then turned her face toward the lamp. Just before it had been quite pale and it was now deep red. She was looking with unseeing eyes. Suddenly she sprang up, rushed off as if she was on fire, and with angry, uncertain steps she dashed out, knocking against things without feeling them, as if into a mist, into a fog. . . . With increasing fear Diederich turned to his wife and his mother. As Guste seemed disposed to be disrespectful he pulled himself together, with his accustomed form, and marched stiffly after Emmi.

He had not reached the stairs when the door above was closed noisily with lock and bolt. Then Diederich's heart began to beat so fast that he had to stop. By the time he reached the top the voice with which he asked permission to enter was weak and breathless. There was no answer, but he heard something clink on the washstand—and suddenly he waved his arms, shouted, banged on the door and yelled madly. Because of his own noise he did not hear her opening the door, and he was still shouting when she stood before him. "What do you want?" she asked angrily, whereupon Diederich recovered himself. From the stairs Frau Hessling and Guste were peering up with horrified curiosity. "Stay downstairs!" he commanded, pushing Emmi back into the room. He shut the door. "The others needn't smell this," he said tersely, and he took out of the wash-jug a small sponge dripping with chloroform. He held it away from him with outstretched arm and asked: "Where did you get this?" She tossed her head and looked at him without replying. The longer this lasted the more unimportant Diederich felt the question, which should, by rights, have been the first to be asked. Finally, he simply went to the window and threw the sponge into the dark courtyard. There was a splash. It had fallen into the brook. Diederich gave a sigh of relief.

Now it was Emmi's turn to ask questions. "What do you think you are doing up here? Kindly allow me to do what I think fit."

This came to him as a surprise. "Yes, but . . . what *are* you doing?"

She looked away and replied with a shrug: "What do you care?"

"Oh, come now!" Diederich was indignant. "Even if you no longer have any shame before your divine Judge, of which I personally would highly disapprove, you might at least have a little regard for us here. You are not alone in the world."

Her indifference offended him deeply. "I will have no scandal in my house! I am the first person who will suffer."

Suddenly she looked at him. "And I?"

He snapped: "My honor—" but stopped suddenly. Her expression, which had never seemed to him so eloquent, seemed to accuse and to mock at the same time. In confusion he went to the door. Here it dawned on him what he had to do.

"At all events, as your brother and a man of honor, I will, of course, do my duty. Meanwhile I expect you to impose upon yourself the utmost reserve." With a glance at the wash-jug, from which there was still a smell:

"Your word of honor!"

"Leave me alone," said Emmi. Then Diederich came back.

"You do not seem to be aware of the seriousness of the situation. If what I fear is true, you have—"

"It is true," said Emmi.

"Then you have not only risked your own existence, at least socially, but you have covered a whole family with shame. And when I stand here in front of you now, in the name of duty and honor—"

"Then that won't change a thing," said Emmi.

He was startled and was preparing to express his loathing of such cynicism, but Emmi's face reflected all that she had been through. Diederich shuddered at the superiority of her desperation.

He felt as if certain springs had snapped inside him. His legs trembled, he sat down, and managed to say: "Can't you tell me?—I will also—" He looked at Emmi's appearance and the word "forgive" stuck in his throat. "I will help you," he said. "How can you help me?" she countered wearily, as she leaned against the wall.

He looked down in front of him. "Of course, you must give me some information. I mean, about certain details. I presume this has gone on since your riding lessons?"

She let him go on surmising; she neither confirmed nor denied any of his guesses. But when he raised his eyes to her, her lips were softly parted and she was gazing at him in wonder. It dawned on him that she was surprised because he was comforting her by putting into words what she had been suffering alone. His heart was seized with an unfamiliar pride; he stood up and said confidingly: "You can leave it to me. First thing tomorrow morning I'll go there." She shook her head gently and fearfully.

"You don't understand. It is all over."

Then he made his voice cheerful. "We are not completely helpless. Let me see what I can do."

He gave her his hand as they parted. She called him back again.

"Are you going to challenge him to a duel?" Her eyes were staring wide open and she held her hands to her lips.

"Why do you ask?" said Diederich, for he had not thought of this.

"Swear that you will not challenge him!"

He promised. At the same time he blushed, for he would like to have known for whom she was afraid, for him or the other. He would not have liked it to be the other, but he stifled the question, because it might have been painful for her to answer, and he all but tiptoed out of the room.

He ordered the two women, who still waited below, sternly to bed. He lay down beside Guste only after she had fallen asleep. He had to think over what he would do the next day. Make an impression, of course! Admit of no possible doubt as to the outcome of the affair! But instead of his own smart figure, Diederich saw again and again in his imagination, a stout man with pale troubled eyes, who begged, raged and finally collapsed: Herr Göppel, Agnes Göppel's father. Now in his terrified soul Diederich understood what the father must then have felt. "You don't understand," said Emmi. He did understand, for he had inflicted such a thing himself.

"God forbid!" he said aloud, as he turned over. "I won't be drawn into this business. Emmi was only bluffing with the chloroform. Women are depraved enough for that. I'll throw her out, as she deserves!" Then Agnes appeared before him in the rainy street and stared up at his window, the pale reflection of the gaslight on her face. He pulled the bedclothes over his eyes. "I can't drive her onto the streets!" Morning dawned and he was amazed at what had happened to him.

"Lieutenants get up early," he thought, and he slipped off before Guste was awake. Beyond the Saxon Gate the gardens were full of perfume and twittering, beneath the spring skies. The villas, still closed, looked as if they had been freshly washed, and as if innumerable newly married couples had moved into them. "Who knows," thought Diederich as he breathed in the pure air, "perhaps it will not be difficult. There are still decent people in the world. The circumstances are also much more favorable than—" He preferred not to complete the thought. There in the distance a cab stopped—before which house was it? Yes, that was the one. The iron gate stood open, and the door as well. The officer's servant came toward him. "That's all right," said Diederich. "I see the Lieutenant already." For in the room straight ahead Herr von Brietzen was packing a trunk. "So early?" he asked, let the lid of the trunk fall and caught his finger: "Damn it!" Diederich reflected with discouragement. "He, too, is busy packing."

"To what do I owe the honor—" began Herr von Brietzen, but involuntarily Diederich made a movement which signified that this was superfluous. Nevertheless, Herr von Brietzen denied everything of course. His denial was longer than Diederich's had been, and Diederich recognized this fact inwardly, for when a girl's honor was at stake a Lieutenant had to be several degrees more punctilious than a Neo-Teuton. When they had finally got the whole situation straight, Herr von Brietzen at once placed himself at Diederich's disposal, as was certainly expected of him. But in spite of his deadly fear, Diederich replied cheerfully that he hoped a decision with arms might be unnecessary, provided Herr von Brietzen—And Herr von Brietzen assumed exactly the expression Diederich had foreseen, and said exactly the words which Diederich had heard in his imagination. When driven into a corner, he uttered the sentence which Diederich dreaded most, and which, he admitted, could not be avoided. A girl who had lost her virtue could not be selected as the mother of one's children! Diederich replied to this as Herr Göppel had replied, and was as crushed as Herr Göppel had been. He did not get really angry until he uttered his big threat, the threat with which he had been promising himself success since yesterday.

"In view of your unchivalrous refusal, Lieutenant, I find myself unfortunately compelled to place your Colonel in possession of the facts."

Herr von Brietzen really seemed to be. hit in a vulnerable spot. He asked hesitantly: "What good do you think that will do? Force me to listen to a moral lecture? Well, all right. But, in any case"— Herr von Brietzen recovered his self-possession—"as far as chivalry is concerned, the Colonel will probably have very different views from those of a gentleman who refuses to accept a challenge."

Then Diederich arose in his wrath. Herr von Brietzen would kindly hold his tongue, otherwise he might find that he would have to deal with the Neo-Teutons! He, Diederich, had proved by his scars that he had joyfully shed his blood for the honor of the colors! He could only wish that Lieutenant von Brietzen would one day be in a position where he would have to challenge a Count von Tauern-Bärenheim! "I challenged him flat out!" And in the same breath he declared that he was far from recognizing the right of an impertinent Junker to shoot down a decent citizen and the father of a family. "You'd no doubt like to seduce the sister and shoot the brother," he shouted, beside himself. In a similar state of rage Herr von Brietzen talked of having his servant smash the tradesman's face, and as the servant stood there ready, Diederich cleared out, but not without a parting shot. "If you think, because of your impertinence, we will pass the military appropriation bill! We'll show you what revolution is!"

Outside in the deserted avenue he continued to rage, shook his fist at the invisible enemy and uttered threats. "You will regret that some day, when we put our foot down!" Suddenly he noticed that the gardens were still full of perfume and twittering beneath the spring skies, and it became clear to him that Nature herself, whether she smiled or snarled, was powerless before Authority, the authority above us, which is quite unshakable. It was easy to threaten revolution, but what about the Emperor Wilhelm Monument? Wulckow and Gausenfeld? Whoever trampled others underfoot must be prepared to be walked on, that was the iron law of might. After his attack of rebellion, Diederich again felt the secret thrill of the man who is trampled upon . . . A cab came along from behind, Herr von Brietzen and his trunk. Before he knew what he was doing Diederich faced about, ready to bow. But Herr von Brietzen looked the other way. In spite of everything Diederich rejoiced in the fresh chivalrous young officer. "Nobody can take the place of the military," he said with conviction.

Now, however, that he had entered Meisestrasse, he became apprehensive. From a distance he could see Emmi looking out for him. All of a sudden he realized all that she must have gone through during the last hour, which had decided her fate. Poor Emmi! Now it was decided. No doubt, Power was elevating, but when it struck down one's own sister ... "I did not know it would touch me so closely." He nodded as encouragingly as possible. She had become much thinner, how was it nobody had noticed? She had big sleepless eyes beneath her pale shimmering hair; her lips twitched as he nodded to her. He noticed this with the sharp eyes of his fear. He all but crept up the stairs. On the first floor she came out of the room and went on in front of him to the floor above. Upstairs she turned around—and when she saw his face she went inside without speaking, went to the window, and remained standing, with her face turned away. He pulled himself together and said aloud: "Oh! Nothing is lost yet." He recoiled at his own words and closed his eyes. As he groaned aloud, she turned, came slowly toward him, laid her head on his shoulder and they wept together.

Afterward he had an encounter with Guste who wanted to nag. Diederich told her point-blank that she was only using Emmi's misfortune in order to have her revenge for the not altogether auspicious circumstances under which she herself had got married. "Emmi, at least, is not throwing herself at anyone." Guste screeched: "Did I throw myself at you?" He cut her short. "In any case, she is my sister!" And as she was now living under his protection, he began to find her interesting, and to show her unusual respect. After meals, he would kiss her hand, in spite of Guste's grins. He compared the two women. How much more common Guste was! Magda, even, whom he had favored because she was successful, no longer compared in his memory with the forsaken Emmi. Through her misfortune Emmi had become more refined and, so to speak, more elusive. When her hand lay there, so white and aloof, and Emmi was sunk silently in her own thoughts, as if in an unknown abyss, Diederich felt touched by the premonition of a deeper world. The attribute of a fallen woman, unnatural and despicable in others, lent Emmi, Diederich's sister, a strange shimmering air of questionable charm. Emmi was now both more touching and more brilliant.

The Lieutenant, who had caused all this trouble, seemed a good deal less important in comparison—and so did the Power, in whose name he had triumphed. Diederich discovered that Power could sometimes present a common and vulgar appearance, Power and everything that went with it, success, honor, unimpeachable sentiments. He looked at Emmi and was forced to question the value of what he had attained or was still striving for: Guste and her money, the monument, the favor of the authorities, Gausenfeld, distinctions and high office. He looked at Emmi and thought of Agnes. Agnes had encouraged tenderness and love in him, she had been the true thing in his life, he should have held it fast. Where was she now? Dead? Sometimes he sat, holding his head in his hands. What had he now? What were the rewards in the service of Power? Once more everything failed him, everyone betrayed him, exploited his purest intentions, and old Buck was master of the situation. Agnes, who could only suffer—the thought insinuated itself that she had won. He wrote to Berlin and made inquiries about her. She was married and in passable health. This relieved him, but somehow, it also disappointed him.

While Diederich sat there thus with his head in his hands, however, election day arrived. Filled with a sense of the vanity of all things, Diederich had lost all desire to occupy himself with what was going on around him. One of the things he failed to notice was the increasing hostility that marked the face of his machinist. Early in the morning on election Sunday, while Diederich was still in bed, Napoleon Fischer walked into his room. Without the least apology he began: "At the eleventh hour, Dr. Hessling, I have something serious to tell you." This time it was he who smelled a rat and reminded Diederich of their agreement. "You are playing a double-faced game. You made certain promises to us, and being men of our word, we did not agitate against you, but only against the Liberals." "So did we," declared Diederich.

"You know that's not true. You have been hobnobbing with Heuteufel. He has already agreed to your monument. If you do not go over to his side with full colors today, you will certainly do so on the second ballot, and shamefully betray the people."

With folded arms Napoleon Fischer took another long stride towards the bed. "All I want to tell you is that we will be keeping our eyes open."

Diederich in his bed found himself completely at the mercy of his political opponent. He tried to soothe him. "I know, Fischer, you are a great politician. You will certainly get into the Reichstag."

"That's right," Napoleon glared from below. "If I don't, there will be a strike in several factories in Netzig. One of those factories you happen to know quite well, Doctor Hessling." He turned on his heel. At the door he stared once more at Diederich, who had sunk down under the bedclothes in terror. "Therefore, long live international Social Democracy!" he shouted as he went out.

From beneath the bedclothes Diederich cried: "Hurrah for His Majesty the Emperor!" After that there was nothing to be done but to face the situation. It looked threatening enough. Oppressed by forebodings he hastened out into the street, to the Veterans' Association, to Klappsch's. Everywhere he was forced to admit that, during the days of his discouragement, the clever tactics of old Buck had achieved wide success. The Emperor's Party had been diluted by accretions from the Liberal ranks, and the difference between Kunze and Heuteufel was negligible compared with the abyss between him and Napoleon Fischer. Pastor Zillich, who exchanged shy greetings with his brother-in-law, Heuteufel, asserted that the Emperor's Party ought to be satisfied with its success, for it had certainly strengthened the national conscience of the Liberal candidate, even if he eventually won. As Professor Kühnchen expressed a similar opinion, there was no ignoring the suspicion that they were not satisfied with the promises they had extracted from Diederich and Wulckow, and that they had allowed old Buck to win them over by promises of greater personal advantage. The corruption of the democratic clique was so great that anything was possible. As far as Kunze was concerned, he was determined to be elected; if necessary, with the help of the Liberals. His ambition had corrupted him, it had brought him to the point of promising to vote for the foundling hospital! Diederich became indignant; Heuteufel was a hundred times worse than any proletarian, and he alluded to the terrible consequences of such an unpatriotic attitude. Unfortunately he could not allow himself to go into details—and with the possibility of the strike before him, in his heart the ruins of the Emperor Wilhelm Monument, of Gausenfeld and all his dreams, he rushed about in the rain from one polling-station to another, drumming up the loyal voters, knowing full well that their loyalty to the Emperor would bear the wrong fruit and would help the worst enemies of the Emperor. At Klappsch's in the evening, splashed with mud from head to foot, in a feverish daze from the noise of the long day, all the beer he had drunk and his anxiety about the final election result, he heard the figures. Around eight thousand votes for Heuteufel, six thousand odd for Napoleon Fischer, but Kunze had three thousand six hundred and seventy-two. The second ballot was between Heuteufel and Fischer. "Hurrah!" shouted Diederich, for nothing was lost and they had gained time.

With a resolute stride he marched off, in his heart the vow henceforth to do his utmost to save the national cause. Time was of the essence, for Pastor Zillich would have liked nothing better than immediately to plaster every wall in town with placards exhorting all adherents of the Emperor's Party to vote for Heuteufel in the second ballot. Kunze, to be sure, cherished the vain hope that Heuteufel would do him the favor of stepping down. What blindness! The very next morning one could read the white handbills on which the Liberals maintained hypocritically that they, too, were devoted to the national cause, which was by no means the privilege of a minority, and for this reason—. Old Buck's trick revealed itself completely; if the entire Emperor's Party was not to return to the bosom of the Liberals, then action was the order of the day. Powerfully tensed with energy, Diederich ran into Emmi in the hallway of their house as he was returning from his reconnoitering. Emmi's face was veiled and she moved as though nothing made any difference now. "Well I beg your pardon," he thought, "but things most certainly do make a difference. Where would we be if they didn't?" He greeted Emmi furtively and with something like awe.

He returned to his office from which old Sötbier had vanished and where Diederich, now his own accountant and answerable only to his God, made his weighty decisions. He strode to the telephone and demanded Gausenfeld. Just then the door opened, the postman laid down his bundle of letters, and Diederich noticed the address of the one on top: Gausenfeld. He hung up the receiver again and, nodding like Destiny, he gazed at the letter. The deed was done! The old chap had not waited to be told; he understood that he no longer dared to give money to Buck and his allies, and that if necessary, he could personally be called to account. Diederich calmly tore open the envelope—but after two lines he was reading feverishly. What a surprise! Klüsing was ready to sell! He was growing old and regarded Diederich as his natural successor!

What did it all mean? Diederich sat down in a corner to think. First of all, it meant that Wulckow had intervened. Old Klüsing was in mortal fear because of the Government contracts; and the strike that Napoleon threatened had done the rest. Gone were the days when he thought he could get out of the dilemma by offering Diederich a share of the paper for the *Netzig Journal!* Now he was offering him the whole of Gausenfeld! "I am a Power," Diederich declared, and he decided that Klüsing's idea that he should buy the factory and pay its full value was simply ridiculous in view of the circumstances; Diederich actually laughed out loud. . . . Then he became aware that at the end of the letter, below the signature, there was something else, a postscript written in smaller writing than the rest and so inconspicuous that Diederich had missed it before. He deciphered it—and his jaw dropped. Suddenly he leaped up. "So that's it!" he shouted, capering triumphantly about his empty office. "Now we have it!" Then he said, with great seriousness: "It is dreadful! An abyss!" He read again, word for word, the fateful postscript, placed the letter in the safe and shut the door sharply. In the safe this poison was lying in wait for Buck and his followers—supplied by their friend. Not only had Klüsing ceased to furnish them with funds; he betrayed them also. But there was no doubt they deserved it; such depravity had probably disgusted even Klüsing. To spare them would be to share their guilt. Diederich examined his conscience. "Mercy would be a downright crime. Let every man look to himself. Ruthless action is called for here. Tear the mask from this excrescence and sweep it out with an iron broom! I undertake the task in the interest of the public welfare. My duty as a loyal patriot leaves me no choice. These are tough times."

The next evening there was a large public meeting, called by the Liberal election committee in the large Valhalla Theater. With the active assistance of Gottlieb Hornung, Diederich had taken steps to ensure that the meeting was not confined to Heuteufel's supporters. He himself did not think it necessary to hear the speech of the candidate, and he did not go until the meeting was open for discussion. In an anteroom he ran into Kunze, who was in a bad humor. "A washed-up old war horse!" he shouted. "Look at me, sir, and tell me if I look like the sort of man who would allow himself to be called that!" As he was too agitated to continue, Kühnchen came to his assistance. "Heuteufel should have said that to me!" he yelled. "I'd have shown him the sort of man Kühnchen is!"

Diederich urged the Major to sue his opponent. But Kunze needed no encouragement: he swore he would simply smash Heuteufel's face. Diederich thought this a good idea, and he agreed most emphatically when Kunze declared that, under the circumstances, he would side with the worst revolutionaries before he sided with the Liberals. Kühnchen and Pastor Zillich, who had joined them, opposed this view. The enemies of their country—and the Emperor's Party! "Corrupt cowards!" said Diederich's look—while the Major continued to swear vengeance. These swine would weep tears of blood! "And they'll do it tonight," said Diederich with such iron determination that they were all astonished. He paused for a moment and glared at each of them in turn. "What would you say, Pastor, if I were to prove certain machinations against your Liberal friends? . . ." Pastor Zillich turned pale. Diederich turned to Kühnchen: "Dishonest use of public funds." Kühnchen jumped. "The devil you say!" he shouted ferociously. Kunze bellowed: "Give me your hand!" and he seized Diederich in his arms. "I am but a simple soldier," he assured him. "The shell may be rough, but the kernel is sound. Prove the knavery of those swine and Major Kunze is your friend, as though we had been under fire together at Mars-la-Tour!"

The Major had tears in his eyes, as did Diederich, and their souls were every bit as highly charged as the atmosphere of the meeting. On entering one could see arms being raised everywhere through the blue haze, and here and there a breast gave vent: "Bah!" "Hear, hear!" or "Disgraceful!" The electoral contest was at its height. Diederich plunged in with extraordinary bitterness, for in front of the table at which old Buck was presiding in person, who was standing at the edge of the platform and speaking? Sötbier, Diederich's dismissed accountant! In revenge Sötbier was making an inflammatory speech which characterized in the most derogatory fashion the alleged worker-friendliness of certain gentlemen. It was nothing but a demagogic stunt, by which, for the sake of certain personal advantages, they wished to divide the middle classes and drive the voters onto the side of the revolution. Formerly the gentleman in question had said: Whoever is born a slave must remain a slave. "Bah!" yelled the organized workers. Diederich pushed his way through until he was beside the platform. "A vulgar libel!" he shouted into Sötbier's face. "You ought to be ashamed of yourself! Since your dismissal you have joined the malcontents." The Veterans' Association, under Kunze's command, shouted as one man:

"Disgraceful!" and "Hear, hear!"—while the organized workers hissed and Sötbier shook a trembling fist at Diederich, who threatened to have him locked up. Then old Buck stood up and rang his bell.

When silence had been restored he said in a gentle voice, which swelled in an ardent crescendo: "Fellow citizens! Do not encourage the personal ambition of individuals by taking them seriously! What is the person? What are classes even? The people's interests are at stake, and the people includes everyone except those who want to be masters. We must stand together. We citizens must not again make the mistake, which was made in my youth, of entrusting our welfare to bayonets, as soon as the workers demand their rights. Because we refused time and again to grant the workers their rights, we have given the masters power to deprive us of our rights as well."

"Quite right!"

"We, the people, are now given what may be our last opportunity—in the face of this demand upon us to increase the size of the army—to assert our freedom against our masters, who are arming us only to keep us in bondage. Whoever is born a slave must remain a slave—that is said not only to you workers, it is said to us all by the masters for whose power we must pay ever more dearly."

"Quite right! Bravo! Not a man, not a penny!" Amidst enthusiastic approval old Buck sat down. Diederich, who was dripping with perspiration as he approached the final struggle, glanced over the audience and saw Gottlieb Hornung, in charge of the contractors for the Emperor Wilhelm Monument. Pastor Zillich was busy among the young churchmen, and the Veterans' Association had rallied around Kunze. Then Diederich launched forth. "Our hereditary foe is raising his head once more," he shouted defiantly. "A traitor to the Fatherland, who refuses our magnificent Emperor what he—" "Ha, ha!" cried the traitors to the Fatherland, but amid the applause of the loyalists, Diederich continued to shout, even as his voice was breaking: "A French general is demanding *revanche!*" From the platform someone asked: "How much is he getting for that from Berlin?" There was laughter, while Diederich clawed the air as if he wanted to climb upon it. "The flash of arms! Blood and iron! Manly ideals! A strong Empire!" His pithy expressions rattled against each other, amidst the din made by the right-thinking patriots. "A powerful regiment, a bulwark against the turbid stream of democracy."

"Wulckow is your bulwark!" cried the voice from the platform again. Diederich turned around and recognized Heuteufel. "Do you mean His Majesty's Government?" "Another bulwark!" said Heuteufel. Diederich pointed his finger at him. "You have insulted the Emperor!" he shouted sharply. Behind him, however, someone screeched: "Informer!" It was Napoleon Fischer, and his comrades repeated it with hoarse shouts. They had jumped up and surrounded Diederich in a threatening fashion. "He is trying to provoke someone again! He wants to get someone else in jail! Throw him out!" They seized him. Callused hands were squeezing his throat as he turned his face, distorted with terror, toward the chairman and begged chokingly for help. Old Buck granted his request; he rang his bell incessantly, and even sent some young men down to rescue Diederich from his enemies. No sooner was he free than Diederich pointed his finger at old Buck. "The corruptness of democracy," he shouted, dancing with passion. "I will prove it to him!" "Bravo!" "Let him speak"—and the camp of the loyalists took to their feet, clambered over the tables and stood face to face with the revolutionaries. A free-for-all seemed imminent. The police officer on the platform reached for his helmet to protect himself; it was a critical moment. Then a command was heard from the platform: "Silence! Let him speak!" It was almost quiet, for people had become aware of an anger greater than any other present. Old Buck, looming above his table on the platform, was no longer a stately old gentleman. Power seemed to give slenderness to his figure, he was pale with hatred, and he shot a glance at Diederich which caused the onlookers to hold their breath.

"Let him speak," the old man repeated. "Even traitors are allowed to speak before they are condemned. That is what traitors to the nation look like. They have changed only in externals since the time when my generation fought and died, and went to prison and the scaffold!" "Ha! ha!" cried Gottlieb Hornung, filled with superior mirth. Unfortunately for him, he was sitting within arm's reach of a powerful workman, who raised his arm so threateningly that, before the blow struck him, Hornung toppled over together with his chair.

"At that time also," intoned the old man, "there were people who preferred profit to honor, and who found no domination humiliating, provided their pockets were the better for it. Servile materialism, the fruit and weapon of every tyranny, that was what defeated us, and you also, my fellow citizens—"

The old man spread out his arms and steeled himself for the final cry of his conscience.

"Fellow citizens, you also are in danger today of being betrayed by that materialism and of becoming its prey. Let this man speak."

"No!"

"He shall speak. Afterwards you can ask him how much in hard cash those opinions are worth, which he has the cheek to call patriotic. Ask him who bought his house, for what purpose, and to whose advantage."

"Wulckow!" The word was shouted from the platform, but the audience took it up. With threatening fists clenched at his back, Diederich ascended—not quite voluntarily—the steps to the platform. He looked around in search of help. Old Buck was sitting motionless, his clenched fist resting on his knee, and his eyes never left Diederich. Heuteufel, Cohn, all the members of the committee were waiting for his collapse, with an expression of cold eagerness on their faces. And the audience shouted, "Wulckow! Wulckow!" Diederich stammered something about slander, his heart was beating furiously, and for a moment he shut his eyes, in the hope that he was going to faint and would thus get out of the dilemma. But he did not faint, and, as there was no alternative, a terrible courage possessed him. He clutched at his breast pocket, to make sure of his weapon, and with the joy of battle he surveyed his enemy, that sly old man who had at last torn off the mask of the paternal friend and confessed his hatred. Diederich glared at him, and, standing before him thrust both his fists toward the floor. Then he faced the audience aggressively.

"Do you want to earn some money?" he bawled, like a street-hawker above the din—and all was silent as if at a magic command. "Everyone can earn some money from me," he yelled with undiminished violence. "To everyone who can prove how much I made on the sale of my house I will pay the same again!"—Nobody seemed prepared for this. The contractors were the first to cry "Bravo!" Then the Christians and the veterans followed suit, but half-heartedly, for the shout of "Wulckow!" had begun again, to the beat of beer glasses which were being pounded on the tables. Diederich saw that this was a prearranged trick directed not only against himself but against much higher authorities as well. He looked around uneasily, and indeed, the police officer was again clutching at his helmet. Diederich made a sign to him with his hand, as much as to say he would attend to this, and bellowed:

"Not Wulckow, but very different people! The Liberal foundling hospital! They wanted me to give up my house for that; that was proposed to me, I am ready to swear it. As a loyal patriot I emphatically repudiated the suggestion that I should cheat the town and share the spoil with certain officials of the municipal administration."

"You lie!" cried old Buck, as he stood up flaming. But Diederich flamed even more fiercely, in the consciousness of being right and of his moral mission. He plunged his hand into his pocket, and in front of the thousand-headed hydra below, whose venom bespattered him: "Liar! Swindler!" he fearlessly waved his document. "Here's the proof!" he shouted, waving the paper until they decided to listen to him.

"It did not work with me, but in Gausenfeld, it did, my fellow citizens. In Gausenfeld ... How can that be? I'll tell you. Two gentlemen from the Liberal Party went to the owner and tried to secure advance purchase rights to a certain piece of property, in case the foundling hospital should be built there."

"Names! Names!"

Diederich thumped his chest, prepared to go to any length. Klüsing had told him everything except the names. With flashing eyes he stared at the members of the committee. One seemed to grow pale. "Nothing ventured, nothing gained," thought Diederich, and he shouted:

"One of them was Cohn, the owner of the department store!"

He stepped off the platform with the air of one whose duty has been fulfilled. Down below Kunze received him and kissed him on both cheeks, oblivious of everything, to which the members of the Emperor's Party applauded. The others shouted: "Proof!" or "Swindler!" But "Let Cohn speak!"—that was the general cry. It was impossible for Cohn to evade the issue. Old Buck looked at him; his cheeks were quivering and he was rigid, and then he called upon him to speak. Cohn, pushed forward vigorously by Heuteufel, came out very indecisively from behind the long committee table, dragged his feet, and created a most unfavorable impression even before he started. He smiled apologetically. "Gentlemen, you will certainly not believe what the previous speaker has said." He spoke so softly that hardly anybody understood. Yet Cohn fancied, even then, that he had gone too far. "I will not exactly contradict the previous speaker, but it was not the way he has described!"

"Aha! He admits it!"—and suddenly there broke loose such an uproar that Cohn, caught off guard, jumped backward. The room was filled with noise and gesticulation. Here and there opponents were falling upon one another. "Hurrah!" screeched Kühnchen as he rushed through the crowd, with streaming hair, swinging his fists and egging on the fight . . . On the platform, too, everyone had jumped up, except the police officer. Old Buck had left the chairman's seat, and with his back to the people, on whose deaf ears the last cry of his conscience had fallen, he turned away so that nobody could see that he was weeping, forsaken and alone. Heuteufel spoke indignantly to the police officer, who did not move from his chair, but informed him that the police alone decided if and when the meeting should be stopped. There was no necessity to do so just when the Liberals were getting the worst of it. Then Heuteufel went to the table and rang the bell, shouting, as he did so: "The second name!" And as everyone on the platform joined in the cry, it was finally audible, and Heuteufel could continue.

"The second person who was in Gausenfeld is Judge Kühlemann! That's right. Kühlemann himself. The same Kühlemann at whose bequest the foundling hospital is to be built. Does anyone want to contend that Kühlemann was stealing from his own bequest? Well, then!" Heuteufel shrugged his shoulders and there was approving laughter. But not for long; passions were soon kindled again. "Proof! Kühlemann himself should explain! Thieves!" Heuteufel explained that Kühlemann was dangerously ill. They were sending a messenger and had already telephoned. "Oh, damn!" whispered Kunze to his friend Diederich. "If it was Kühlemann then it is all over, we can just pack up and leave."—"Not at all," Diederich answered with reckless confidence. Pastor Zillich, for his part, had now no other hope than the hand of God. "We don't need it," said Diederich in his recklessness, as he buttonholed a sceptic. He egged on the Nationalists to take a more decisive stand. He even shook hands with Social Democrats in order to strengthen their hatred of the corrupt Liberal bourgeoisie, and everywhere he displayed Klüsing's letter. He whacked the paper so vigorously with the back of his hand that nobody could read it, and shouted: "Does that say Kühlemann? It says Buck! If Kühlemann has a last gasp left in him he will have to admit that he wasn't the one. It was Buck!"

As he spoke he nevertheless kept his eye on the platform, where a remarkable silence had ensued. The gentlemen of the committee were rushing about, but they talked in whispers. Old Buck was nowhere to be seen. "What is wrong?" The hall had also grown quieter, nobody knew why. Suddenly word came: "They say Kühlemann is dead!" Diederich felt it rather than heard it. He suddenly stopped talking and exerting himself. His face was contorting into grimaces from excitement. He did not reply when he was asked a question. Around him he could hear a surreal jumble of sounds, and he no longer knew exactly where he was. Then Gottlieb Hornung came up and said: "God's truth, he's dead. I was upstairs, they telephoned. At that very moment he died."

"At the right moment," said Diederich, looking around in astonishment, as if waking from a dream. "The hand of God has again proved itself." Pastor Zillich affirmed, and Diederich became aware that this was a hand not to be disdained. What if it had given a different turn to the wheel of fate? . . . The parties in the hall were dispersing. The intervention of death in politics had turned the parties into human beings. They spoke in hushed tones and withdrew. When Diederich reached the street he heard that old Buck had fainted.

The *Netzig Journal* reported on the "tragically ending electoral assembly" and followed with a respectful obituary for the highly distinguished citizen Kühlemann. The reputation of the deceased remained untarnished, even if things had occurred which required further illumination. . . . Events took their course after Diederich and Napoleon Fischer had held a private conference. On the evening before the election the "Emperor's Party" held an assembly from which the opponents were not excluded. Diederich spoke and scourged with fiery phrases the democratic corruption as well as its chief perpetrator in Netzig, whose name it was the duty of a true patriot to speak aloud—but then Diederich thought the better of speaking it aloud. "For gentlemen, within my breast swells the elation that I might prove myself worthy of our magnificent Emperor by tearing the mask from his most dangerous enemy and proving to you that he, too, has nothing but his own profit at heart." At this point he was struck by an inspiration, or was it a memory? He was not sure. "His Majesty has uttered the exalted words: 'I would give my African colonial empire for an arrest warrant for Eugen Richter!' But I, gentlemen, shall deliver into the hands of his Majesty Richter's closest friends!" He allowed the enthusiasm to subside; then, in relatively hushed tones: "And therefore, gentlemen, I am in a position to harbor a particularly well-grounded guess as to what is expected of the Emperor's Party by higher circles—by much higher circles, I might add!" He reached for his breast pocket as though he carried there once again the decisive document, and suddenly, at the top of his lungs: "Anyone who still thinks he should cast his vote for the Liberals is no patriot!" Since those assembled gave every indication that they were convinced of this, Napoleon Fischer, who happened to be present, made an attempt to demonstrate to them the necessary consequences of their position. Diederich cut him off immediately. The nationally minded voters would do their duty with a heavy heart and choose the lesser evil. "But let me say that I am the first to denounce categorically any deals made with the Revolution!" He pounded on the podium until Napoleon beat a hasty retreat. One could see that Diederich's indignance had been genuine when one opened the Social Democratic *Volksstimme* early in the morning on the day of the second ballot. Amidst derisive attacks on Diederich appeared everything he had said against old Buck, but this time names were named. "Hessling's going to fall," said the voters, "for Buck has to sue him now." But many replied: "Buck is the one who is going to fall, the other knows too much." The Liberals, too, insofar as they were susceptible to reason, felt that the time had come to proceed with caution. So if the Nationals, whom by all appearances were not to be toyed with, felt that one should vote for the Social Democrats. . . . And if the Social Democrat was elected, then it was a good thing to have voted for him, if one did not want to be boycotted by the workers. . . .

The final voting took place at three o'clock in the afternoon. An alarm was sounded in Kaiser Wilhelm Strasse, and everyone rushed to the windows and shop doors to see where the fire was. It was the Veterans' Association marching past in uniform. Their flag pointed the way of honor. Kühnchen, who was in command, wore his helmet at a rakish angle on the back of his neck and was swinging his sword in a frightening manner. Diederich tramped along in rank and file and rejoiced at the thought that from now on everything would be done in rank and file, mechanically, and according to command. One needed only to march, and old Buck would be trampled to a pulp under the goose-stepping jackboots of Power! . . . At the other end of the street they received the new colors, which were presented with thunderous music and cheers of pride. The procession, lengthened by unforeseen reinforcements of patriots, reach Klappsch's premises. Here they formed into sections and Kühnchen gave the command: "To the urns." The election committee, with Pastor Zillich at the head, was waiting in the hall, festively attired. Kühnchen issued his commands in martial tones. "On, comrades, to the poll! We vote for Fischer!" Whereupon the music became louder and they marched from the right wing into the polling place. The entire procession followed the Veterans' Association. Klappsch was not prepared for so much enthusiasm, and had run out of beer. Finally, when the national cause seemed to have brought forth all that it was capable of producing, Mayor Scheffelweis arrived amidst cheers. He demonstratively allowed a red ballot to be thrust into his hand, and when he returned from casting his vote he was seen beaming with joy. "At last!" he said, pressing Diederich's hand. "We have this day conquered the dragon." Diederich's reply was merciless. "You, Mr. Mayor? Why, you are still halfway down its throat. Mind it doesn't take you with it when it dies!" As Dr. Scheffelweis paled, another cheer arose. "Wulckow! . . ."

Five thousand and more votes for Fischer! Heuteufel, with barely three thousand, was swept aside by the patriotic tide, and the Social Democrat went to the Reichstag. The *Netzig Journal* declared this result a victory for the "Emperor's Party," for thanks to the latter, a stronghold of Liberalism had fallen. With this, however, Nothgroschen aroused neither great satisfaction nor definite opposition. Everyone found the accomplished fact natural but uninteresting. After the uproar of the election it was time to go back to making money. The Emperor Wilhelm Monument, only yesterday the focal point of a civil war, no longer aroused the slightest excitement. Old Kühlemann had left the town six hundred thousand marks for public purposes; very decent. A foundling hospital or a monument, that was the same as sponges and toothbrushes to Gottlieb Hornung. At the decisive meeting of the town councillors it turned out that the Social Democrats were in favor of the monument; well and good. Somebody proposed that a committee be formed at once, and that the honorary chairmanship be offered to Governor von Wulckow. Here Heuteufel, who was probably annoyed, after all, by his defeat, got up and expressed a doubt as to whether the Governor, who was mixed up in a certain property deal, would himself think it fitting that he should help to decide on the site on which the monument was to stand. There were grins and winks, and Diederich felt a cold shiver down his spine as he waited to see if the scandal would now come out. He waited in silence, secretly thrilled at the thought of what would happen to Authority if somebody disclosed the scandal. He could not have said what he really wished. As nothing happened, he stood up very straight and protested, without any exaggerated effort, against the insinuation he had once before publicly refuted. The other side, on the contrary, had done nothing at all to counter the charges of irregularity which had been brought against them. "Don't you worry," replied Heuteufel. "You will soon be satisfied. A writ has already been served."

This, at least, caused a sensation, but the impression was weakened when Heuteufel admitted that his friend Buck had taken action not against Councillor Hessling, but merely against the Socialist paper *Die Volksstimme.* "Hessling knows too much," people said—and after Wulckow, who was made honorary chairman, Diederich was appointed chairman of the Emperor Wilhelm Monument Committee. In the municipal administration these decisions received the warmest support from Mayor Scheffelweis; they were passed in the noticeable absence of old Buck. If he himself did not think more of his own cause! Heuteufel said: "Is he to look on in person at dirty work which he cannot prevent?" This merely harmed Heuteufel himself. Since old Buck in recent times had suffered two defeats, it was expected that his action against the Socialist newspaper would be the third. The statements that had to be made in court were adapted by everyone in advance to fit the given circumstances. Of course, Hessling had gone too far, the more reasonable people said. Old Buck, who was long known to them all, was not a swindler and a cheat. He may have been guilty of imprudence, especially now, when he was paying his brother's debts, and was himself up to his neck in debt. Did he really go with Cohn to Klüsing about the site? It was a good stroke of business—only it should not have been found out. And why did Kühlemann have to die at the exact moment when he ought to have declared his friend's innocence? Such bad luck was not without cause. Herr Tietz, the business manager of the *Netzig Journal,* who had the run of Gausenfeld, said point-blank that it was a crime against oneself to take up the defense of people whose number was up. Tietz also drew attention to the fact that old Klüsing, who could have ended the whole thing with a word, took good care to say nothing. He was ill, and, on his account, the hearing was postponed indefinitely.

That, however, did not prevent him from selling his factory. This was the latest, this was what constituted the "significant changes in a large enterprise of the utmost importance to the economic life of Netzig" to which the *Netzig Journal* made occult reference. Klüsing had joined a Berlin syndicate. When asked why he did not take advantage of the opportunity, Diederich produced a letter in which Klüsing offered him the sale before anyone else. "And on terms that occur once in a lifetime," he added. "Unfortunately, I am in quite deep with my brother-in-law in Eschweiler, I am not even sure that I shall not have to leave Netzig." But as an expert he answered an inquiry of Nothgroschen's, who made the reply public that the prospectus was, if anything, an understatement of the facts, and that Gausenfeld was a veritable gold mine. The purchase of shares, which were put on the open market, could be strongly recommended. And so it happened that there was a great demand for the shares in Netzig. How impartial and untainted by personal interest Diederich's opinion was became apparent on one occasion in particular, when old Buck was looking for a loan. His family responsibilities and his sense of public duty had brought him to the point where even his friends refused to help him. Then Diederich intervened. He gave the old man a second mortgage on his house in the Fleischhauergrube. "He must have been desperately in need of the money," Diederich would remark whenever he told the story, "if he accepted it from me, his strongest political opponent! Who would have believed it?" Diederich contemplated the vagaries of fate. . . . He added that the house would be an expensive luxury if it came into his hands. Of course, he would soon have to leave his own, and this too showed that he was not counting on Gausenfeld. "But," declared Diederich, "the old man is not lying on a bed of roses. Who knows how his lawsuit will end. And just because I have to fight him politically, I want to show—you understand." People understood and congratulated Diederich on his more than creditable action. Diederich modestly demurred. "He accused me of lacking idealism, and I had to prove that he was wrong." A note of virile emotion trembled in his voice. People's fates pursued their courses, and if in many cases they encountered rough terrain, it was all the more pleasant for Diederich to find his own running smoothly. Diederich fully realized this on the day Napoleon Fischer left for Berlin to vote against the military-appropriations bill. The Socialist paper had announced a mass demonstration, and the station was to be guarded by the police. It was the duty of every loyal citizen to be present. Diederich ran into Jadassohn en route. They greeted one another formally as befitted the coolness which had sprung up between them. "Are you also going to have a look at the show?" asked Diederich.

"I am going on a holiday—to Paris." And indeed, Jadassohn was wearing knickerbockers. "If only to avoid the political imbecilities which have been going on here," he added. Diederich resolved to ignore urbanely the vexation of a man who had had no success. "One would have thought you were about ready to settle down."

"I? Why so?"

"Isn't Fräulein Zillich away at her aunt's?"

"At her aunt's? That's a good one!" Jadassohn leered. "And people thought. . . . I suppose you did, too?"

"Leave me out of it." Diederich assumed a knowing expression. "But if she's not at her aunt's then where has she gone?"

"She's flown the coop," said Jadassohn. Diederich stood still and gasped. Käthchen Zillich had run away! In what adventures he might have been involved! . . . Jadassohn spoke as a man of the world:

"Yes, she's gone to Berlin. Her fond parents are still in ignorance. I have no quarrel with her, you understand; things had to come to a head, sooner or later."

"In one way or another," Diederich added, having recovered himself. "I prefer this way to any other," Jadassohn declared. To which Diederich replied in a confidential whisper: "I don't mind telling you now that it always looked as if that girl was rather sweet on you." Jadassohn denied it, but not without a touch of *amour-propre.* "What do you take me for? I myself gave her letters of introduction. Just you wait. She will be a big success in Berlin."

"I do not doubt it." Diederich winked. "I know her good points . . . You certainly thought I was naive." He would not listen to Jadassohn's defense. "You thought me naive, but at the same time I put a damned big spoke in your wheel, I can tell you." He gave the other, who was becoming more and more uneasy, an account of his adventure with Käthchen in the Cabinet of Love—an account which was much more detailed than the facts warranted. With a smile of satisfied vengeance he watched Jadassohn, who was obviously in doubt as to whether his honor were not involved. Finally he decided to clap Diederich on the shoulder, and in the friendliest manner they drew the obvious conclusions. "Of course, the matter is strictly between ourselves . . . Such a girl must be judged fairly, for where would the *demi-monde* get recruits? . . . Her address? Well, as a favor to you. So if you ever happen to be in Berlin, there will be at least one familiar face." "It would actually have a certain charm," Diederich said reflectively. And as Jadassohn saw his luggage, they said goodbye. "Politics, unfortunately has driven something of a wedge between us, but, thank God, we can come together in human affairs. Have a good time in Paris."

"It is not a pleasure trip." Jadassohn turned around, with an expression as if he were about to entrap a witness. When he saw how disturbed Diederich looked he came back. "In four weeks you will see for yourself," he said with curious solemnity and self-possession. "Perhaps it would be best if you were to begin now to prepare the public." Impressed in spite of himself, Diederich asked: "What do you propose to do?" Jadassohn answered portentiously and with a smile of resigned determination: "I am about to adapt my outward appearance more appropriately to my patriotic convictions . . ." When Diederich had grasped the significance of these words, he could only incline his head respectfully. Jadassohn had already gone. In the background, as he entered the station, his ears glowed once more—for the last time!—like two church windows in the light of the setting sun.

A group of men was approaching the station, a banner flying in their midst. A number of policemen lumbered down the steps and faced off against them. Immediately the group began to sing the Internationale. All the same, their advance was successfully repelled by the representatives of law and order. Some, it is true, got through and rallied around Napoleon Fischer, whose arms were so long that he seemed to drag his carpet bag almost along the ground. The men were recovering in the refreshment room from their exertions in the July sun on behalf of the revolution. Then Napoleon Fischer tried to make a speech on the platform, since the train was late anyway, but the Parliamentary Representative was forbidden to do so by a policeman. Napoleon put down his carpet bag and bared his teeth. He was evidently on the point of resisting the power of the State, which did not surprise Diederich in the least. Fortunately for Napoleon Fischer the train drew up. Only then did Diederich notice a small gentleman, who turned away whenever people passed near him. He was holding a large bouquet in front of him and looking in the direction of the train. Those shoulders seemed familiar to Diederich . . . Something awfully strange was going on here! Judith Lauer waved from a carriage, her husband helped her out, and actually handed her the bouquet, which she accepted with that serious smile of hers. As the couple turned toward the exit, Diederich hastened, fuming, to get out of their way. Nothing strange was going on; Lauer's term was simply up, and he was a free man once more. Not that there was anything further to fear from him; but one would have to become accustomed again to the thought that he was at large . . . And he received her with flowers! Did he not know anything? Surely he had had time to reflect. And she, returning to him after he had served his sentence! There were relationships which no decent man could ever fathom in his wildest dreams. In any case, the matter did not concern Diederich any more than everybody else. He had only done his duty on that occasion. "Everybody will be as painfully affected as myself. Everyone will give him to understand that he would do best to remain quietly at home. . . . He has made his bed and now he must lie in it." Käthchen Zillich had understood that and drawn the right conclusion. What was right in her case applied to others as well, and not only to Herr Lauer.

Diederich himself, who walked through the town to the accompaniment of respectful greetings, now accepted as a matter of course the position to which his accomplishments had entitled him. During these tough times he had fought so hard that it now only remained for him to reap his reward. Others had begun to believe in him, and forthwith his own doubts vanished . . . Lately there had been unfavorable rumors about Gausenfeld, and the stocks fell. How had people heard that the Government had withdrawn its contracts and entrusted them to Hessling's firm? Diederich had not breathed a word about it, but it became known even before the dismissal of the workmen, which the *Netzig Journal* regretted so deeply. Old Buck, as chairman of the board of directors of Gausenfeld, had to initiate these dismissals which harmed his reputation. Presumably it was only because of old Buck that the Government was acting so harshly. It had been a mistake to elect him chairman. In any case, he should have paid his debts with the money Hessling had so decently given him, instead of buying Gausenfeld stock. Diederich himself repeatedly expressed this opinion. "Who would ever have believed it?" he remarked again in this connection; and again he contemplated the vagaries of fate. "It is easily seen what a man is capable of when he feels the ground slipping from under his feet." This gave everybody the unpleasant impression that old Buck would drag them down, as shareholders, into his own ruin. For the stocks were falling. As a result of the dismissals, a strike was threatened, and they fell still further . . .

At this juncture Kienast made a number of friends. Kienast had arrived unexpectedly in Netzig, for a rest, as he said. Nobody liked admitting that they had Gausenfeld stock and had been outwitted. Kienast told one shareholder that another had already sold out. His personal opinion was that it was high time to do so. A broker, whom he did not know, by the way, came into the cafés from time to time and bought stock. Some months later the newspaper published a daily advertisement of the banking house of Sanft and Co. Anyone who still had Gausenfeld shares could unload them here without any trouble. By the beginning of the autumn not a soul held any more of those rotten stocks. But there was talk of a merger between Hessling and Gausenfeld. Diederich professed to be astonished. "What about old Herr Buck?" he asked. "As chairman of the board of directors he will certainly have something to say in the matter. Or has he also sold out?" Then it was said: "He has other troubles," for his action for libel against the Socialist paper had now come up for hearing. "He will probably lose," people said, and Diederich, with perfect impartiality: "It is a pity. In that case he will never sit on another board of directors."

With this idea in mind everyone went to the trial. The witnesses who appeared could remember nothing. Klüsing had long since spoken to everyone about the sale of the factory. Did he specifically mention the site? And had he mentioned old Buck as the go-between? All this remained doubtful. Among the Town Council members it was known that the site was under discussion for the then projected foundling hospital. Had Buck been in favor of it? Certainly he had not opposed it. Several people had been struck by his lively interest in that site. Klüsing himself, who was still ill, had declared in his affidavit that his friend Buck had been in and out a good deal a short while before. If Buck had spoken to him about an option on the site he had certainly not understood it in any sense detrimental to Buck's honor ... The plaintiff, Buck, wished to establish the fact that it was the late Kühlemann who had negotiated with Klüsing: Kühlemann, the benefactor himself. The point, however, was not proven; here as well Klüsing's testimony was indecisive. That Cohn said so was immaterial, since Cohn had an interest in proving that his own visit to Gausenfeld was innocent. Diederich remained as the most important witness. Klüsing had written to him and immediately afterwards had had a conversation with him. Was any name mentioned on that occasion? Diederich testified:

"I had no wish to learn one name or another. I declare, as all the witnesses can confirm, that I have never publicly mentioned the name of Herr Buck. My sole interest in the matter was that the town must not be injured by the actions of individuals. I intervened on behalf of political morality: I bear no personal malice whatever, and I should be sorry if the plaintiff did not leave this court without a stain on his character."

A murmur of approval greeted his words. Only Buck seemed dissatisfied. He jumped up, red in the face. . . . Diederich was now asked for his personal view of the matter. He was preparing to speak, when old Buck stepped forward, holding himself erect, and his eyes flaming as they did at that fateful electoral assembly.

"I forbid this witness to give a favorable testimony to myself and my life. He is not qualified to do so. His success has been attained by methods very different from mine, and they have a very different aim. My house was always open and free to everyone including the witness. For more than fifty years my life has not been my own, it has been devoted to one idea, which was shared by many in my time: to justice and the common welfare. I was well off when I entered public life; when I leave it I shall be poor. I need no defense." He fell silent and his face trembled—but Diederich merely shrugged his shoulders. To what success was the old man referring? He had long since failed, and now he was spinning sonorous phrases, upon which no one would bank. He pretended to be superior, but he was already under the wheels. How could a man so misunderstand his position? "If one of us is to condescend the other—"Diederich glared. The old man flamed up in vain, he simply glared him down, and with him justice and the common welfare. Every man for himself—and just was the cause that prevailed in the end . . . He had the distinct impression that everyone shared this conviction. The old man had the same impression; he sat down, his shoulders slumped, and in his face appeared a look of something like shame. Turning to the magistrates he said: "I do not claim any privileged position. I submit to the judgment of my fellow citizens."

Diederich thereupon continued his testimony as if nothing had happened. It was indeed quite favorable and made an excellent impression. Since the Lauer trial people found him changed for the better, he had acquired a calm self-assurance, which was, after all, not surprising, for he was now a made man and had come out on top of the heap. It was just striking noon when the latest news from the *Netzig Journal* spread through the courtroom. It was revealed that Hessling, a major shareholder in Gausenfeld, had been made general manager of the company ... The crowd eyed him with great curiosity, and then looked over at old Buck sitting opposite, at whose expense he had prospered. He now got back with a hundred percent interest the twenty thousand which he had lent the old man, and yet retained his reputation for virtue. That the latter should have invested the money in Gausenfeld of all places was regarded as a good joke on Hessling's part, and was a momentary consolation to many for their own losses. When Diederich left he did so amidst a respectful silence. He was greeted with that degree of respect which is almost servility. The cheated shareholders were saluting success.

They were by no means so lenient with old Buck. When the presiding magistrate pronounced the verdict, there was applause. The newspaper was fined only fifty marks! The case was not proven and the plea of good faith was admitted. The legal experts pronounced this a devastating blow to the plaintiff, and as Buck left the courthouse even his friends avoided him. Humble folks who had lost their savings in Gausenfeld shook their fists at him. This verdict convinced them all that they were right to be through with old Buck. A deal like that on the site for the foundling hospital ought, at least, to be successful; Hessling pointed this out and he was right. But that was just it. All his life old Buck had never had real success. He thought himself a wonder because as a city father and party leader he was retiring in debt. There were plenty of other good-for-nothing customers. His questionable business capacity had its counterpart in morals, the proof of which was that still unexplained story of the engagement of his son, who was now hanging around the theater. And Buck's politics? An international standpoint, always demanding sacrifices for demagogic purposes, and on the worst terms with the Government, which in its turn had a bad effect on business. That was the policy of a man who had nothing more to lose, and who lacked a good citizen's sense of responsibility in regard to investments. With indignation people realized that they had delivered themselves entirely into the hands of an adventurer. There was a general, heartfelt desire to prevent him from doing further harm. As he himself did not draw the obvious conclusion from the devastating verdict, it became necessary for others to drive it home. The right to hold administrative office must surely be conditioned by the provision that a public official must prove himself worthy of the dignity demanded by his position, by his conduct both in and out of office. Did old Buck fulfill this condition? To ask the question was to answer it, as the *Netzig Journal* observed, of course, without mentioning names. But things had to reach the point where the matter was brought to the attention of the Town Council. Finally, one day before the discussion, the obstinate old man listened to reason and resigned his position as town councillor. After that his political friends could not risk losing their remaining supporters by retaining him as the leader of the party. It appeared that he did not make their task any easier. Several visits and some gentle pressure were necessary before a letter appeared in the press saying that he placed the welfare of democracy above his own. As the former was threatened with harm, through his name, owing to the influence of passions which he hoped were only temporary, he would retire. "If the general good demands, I am prepared to bear the unjustified slur which a deceived public opinion has put on me, in the belief that the eternal justice of the people will one day absolve me again."

This was regarded as imperiousness and hypocrisy. Well-meaning observers excused it on the ground of old age. In any case what he wrote or did not write was of no consequence, for what was he now? People who had him to thank for their jobs or other personal gain looked him in the face without raising their hats. Many laughed and commented aloud—these were the people to whom his outright authority did not extend, but who had nevertheless been full of devotion as long as he enjoyed general esteem. In place of the old friends whom he never encountered on his daily walk, new and strange friends appeared. They met him as he was returning home in the twilight; sometimes it was a small tradesman with haggard eyes, threatened with bankruptcy; or a somber drunkard or some shadowy figure slinking along by the walls of the houses. They would slacken their pace and meet his gaze with shy or insolent familiarity. They lifted their hats, no doubt hesitantly, and then old Buck would totter up to them and shake the hand extended toward him, no matter whose it might be.—As time went on he was no longer even an object of people's hate. Those who had purposedly cut him now passed him indifferently, and sometimes even greeted him again by force of habit. A father out for a walk with his young son assumed a pensive air, and when they had passed him, he explained to his child: "Did you see that old gentleman slinking along all by himself and looking at nobody?

Let that be a lesson to you for the rest of your life, of what disgrace can do to a man." Henceforth at the sight of old Buck the child was seized with a mysterious thrill of horror, just as the older generation, when it was young, had experienced an inexplicable feeling of pride on seeing him. There were, it is true, young people who did not follow the prevailing opinion. Sometimes, when the old man left the house, school was just letting out. The schoolchildren would trot off in droves, stepping respectfully aside to make room for their teachers; and Kühnchen, now an unrestrained Nationalist, or Pastor Zillich, more puritanical than ever since Käthchen's misfortune, would hurry on, without even a glance at the man in disgrace. Then these few youngsters would stop on the road; each, by all appearances, for himself and on his own initiative. Their brows were not as smooth as those of their schoolmates; they had expression in their eyes when they turned their backs on Kühnchen and Zillich and took off their caps to old Buck. Involuntarily he would stop and gaze into these faces bright with promise, inspired once more by the hope with which, all his life long, he had looked into the face of every fellow creature.

In the meantime Diederich had little time indeed to pay much attention to the secondary phenomena accompanying his rise to power. The *Netzig Journal,* now unreservedly at Diederich's disposal, maintained that it was Herr Buck himself who, before his resignation as chairman of the board of directors, had proposed the appointment of Dr. Hessling as general manager. The fact left a rather peculiar taste in the mouths of many people. But Nothgroschen drew attention to Dr. Hessling's great and undeniable services to the community in that capacity. But for him, who had quietly acquired more than half the shares, they would certainly have fallen still more, and a great many families had only Dr. Hessling to thank if they were saved from ruin. The strike had been prevented by the energetic action of the new chairman. His loyalty to Emperor and country was a guarantee that for the future the sun of governmental approval would never set on Gausenfeld. In brief, glorious days were dawning for the industrial life of Netzig, and especially for the paper industry—the more so, as the rumor of a merger between Hessling's business and Gausenfeld proved to be true. Nothgroschen was able to state that only on this condition could Dr. Hessling be prevailed upon to take charge of Gausenfeld.

As a matter of fact Diederich lost no time in increasing the share capital. The Hessling factory was put in as new capital. Diederich had pulled off an excellent stroke of business. Success had crowned his first act of administration. He was master of the situation, with his docile board of directors, and could proceed to impress his commanding personality upon the internal organization of the business. At the outset he assembled the entire populace of workers and employees. "Some of you," he said, "already know me from the Hessling factory. Well, the rest of you will get to know me soon enough! Whoever is prepared to cooperate with me is welcome, but I will stand no radicalism! Not quite two years ago I said that to a few of you, and now you can see how many I have at my command. You may be proud to have such a master! You can rely on me. I will undertake the responsibility of arousing you to a sense of patriotism, and of making you faithful supporters of the existing order." He promised them dwellings, medical benefits, and cheap groceries. "But I forbid socialist agitation! In the future you will vote as I tell you, or you will be fired!" Diederich also said that he was determined to curb atheism. He would note every Sunday who went to church and who did not. "So long as unredeemed sin prevails in the world, there will be war and hatred, envy and discord. Therefore, there must be one master!"

In order to enforce this fundamental principle every room in the factory was adorned with inscriptions to drive it home: No thoroughfare! It is strictly prohibited to fetch water in the fire buckets! They were especially not allowed to send out for bottles of beer, for Diederich had not failed to make a contract with a brewer which ensured him a profit on what his employees consumed. . . . Eating, sleeping, smoking, children, "courting, flirting, petting, and every other indecent act", were strictly prohibited! In the workmen's dwellings, even before they were built, foster children were forbidden. An unmarried couple living together, who had evaded detection for ten years under Klüsing, were solemnly dismissed. This occurrence even inspired Diederich to invent a new means of raising the moral tone of the people. In the appropriate places he had paper hung up, which was manufactured in Gausenfeld itself, and which nobody could use without noticing the moral and patriotic maxims imprinted upon it. At times he would hear the men shouting to one another some lofty dictum or singing a patriotic song which had been impressed upon their memory on a like occasion. Encouraged by this success Diederich put his invention on the market. It appeared under the name of "World Power," and, as a grandiloquent advertisement announced, it carried the German spirit, supported by German technology, in triumph all over the world.

Even this educational toilet paper could not remove all possibility of conflict between master and men. One day Diederich was compelled to announce that he would pay only for dental treatment, but not for tooth replacement, out of the insurance fund. One man had had an entire set of dentures made! When Diederich insisted upon his policy, which admittedly had been issued after the fact, the man sued him, and by some fluke actually won his case. His faith in the existing order thereby shaken, he became an agitator, his morals declined, and he would certain have been dismissed under normal circumstances. But Diederich could not bring himself to abandon the set of teeth, which had cost him so much, and so he retained the man as well. . . . The whole business, as he had to admit to himself, was most injurious to the spirit of the labor force. Added to this came the influence of dangerous political events. When several Social Democrats in the newly opened Reichstag building remained seated while cheers for the Emperor were called, there was no longer any doubt that the necessity for antirevolutionary legislation was established. Diederich publicly advocated the idea, and prepared his employees for it in an address which was received in brooding silence. The majority in the Reichstag was so unprincipled as to defeat the measure, and the result was not long in making itself known; an industrial magnate was murdered. Murdered! An industrial magnate! The assassin declared he was not a Social Democrat, but Diederich knew from experiences with his own workmen what that denial meant. The murdered man was supposed to have been well disposed toward the workers, but Diederich knew from his experience what that meant. For days and weeks he never opened a door without the fear that a drawn dagger lurked behind it. His office was fitted with spring-guns, and in Guste's company he crawled every evening around the bedroom and searched for murderers. His telegrams to the Emperor, whether emanating from the Town Council, the committee of the "Emperor's Party," the Trade Association, or the Veterans' Association, the telegrams with which Diederich bombarded His Imperial Highness shouted for help against the revolutionary movement, fanned by the Socialists, which had claimed yet another victim; they shouted for relief from this plague;

for immediate legal action and military protection for authority and property; for the imprisonment of strikers who prevented anyone from working . . . The *Netzig Journal,* which duly reported all this, did not fail to acknowledge the great services Dr. Hessling had rendered in the cause of social peace and the welfare of the workers. Every new workman's dwelling Diederich built was displayed by Nothgroschen in a highly flattering picture and was made the subject of a laudatory article. Certain other employers, whose influence in Netzig fortunately was no longer of any account, might encourage subversive tendencies in their employees by sharing profits with them. The principles for which Dr. Hessling stood embodied the best relationship imaginable between employer and employee, such as His Majesty the Emperor wished to see everywhere in German industry. Strong resistance to the unjust demands of the workers, together with joint action on the part of the employers, was a part, as everyone knew, of the Emperor's social program, which it was the honorable ambition of Dr. Hessling to carry out. A picture of Diederich was published with the article.

Such recognition spurred him on to ever greater zeal—in spite of the unredeemed sin, the powerful effects of which were visible not only in business but in domestic life as well. Here, unfortunately, it was Kienast who sowed envy and discord. He declared that but for him and his discreet assistance in the purchase of the stock Diederich could never have attained his brilliant position. To this Diederich retorted that Kienast had been compensated by a number of shares proportionate to his means. His brother-in-law repudiated this and professed to have found a legal basis for his unconscionable demands. Was he not, as Magda's husband, part-owner of the old Hessling factory, to the extent of one-eighth of its value? The factory was sold and Diederich had received cash and preferred Gausenfeld shares in exchange. Kienast demanded one-eighth of the capital income and of the yearly dividends from the preferred shares. To this outrageous demand Diederich replied emphatically that he owed nothing more either to his sister or his brother-in-law. "I was bound to pay you only your share of the annual profits of my factory. My factory is sold. Gausenfeld does not belong to me but to a company of shareholders. So far as the capital is concerned, that is my private fortune. You have no claim on it." Kienast called this barefaced robbery. Fully convinced by his own argument Diederich talked of extortion, and then came a lawsuit.

The lawsuit lasted three years. It was fought with increasing bitterness, especially by Kienast, who gave up his post in Eschweiler and moved with Magda to Netzig in order to devote himself entirely to it. As chief witness against Diederich he had cited old Sötbier, who, in his desire for vengeance, was actually prepared to prove that even earlier Diederich had not given his relations the money which was due them. Kienast also hit upon the idea of illuminating certain incidents in Diederich's past with the assistance of Napoleon Fischer, now a deputy in the Reichstag. In this, however, he never quite succeeded. Nevertheless, these tactics compelled Diederich on different occasions to pay over considerable sums to the party funds of the Social Democrats. And he conceded to himself that his personal loss grieved him less than the injury which the national cause suffered thereby. Guste, who could not see quite so far, egged on the men in their fight primarily from feminine motives. Her first child was a girl, and she could not forgive Magda for having a boy. Magda, whose interest in the money question was initially lukewarm at best, traced the beginning of hostilities to the time when Emmi appeared with a scandalous hat from Berlin. Magda remarked that Emmi was now favored by Diederich in the most shameful fashion. Emmi had her own flat in Gausenfeld where she gave tea parties. The amount of her dress allowance was nothing less than an insult to her married sister. Magda had to witness the advantage which her marriage had conferred upon her being turned into the very opposite, and she accused Diederich of having expediently got rid of her just before his success began. If Emmi could still not find a husband there appeared to be good reasons for it—which were even being whispered about in Netzig. Magda saw no reason why she should not say them out loud. Inge Tietz brought the story to Gausenfeld, but at the same time she brought with her a weapon against Magda, because she happened to meet the midwife at the Kienasts', and the first child was born hardly six months after they were married. A terrible commotion ensued, telephonic vituperation from one house to the other, threats of legal proceedings, for which material was collected by each sister from the other's servants.

* * *

But soon after Diederich and Kienast had managed with manly levelheadedness to ward off for the time being a full-blown family scandal, one broke out nonetheless. Guste and Diederich received anonymous letters which they had to conceal from every third party and even from each other, so utterly risqué was their content. What is more, the drawings with which they were illustrated transgressed the bounds of propriety for even realist art. Every morning without fail the innocent grey envelopes lay on the breakfast table, and each whisked his own into concealment while acting as though he did not see the other's. Their little hiding-game was brought to an end, however, when Magda had the audacity to show up in Gausenfeld with a bundle of letters, closely resembling those sent to Diederich and Guste, that she claimed to have received. This was too much for Guste. "I'm sure you have a very good idea of who's been writing them to you!" she sputtered, choked with rage and red in the face. Magda said that she could well imagine and that that was why she had come. "If you get your jollies by writing letters like that to yourself," hissed Guste, "then do me a favor and don't write them to people who don't get their jollies that way!" Magda protested and, turning green, countered with a barrage of accusations. But Guste had made a dash for the telephone; she called Diederich in his office and asked him to come at once, then ran off and returned with a bundle of letters. Diederich came in the other door and had brought his along as well. When the three fascinating collections had been spread out to great effect upon the table, the three relatives stared aghast at one another. Then they collected their wits and began vociferously and in unison to give vent to the same charges. To avoid losing ground, Magda appealed to the witness of her husband, who was likewise being plagued with the letters. Guste claimed to have seen something of the like in Emmi's possession as well. Emmi was sent for, and after little prodding confessed in her deprecatory manner that she too had been receiving such smutty missives. She had destroyed most of them. Not even old Mrs. Hessling had been spared! Although she held out for as long as she could in tearful denial, the others eventually brought her around . . . Since all of this served only to broaden the affair without leading to any resolution, the two family factions separated with threats that were at bottom hollow, but nonetheless fearsome. To shore up their respective positions, each of the two parties kept an eye out for possible confederates. One of the first items of intelligence that resulted was that Inge Tietz also numbered among the recipients of the inappropriate offerings. The hypothesis that then suggested itself found increasing confirmation. The mysterious letter-writer had wormed his way into private lives everywhere, even into Pastor Zillich's; indeed, even into the Mayor's and his family's. As far as the eye could see, he had conjured up around the Hessling household and around the households of all the better families associated with it an atmosphere of the crassest obscenity. For weeks thereafter, Guste did not dare venture out of the house. She and Diederich cast in horror their suspicion upon this neighbor and that. All over Netzig, no one trusted any longer those they had trusted most. Then came the day and the breakfast hour when within the bosom of the Hessling family, suspicion violated the ultimate boundary. A document, more accurate than any that had gone before it, trembled in Guste's hand; it captured moments that in their particularity were known—but never, ever spoken of aloud—only to her and her husband. These were things of which no third party could ever have been aware; if they had, it would mean the end of everything. But what then?. . . Guste sent a scrutinizing glance over the breakfast table to Diederich: in his hand trembled the same paper, and his glance scrutinized as well. Both of them, seized with fear, quickly cast their eyes downward.

The betrayer was everywhere. Where no one else was, there he stood as an alter ego. Through him, all bourgeois respectability was thrown into question in an undreamt-of manner. His activity would have led to an utter breakdown of all moral self-respect and all mutual regard if it were not for countermeasures, taken as though by universal, silent agreement, that brought about their restitution. The thousandfold fears, churning and working underground in search of a way out, converged from all sides, formed with the power of the united fear the canal that led to daylight and were finally able to pour their dark torrents over one man. Gottlieb Hornung did not even know what hit him. Speaking in private with Diederich, he boasted with his customary swagger of a number of letters he claimed to have written. His only reply to Diederich's harsh remonstrations was that everyone was writing such letters these days; it was the fashion, a parlor game—which Diederich repudiated with all due severity. The conversation left him with the impression that his old friend and compatriot Gottlieb Hornung, who had performed so many useful services in the past, was just the man to perform one here as well, even if it were involuntary; and so he dutifully turned him in. And when Hornung's name was made public in connection with the affair, it turned out that he had been a universal object of suspicion for quite some time. His activity during the elections had afforded him many an insight into people's lives; on top of that he was a native of Netzig and had no relatives, which had apparently made it all the easier for him to carry out his mischief. And then there was the desperate struggle for his right to refuse to sell sponges and toothbrushes. This struggle embittered him noticeably; in the course thereof he had let slip certain derisive remarks about prominent citizens whose need for the sponges was more than external, and for whom it would take a lot more than a toothbrush to scrub away what needed to be scrubbed away. He was indicted and he readily confessed his authorship of a number of the letters. He stoutly denied his complicity in most of the cases, to be sure, but the court called upon the testimony of handwriting experts. The opinion of a witness such as Heuteufel, who spoke of an epidemic and who maintained that no single person would ever be able to produce such an appalling mass of filth, was countered by the testimony of all the other witnesses and by the public will. The latter was represented most effectively by Jadassohn, who since his return from Paris had smaller ears and had been promoted to Public Prosecutor. Success and the confidence bred by the removal of his outward blemish even taught him moderation; he recognized that it would be in the best interests of the community at large to consider the arguments put forth by those who contended that Gottlieb Hornung was suffering from overwrought nerves. Diederich was the most ardent proponent of this view, and he did everything he could do to help the unfortunate friend of his youth. Hornung got off with a stay in the sanatorium, and upon his release Diederich provided him, on the condition that he leave Netzig, with funds sufficient to deliver him for a time from sponges and toothbrushes. In the long run, to be sure, the sponges and toothbrushes won out, the things looked very bleak indeed for Gottlieb Hornung. . . . The letters stopped of course as soon as he was safely interned in the asylum. Or at least if someone did receive one, he did not make it known, and the affair was officially over.

Diederich could once again regard his home as his castle. No longer subjected to this filthy encroachment upon their private life, the family blossomed forth in the purest manner. After Gretchen, who was born in 1894, and Horst in 1895, came Kraft in 1896.

A just father, Diederich kept an account for each child, even before it was born, and the first things he deducted were the cost of the midwife and the expenses of providing for each child. His view of married life was very strict. Horst's birth was not an easy one. When it was all over Diederich informed his wife that, if it had been necessary to choose, he would have simply allowed her to die, "painful as that course would have been," he added. "But the race is more important, and I am responsible to my Emperor for my sons." Women were there to produce children and Diederich refused them any license for frivolity and impropriety, although he graciously allowed them opportunities for edification and recreation. "Keep to the woman's sphere," he would say to Guste, "religion, cooking and children." On the red-checked tablecloth, with the imperial eagle and crown on each square, the Bible always lay beside the coffee pot, and it was Guste's duty to read aloud a passage from it every morning. On Sundays they went to church. "The authorities wish it," said Diederich seriously when Guste balked. As Diederich lived in the fear of his Lord and Master, so Guste was ordered to live in the fear of hers. When they entered a room she knew that the right of precedence properly belong to her husband. The children, in turn, had to treat her with respect, and Männe, the dachshund, had to obey everyone. At meals, therefore, the children and the dog had to observe silence. Guste's duty was to discern from the wrinkles upon her husband's brow whether it was advisable to leave him undisturbed or to drive away his cares with chatter. Certain dishes were prepared only for the master of the house, and when he was in a good humor, Diederich would throw a piece across the table and, laughing heartily, would watch to see who caught it, Gretchen, Guste or the dog. His afternoon nap was often troubled by gastronomical disturbances, and Guste's duty then commanded her to put warm poultices on his stomach. Groaning and terribly frightened he vowed he would make his will and appoint a trustee. Guste would not be allowed to touch a penny. "I have worked for my sons, not in order that you may amuse yourself after I am gone!" Guste objected that her own fortune was the foundation of everything, but it availed her nothing . . . Of course, when Guste had a cold, she could not expect Diederich to nurse her back to health. She had to keep as far away from him as possible, for Diederich was determined not to have any germs near him. He would not go into the factory unless he had antiseptic lozenges in his mouth, and one night he kicked up a row because the cook had come down with influenza, and had a temperature of one hundred four degrees. "Get that filth out of the house at once!" Diederich commanded, and when she had gone he wandered about the house for a long time spraying it with disinfecting fluids. When he read the *Lokal-Anzeiger* in the evening he would frequently say to his wife that human life was less important than a German Navy—to which Guste agreed, for the simple reason that she did not like the Empress Victoria, who was betraying Germany to England, as everyone knew, quite apart from certain domestic conditions, of which Guste strongly disapproved, in Friedrichskron Castle. We needed a strong fleet against England, which must be absolutely smashed; it was the deadliest enemy of the Emperor. And why? In Netzig they knew all about it. Simply because His Majesty had once, in a lively mood, given the Prince of Wales a friendly kick in a tempting portion of his anatomy. Besides, certain kinds of high-quality paper came from England, whose importation could best be stopped by a victorious war. Looking over the top of his paper Diederich would say to Guste: "I hate England as only Friedrich the Great hated that nation of thieves and shopkeepers. Those are His Majesty's sentiments and I subscribe to them." He subscribed to every word in every speech of the Emperor's, and always in their first and strongest form, not in the toned-down version which appeared the next day. All these words so expressive of German character, so in tune with the times—Diederich lived and breathed in them, as if they had been manifestations of his own nature; they remained in his memory as if he himself had spoken them. Sometimes he really had spoken them. Others he mixed up on public occasions with his own remarks, and neither he nor anybody else could tell what came from him and what from one more exalted... "This is sweet," said Guste, who was reading the miscellaneous column. "We must grasp Neptune's trident," declared Diederich unperturbed, while Guste read aloud some anecdote about the Empress which filled her with deep satisfaction. At Hubertusstock, the exalted lady liked to dress in simple, almost middle-class style. A postman to whom she revealed her identity on a country road did not believe who she was and laughed in her face. Afterward he was devastated and fell upon his knees, only to be rewarded with a mark. This delighted Diederich as well, just as his heart was touched when the Emperor went out into the street on Christmas Eve, with fifty-seven marks in newly minted money, to give the poor of Berlin a happy Christmas; or as an ominous thrill ran through him on learning that the Emperor had become an Honorary Bailiff of the Knights of Malta. The *Lokal-Anzeiger* opened up new worlds, and then, again, it brought the highest rulers comfortably close to one. There in the alcove the three-quarter life-size figures in bronze of their Majesties seemed to smile and move closer, and the bronze Trumpeter of Säckingen, who accompanied them, could be heard blowing a cordial blast. "It must be heavenly on laundry-day at the Emperor's," said Guste. "They have a hundred people for washing!" Diederich, on the other hand, was filled with profound pleasure because the Emperor's dachshunds were not obliged to respect the trains of the court ladies. He conceived the plan of giving full liberty to his own Männe in this respect at their next evening party. But a telegram in the next column made him uneasy, because it was still uncertain whether the Emperor and the Tsar would meet. "If it doesn't happen soon," said Diederich importantly, "we shall have to be prepared for the worst. One cannot trifle with world history." He liked to linger over imminent catastrophes, for "the German spirit is serious, almost tragic," he would declare.

But Guste's interest was waning visibly, and her yawns were growing more frequent. Under Diederich's chastising gaze she seemed to remember some duty; she narrowed her eyes to a defiant squint and even began to beleaguer him with her knees. He had one more patriotic thought he wanted to utter, but Guste cut him off with unusual severity: "Rubbish!" Diederich, however, far from wanting to punish this transgression, cringed up at her as though he were expecting more. . . . His attempt to embrace her about the hips was rewarded with a sudden and resounding slap to the cheek—to which he gave no reply, but stood up and crept behind the draperies, where he stood panting. And as he reemerged into the light, it became apparent that his eyes were not glaring at all, but staring in fear and dark desire. . . . This seemed to free Guste from the last of her misgivings. She rose, and shaking her hips in the most wanton manner began for her part to glare emphatically, and pointing her sausagelike finger imperiously toward the floor she hissed: "On your knees, you wretched slave!" And Diederich did what she commanded! In an outrageous inversion of every law, Guste was allowed to give him orders: "You will worship my magnificent form!"—And then, lying on his back, he would let her stomp on his stomach. She would, to be sure, interrupt herself in the midst of this activity and suddenly ask quite prosaically, without her cruel pathos: "Have you had enough?" Diederich did not move; immediately Guste was the complete mistress once again. "I am the mistress, you are the subject," she assured him expressly. "Get up! March!"—and she goaded him onward with her dimpled fists all the way to the conjugal bedroom. "You'd better be enjoying this!" she commanded, but Diederich managed to slip away and turn off the light. Standing in the dark, his heart skipping beats, he listened while Guste, from behind, called him the most indecent names, in the course of which, however, she began again to yawn. Somewhat later she had perhaps already gone to bed and fallen asleep—but Diederich, still intensely awake, crawled on all fours to the estrade in the parlor and hid himself behind the bronze Emperor. . . .

After every one of these nocturnal fantasies he had the household ledger brought to him the next morning, and woe to Guste if the books did not balance perfectly. He invoked a terrible reprisal in front of all the servants and put a decisive end to her brief presumption of power, if she still had any memory of it. Authority and morals triumphed once more. Diederich took other measures as well to ensure that things in their marital relations did not turn out too much to her advantage. Every second or third evening, sometimes even more often, Diederich went out—to his *stammtisch* in the Ratskeller, or so he told Guste, even if that was not always the case. . . . Diederich's seat at the *stammtisch* was underneath a Gothic arch, on which one could read the words "The tavern's rough but cozy bench—a haven from your nagging wench." The pithy old maxims on the other arches as well offered gratifying compensation for the concessions that one was forced by nature to make to one's wife at home. "He who loves not wine and song deserves a wife his whole life long," or "Deliver thee God from pain and scourge, evil women and evil curs." On the other hand, anyone sitting between Jadassohn and Heuteufel and raising his eyes to the ceiling could read: "A crackling fire, cheerful accord, and against the wall a well-honed sword. As our fathers did in days gone by, come drink your troubles and sorrows dry." This advice was being taken everywhere one looked, regardless of creed or party affiliation. For even Cohn and Heuteufel, together with their close friends and supporters, had turned up over the course of time, one by one and without making much of a stir, for the simple reason that in the long run, it was impossible for anyone to dispute or overlook the success which lent wings to the national cause and carried it ever higher aloft. Heuteufel's relationship to his brother-in-law Zillich was still marked with the dissention that had always troubled it. It seemed that the barriers between the *weltanschauungen* were insurmountable after all, and both sides could confirm the sentiment that "the German does not brook any challenge to his religious convictions." In politics, on the other hand, the concensus was that every ideology was anathema. In its day, the Frankfurt Parliament could count among its ranks some truly illustrious men, granted, but there were no true *realpolitiker*, and therefore their works amounted to nothing but rubbish, as Diederich pointed out. But leniently disposed by his success, he conceded for the rest that the Germany of thinkers and poets might well have had some justification for its existence after all. "But that was only a preliminary phase; our intellectual achievements of today belong to the realms of industry and technology. Our success proves it." Heuteufel had to admit it. His remarks about the Emperor, about the effectiveness and the significance of His Majesty, sounded appreciably more guarded than before. By each successive public speech made by His Highness he was taken aback; he began after his usual manner to find fault but soon gave every indication that he would have liked nothing better than simply to jump on the band wagon. The notion was gaining increasing currency that resolute liberalism could only win the day when it, too, filled itself with the energy of the national way of thinking; when it distinguished itself with a spirit of positive cooperation and while single-mindedly holding high the liberal banner nevertheless called out a resounding *quos ego* to the enemies who begrudged us our place in the sun. For it was not only our hereditary enemy France which raised its head time and again; the day of reckoning with the impudent English was drawing closer as well! We sorely needed the fleet, for the expansion of which the brilliant propaganda of our brilliant Emperor tirelessly agitated, and our future lay indeed on the water; this realization was gaining more and more ground. The idea of the fleet seized the imagination of one man after another around the *stammtisch* and grew to a raging flame which, fed and fed anew with German wine, burned in homage to its originator. The fleet, these ships, amazing machines of bourgeois invention which, once set in operation, produced world power, just as in Gausenfeld certain machines produced a certain paper known as "World Power"; this was what meant more to Diederich than anything else, and it was above all the fleet that won over Cohn as well as Heuteufel to the national way of thinking. A beachhead in England was the dream that wafted through the Gothic vaults of the *Ratskeller*. Eyes sparkled, and the bombardment of London was planned out. The bombardment of Paris was a by-product of the process and fulfilled the plans God had made for us. For "the Christian cannons do their work well," as Pastor Zillich said. Only Major Kunze expressed doubt; he gave vent to dark forebodings. Ever since he, Kunze, had been defeated by Comrade Fischer, he considered any defeat possible. But he remained the only grumbler. The one who triumphed the most was Kühnchen. The deeds that the horrid little man had once carried out in the Great War, met now, at long last, a quarter-century later, with their true confirmation in the sentiments currently being espoused. "The seeds," he said, "that we sowed back then, are all starting to sprout. I'm a very lucky man, that these old eyes have lived to see the day!"—and he fell asleep in the middle of his third bottle.

On the whole, Diederich's relations with Jadassohn were turning out very well. The erstwhile rivals, having matured and advanced to the ranks of the sated, interfered with one another neither politically nor socially, nor in that discreet villa which Diederich visited the one evening in the week when without Guste's knowledge he did not appear at the *stammtisch*. It lay beyond the Saxon Gate, was known previously as the von Brietzen villa, and was inhabited by a single lady who was rarely seen in public, and then never on foot. In a proscenium box at the Valhalla Theatre she sometimes sat in great state, was subjected to general scrutiny with opera glasses, but was never bowed to by anyone. For her own part she behaved like a queen preserving her incognito. In spite of her splendor, everybody knew that it was Käthchen Zillich who had trained for her profession in Berlin, and now pursued it successfully in the old von Brietzen villa. Nobody denied that this situation did not enhance the prestige of Pastor Zillich. His parishioners were deeply offended, and the sceptics were delighted. In order to avoid a catastrophe, the Pastor appealed to the police to put an end to the scandal, but he encountered opposition which could only be explained by certain connections between the von Brietzen villa and the highest officials in the town. Despairing of human no less than divine justice, the father swore he would discharge the duties of a judge himself, and one afternoon he was reported to have inflicted chastisement on his wayward daughter as she lay in bed.

Had it not been for her mother, who guessed everything and followed him, Käthchen would not have got off with her life, the parishioners declared. It was said that the mother still had a reprehensible weakness for the daughter in her wicked splendor. So far as the pastor was concerned, he declared from the pulpit that Käthchen was dead and buried, thus saving himself from the intervention of the ecclesiastical court. In time this ordeal served to strengthen his authority . . . Of the gentlemen who had acquired a stake in Käthchen's career Diederich knew officially only Jadassohn, although the latter had invested less money than anyone. In fact, Diederich suspected that he had invested nothing at all. Jadassohn's former relations with Käthchen served as a sort of mortgage on the enterprise. Accordingly, Diederich had no scruples in discussing with Jadassohn the anxiety it caused him. At the *stammtisch* the pair pulled their chairs together into an alcove, over which the motto stood: "What lovely woman does for love of man must e'er succeed accordingly to plan." With due respect for Pastor Zillich, who was in the room holding forth on the cannons of Christianity, they discussed the affairs of the villa. Diederich complained of Käthchen's insatiable demands upon his purse, and he expected Jadassohn to exercise some favorable influence upon her in this regard. But Jadassohn merely said: "Why do you keep her then? Isn't she supposed to be expensive?" And this was true. After his first fleeting satisfaction at having won Käthchen in this fashion, Diederich had come to regard her nothing more than as a debit, a substantial debit, in his advertising account. "My position," he said to Jadassohn, "obliges me to maintain a certain image. Otherwise I would—honestly—drop the whole thing, for, between ourselves, Käthchen does not offer enough." At this Jadassohn smiled eloquently, but said nothing. "In any case," continued Diederich, "she is of the same genre as my wife, and my wife"—here he whispered behind his hand—"has a better technique. I suppose my heart is just too big for its own good—after every escapade at the von Brietzen villa I have the feeling that I owe my wife something. You may laugh, but as a matter of fact, I always make her a present. I just hope she doesn't get suspicious." Jadassohn laughed with more knowledge than Diederich suspected, for he had long since regarded it as his moral duty to enlighten Frau Hessling with this relationship with Käthchen.

In political matters a similarly advantageous cooperation was established between Diederich and Jadassohn as in the case of

Käthchen. They jointly did their utmost to purge the town of unpatriotic elements, especially of those who spread the plague of *lèse-majesté*. With the help of his many connections Diederich discovered the offenders, while Jadassohn led them to the slaughter. When the *Song to Aegir* appeared, their activities proved especially fruitful. In Diederich's own house the piano-teacher, with whom Guste practised, spoke disrespectfully of the *Song to Aegir* and endured appropriate punishment ... Even Wolfgang Buck, who had recently come back to live in Netzig again, declared that the guilty verdict was quite just, for it satisfied imperial sentiment. "People would not have understood a pardon," he said at the *stammtisch*. "The monarchy is among political regimes what severe and energetic women are in love. Anyone so disposed will insist on something being done and cannot be satisfied with half-measures." Diederich blushed at this.... Unfortunately, Buck confessed to such sentiments only so long as he was sober. Later on he gave sufficient grounds for being excluded from all decent society by his well-known way of dragging the most sacred things in the dust. It was Diederich who saved him from that fate. He defended his friend." "You must remember, gentlemen, that he has a hereditary taint, for the family shows signs of advanced degeneracy. On the other hand, a proof of the healthy kernel in him is the fact that he was not satisfied with an actor's existence and has resumed his profession as a lawyer." The reply was that it looked suspicious that Buck should maintain such absolute silence concerning his experiences of almost three years on the stage. Was he even qualified to give satisfaction any more? Diederich could not answer this question. A logically inexplicable yet profound impulse compelled him time and again to seek the company of the son of old Buck. Again and again he eagerly renewed a discussion which abruptly terminated on each occasion, after having revealed irreconcilable differences of opinion. He even invited Buck into his home, but was not prepared for what happened next. For if Buck came at first merely for the sake of a particularly good glass of cognac, he was soon obviously coming on account of Emmi. They communicated on a level over Diederich's head, and in a way that offended him. They carried on clever and caustic conversations, apparently without the warmheartedness or the other factors that normally animated conversation between the sexes. When they lowered their voices and became confidential Diederich found them absolutely sinister. He had the choice of intervening in the interest of propriety or simply leaving the room. To his own astonishment he chose the latter. "Each of them has come to know the perils of fate, even if their fates have been well-deserved," he said to himself with the sense of superiority that befitted him, and without giving much thought to the fact that deep down, he was proud of Emmi, because his own sister, Emmi, was refined enough, exceptional enough, indeed, dubious enough to get on with Wolfgang Buck. "Who knows?" he thought hesitantly, and finally decided: "Why not! Bismarck did the same thing with Austria; first a defeat and then an alliance!"

These obscure reflections prompted Diederich again to take a certain interest in Wolfgang's father. Old Buck had developed a heart condition. He was now rarely seen, and when he was, he was usually standing in front of a shop window apparently absorbed in the display, but in reality solely trying to conceal the fact that he could not breathe. What did he think? How did he judge the new commercial prosperity of Netzig, the renaissance of nationalism, and those who now held the reins of power? Was he convinced and inwardly vanquished? From time to time it happened that Dr. Hessling, the Managing Director and the most powerful person of his class, would duck surreptitiously into a doorway, and then creep along unobserved behind this powerless, half-forgotten old man: Diederich, at the height of his power, mysteriously disturbed by a dying man. . . . As old Buck was in arrears with the interest on his mortgage, Diederich proposed to the son that he take over the house. Of course he would allow the old gentleman to occupy it so long as he was alive. Diederich wanted also to buy the furniture and pay for it at once. Wolfgang induced his father to accept.

Meanwhile March 22 passed, the one hundredth birthday of Wilhelm the Great had come and gone and his monument had still not been erected in the public park. Interpellations were raised to no end at the meetings of the Town Council, and several times additional credits were sanctioned after great difficulty, only to be vetoed again. The worst blow the community received was when His Majesty refused to have his lamented grandfather portrayed as a pedestrian and demanded an equestrian statue. Spurred on by his impatience, Diederich often went to Meisestrasse in the evening to see how the work was progressing. It was the month of May and unpleasantly warm even in the twilight, but there was a breeze blowing through the deserted, newly planted area of the public park. With feelings of irritation Diederich thought again of the excellent stroke of business which the lord of the manor, Herr von Quitzin, had done here. That fellow had it all his own way. It was not very difficult to speculate in landed property when one's cousin was Governor! The town had no alternative but to take over the whole lot for the monument and pay whatever he demanded. . . . Then two figures appeared. Diederich saw in time who it was, and drew back among the shrubbery.

"We can breathe here," said old Buck. His son answered:

"Unless the place takes away all desire to do so. They have contracted a debt of a million and a half to create this rubbish heap." And he pointed to the unfinished arrangement of stone pedestals, eagles, circular benches, lions, temples, and figures. With beating wings, the eagles had dug their talons into the still empty pedestal, others were perched on top of those temples which were set at symmetrical distances within the row of circular benches; within these temples crouched lions ready to spring into the foreground, where there was already enough movement, caused by fluttering flags and people in violent agitation. Napoleon III, in the stooped attitude of Wilhelmshöhe, adorned the rear of the pedestal, as the vanquished in the rear of the triumphal chariot. He was also threatened by an attack from one of the lions, which was arching its back most ferociously on the steps of the monument just behind him. Bismarck and the other paladins, very much at home in the midst of the menagerie, stretched up their hands from the base of the pedestal in order to share in the deeds of the as yet absent ruler.

"Who really ought to jump into that vacant place up there?" asked Wolfgang Buck. "The old man was merely a forerunner. Afterward this mystic-heroic spectacle will be cordoned off with chains, and we shall have something to gape at—which was the main object of the whole thing. Theatrics, and not even good ones at that."

After a while—as twilight deepened—the father said: "And you, my son? Acting also seemed to you to be the main object."

"As it does to all my generation. That's all we can do. We should not take ourselves too seriously nowadays. That is the safest attitude in view of the future, and I will not deny that it was for no other reason than vanity that I abandoned the stage again. It is laughable, father. I left because once, when I was acting, a chief of police wept. Can you imagine that being tolerable? I represent the last degree of refinement, an insight into the heart of man, lofty morality, modernity of the intellect and soul, to people who seem to be my equals, because they nod to me and look as if they felt something. But afterward they pursue revolutionaries and open fire on strikers, for my chief of police is typical of them all."

Here Buck turned straight toward the bush which concealed Diederich.

"Art remains art to you, and the whole tumult of the intellect never touches your lives. On the day the masters of your culture understood that, as I do, they would leave you alone with your wild animals, as I do." As he pointed to the lions and eagles, the old man also looked at the monument and said:

"They have become very powerful, but their power has brought neither more intelligence nor more kindness into the world. It has been in vain. We also were born in vain, apparently." He glanced at his son. "Nevertheless you should not leave the field to them."

Wolfgang sighed heavily. "What is there to hope for, father? They took good care not to push things too far as the privileged classes did before the revolution. History has unfortunately taught them moderation. Their social legislation prepares the way and corrupts. They satisfy the masses just enough to make it not worth their while to put up a serious fight for bread, let alone freedom. Who is left to testify against them?"

Then the old man drew himself up, and his voice was sonorous once again. "The spirit of humanity," he said, and, after a moment, as the younger man held his head down:

"You must believe in that my son. When the catastrophe is over which they think they can avoid, you may be sure that humanity will not consider the causes leading to the first revolution any more shameless and stupid than the conditions which were ours."

Softly as a voice from the distance he said: "He who lived only in the present would not have lived at all."

Suddenly he seemed to totter. The son hastened to hold him up and on his arm the old man disappeared in the darkness, with bowed figure and halting step. Diederich, who hurried off by a different route, had the sensation of emerging from a bad but largely incomprehensible dream, in which the very foundations had been shaken. And in spite of the unreality of all that he had heard, it seemed to shake things more profoundly than the tremors of the revolution as he had known it had ever shaken them. The days of one of these two men were numbered, the other had not very much to look forward to either, yet Diederich felt it would have been better if they had stirred up a healthy uproar in the country, than to have whispered, here in the dark, things which were concerned only with the soul and the future.

The present certainly offered more tangible matters. Together with the creator of the monument Diederich planned the artistic arrangements for the unveiling ceremony, in which the artist proved to be more accommodating than might have been expected of him. Generally speaking, he had so far shown only the good side of his profession, namely genius and a dignified political viewpoint, while, for the rest, he turned out to be polite and competent. The young man, a nephew of Mayor Scheffelweis, was a proof that, in spite of outdated prejudices, there were still decent people in every walk of life, and that there is no need to despair of a young man who is too lazy to earn an honest living and becomes an artist. The first time he returned from Berlin to Netzig he still wore a velvet jacket and brought nothing but embarrassment to his family. But on his second visit he was already the proud possessor of a silk hat, and before long he was discovered by His Majesty, and was permitted to sculpt the successful likeness of the Margrave Hatto the Powerful for the Siegesallee, together with the likeness of his two most important contemporaries, the monk Tassilo, who could drink one hundred liters of beer in a day, and the Knight Klitzenzitz, who introduced compulsory labor among the inhabitants of Berlin, although they hung him afterward. His Majesty had drawn the special attention of the Lord Mayor to the achievements of the Knight Klitzenzitz, and this had again redounded to the advantage of the sculptor's career. One could not do too much for a man who basked in the direct rays of the imperial sunshine. Diederich placed his house at his disposal, he also hired the horse which the artist required to keep in good health. And what ambitions were conceived when the famous guest described as very promising little Horst's first attempts to sketch! Diederich decided on the spot that Horst should follow art, that most opportune career.

Wulckow, who had no feeling for art, and did not know what to say to His Majesty's protégé, received from the Monument Committee an honorarium of two-thousand marks, to which he was entitled as honorary chairman. The oration to be made at the unveiling, however, was entrusted by the Committee to the proper chairman, the spiritual creator of the monument and the founder of the national movement which had led to its erection, Dr. Hessling, Municipal Councillor and Managing Director of Gausenfeld, hurrah! Moved and elated, Diederich saw himself on the eve of further promotion. The Governor-General himself was expected, and Diederich would have to speak before His Excellency; what results that promised! Wulckow, it is true, tried to thwart them. He was irritated because he had been passed over, and went so far as to refuse to admit Guste to the stand with the officials' wives. Diederich, on this account, had an exchange with him which was stormy, but fruitless. Fuming with rage he returned home to Guste. "He won't budge. He says you won't be an official lady. We shall see who is more official, you or he! He shall beg you to come! Thank heaven I no longer have need of him, but he may need me." And so it was, for when the next number of *Die Woche* appeared, what did it contain besides the usual pictures of the Emperor? The reproduction of two portraits, one showing the creator of the Emperor Wilhelm Monument in Netzig, as he was just putting the final touches to his work, the other showing the chairman of the committee and his wife, Diederich and Guste together. Not a mention of Wulckow—which was widely noticed and regarded as a sign that his position had been weakened. He must have felt it himself, for he took steps to get into *Die Woche*. He called on Diederich, but Diederich sent word he was not at home. The artist made excuses. Then it so happened that Wulckow actually approached Guste in the street. That business about the seat with the officials' wives was all a misunderstanding. . . . "He begged like our dachshund," Guste reported. "Just for that very reason, no!" decided Diederich, and he had no scruples in telling the story to everybody. "Should I show restraint, when the man is in my power?" he said to Wolfgang Buck. "Colonel von Haffke is giving up on him as well." He boldly added: "Now he sees that there are people more powerful than himself. To his own disadvantage Wulckow did not learn in time to adapt himself to the modern conditions of large-scale publicity that characterize our present course!" "Absolutism tempered by the craving for notoriety," added Buck.

In view of Wulckow's decline Diederich took more and more offense at that real-estate deal that had been so disadvantageous to himself. His indignation grew to such a point that the visit which Reichstag Deputy Napoleon Fischer happened to be paying to Netzig became a truly liberating opportunity for Diederich. Parliamentary immunity had its advantages, after all! For Napoleon Fischer repaired immediately to the Reichstag and made revelations. In perfect safety he exposed the maneuvers of Governor von Wulckow in Netzig, his immense profit on the site of the Emperor Wilhelm Monument, which, Napoleon declared, had been extorted from the town, and the honorarium which allegedly amounted to five-thousand marks and which he described as "a bribe." According to the press this caused an enormous sensation among the representatives of the people. It is true, this anger was not directed against Wulckow but against the man who had exposed him. There was a furious demand for proof and witnesses. Diederich trembled lest the next line should mention his name. Happily it did not appear. Napoleon Fischer did not betray the duty of his office. Instead the Minister spoke. He left to the judgment of the House this outrageous attack, unfortunately made under cover of immunity, against one who was absent and could not defend himself. The House gave judgment by applauding the Minister. The matter was at an end, so far as Parliament was concerned, and it remained only for the press also to express its horror and, where it was politically not entirely irreproachable, to wink its eye gently. The editors of several Social Democratic papers which had been incautious had to appear in court, including the editor of the *Netzig Volksstimme.* Diederich seized this occasion to draw a sharp line between himself and those who had doubted Governor von Wulckow. He and Guste called on the Wulckows. "I know at first hand," he said afterward, "that the man is assured of a brilliant future. He went hunting recently with His Majesty and brought off an excellent joke." A week later *Die Woche* published a full-page portrait, a bald head and beard in one half, a paunch in the other, and underneath the legend "Governor von Wulckow, the spiritual creator of the Emperor Wilhelm Monument in Netzig, who was recently the object of an attack in the Reichstag which excited universal indignation, and whose appointment as Governor-General is expected. . . ." The picture of Dr. Hessling and his wife had only been given a quarter page. Diederich was satisfied that due proportion in rank had been restored. Authority remained as impregnable as ever, even under modern conditions of large-scale publicity. In spite of everything he was profoundly contented. In this way he was spiritually most appropriately prepared for his oration.

The latter was conceived during the ambitious visions of nights snatched from sleep, and as a result of a lively exchange of ideas with Wolfgang Buck, and especially with Käthchen Zillich, who showed a remarkably clear perception of the importance of the approaching event. On the fateful day, when Diederich, his heart beating against the copy of his speech, drove up with his wife at half-past ten to the festive scene, the latter presented a not yet bustling but all the more orderly spectacle. Above all, the military cordon had already been drawn up! And if one only got through after showing all the required credentials, it nevertheless represented an impressive distinction over against the unprivileged mob, who had to crane their perspiring necks in the sun behind the soldiers and at the foot of the large black firewall of an adjoining building. The stands to the right and left of the long white cloths, behind which Wilhelm the Great could be divined, were sheltered by awnings and innumerable flags. On the lefthand side, as Diederich noticed, the officers proved themselves quite capable of seating themselves and their ladies without outside help, thanks to the sense of discipline which was in their very blood. All the rigors of police supervision were transferred to the righthand side where the civilians pushed and shoved for the best seats. Then Guste expressed dissatisfaction with hers. It seemed to her that only the official marquee, facing the statue, was fit to receive her. She was an official lady; Wulckow had admitted it. Diederich must go there with her or appear a coward; but, of course, his daring assault was repulsed as emphatically as he had anticipated. For form's sake, and so that Guste should not lose faith in him, he protested against the tone of the police officer, and was almost arrested. His order of the Crown, fourth class, his black-white-and-red sash and his speech, which he produced, just managed to save him, but they could never pass as a satisfactory substitute, either in his own eyes or those of the world, for a uniform. This one real distinction was lacking, and Diederich was once more compelled to notice that without a uniform one went through life with a bad conscience, notwithstanding one's other first-class qualifications.

In a state of disarray the Hesslings beat a conspicuous retreat, with Guste looking blue and swollen in her feathers, lace, and diamonds. Diederich was fuming and he shoved forward his paunch with its sash as much as possible, as if he were spreading the national colors over his defeat. Thus they passed between the Veterans' Association, with wreaths of oak around their tall hats, who were placed in the lower half of the military stand, under the command of Kühnchen, as a *Landwehr* Lieutenant, and the maids of honor in white, with black-white-and-red sashes, under the orders of Pastor Zillich in his official robes. But when they reached their places, who was sitting, with the air of a queen, in Guste's seat? They were flabbergasted: Käthchen Zillich! Here Diederich felt bound to speak a word of authority. "This lady has made a mistake; the seat is not for her," he said, not to Käthchen Zillich, whom he appeared to take for a stranger, no less than for a doubtful character, but to the official in charge—and even if public opinion about him had not supported him, Diederich represented in this matter the unspoken power of order, morals and law. As far as he was concerned the stand could collapse rather than that Käthchen Zillich should remain there. . . . Nevertheless, the incredible occurred. The steward shrugged his shoulders, while Käthchen smiled ironically, and even the policeman whom Diederich had called gave further incomprehensible support to this clear breach of morality. Diederich was stunned by a world whose normal laws appeared to be suspended, and he submitted when Guste was moved up to a row away at the top, the latter exchanging a few choice words with Käthchen Zillich concerning their contrasted treatment. This exchange of opinions was taken up by a number of other people nearby and threatened to get out of hand, when the band began to crash out the March of the Wartburg Procession, for the procession to the official marquee was actually in progress; Wulckow at the head, unmistakable despite his red hussar uniform, with an important general on one side of him, and on the other, a gentleman in a dress suit with decorations. Was it possible? Two more important generals! And their adjutants, uniforms of every color, glittering medals and tremendously tall men. "Who is that tall one in the yellow?" asked Guste anxiously. "Isn't he a fine man!—" "Would you kindly not walk on my feet!" Diederich demanded, for his neighbor had jumped up; everybody was straining forward, exalted and excited. "Just look at them, Guste! Emmi is a silly goose not to have come. This is the only first-class theater. It is superb; there is no denying it!"—"But that one with the yellow facings!" Guste raved. "That slim man! He must be a real aristocrat. I can see it at once." Diederich laughed rapturously. "There is not one of them who isn't a blue-blooded aristocrat, you can be sure. When I tell you that His Majesty's aide-de-camp is here!" "The one in yellow!" "Here in person!"

Everyone scanned the procession. "The aide-de-camp! Two major generals! By Jove!" And the graceful smartness of the salutes! Even Mayor Scheffelweis was dragged out of his modest obscurity and could stand stiffly in front of his superiors in the uniform of a Lieutenant in the Army Service Corps Reserve. Dressed as a lancer Herr von Quitzin thoroughly examined through his monocle the plot of ground which had temporarily belonged to him. But Wulckow, the red hussar, only now brought into evidence the full significance of a Governor, as he saluted, thrusting out the immense profile of his posterior framed with cords. "These are the pillars of our strength!" shouted Diederich, his words drowned by the powerful sounds of the march. "So long as we have such rulers we shall be the terror of the world!" Driven by an overpowering impulse, in the belief that his hour had come, he rushed down toward the speaker's platform. But the policeman on guard intercepted him. "No, no! It ain't your turn yet," said the policeman. Suddenly checked in his course, he ran into a steward, who had been keeping an eye on him, the same one as before, a municipal employee, who assured him that he knew very well that the seat of the lady with the yellow hair belonged to Diederich: "But the lady got it according to superior orders." The rest was told in a faint whisper, and Diederich let him go with a gesture implying: "Of course, in that case!" His Majesty's aide-de-camp! Of course, in that case! Diederich wondered whether it would not be well to turn around and openly pay homage to Käthchen Zillich.

He did not have time to do so. Colonel von Haffke commanded the color guard to stand at ease, and Kühnchen gave his veteran warriors the same command. Behind the marquee the regimental band played a call to prayers, which was obeyed by the maids of honor and the Veterans' Association. Kühnchen in his historical *Landwehr* uniform, which was decorated not only with an iron cross but also with a distinguished patch—where a French bullet had penetrated—met the berobed Pastor Zillich in the middle of the open space. The color guard also fell in and, under Zillich's guidance, they did honor to their ancient Ally. On the stand for the civilians the public were prompted by the officials to rise. The officers did so of their own accord. Then the band played "A Mighty Fortress Is Our God." Zillich seemed anxious to do something more, but the Governor-General, obviously convinced that the ancient Ally had had enough, fell back in his seat a bit yellow in the face, with the lusty aide-de-camp on his right and the major-generals on his left. When the whole company had formed groups, according to their natural laws, in the official marquee, Governor von Wulckow was seen to give a sign, as a result of which a policeman was set in motion. He betook himself to his colleague in charge of the speaker's platform, whereupon the latter passed the word to Diederich. "Come on, it's your turn," said the policeman.

Diederich was careful not to stumble as he climbed up, for his legs had suddenly become weak, and everything swam before his eyes. After gasping for a moment, he distinguished in the bare circle around him a little tree, which had no leaves, but was covered with black-white-and-red paper flowers. The sight of the little tree brought back his strength and his memory. He began:

"Your Excellencies, my Lords and gentlemen, it is a hundred years since the great Emperor, whose monument is being unveiled by His Majesty's representative, was given to us and to the Fatherland. At the same time—to lend more significance to this hour—it is almost a decade since his illustrious grandson ascended the throne! Why should we not first of all cast back a proud and grateful glance over the great times which we ourselves have been privileged to experience?" Diederich glanced back. He alternately celebrated the unparalleled upsurge of commerce and of nationalism. He discussed the ocean for a considerable time. "The ocean is indispensable to the greatness of Germany. In the ocean we have a proof that there can be no decision, on the seas or beyond them, without Germany and the German Emperor, for today world commerce is our chief concern." Not only from an industrial standpoint, however, but even more from a moral and intellectual standpoint, this upsurge could be described as unique. What was our former condition? Diederich drew an unflattering picture of the previous generation which, led astray to licentious beliefs by a one-sided humanitarian education, had no sense of dignity in national affairs. If that had now been fundamentally changed, if we now formed one single national party, in the just consciousness that we were the most competent people in Europe and the whole world, despite mean-spirited and captious critics—whom had we to thank for it? Only His Majesty, Diederich answered. "He has aroused the citizen from his slumbers, his lofty example has made us what we are." As he said this he struck himself on the chest. "His personality, his unique, incomparable personality, is so powerful that we can all creep up around it, like clinging ivy!" he shouted, although this was not in the draft he had written. "In whatever His Majesty the Emperor decides for the good of the German people, we will joyfully cooperate, be we nobles or commoners. The simple man from the workshop is also welcome!" he added, again at the inspiration of the moment, suddenly stimulated by the smell of the perspiring populace behind the military cordon, which was borne in his direction by the wind.

"Rendered efficient to an astonishing degree, full of the highest moral strength for positive action, and in our shining armor, the terror of all enemies who enviously threaten us, we are the elite among the nations and represent an unprecedented height of Germanic master-culture which will never be surpassed by any people be they who they may!"

At this point the Governor-General was observed to make a sign with his head, while the aide-de-camp moved his hands against one another: The stands erupted in applause. Handkerchiefs were waved among the civilians. Guste allowed hers to flutter in the breeze, and so did Käthchen Zillich, in spite of the earlier unpleasantness. His heart as light as the fluttering handkerchiefs, Diederich resumed his lofty flight.

"A master-nation, however, does not achieve such an incomparable flowering in the slackness of peaceful ease. No. Our ancient Ally has deemed it necessary to test the German gold with fire. We had to pass through the fiery furnaces of Jena and Tilsit, and in the end we have been able to plant our victorious colors everywhere, and to forge the imperial crown of Germany upon the field of battle."

He recalled the many trials in the life of Wilhelm the Great, from which, Diederich asserted, we could see that the Creator does not lose sight of His chosen people, and that He builds up the instrument suitable to His purpose. The great Emperor, for his part, had never been mistaken about this, as was particularly evident on that great historical occasion when, as Emperor by the grace of God, with his scepter in one hand and his imperial sword in the other, he paid honor only unto God and received his throne from Him. With a lofty sense of duty he had scorned to pay honor to the people and to accept the crown at their hands. Nor did he shrink back before the awesome responsibility to God alone, from which no minister and no Parliament could relieve him. Diederich's voice trembled with emotion. "The people themselves recognize that, to the extent that their reverence for the personality of the deceased Emperor approaches deification. Did he not succeed? And where success is, there is God! In the Middle Ages Wilhelm the Great would have been canonized. Today we erect a first-class monument to his memory."

Again the Governor-General made a sign, which was again the signal for tumultuous applause. The sun had disappeared and it grew colder, and as if inspired by the darkening skies Diederich turned to a deeper question.

"Who, then, stood in the way of his exalted purpose? Who was the enemy of the great Emperor and of his loyal people? Napoleon, whom he succeeded in smashing, received his crown not from God but from the people. That fact gives to the judgment of history its eternal and overpowering significance." Then Diederich took it upon himself to describe conditions in the empire of Napoleon III, poisoned by democracy and therefore abandoned by God. Crass materialism, concealed by hollow piety, had given rise to the most unscrupulous commercialism. This contempt for the soul found its natural ally in a degraded hedonism. Publicity-mongering was the dominant impulse of public life, and at every moment it degenerated into a mania for persecution. Relying outwardly upon prestige, but inwardly upon the police, with no other creed but force, one strove only for theatrical effects, making great pomp with the heroic periods of the past, but chauvinism was the only pinnacle which was ever attained. . . "Of all that we know nothing," cried Diederich raising his hand toward the Witness above. "Therefore, there can never, never be for us that terrible end which awaited the empire of our hereditary foe."

At this point a flash of lightning glared. Between the military cordon and the firewall, in the area where he assumed the masses to be, there was a lurid flash in the dark cloud, and a peal of thunder followed which had clearly gone too far. The gentlemen in the official marquee began to look about in disapproval and the Governor-General had winced. On the stand reserved for the officers there was, naturally, no falling off of discipline, though among the civilians a certain uneasiness became apparent. Diederich silenced the outcry, for he shouted, likewise thundering: "Our ancient Ally bears witness! We are not like the others. We are serious, loyal and true! To be a German is to do a thing for its own sake. Who among us has ever made money out of his loyalty? Where could corrupt officials be found? Here masculine honesty is united with feminine purity, for woman leads us ever onward and is not the tool of ignoble pleasure. This radiant picture of true German character, however, rests upon the solid earth of Christianity, and that is the only true foundation; for every heathen civilization, however beautiful and fine, will collapse at the first breath of disaster. And the soul of the German being is the veneration of power, power transmitted and hallowed by God, against which it is impossible to revolt. Therefore we must, now as always, regard the defense of our country as the highest duty, the Emperor's uniform as the supreme distinction, and the craft of war as the most dignified labor."

The thunder rumbled, though it seemed intimidated by Diederich's increasingly powerful voice. But drops began to fall, which could be heard separately, they were so large.

"The turbid stream of democracy," Diederich screamed, "flows inceasingly from the land of our hereditary foe, and German manliness and German idealism alone can dam the tide. The unpatriotic enemies of the divine world order however, who wish to undermine our political system—they must be exterminated, root and branch, in order that, when one day we are called before our heavenly Judge, each of us can appear with a clear conscience before his God and his old Emperor, so that when asked if he has worked wholeheartedly for the welfare of the Empire, he can strike his chest and answer with an unreserved YES."

At these words Diederich hit his chest so hard that he knocked the wind out of himself. The civilian stand seized upon the unavoidable pause which ensued and showed by its restlessness that it regarded the speech as finished. The storm had now come up directly over the heads of the festive gathering, and in the sulfurous light these raindrops, as big as hens' eggs, kept falling singly, slowly, like a warning ... Diederich had recovered his breath.

"Now, when this monument is unveiled," he began with renewed vigor, "when flags and standards are drooped in reverence, swords are lowered and bayonets flash at the command: present arms—" Just at this moment there was such a formidable crash in the heavens that Diederich ducked his head, and before he knew what he was doing he had crept under the podium. Fortunately he emerged again before anyone had noticed him disappear, for everyone had been similarly affected. They scarcely paid any attention as Diederich requested His Excellency, the Governor-General, to be so kind as to order that the monument be unveiled. The Governor-General did manage to step out in front of the official marquee, but his face was a shade yellower than usual and the glitter of his star was extinguished. In a feeble voice he said: "In the name of His Majesty I declare this monument to be unveiled"—and the covering fell, to the strains of "The Sentry on the Rhine." Wilhelm the Great, riding through the air, looked like a good paterfamilias, though surrounded by all the terrors of authority, and the sight of the Emperor again steeled his loyal subjects against the threats from the sky. They joined heartily in the cheers of the Governor-General for the Emperor. The air of the national anthem was the cue for His Excellency to go up to the foot of the monument, examine it and reward the expectant sculptor with a few appropriate words of recognition. People found it natural that this exalted personage should glance up dubiously at the sky, but, as might be expected, his sense of duty triumphed—a victory all the more brilliant because among that crowd of gallant soldiers he was the only civilian in a dress-suit. He ventured boldly forth, advancing beneath those huge, slow drops of rain, surrounded by lancers, cuirassiers and army service corps. . . . The inscription "Wilhelm the Great" had already been inspected, the sculptor had been favored with a few words and received his decoration, and it was Hessling's turn to be introduced as the spiritual creator of the monument, and to be decorated, when the heavens burst. They burst completely, all at once, and with such force as to suggest a long-delayed explosion. Before the gentlemen could turn around they were up to their ankles in water, and water poured from His Excellency's sleeves and trouser legs. The stands disappeared beneath the downpour, and as if on a distant billowing sea it could be seen that the awnings had collapsed beneath the fury of the cloudburst. Shrieking crowds struggled right and left in the moist entanglement. The officers brought their bared swords to play against the elements and were able to cut their way through the canvas to freedom. The civilians could only descend as one gray, writhing serpent, which bathed in the flooded field with spasmodic twists.

Under these circumstances, the Governor-General consented to omit the remainder of the festive program for reasons of expediency. While the lightning flashed all around him and water sprang from him as from a fountain, he beat a hasty retreat, with the aide-de-camp, the two major-generals, dragoons, hussars, lancers and army service corps bringing up the rear.

On the way His Excellency remembered that the decoration for the spiritual creator was still hanging from his finger. Faithful to his duty in the extreme but determined not to be detained, he passed it on, as he ran in his dripping clothes, to Governor von Wulckow. Wulckow, in turn, met a policeman who was still clinging to his post, and entrusted him with the bestowal of this sign of His Highness's approval, whereupon the policeman wandered through the storm and rain in search of Diederich. Finally he found him crouching in the water underneath the podium. "Here you go, the order of Wilhelm," said the policeman, making off, for just then a flash of lightning came so near that it seemed as if it were trying to prevent the decoration from being bestowed. Diederich could only heave a sigh. When he finally ventured, with half of his face, to peer out at the world, it presented a spectacle of increasing revolutionary upheaval. The large black firewall opposite had cracked open and threatened to topple over, along with the house to which it belonged. Above a seething mass of people, in the erratic ghostly light of sulphur-yellow and blue, the carriage horses reared and dashed away. Happy were the unprivileged crowd outside who had managed to get away. The cultivated and wealthy classes, on the other hand, could feel the flying wreckage of the upheaval falling about their heads, as well as fire from above. It was hardly surprising that the circumstances determined their behavior and many ladies, hurled back from the exit in the most ungentlemanly fashion, simply rolled over one another. The officers, relying upon their bravery alone, made use of their weapons of offense against everyone who opposed them, while buntings torn by the storm from what remained of the stands and the official marquee whistled through the air, black-white-and-red, about the ears of the strugglers. Hopeless though everything was, the regimental band continued to play the national anthem, even after the military cordon and the world order had collapsed. They played like the orchestra on a sinking ship to the accompaniment of terror and dissolution. Another burst of the hurricane dispersed even them—and Diederich, with his eyes squeezed shut, and a dizzying sense that the end of everything was imminent, sank back into the cool depths beneath the podium, to which he clung like it was the last thing on earth. But his farewell glance had embraced something that passed all understanding: the fence hung with black-white-and-red, which enclosed the park, had collapsed beneath the weight of the people on it, and then this clambering up and down, this rolling about, this piling-up and sliding-back of people, standing on their heads and sitting on one another's faces—and then being swept along by the whips from on high, under streams of fire, this clean-out like the end of a drunken masquerade: a swept-together heap of nobles and commoners, the most distinguished uniform and the citizen aroused from his slumbers, pillars of the State and heaven-sent statesmen, ideal riches, hussars, lancers, dragoons and army service corps!

The horsemen of the apocalypse rode on, however, as Diederich noticed. They had only held maneuvers for the Judgment Day; the real emergency had not yet arrived. Cautiously he left his hiding place and discovered that it was now only raining and that Emperor Wilhelm the Great was still there, with all the paraphernalia of power. All the time Diederich had had a feeling that the monument had been smashed and washed away. The scene of the festivities, of course, looked like a desolate memory; not a soul stirred among the ruins. But, yes, there was someone moving in the background, someone wearing a lancer's uniform. It was Herr von Quitzin, who was examining the house that had collapsed. It had been struck by lightning and sat smoking beside the remains of its large black firewall. In the general exodus only Herr von Quitzin had stood his ground, for an idea had given him strength. Diederich read his mind. Herr von Quitzin was thinking: "We should have unloaded the house on those fellows as well. But nothing doing, we tried as hard as we could. Well at least I'll get the insurance money. There is a God!" And then he walked over to the fire brigade, which, fortunately, could no longer intervene with much effect, or spoil his business plans.

Encouraged by this example Diederich also set out for home. He had lost his hat, his shoes were full of water, and in the seat of his trousers he carried a puddle. As no conveyance seemed to be available he decided to cut through the center of town. The crooked old streets shielded him from the wind and he began to feel warmer. "There is no danger of catarrh. I'll get Guste to put a poultice on my stomach. She had better not bring the flu into the house, though!" After this worry he remembered his decoration. "The order of Wilhelm, created by His Majesty, is given only for exceptional services on behalf of the welfare and improvement of the people. . . . That's what I've got!" said Diederich out loud in the empty street. "Even if it rains dynamite!" The attempt by nature to overthrow the existing authority had been an attempt with inadequate means. Diederich showed Heaven his order of Wilhelm and said, "Ha, ha!" Whereupon he pinned it on, beside the order of the Crown, fourth class.

In the Fleischhauergrube several carriages had stopped, curiously enough, in front of old Buck's house. One of them, moreover, was a country cart. Could he. . . ? Diederich peered into the house. The glass hallway door stood open, strange to say, as if someone were expected who did not often come. Solemn silence in the wide hall; it was only when he crept past the kitchen that he heard sobbing: the old servant, with her face resting on her arms. "So things are as bad as that!"—Diederich suddenly shuddered and stopped, ready to retreat. "This is no place for me. . . . Wait a minute, my place *is* here, for everything here is mine, and it is my duty to see that they do not take anything away afterward." But this was not the only thing that impelled him. Something less obvious and more profound made him gasp for breath and caught him in the stomach. He stepped carefully up the flat old stairs and thought: "Respect for a brave enemy when he falls on the field of honor! God has judged him. Yes, indeed, such is life. Nobody can tell whether some day—But, come now, there is a difference, either a thing is right or it isn't. One must neglect nothing that can add to the fame of what is right. Our old Emperor probably also had to pull himself together when he went to Wilhelmshöhe to meet the utterly defeated Napoleon."

By this time he had reached the mezzanine floor, and he walked cautiously down the long corridor at the end of which the door—here also—stood open. He kept close up against the wall and peered in. A bed with the foot turned towards him, and in it old Buck was reclining against a heap of pillows, apparently no longer in his right mind. Not a sound. Was he alone? He moved carefully to the other side. Now he could see the curtained windows and in front of them, the family in a semicircle: Judith Lauer, stock-still, nearest the bed, then Wolfgang, with an expression on his face which nobody would have expected. Between the windows was huddled the herd of five daughters and their bankrupt father, who was no longer even elegant any more; further off stood the countrified son and his dull-eyed wife, and finally Lauer, who had sat down. With good reason they all kept so quiet, at that moment they were losing their last prospect of ever having a say in anything again! They had been successful and very sure of themselves, so long as the old man held out. He had fallen and they with him; he was disappearing and so were they, every one of them. He had always built upon quicksand, for he had not relied upon Power! How empty were his goals, which had led away from Power! How fruitless his spirit, which had left behind nothing but decay! How blind any ambition which had no fists nor money in those fists!

But what was that look on Wolfgang's face? It did not look like grief, although tears were falling from his yearning eyes; it looked like envy, sorrowful envy. What about the others? Judith Lauder, whose brows frowned darkly; her husband who was sighing aloud—even the eldest son's wife had folded in front of her face her working-woman's hands. Diederich stepped into the center of the doorway in a determined attitude. It was dark in the passage and they could not see him—not that it mattered—but the old man? His face was turned in Diederich's direction, and where his eyes were fixed one divined more than was actually there, visions that no one could obstruct. As these visions appeared reflected in his astonished eyes he opened out his arms on the pillows, tried to lift them, and did so, moving them in a gesture of welcome. Whom was he welcoming? How many were there to whom he made these prolonged signs of beckoning? A whole nation, apparently, but of what character, that its coming should awaken this spectral joy in the countenance of old Buck?

Then he suddenly gave a start, as if he had met a stranger with a message of terror. He was frightened, and struggled for breath. Facing him, Diederich held himself even more stiffly, puffed out his chest with its black-white-and-red sash and its decorations, and glared, on general principles. Suddenly the old man's head dropped; he fell forward, right over, as though he had been broken. His family shrieked. In a horrified whisper the eldest son's wife cried: "He has seen something! He has seen the Devil!" Judith Lauer got up slowly and shut the door. Diederich had vanished.

Translated by Ernest Boyd
Adapted, with New Portions
Translated by Daniel Theisen

THE GERMAN LIBRARY
in 100 Volumes

All volumes available in hardcover and paperback editions at your bookstore or
from the publisher. For more information on The German Library write to: The
Continuum Publishing Company, 370 Lexington Avenue, New York, NY 10017.